Somewhere Special

★ Premier Hotels ◆ B&B Guest Accommodation ★ Self-Catering Holiday Homes

England

To Begin

All you need to know about the guide and how to use it

Contents

Plus... Useful Information

'Somewhere Special' 2002

Published by: **English Tourism Council**, Thames Tower, Black's Road, London W6 9EL *in association with* **Celsius**, St Thomas House, St Thomas Street, Winchester SO23 9HE.

Managing Editor, ETC: Michael Dewing
Design, compilation and production: Celsius
Editorial contributors: Tessa Lecomber, Hugh Chevallier
Cartography (regional base maps): Colin Earl
Printing: Belmont Press

© English Tourism Council (except where stated), 2001

ISBN 0 86143 253 3

Important:

The English Tourism Council

English Tourism Council is the national body for English tourism. Its mission is to drive forward the quality, competitiveness and wise growth of England's tourism by providing intelligence, setting standards, creating partnerships and ensuring coherence. ETC sets out: to provide leadership and support for the industry – creating the right framework for tourism to flourish and providing a clear focus for tourism policy and promotion; to raise the quality of English tourism – ensuring consumers expectations are met and that tourism contributes to the quality of life; to improve the competitiveness of the industry; to ensure the wise growth of tourism – helping the tourism industry to take better account of the natural and built environment and the communities within which it operates.

Front cover: The Goring (page 219) and The Old Convent (page 128)
Title page: Linthwaite House Hotel (page 35)
Back cover: Broomhill Manor Country Estate (page 192) and Montgomery House (page 112)

Somewhere Special is the guide for the discerning traveller, featuring hundreds of hotels, B&Bs, inns, farmhouses, guest accommodation and self-catering all offering their guests that little bit extra. The format is easy to use, with attractive, detailed entries cross-referenced to full-colour maps, plus articles and features as well as helpful hints. Whatever your budget, and whether you want a short get-away or a longer break, **Somewhere Special** offers a choice of accommodation that promises a warm welcome and a stay that's special.

Welcome...

Your sure signs of where to stay

As in other English Tourism Council guides, all accommodation included in this invaluable title has been assessed under the Council's National Rating Standard (see page 9). In **Somewhere Special**, however, you are promised something extra, for every single entry has achieved a top quality Star or Diamond rating or a Gold or Silver Award (see page 9). This means that the full range of facilities on offer will be presented with exceptional care, individuality and quality of service.

Quality first

Whether you're looking for no-holds-barred luxury on a grand scale, a short break in a cosy cottage with character or an intimate bed and breakfast that gives personal attention to perhaps only three or four guests, you're looking in the right guide. The criterion for inclusion in **Somewhere Special** is excellence rather than the range of facilities available – though of course you'll be able to see at a glance exactly what's on offer.

How to use the guide

Somewhere Special will enable you to find that special place to stay – whichever part of the country you are planning to visit. Even if you only have a rough idea of where you wish to go, you can easily use this guide to locate a quality place to stay.

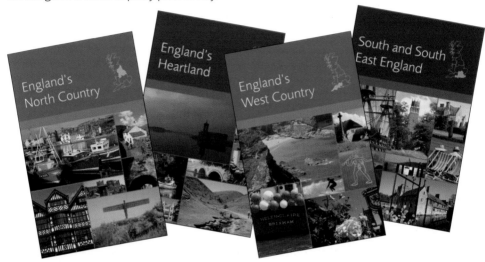

The guide is divided into four distinct sections:
England's North Country, England's Heartland, England's West Country, and South & South East England.

Overleaf you will find a break-down of which county is in which region, together with an accompanying 'England-at-a-glance' map.

Regional listings

Entries are listed by their geographical position, so you'll find that the places you are interested in are usually close to each other in the guide. Serviced establishments (hotels and B&B guest accommodation) are listed separatley from self-catering properties and appear first within each regional section. Each of these sub-sections is preceded by a full-colour regional map which clearly plots by number the location of all the **Somewhere Special** entries, as well as the positions of major roads, towns, stations and airports. If you know the area you want to visit, first locate the possible establishments on the regional map and then turn to the appropriate pages in the regional section.

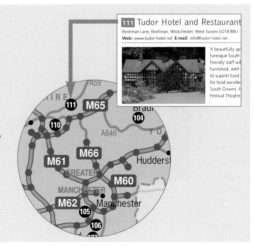

111 Tudor Hotel and Restaurant
Boshman Lane, Boshman, Wickchester, West Sussex SO18 8BU
Web: www.tudor-hotel.net **E-mail:** info@tudor-hotel.net

A beautifully ap
turesque South
friendly staff wi
its superb food
for food excelle
South Downs. H
Festival Theatre

The entries in more detail

The entries are designed to convey as much information as possible in a clear, attractive and easy-to-read format. A fictional sample entry is shown below, together with an explanation of the layout of information.

Each entry shows the establishment's Star or Diamond rating. In **Somewhere Special**, of course, every entry will have a rating of either Four or Five Stars or Diamonds, or a Gold or Silver Award.

1 Entries cross-referenced by number to full-colour maps at the beginning of each regional sub-section

2 Establishment name plus Star or Diamond rating

3 Address and full contact details

4 Full description of establishment

5 Detailed information on prices and facilities, including months open (note: only shown if establishment is **not** open all year) and any credit or charge cards accepted

6 Symbols showing the full range of facilities and services available (see the back cover flap for a key)

111 Tudor Hotel and Restaurant ★★★ Silver Award

Boshman Lane, Boshman, Wickchester, West Sussex SO18 8BU **Tel:** (01842) 173234 **Fax:** (01842) 173459
Web: www.tudor-hotel.net **E-mail:** info@tudor-hotel.net

A beautifully appointed country manor house dating from 1501, set in a picturesque South Downs village, only four miles west of Wickchester. The friendly staff will make you feel very welcome. Bedrooms are all individually furnished, with every modern facility. The Tudor Restaurant is renowned for its superb food and extensive wine list and has been awarded an AA Rosette for food excellence. Enjoy walking on the beautiful riverside or the rolling South Downs. Hambourne Roman Villa, Brickwood House and Wickchester Festival Theatre are all within easy reach.

Bed & Breakfast per night: single room from £59.00–£62.00; double room from £92.00–£115.00
Dinner, Bed & Breakfast per person, per night: £60.00–£75.00
Lunch available: 1230–1400
Evening meal: 1900 (last orders 2130)

Bedrooms: 5 single, 16 double, 10 twin, 2 family
Bathrooms: 33 en-suite
Parking: 44 spaces
Open: All year except Christmas
Cards accepted: Mastercard, Visa, Switch/Delta, Amex, Diners, Eurocard

Other features of the guide

As well as the entries – 543 in all – you'll find many interesting and informative features on a wide variety of subjects scattered throughout the book. The four comprehensive introductions to the regions start on pages 13, 85, 145 and 203. At the back of the book (starting on page 253) you will find more detailed information about booking accommodation. You are strongly recommended to read this before committing yourself to any firm arrangements, bearing in mind the fact that all details have been supplied by proprietors themselves. Finally, you will find a complete alphabetical index to all the establishments featured in the guide, cross-referenced to the page number on which they appear.

England at a glance

This guide is divided into four main regional sections. A map of the area, showing each entry and its nearest town or city, as well as nearby major roads or motorways, can be found after the regional introduction.

England's North Country
Cheshire, Cumbria, County Durham, East Riding of Yorkshire, Greater Manchester, Lancashire, Merseyside, North & North East Lincolnshire, North, South & West Yorkshire, Northumberland, Tees Valley, Tyne & Wear, York.

England's Heartland
Bedfordshire, Cambridgeshire, Derbyshire, Essex, Gloucestershire, Herefordshire, Hertfordshire, Leicestershire, Lincolnshire, Norfolk, Northamptonshire, Nottinghamshire, Rutland, Shropshire, Staffordshire, Suffolk, Warwickshire, West Midlands, Worcestershire.

England's West Country
Bath & North East Somerset, Bristol, Cornwall, Devon, Isles of Scilly, North Somerset, Somerset, South Gloucestershire, Western Dorset, Wiltshire.

South & South East England
Berkshire, Buckinghamshire, East & West Sussex, Eastern Dorset, Hampshire, Isle of Wight, Kent, London, Oxfordshire, Surrey.

The Connaught Hotel (page 226)

The National Rating Standard

Lakefield (page 66)

When you're looking for a place to stay, you need a rating system you can trust. The English Tourism Council's ratings give you a clear guide to what to expect, in an easy-to-understand form. Properties are visited annually by trained, impartial assessors who award ratings based on the overall experience of their visit. There are strict guidelines to ensure every property is assessed to the same criteria, so you can have the confidence that your accommodation has been thoroughly checked and rated for quality before you make your booking. After all, meeting customer expectations is what makes happy guests.

Tide's Reach (page 196)

Gold and Silver Awards

Look out for the Gold and Silver Awards which are exclusive to the English Tourism Council. They are awarded to hotels and guest accommodation establishments which not only achieve the overall quality within their Star or Diamond rating, but also reach the highest level of quality in those specific areas which guests identify as being really important for them. They will reflect the quality of comfort and cleanliness you will find in the bedrooms and bathrooms and the quality of service you'll enjoy throughout your stay.

An assessor calls

Before a quality rating is awarded, one of our qualified assessors visits the establishment to make an independent assessment. For serviced accommodation, the assessor books in advance as a 'normal' guest and does not reveal his or her identity until after settling the bill following an overnight stay. Self-catering properties are generally assessed on a day visit arranged in advance with the owner.

Each assessment will involve a thorough tour of the property together with the proprietor. At the end of the tour, they discuss the conclusions, with the assessor making suggestions where helpful.

Only after the visit does the assessor arrive at a conclusion for the quality rating – so the assessment is 100% independent and reliable.

Tylney Hall Hotel (page 218)

Millstream Hotel and Restaurant (page 230)

Stars for Hotels

Star ratings are your sign of quality assurance, giving you the confidence to book the accommodation that meets your expectations. Based on the internationally recognised rating of one to five Stars, the system puts great emphasis on quality and is based on research which shows exactly what consumers are looking for when choosing a hotel. Ratings are awarded from one to five Stars – the more Stars, the higher the quality and the greater the range of facilities and level of services provided.

> Remember that only Star rated hotels with a Gold or Silver Award qualify for entry in Somewhere Special.

Hotel Star ratings explained

At a ★ hotel you will find:
Practical accommodation with a limited range of facilities and services, and a high standard of cleanliness throughout. Friendly and courteous staff to give you the help and information you need to enjoy your stay.
Restaurant/eating area open to you and your guests for breakfast and dinner. Alcoholic drinks will be served in a bar or lounge. 75% of bedrooms will have en-suite or private facilities.

At a ★★ hotel you will find:
In addition to what is provided at ★
Good overnight accommodation with more comfortable bedrooms, better equipped – all with en-suite or private facilities and colour television. A relatively straightforward range of services, including food and drink and a personal style of service. A restaurant/dining room for breakfast and dinner. A lift is normally available.

At a ★★★ hotel you will find:
In addition to what is provided at ★ and ★★
Very good accommodation offering greater quality and range of facilities and services, and usually more spacious public areas and bedrooms. A more formal style of service with a receptionist on duty and staff responding well to your needs and requests. Room service of continental breakfast. Laundry service available. A wide selection of drinks, light lunch and snacks served in a bar or lounge.

At a ★★★★ hotel you will find:
In addition to what is provided at ★, ★★ and ★★★
Excellent accommodation offering superior comfort and quality; all bedrooms with en-suite bath, fitted overhead shower and WC. The hotel will have spacious and very well appointed public areas and will put a strong emphasis on food and drink. Staff will have very good technical and social skills, anticipating and responding to your needs and requests. Room service of all meals and 24 hour drinks, refreshments and snacks. Dry cleaning service available.

At a ★★★★★ hotel you will find:
In addition to what is provided at ★, ★★, ★★★ and ★★★★
A spacious, luxurious establishment offering you the highest international quality of accommodation, facilities, services and cuisine. It will have striking accommodation throughout, with a range of extra facilities. You will feel very well cared for by professional, attentive staff providing flawless guest services. A hotel that fits the highest international standards for the industry, with an air of luxury, exceptional comfort and a sophisticated ambience.

Marriott Sprowston Manor Hotel & Country Club (page 123)

Diamonds for Guest Accommodation

The Diamond ratings for Guest Accommodation reflect visitor expectations of this sector – a wide variety of serviced accommodation, embracing B&Bs, inns, farmhouses and guest accommodation, for which England is renowned.

The quality of what is provided is more important to visitors than a wide range of facilities and services. Therefore, the same minimum requirement for facilities and services applies to all Guest Accommodation from one to five Diamonds, while progressively higher levels of quality and customer care must be provided for each rating.

In Somewhere Special, only those establishments with a Four or Five Diamond rating, or a Diamond rated property with a Gold or Silver Award, qualify for entry in the guide.

Walnut Tree Cottage Hotel (page 119)

Guest accommodation Diamond ratings explained

At ◆◆◆ guest accommodation you will find:
A good overall level of quality. For example, good quality, comfortable bedrooms; well maintained, practical décor; a good choice of quality items available for breakfast; other meals, where provided, will be freshly cooked from good quality ingredients. A good degree of comfort provided for you, with good levels of customer care. A comfortable bed, with clean bed linen and towels and fresh soap. Adequate heating and hot water available at reasonable times for baths or showers at no extra charge. A sound overall level of quality and customer care in all areas.

At ◆◆◆◆ guest accommodation you will find:
In addition to what is provided at ◆◆◆
An excellent overall level of quality in all areas and customer care showing very good levels of attention to your needs.

At ◆◆◆◆◆ guest accommodation you will find:
In addition to what is provided at ◆◆◆ *and* ◆◆◆◆
An exceptional overall level of quality. For example, ample space with a degree of luxury, an excellent quality bed, high quality furniture, excellent interior design. Breakfast offering a wide choice of high quality fresh ingredients; other meals, where provided, featuring fresh, seasonal, and often local ingredients. Excellent levels of customer care, anticipating your needs.

Bradfield Manor (page 167)

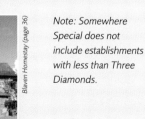

Blaven Homestay (page 36)

Note: Somewhere Special does not include establishments with less than Three Diamonds.

Dairy Cottage (page 76)

Stars for Self-Catering

The Star ratings for self-catering reflect the quality that you're looking for when booking accommodation. All properties have to meet an extensive list of minimum requirements to take part in the scheme. Ratings are awarded from one to five Stars – the more Stars, the higher the quality. Establishments at higher rating levels also have to meet additional requirements for facilities. Some self-catering establishments have a range of accommodation units in the building or on the site and the individual units may have different Star ratings. In such cases the entry shows the range available.

> Remember that only Four and Five Star properties qualify for entry in Somewhere Special.

Self-catering Star ratings explained

At a ★★★★ property you will find:
An excellent overall level of quality with very good care and attention to detail throughout. There will be a microwave cooker and access to a washing machine and drier if it is not provided in the unit, or a 24-hour laundry service.

At a ★★★★★ property you will find:
In addition to what is provided at ★★★★
An exceptional overall level of quality with high levels of décor, fixtures and fittings, with personal touches. Excellent standards of management efficiency and guest services.

Accessibility

If you find difficulty in walking or are a wheelchair user, then you also need to know how accessible a particular establishment is. If you book your accommodation at an establishment displaying the Accessible symbol, there's no longer any guesswork involved. The National Accessible Scheme forms part of the *Tourism for All* campaign that is being promoted by all National and Regional Tourist Boards throughout Britain. There are three categories of accessibility, based upon what are considered to be the practical needs of wheelchair users. The National Accessible Scheme is currently in the process of being updated. Consultation has been conducted throughout 2001 with introduction during 2002.

 Category 1: accessible to all wheelchair users including those travelling independently

 Category 2: accessible to a wheelchair user with assistance

Category 3: accessible to a wheelchair user able to walk short distances and up at least three steps.

Old Vicarage Hotel ₤ Category 2 (page 102)

Additional help and guidance for those with special needs can be obtained from:

Holiday Care, 2nd Floor, Imperial Buildings, Victoria Road, Horley, Surrey RH6 7PZ
Telephone (01293) 774535
Fax (01293) 784647
Minicom (01293) 776943
Web: www.holidaycare.org.uk
E-mail: holiday.care@virgin.net

England's North Country

Peak after peak

The soul of England's North Country lies in the Pennines, England's mountainous backbone stretching from the borders of Scotland to the borders of the Midlands. The North boasts the Lake District, two glorious coastlines, countless imposing castles and, in York, one of the most perfect cities one could ever wish for, but somehow the sheer scale of the Pennine ridge dominates. The mountains run for around 200 miles (320km), the peaks rising above 2,000ft (610m), too many to count.

▶ Humber Bridge

Parliament approved construction of a Humber bridge in 1959, but it took 22 years to open, and cost £98 million, almost four times the original estimate. The result, however, is impressive. With a central span of almost a mile (4,626ft, 1,410m), the Humber Bridge was until very recently the longest unsupported section of bridge in the world. Visitor facilities include viewing areas at both ends; the northern side also has a tourist information centre and country park; views of and from the bridge are magnificent.

Exploring on foot

The most famous way to savour the Pennine experience, fitness and time permitting, is to walk Britain's oldest long-distance path. About 10,000 people each year complete the 268 miles (431km) of the Pennine Way, though many more – perhaps 300,000 – join it for a mile or two from one of 535 separate access points. Two of these are intersections with other long-distance waymarked paths. The Coast-to-Coast Walk, as its name suggests, links the Irish Sea with the North Sea, traversing the Lake District, Yorkshire Dales and North York Moors national parks on its 190 mile (306km) route, while the Dales Way (81 miles, 130km) is a low-level path along the banks of the Wharfe, Dee, Lune and Kent rivers. The Cumbria Way (Ulverston to Carlisle) guides you through Lakeland grandeur. The Cleveland Way falls almost entirely within the North York Moors national park, but still extends over 100 miles (160km). Roughly following the river from its source high in the Dales to the sea near Preston, the wise walker tackles the Ribble Way in a downhill direction. Altogether quieter and less dramatic is the Wolds Way, wending from near Hull to Filey, where it joins the Cleveland Way. Needless to say, all these – as well as Hadrian's Wall, which can be walked for its entire length – explore scenery of the utmost beauty. All make an ideal starting point for shorter strolls, too.

▶ Bowes Museum

In the entrance hall, on the stroke of every hour, a large silver swan whirrs into action, slowly bending its articulated silver neck to swallow a silver fish. This bizarre mechanical toy is one of many valuable treasures amassed by John Bowes, Earl of Strathmore, who in 1869 began building this outrageously inappropriate French château-style mansion to house his possessions. The imposing rooms contain paintings by El Greco, Goya, Boucher and Courbet, together with superb displays of furniture, ceramics and tapestries (tel: 01833 690606).

Mills to museums

Towards the southern end of the Pennines the valleys become more populated. The fast-flowing rivers that long ago powered the mills are lined with the characterful small houses built for the workers. Once reviled but now revered, towns such as Holmforth and Hebden Bridge have justly become visitor attractions in their own right. And the factories have in many instances been turned into imaginative museums and galleries. The Armley Mills Industrial Museum, Leeds, occupies what was once the largest woollen mill in the world; Saddleworth Museum and Art Gallery houses working woollen textile machinery; much of Salts Mill, near Bradford is devoted to the works of the artist, David Hockney; and, at Macclesfield, Paradise Mill produced silk until the 1980s. At Sheffield, those with an interest in industrial archaeology can indulge themselves at either the Abbeydale Industrial Hamlet or Kelham Island Industrial Museum. If you prefer more modern scientific endeavour, then try the Jodrell Bank Science Centre & Arboretum, south of Manchester, home of a massive steerable radio telescope.

On a grand scale

A few miles from Jodrell Bank lies Tatton Park, one of the finest country houses of the North, and built on the decidedly grand scale. Other lesser-known properties to explore include: medieval Raby Castle with its nine towers (near Staindrop, County Durham); the very Victorian Lady Waterford Hall, decorated with murals depicting familiar Bible stories (Ford, Northumberland); Dalemain, a stately home intriguingly adapted from the original pele tower, now home of the Westmorland and Cumberland Yeomanry Museum (Penrith, Cumbria); Burton Constable Hall, an Elizabethan setting for a remarkable collection of scientific instruments (Sproatley, East Riding of Yorkshire); Croxteth Hall, where visitors can join an Edwardian house party or look at an extensive collection of rare breed animals (Liverpool, Merseyside); and Browsholme Hall, full of unusual objects squirrelled by the Parker family, owners of the hall for over 400 years (near Whitewell, Lancashire).

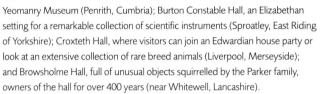

For art's sake

The North Country has a range of arts and music festivals to rival the rest of England. As always, the breadth of entertainment is prodigious. For concerts devoted to early music – and played in some of England's most glorious medieval churches – visit either the York Early Music Festival (July) or, 25 or so miles (40km) further east, the Beverley and East Riding Early Music Festival (May). At the other end of the spectrum, go south to Huddersfield in November for the Contemporary Music Festival. The Lake District hosts jazz, orchestral and chamber concerts at a number of venues as part of its Summer Music festivities (August), while Chester does broadly the same – as well as throwing in a fringe element, too – in July. Bradford (late June and early July) and Harrogate (late July and early August) both add comedy and street theatre to a range of musical concerts. Manchester, meanwhile, devotes three weeks in May to its Streets Ahead festival. Circus events and fireworks provide alternatives to the music, dance and theatre – and everything is free. And, if you thought the Aldborough Festival was exclusive to Suffolk, look closely at the spelling. A village near Boroughbridge, North Yorkshire, holds the Northern Aldborough (not Aldeburgh) Festival each July; classical music is once again the subject.

Fishing villages and golden sands

The coastline of Northumberland, England's north eastern extremity, bears an intriguing resemblance to Cornwall, in the extreme south west. Fine sandy beaches, a history peopled by saints and martyrs, and a rural interior characterise both. In Northumberland it is a simple matter to escape the throng, but take a trip to the Farne Islands, and you will be outnumbered by

► Settle–Carlisle railway

When the railway between Settle and Carlisle opened in 1876 it had taken over six years to build, cost more than £3.5 million, and claimed the life of one navvy per week. Crossing perhaps the most inhospitable terrain in England, including the summit of Ais Gill (1,169ft, 356m), the line stretched Victorian engineering to the limits. Today it affords passengers views of enormous beauty, and provides opportunities for walking the dramatic scenery along its route. Excursions are available; for general information call 08457 484950.

► Port Sunlight

Lord Leverhulme employed 30 or so architects to design Port Sunlight, 3 miles (5km) south east of Birkenhead, including a young Edwin Lutyens. Opened on 3 March 1888, Port Sunlight provided high-quality homes at affordable rents for workers at his Lever Brothers' soap factory. Visiting the garden village, with its varied architectural styles, is a fascinating day out. One highlight is the Lady Lever Art Gallery, containing magnificent works by English painters, including some leading pre-Raphaelite artists (tel: 0151 644 6466).

both birds and seals. The golden shores south of Bamburgh and north of Dunstanburgh, two glorious beaches that never seem busy, have the added attraction of offering views of their respective castles. Further south, into the North York Moors national park, the coastline is more for the fossil hunter and the walker – the Cleveland Way here follows the sea – than the sun-seeker. Many of the picturesque villages, such as Ravenscar, Runswick Bay, Staithes and Robin Hood's Bay, tumble down cliffs that yield an array of fossils. Then come the famous resorts of Scarborough, Filey and Bridlington, each with magnificent golden beaches ideal for family outings. Southport,

► Grace Darling

Few women have attracted such uninvited public adulation as Grace Darling. Daughter of a lighthouse keeper, Grace lived a lonely life on the Farne Islands, off the Northumberland coast. On 7 September 1838 she and her father risked their lives to rescue nine survivors from the wrecked steamer *Forfarshire*, putting out in heavy seas in a tiny rowing-boat. The newspapers made her a national heroine overnight. At Bamburgh are the Grace Darling Museum and the cottage where she was born. Weather permitting, a boat trip around the Farne Islands is an unforgettable experience (tel: 01665 720884).

on the southern Lancashire shores, has endless sand, as does its illustrious neighbour, Blackpool, over the Ribble Estuary. North again is Morecambe Bay, at low tide around 150 square miles (38,850 hectares) of gleaming but potentially treacherous sand. Away from the bustle of Blackpool and the teeming birdlife of Morecambe Bay, try Annaside or Gutterby Spa, two of the region's remoter beaches.

Former glories

Hidden away on Cumbria's westernmost point is an elegant port that, 250 years ago, was busier than Liverpool. Retaining many 17th- and 18th-century buildings, and with pleasure craft bobbing up and down in the old harbour, Whitehaven makes an unusual excursion from the Lake District. The North has countless towns that invite unhurried exploration. One is Hexham, whose focal point is the magnificent abbey, dating largely from the 12th century, but it also has Georgian streets surrounding the Shambles, the shelter for the lively Tuesday market. Others to consider are: Rothbury, in Northumberland, an attractive small market town with a medieval bridge; Barnard Castle (County Durham), where visitors can marvel at the exhibits in the Bowes Museum, then clamber over the ruins of the lofty castle to admire the views of the River Tees; Beverley (East Riding of Yorkshire), a superb mixture of medieval and Georgian architecture; Pickering (North Yorkshire), whose ancient coaching inns reflect its heyday as an important stop on the way to Scarborough and Whitby; Clitheroe (Lancashire), where a diminutive Norman castle watches over the stone-built houses; and Macclesfield (Cheshire), a former weaving centre in the shadow of the southern Pennines with fine 18th-century townhouses.

► Lawnmowers on Display

The British Lawnmower Museum (tel: 01704 501336) is based in the seaside resort of Southport, Merseyside. Prized exhibits include some of the first machines dating from the early 19th century, mowers once belonging to Nicholas Parsons and to Prince Charles, another capable of cutting a 2 inch (5cm) wide strip, and what is believed to be the only hand-powered rotary lawnmower in existence. Also on view is the world's largest collection of toy mowers and one of the oldest surviving racing lawnmowers (built by the curator).

North Country fare

The region produces a number of edible specialities, confectionery and cheeses in particular. Cumbria, renowned for its coiled, smoky sausage, also produces Cumberland rum butter – originally eaten to celebrate the arrival of a newborn child and still made in Whitehaven – as well as Kendal mint cake, famously taken on expeditions to Mount Everest. Pontefract was once the centre of liquorice cultivation and, although the plant is no longer grown nearby, Pontefract cakes are manufactured in the town. Nantwich Museum devotes a room to Cheshire cheese, while three Yorkshire Dales – Swaledale, Wensleydale and Coverdale – give their names to crumbly cheeses made within the national park. Traditionally, the finest kippers are sold on the quayside at Whitby.

A Northern miscellany

The North Country can also offer many other curiosities. Around Ingleton are a number of cave systems, of which the vast Gaping Ghyll cavern is perhaps the most impressive. Also in North Yorkshire, but west of Masham, is the Druid's Temple, a 19th-century folly built in imitation of a miniature Stonehenge. Hale, just over the Mersey from Runcorn, boasts the grave of John Middleton, a local giant reputedly 9 ft 3 inches (2.8m) tall, while at Lower Heysham, near Morecambe, on a promontory above the sandy beach, are some strange rock 'coffins', perhaps carved by 9th-century missionaries from Ireland. And in one of England's furthest-flung spots, high up in the Pennines where Cumbria and Durham meet, is Cauldron Snout, a magnificent waterfall and series of cataracts.

Some useful contact numbers

Lake District National Park Visitors' Centre (tel: 01539 446601)
Yorkshire Dales National Park (tel: 01756 752774)
North York Moors National Park (tel: 01439 770657)
Hadrian's Wall (tel: 01434 344363)
The Armley Mills Industrial Museum, Leeds (tel: 0113 263 7861)
Saddleworth Museum and Art Gallery, Uppermill (tel: 01457 874093)
Salts Mill, Bradford (tel: 01274 531163)
Paradise Mill, Macclesfield (tel: 01625 618228)
Abbeydale Industrial Hamlet, Sheffield (tel: 0114 236 7731)
Kelham Island Museum, Sheffield (tel: 0114 272 2106)
Jodrell Bank Science Centre & Arboretum (tel: 01477 571339)
Raby Castle, Staindrop (tel: 01833 660202)
Lady Waterford Hall, Ford (tel: 01890 820338)
Dalemain, Penrith (tel: 01768 486450)
Burton Constable Hall, Sproatley (tel: 01964 562400)
Croxteth Hall, Liverpool (tel: 0151 228 5311)
Browsholme Hall, Whitewell (tel: 01254 826719)
York Early Music Festival (tel: 01904 645738)
Beverley and East Riding Early Music Festival (tel: 01904 645738)
Huddersfield Contemporary Music Festival (tel: 01484 472103)
Lake District Summer Music (tel: 01539 724441)
Chester Summer Festival (tel: 01244 320722)
Bradford Festival (tel: 01274 309199)
Harrogate International Festival (tel: 01423 562303)
Manchester International Arts (tel: 0161 224 0020)
Northern Aldborough Festival (tel: 01423 324899)
Nantwich Museum (tel: 01270 627104)

▶ Grizedale Sculpture Trail

A walk through Grizedale Forest offers a fascinating trail of discovery in the hunt for 80 or so large-scale sculptures dotted

along its pathways. The Sculpture Trail began as an opportunity for artists to develop diverse works on the theme of the Forest, and the sculptures are inspired by the materials and forms which naturally occur here: wildlife, rock formations, drystone walls, and, of course, trees. Most are sited on the Silurian Way, a 9½-mile (15km) circular walk starting at the Visitor Centre (tel: 01229 860010) where maps (including short-cuts) may be purchased.

▶ Berwick-upon-Tweed

Berwick-upon-Tweed, though still in England, is further north than much of the Hebridean island of Islay. Oddly, it is cut off from the county which bears its name, for Berwickshire lies in Scotland. Less surprisingly, Berwick's history is intractably bound up with the struggle between the English and the Scots; between 1147 and 1482, the town changed hands 13 times. The 16th century saw the walls comprehensively fortified against a Scots-French attack which never materialised, hence their amazing state of preservation. A 2 mile (3km) walk around these ramparts gives spectacular views of the historic town.

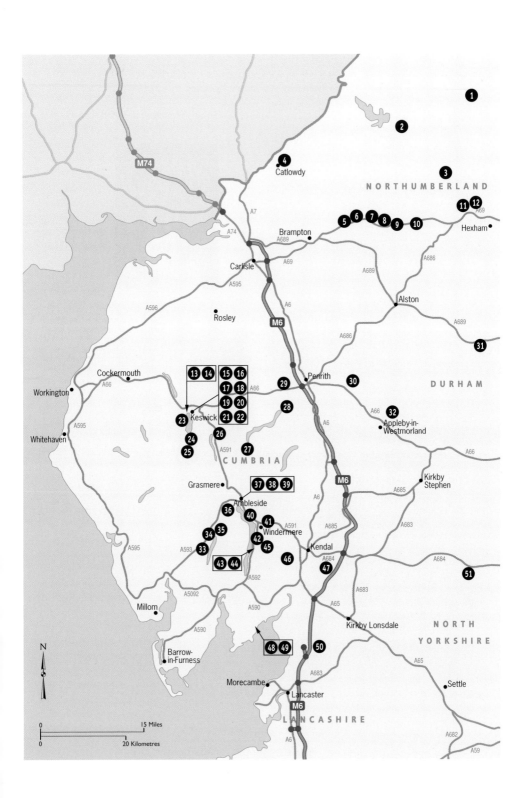

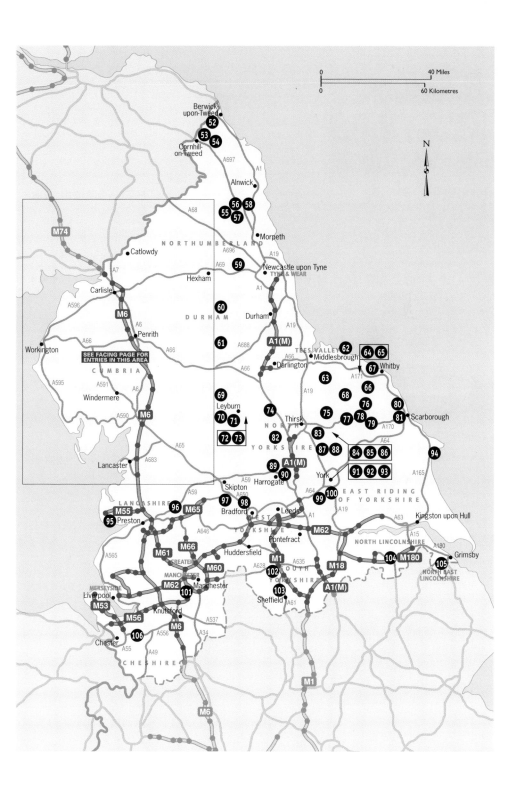

1 Dunns Houses Farmhouse Bed and Breakfast   ◆◆◆◆

Dunns Houses, Otterburn, Newcastle upon Tyne, NE19 1LB **Tel:** (01830) 520677 **Fax:** (01830) 520677
Web: www.northumberlandfarmholidays.co.uk **E-mail:** dunnshouses@hotmail.com

Warm, friendly, peaceful Victorian farmhouse with spacious en-suite bedrooms and lounge in self-contained part of the house. Traditional English breakfast made with local produce. Magnificent countryside. Activities include on-site fishing and stables. Nearby is excellent walking, cycling, fishing, birdwatching and golf. Racing at Hexham, Kelso or Newcastle. Kielder, Hadrian's Wall, historical houses and castles. Situated in the heart of Northumberland, surrounded by the Northumberland National Park. Newcastle airport 30m. Royal Quays international ferry services 45m. Children and pets welcome.

Bed & Breakfast per night: single occupancy from £25.00–£30.00; double room from £40.00–£60.00

Bedrooms: 1 double, 1 family
Bathrooms: 2 en-suite
Parking: 10 spaces

2 The Pheasant Inn (by Kielder Water)   ◆◆◆◆

Stannersburn, Falstone, Hexham, Northumberland NE48 1DD **Tel:** (01434) 240382 **Fax:** (01434) 240382
Web: www.the pheasantinn.com **E-mail:** thepheasantinn@kielderwater.demon.co.uk

Traditional 17th-century inn, 375 years old, run by the Kershaw family for the last 16 years. Beamed ceilings, exposed stone walls, centrally heated, open fires provide its cosy atmosphere. An emphasis is maintained on home cooking, using carefully prepared local produce. Eight en-suite bedrooms offer comfortable accommodation with all the modern conveniences you would expect. An ideal location for visiting Kielder Water, Hadrian's Wall, Rothbury (Cragside) and the Scottish Border country.

Bed & Breakfast per night: single occupancy from £30.00–£40.00; double room from £60.00–£65.00
Dinner, Bed & Breakfast per person, per night: £45.00 (min 2 nights October–May)
Lunch available: 1200–1430

Evening meal: 1900 (last orders 2100)
Bedrooms: 4 double, 3 twin, 1 family
Bathrooms: 8 en-suite
Parking: 30 spaces
Cards accepted: Mastercard, Visa, Switch/Delta, Eurocard, JCB

3 Hetherington   ◆◆◆◆

Wark-on-Tyne, Hexham, Northumberland NE48 3DR **Tel:** (01434) 230260 **Fax:** (01434) 230260
E-mail: a_nichol@hotmail.com

A warm welcome awaits visitors to Hetherington, situated in beautiful South Northumberland. Pamper yourself in our genuine four-poster en-suite bedroom. A spa bath is also available for guests. Approximately 40 miles from the ferry terminal and centrally situated for Hadrian's Wall and Kielder Water. An ideal base for walking, touring or cycling. Visit castles, churches and gardens. Catherine Cookson's television dramas are often filmed in this locality. There is a very good selection of pubs and restaurants close at hand.

Bed & Breakfast per night: single occupancy £22.00; double room from £46.00–£52.00

Bedrooms: 2 double, 1 twin
Bathrooms: 2 en-suite, 1 public
Parking: 6 spaces
Open: March–November

4 Bessiestown

♦♦♦♦♦ Silver Award

Catlowdy, Longtown, Carlisle, Cumbria CA6 5QP **Tel:** (01228) 577219 or (01228) 577019 **Fax:** (01228) 577219 or (01228) 577019
Web: www.bessiestown.co.uk **E-mail:** bestbb2000@cs.com

As featured on BBC and GMTV. Multi award-winning best guesthouse. Warm and welcoming, peaceful and quiet. Pretty en-suite bedrooms. New honeymoon suite. Delightful public rooms. Delicious food. Drinks licence. Open all year with indoor heated swimming pool from mid-May to mid-September. Excellent touring base or stop off for Scotland or Northern Ireland. Easy access from M6 junction 44, M74 junction 22 and A7.

🕆 Category 3

Bed & Breakfast per night: single occupancy £35.00; double room from £55.00–£98.00
Dinner, Bed & Breakfast per person, per night: from £41.00
Evening meal: 1900 (last bookings 1600)

Bedrooms: 5 double/twin, 1 family
Bathrooms: 6 en-suite
Parking: 10 spaces
Cards accepted: Mastercard, Visa

5 Bush Nook Guest House

♦♦♦♦

Upper Denton, Gilsland, Brampton, Cumbria CA8 7AF **Tel:** (01697) 747194 **Fax:** (01697) 747790
Web: www.hadriansway.co.uk **E-mail:** paulaibarton@bushnook.freeserve.co.uk

Set in beautiful open countryside and dating back to 1760, Bush Nook provides comfortable accommodation in a peaceful, relaxing environment. A former farmhouse, the two hay loft rooms feature open beams, whilst there is a delightful conservatory and quiet lounge for your use. Licensed, our award-winning evening meals are a speciality. Close to Hadrian's Wall, Bush Nook is a perfect base for touring this unspoilt area, or is an ideal stopover when travelling to or from Scotland.

Bed & Breakfast per night: single room from £18.00–£20.00; double room from £40.00–£50.00
Dinner, Bed & Breakfast per person, per night: £28.00–£37.50
Evening meal: 1900

Bedrooms: 1 single, 2 double, 1 twin
Bathrooms: 2 en-suite, 2 shared
Parking: 4 spaces
Cards accepted: Mastercard, Visa, Switch/Delta

6 The Hill on the Wall

♦♦♦♦

Gilsland, Carlisle CA8 7DA **Tel:** (01697) 747214 **Fax:** (01697) 747214
Web: www.hadrians-wallbedandbreakfast.com **E-mail:** thehill@hadrians-wall.demon.co.uk

A fascinating 16th-century fortified farmhouse overlooking the beautiful Irthing Valley and Hadrian's Wall at Birdoswald, an area rich in Roman history with an outstanding natural landscape. The location is ideal for exploring the north Pennines, Northumberland, the Scottish Borders and the Lake District. Good stopover for Scotland. Comfortable and peaceful with excellent home cooking. Evening meals available.

Bed & Breakfast per night: single occupancy from £20.00–£22.00; double room from £48.00–£52.00
Dinner, Bed & Breakfast per person, per night: £37.50–£40.00

Bedrooms: 3 double/twin
Bathrooms: 2 en-suite, 1 shared
Parking: 10 spaces

7 Holmhead Guest House ◆◆◆◆

on Thirlwall Castle Farm, Hadrian's Wall, Greenhead, via Brampton, Nr. Carlisle CA8 7HY **Tel:** (016977) 47402 **Fax:** (016977) 47402
Web: www.bandbhadrianswall.com **E-mail:** Holmhead@hadrianswall.freeserve.co.uk

Holmhead Farm Guest House is a 200-year-old farmhouse built of stone from Hadrian's Wall and situated near spectacular Roman remains, museums and excavations. Your host, Pauline Staff, is a qualified tour guide and a expert on Hadrian's Wall and is happy to help plan your itinerary or arrange personally guided tours. Offering cosy en-suite bedrooms with lovely views, award-winning breakfasts and, by arrangement, candlelit dinner parties using fresh local produce. Every effort is made to ensure you get the very best combination of local historical interest, comfort and catering from your holiday. Licensed. Non-smoking. AA Special Breakfast Award.

Bed & Breakfast per night: single occupancy from £39.00–£40.00; double room from £58.00–£59.00
Dinner, Bed & Breakfast per person, per night: £49.00–£50.00
Lunch available: packed lunches £2–£5

Bedrooms: 1 double, 2 twin, 1 triple
Bathrooms: 4 en-suite
Parking: 6 spaces
Cards accepted: Mastercard, Visa, JCB

8 Broomshaw Hill Farm ◆◆◆◆◆ Gold Award

Willia Road, Haltwhistle, Northumberland NE49 9NP **Tel:** (01434) 320866 **Fax:** (01434) 320866
Web: www.broomshaw.co.uk **E-mail:** stay-broomshaw@ntlworld.com

For visitors looking for luxury and value. An 18th-century farmhouse enlarged and modernised to very high standards, but still retaining its old world charm. The house is set on the side of a wooded valley through which runs the Haltwhistle Burn. It stands on the conjunction of a footpath and bridleway, both leading to Hadrian's Wall. You can be assured of a warm welcome, with every effort made to ensure your stay is enjoyable.

Bed & Breakfast per night: double room from £46.00–£48.00

Bedrooms: 2 double, 1 twin
Bathrooms: 2 en-suite, 1 private
Parking: 8 spaces
Open: March–October

9 Ashcroft ◆◆◆◆ Silver Award

Lantys Lonnen, Haltwhistle, Northumberland NE49 0DA **Tel:** (01434) 320213 **Fax:** (01434) 320213
Web: www.ashcroftguesthouse.co.uk **E-mail:** enquiries@ashcroftguesthouse.freeserve.co.uk

Elegantly furnished former vicarage, set in large award-winning, terraced gardens. Ample private parking within grounds. Warm, friendly welcome with expert local knowledge. Extensive breakfast choice served in our beautiful dining room overlooking the garden and the hills beyond. Conveniently situated on the southern edge of our small market town, yet only 200 yards from the market square. The perfect base from which to explore Hadrian's Wall and surrounding area. Non-smoking throughout. Colour brochure available.

Bed & Breakfast per night: single room from £25.00–£35.00; double room from £50.00–£56.00

Bedrooms: 1 single, 2 double, 3 twin, 1 family
Bathrooms: 7 en-suite
Cards accepted: Mastercard, Visa, Eurocard

10 Montcoffer

 ◆◆◆◆ Silver Award

Bardon Mill, Hexham, Northumberland NE47 7HZ **Tel:** (01434) 344138 or (07715) 911024 **Fax:** (01434) 344730
Web: www.montcoffer.co.uk **E-mail:** john-dehlia@talk21.com

A warm and relaxed welcome awaits in our tastefully converted stable block. Enjoy an excellent breakfast in our beamed dining room. Our bedrooms offer comfort, privacy and style. We are renowned for providing the highest standards of customer care. We are in a very peaceful location but close to village facilities and the major Roman sites. **Category 2**

Bed & Breakfast per night: single occupancy from £26.00–£32.00; double room from £52.00–£56.00

Bedrooms: 1 double, 1 family
Bathrooms: 2 en-suite
Parking: 8 spaces

11 Newbrough Park

 ◆◆◆◆◆ Gold Award

Newbrough, Hexham, Northumberland NE47 5AR **Tel:** (01434) 674545 **Fax:** (01434) 674544
E-mail: pattie@newbrough.demon.co.uk

Newbrough Park is a beautifully appointed house, dating from 1790 and set in wonderful gardens and grounds. Visit nearby Hexham, with its fine Abbey and racecourse. Also nearby Hadrian's Wall and Vindalanda Roman fort. An ideal base for visiting Newcastle or stopping en-route to Scotland, The Lake District or the south of England. Pattie Shield is a trained cordon bleu cook and will make you feel most welcome.

Bed & Breakfast per night: single occupancy from £35.00–£45.00; double room from £70.00–£90.00
Dinner, Bed & Breakfast per person, per night: £55.00–£70.00
Evening meal: 2000

Bedrooms: 4 double/twin
Bathrooms: 4 en-suite
Parking: 16 spaces
Cards accepted: Mastercard, Visa, Switch/Delta

12 8 St Aidans Park

 ◆◆◆◆

Fourstones, Hexham, Northumberland NE47 5EB **Tel:** (01434) 674073 **Fax:** (01434) 674073
Web: www.hadrians-wall.co.uk **E-mail:** janet@hadrians-wall.co.uk

You will be warmly welcome to stay in this modern stone-built house, situated very close to Hadrian's Wall and the Medieval town of Hexham. We are keen to introduce people to our beautiful and historical region and any visit can be enhanced by being personally conducted around the area (see our website). Walkers, fishermen and guests just wanting to relax will enjoy the good local food.

Bed & Breakfast per night: double room £50.00

Bedrooms: 1 double, 1 twin
Bathrooms: 1 en-suite, 1 private
Parking: 4 spaces
Cards accepted: Mastercard, Visa, Switch/Delta

13 Derwent Cottage

 ◆◆◆◆◆ Gold Award

Portinscale, Keswick, Cumbria CA12 5RF **Tel:** (017687) 74838
E-mail: dercott@btinternet.com

Gleaming silver, cut glass, spacious en-suite bedrooms and elegant furnishings are all to be found at Derwent Cottage. This Lakeland house, dating from the 18th century, stands in large, secluded gardens in the quiet village of Portinscale, one mile from Keswick. A four-course, candle light table d'hôte is served at 1900 each evening with classical music in the background. A residential licence is held, and drinks and wine are available throughout the evening. We are a totally non-smoking establishment.

Bed & Breakfast per night: single occupancy from £37.00–£50.00; double room from £54.00–£80.00
Dinner, Bed & Breakfast per person, per night: £42.00–£55.00
Evening meal: 1900

Bedrooms: 4 double, 2 twin
Bathrooms: 6 en-suite
Parking: 10 spaces
Open: March–October
Cards accepted: Mastercard, Visa, Switch, Solo, Electron

14 Rickerby Grange

◆◆◆◆

Portinscale, Keswick, Cumbria CA12 5RH **Tel:** (01768) 772344 **Fax:** (01768) 775588
Web: www.ricor.co.uk **E-mail:** val@ricor.co.uk

A warm, friendly welcome awaits you at Rickerby Grange, peacefully situated off a private lane in the attractive village of Portinscale. Easy access to the Lakes by car or on foot. Derwent and Keswick are a short walk from our attractive gardens and car park. This family-run hotel prides itself on an excellent choice of freshly prepared food, served to your liking in our elegant dining room. Guest lounge, well stocked bar and first class service are the essential qualities supplied by the resident proprietors.

Bed & Breakfast per night: single room from £30.00–£32.00; double room from £60.00–£64.00
Dinner, Bed & Breakfast per person, per night: £43.00–£45.00
Evening meal: 1900 (last orders 1930)

Bedrooms: 2 single, 8 double, 3 twin, 3 family
Bathrooms: 11 en-suite, 1 private, 1 shared
Cards accepted: Mastercard, Visa, Switch/Delta

15 Lairbeck Hotel

★★ Silver Award

Vicarage Hill, Keswick, Cumbria CA12 5QB **Tel:** (01768) 773373 **Fax:** (01768) 773144
Web: www.lairbeckhotel-keswick.co.uk **E-mail:** ss@lairbeckhotel-keswick.co.uk

A traditional country house hotel in an attractive, secluded garden. With magnificent views of Skiddaw and the surrounding countryside, Lairbeck is only a few minutes' walk from Keswick town centre. We offer a friendly, relaxed atmosphere and excellent home cooking. All bedrooms are en-suite, non-smoking, with television, telephone, hairdryer and tea/coffee facilities. Ground floor accommodation available. No supplement for single rooms. Log fires, full central heating and licensed bar. Special Breaks available. Featured on 'Wish You Were Here?' TV programme.

Bed & Breakfast per night: single room from £34.00–£40.00; double room from £68.00–£80.00
Dinner, Bed & Breakfast per person, per night: £51.00–£57.00
Evening meal: 1830 (last orders 1930)

Bedrooms: 4 single, 7 double, 2 twin, 1 family
Bathrooms: 14 en-suite
Parking: 15 spaces
Cards accepted: Mastercard, Visa, Switch/Delta, Electron, Solo

16 Abacourt House   ◆◆◆◆

26 Stanger Street, Keswick, Cumbria CA12 5JU **Tel:** (01768)772967
Web: www.abacourt.co.uk **E-mail:** abacourt@btinternet.com

In 1992 Abacourt House was created by converting a former private Victorian town house – retaining many of the original features such as pitch-pine doors and staircase – whilst upgrading the property to provide a high standard of accommodation and comfort. We are ideally situated in a cul-de-sac which is quiet at night, yet we are only a few minutes' walk from the town centre shops and restaurants, the lake and the parks.

Bed & Breakfast per night: double room from £44.00–£46.00

Bedrooms: 5 double
Bathrooms: 5 en-suite
Parking: 5 spaces

17 Badgers Wood   ◆◆◆◆

30 Stanger Street, Keswick, Cumbria CA12 5JU **Tel:** (01768) 772621
Web: www.badgers-wood.co.uk **E-mail:** enquiries@badgers-wood.co.uk

Badgers Wood is a fine example of extensive and sympathetic restoration. Situated in a quiet cul-de-sac just minutes from the town centre, bus station and restaurants. Special diets are catered for by arrangement. Our Heartbeat Award assures you of our committment to healthy eating and high standards of kitchen hygiene and our Welcome Host Award assures you of a friendly welcome and comfortable accommodation. All of our bedrooms have views of the beautiful Cumbrian mountains.

Bed & Breakfast per night: single room £18.00; double room from £40.00–£46.00

Bedrooms: 2 single, 3 double, 1 twin
Bathrooms: 2 en-suite, 1 shared

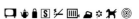

18 Ellergill Guest House   ◆◆◆◆

22 Stanger Street, Keswick, Cumbria CA12 5JU **Tel:** (01768) 773347
Web: www.ellergill.uk.com **E-mail:** stay@ellergill.uk.com

Ellergill is a period town house situated in a quiet location, just a couple of minutes stroll from the centre of Keswick. The centrally-heated accommodation is decorated to a high standard, tastefully furnished with spacious bedrooms offering every comfort with either en-suite or private bathroom, king-size double bed, tea/coffee making facilities, colour television with teletext and radio alarm clock. Ellergill, especially for non-smokers, is open all year.

Bed & Breakfast per night: double room from £40.00–£44.00

Bedrooms: 2 double, 1 twin
Bathrooms: 2 en-suite, 1 private
Parking: unrestricted in Stanger Street

19 Shemara Guest House   ◆◆◆◆

27 Bank Street, Keswick, Cumbria CA12 5JZ **Tel:** (01768) 773936 **Fax:** (01768) 780785
Web: www.shemara.uk.com **E-mail:** shemaraguesthouse@yahoo.co.uk

Quiet, centrally located, all rooms are en-suite and furnished to a very high standard with television, tea/coffee tray, radio, hairdryer, controllable central heating and beautiful mountain views. Cleanliness and hospitality are second to none. Full Cumbrian or continental breakfast is served in our cosy dining room. Strictly no smoking. Private parking available. Once you have stayed at Shemara, we are sure you will return again and again.

Bed & Breakfast per night: single occupancy £25.00; double room from £39.00–£50.00

Bedrooms: 5 double, 1 twin, 1 family
Bathrooms: 7 en-suite
Parking: 4 spaces
Open: February–December
Cards accepted: Mastercard, Visa, Switch/Delta, Visa Electron

The Lake District

To many, the Lake District is a landscape untainted by human hand, a rare example of Nature left gloriously to her own devices. So it may seem, but the reality is different. The breath-taking splendour of the bare mountains, closely cropped turf criss-crossed by drystone walls and lush lowland pasture is as much a product of human activity as the Fens or the Cotswolds. Wind the clock back 5,000 years, and a very different Lakeland scene appears.

The lower slopes were carpeted with mixed oak forest, giving way to birch and pine to a height of about 2,000ft (600m). Above this, only the highest peaks rose above the trees. Down below, the valley bottoms were swamps clogged with sedge and alder. Then our ancestors ventured inland from the more hospitable coastline and began to transform the terrain, a process that has already lasted perhaps five millennia. These New Stone Age peoples knew the volcanic rocks of the Langdale Pikes made the best axe-heads. And with them they cleared land for the grazing of their animals and the planting of their crops.

They left other signs, too. Castlerigg Stone Circle, near Keswick, is the most marvellously situated Neolithic remain, while Long Meg and her Daughters (shown below), near Salkeld, is even larger. With the advent of the Iron Age, around 500BC, trees disappeared at a faster rate. Settlements grew up on limestone areas, where loose rocks were used for round, drystone huts and hillforts. Again, remains can be seen at Carrock Fell in Mungrisdale and at two separate Castle Crags, one in Borrowdale, the other by Haweswater.

To help subjugate the local tribe, the Romans built an astonishing road, still in use today, over Wrynose and Hardknott Passes. The soldiers (apparently from present-day Croatia) stationed at the spectacularly sited Hardknott Fort marvelled at views stretching to the Isle of Man. Today's visitors can do the same. After the Romans came the shadowy Celts and, in the seventh century, the Angles. They left beautiful carved stone crosses, as at Bewcastle, an isolated hamlet north of Brampton, and place-names ending in -ton, -ham, and -ington.

John Morrison

20 | Anworth House

27 Eskin Street, Keswick, Cumbria CA12 4DQ **Tel:** (017687) 72923
Web: www.anworthhouse.co.uk

In a quiet location and ideally situated for Keswick town centre, theatre, lake and fells, this small, friendly Victorian guest house offers excellent en-suite accommodation, a relaxed atmosphere and good food. Each of the five bedrooms is individually co-ordinated and very tastefully furnished to the highest standards. Superb home-cooked meals are served and special diets are catered for. For the comfort of guests, Anworth House is a no smoking establishment. Special winter breaks are available.

Bed & Breakfast per night: single occupancy £25.00; double room from £46.00– £54.00

Bedrooms: 4 double, 1 twin
Bathrooms: 5 en-suite
Cards accepted: Mastercard, Visa, Switch/Delta, Eurocard, JCB, Maestro, Visa Electron, Solo

---

The next wave of settlers was the Vikings, a more peaceable lot than often imagined. They too hewed crosses from stone (Gosforth churchyard has a superb tenth-century example) and gave us words to describe the landscape: *fell, gill* and *beck* are all Norse in origin, as is the ubiquitous *-thwaite* place-name element, meaning a forest clearing. Throughout the twelfth century, the Normans, who had ousted the Scots from Lakeland in 1092, established several Cumbrian monasteries, of which Furness Abbey (extensive ruins still stand) was the most important. The Cistercian monks continued deforestation and, through efficient farming methods, increased the prosperity of the area, so encouraging raids by the Scots. To defend themselves, 14th-century landowners built large fortified (pele) towers, some of which have since been incorporated into stately homes. Sizergh Castle (near Kendal), Hutton-in-the-Forest (north west of Penrith) and Muncaster Castle are three open to the public. Other pele towers have been absorbed into farm buildings.

For about 100 years between the mid-17th and 18th centuries, there occurred a significant change in the vernacular architecture. Farmhouses, long constructed with wooden frames, were rebuilt in the durable and abundant local stone. To the modern eye, the results are quintessentially Lakeland – and very beautiful. Townend, owned by the National Trust and dating from 1626, is a fine example standing in the magnificent village of Troutbeck, near Windermere. If the 'Great Rebuilding in Stone' was architecture's major event, the enclosures of the 18th and 19th century had as great an impact on the landscape. Gangs of itinerant craftsmen were kept busy for decades enclosing the open fells with drystone walls.

Around the turn of the 19th century, the first tourists arrived in search of wild beauty. Leading artists such as Gainsborough, Turner and Constable all visited, while the poets tended to stay longer. Wordsworth (whose birthplace at Cockermouth and homes at Grasmere and Rydal all welcome visitors), Coleridge, Southey and De Quincey formed a literary coterie that has inspired millions. Other luminaries to move here included the art critic and social reformer, John Ruskin, and Beatrix Potter. Both their houses (at Brantwood, by Coniston Water, and at Near Sawrey, Hawkshead, respectively) make fascinating outings.

An important arrival in 1847 was the railway. Windermere (or Birthwaite as it was known till the trains steamed into town) was transformed into a thriving Victorian resort above the lakeshore. Ever since, people have idled away endless hours simply messing about in boats, as immortalised in *Swallows and Amazons* by Arthur Ransome, another literary incomer. Or you can take a leisurely ride on the steam yacht *Gondola* (National Trust), which plies the waters of Lake Coniston.

The landscape continues to change. After thousands of years of deforestation, the process is being reversed: at Grizedale, visitors can follow a nine-mile sculpture trail – one of the earliest and one of the best – through a new forest. And new lakes have been created too: Thirlmere is an artificial, but beautiful, reservoir designed to slake the thirst of the north west. But over and above all this are the mountains. They may have changed their outward appearance, but their rocks, and their majesty, are timeless.

21 Whitehouse Guest House ◆◆◆◆

15 Ambleside Road, Keswick, Cumbria CA12 4DL **Tel:** (01768) 773176
Web: www.whitehousekeswick.co.uk **E-mail:** whitehousekeswick@hotmail.com

Run by the proprietors, Jim and Joan Taylor, the Whitehouse is a traditional Lakeland house in a quiet residential area of Keswick, yet only minutes away from the lake, falls and the amenities of the town, including the theatre, good pubs and restaurants. Local produce and home-made preserves are served in our comfortable dining room and the bedrooms are all tastefully furnished to a very high standard.

Bed & Breakfast per night: double room from £42.00–£46.00

Bedrooms: 2 double, 1 twin
Bathrooms: 3 en-suite
Parking: 3 spaces
Open: February–November

22 Parkfield Guesthouse ◆◆◆◆ Silver Award

The Heads, Keswick, Cumbria CA12 5ES **Tel:** (01768) 772328 **Fax:** (01768) 771396
Web: www.kencomp.net/parkfield **E-mail:** parkfield@kencomp.net

Delightful Lakeland guest house set in one of the most beautiful locations in Keswick. Quiet, yet central, Parkfield is only two minutes' walk from the lake, New Theatre, town centre and bus station. All rooms have en-suite facilities and are individually decorated with high quality furnishings, colour television and tea/coffee tray. Large, beautifully furnished guest lounge with superb views overlooking the golf course and mountains beyond. Private parking to the rear of the property. Exclusivley for non-smokers.

Bed & Breakfast per night: single occupancy from £30.00–£45.00; double room from £52.00–£55.00

Bedrooms: 6 double, 2 twin
Bathrooms: 8 en-suite
Parking: 7 spaces
Cards accepted: Mastercard, Visa, Switch/Delta, Amex

23 Swinside Lodge ★ Gold Award

Newlands, Keswick, Cumbria CA12 5UE **Tel:** (017687) 72948 **Fax:** (017687) 72948
Web: www.swinsidelodge-hotel.co.uk **E-mail:** info@swinsidelodge-hotel.co.uk

Swinside Lodge is a delightful Victorian house in a beautiful and tranquil corner of the Lake District, just beneath Cat Bells and a five-minute stroll from the shores of Derwent Water. Relax in this most comfortable and elegantly furnished, licensed country house hotel which offers guests peace and an idyllic location. We provide the highest standards of comfort, service and hospitality. The hotel is renowned for its superb award-winning cuisine. A warm welcome awaits you.

Bed & Breakfast per night: single occupancy from £45.00–£65.00; double room from £90.00–£125.00
Dinner, Bed & Breakfast per person, per night: £70.00–£90.00
Evening meal: 1930

Bedrooms: 5 double, 2 twin
Bathrooms: 7 en-suite
Parking: 12 spaces
Cards accepted: Mastercard, Visa, Switch/Delta

24 Greenbank Country House Hotel

◆◆◆◆ Silver Award

Borrowdale, Keswick, Cumbria CA12 5UY **Tel:** (017687) 77215 **Fax:** (017687) 77215

Greenbank is a lovely Victorian house in a peaceful setting. Here you can enjoy magnificent views of Derwentwater and the Borrowdale Valley. There are nine comfortable well-appointed bedrooms, each with an en-suite bathroom. Log fires, honesty bar, newspapers to browse through. We particularly enjoy providing imaginatively presented meals, with interesting menues using lots of local fresh produce. Also two well-equipped, warm and comfortable self-catering cottages. Meals available in the hotel.

Bed & Breakfast per night: single room from £25.00–£35.00; double room from £60.00–£70.00
Dinner, Bed & Breakfast per person, per night: £45.00–£50.00
Evening meal: 1900 (last bookings 1700)

Bedrooms: 1 single, 5 double, 2 twin, 1 triple
Bathrooms: 9 en-suite
Parking: 15 spaces
Open: All year except January
Cards accepted: Mastercard, Visa, Switch/Delta, Maestro

25 Hazel Bank

◆◆◆◆◆ Gold Award

Rosthwaite, Borrowdale, Keswick, Cumbria CA12 5XB **Tel:** (017687) 77248 **Fax:** (017678) 77373
Web: www.hazelbankhotel.co.uk **E-mail:** enquiries@hazelbankhotel.co.uk

Hazel Bank stands amidst beautiful four acre gardens overlooking dramatic Borrowdale, with outstanding views of Great Gable and other lakeland peaks. A secluded and tranquil position with direct access to the fells for walkers. Built as the dream house for a wealthy businessman, it is luxuriously furnished providing quality, well-proportioned bedrooms all with stunning views and full en-suite bathrooms. Sample superb meals using fresh local produce and some fine wines in the elegant dining room. Vegetarian meals by arrangement. Non-smoking. Cumbria Tourist Board 'Bed & Breakfast of the Year' 2001.

Dinner, Bed & Breakfast per person, per night: £50.00–£69.50
Evening meal: 1900

Bedrooms: 5 double, 3 twin
Bathrooms: 8 en-suite
Parking: 12 spaces
Cards accepted: Mastercard, Visa, Switch/Delta, Eurocard, JCB

26 Dale Head Hall Lakeside Hotel

★★★ Silver Award

Lake Thirlmere, Keswick, Cumbria CA12 4TN **Tel:** (017687) 72478 **Fax:** (017687) 71070
Web: www.dale-head-hall.co.uk **E-mail:** onthelakeside@dale-head-hall.co.uk

Dale Head Hall occupies a stunning position on the shores of Lake Thirlmere, one of Cumbria's quietest, most pastoral lakes. It provides an idyllic base for exploring this most beautiful corner of England. The bedrooms at the front of the hotel (three with four-poster beds) offer gorgeous lake views. With roaring log fires in the winter and refined cuisine served in the hotel's oak panelled dining room, it is a most romantic place for a few quiet days away.

Bed & Breakfast per night: single occupancy from £57.50; double room from £65.00–£105.00
Dinner, Bed & Breakfast per person, per night: £65.00–£85.00
Evening meal: 1930 (last orders 2000)

Bedrooms: 9 double, 2 twin, 1 triple
Bathrooms: 12 en-suite **Parking:** 20 spaces
Open: All year except January
Cards accepted: Mastercard, Visa, Switch/Delta, Amex, Eurocard, JCB, Maestro, Visa Electron, Solo

At-a-glance symbols are explained on the flap inside the back cover

27 Deepdale Hall

◆◆◆◆

Patterdale, Penrith, Cumbria CA11 0NR **Tel:** (01768) 482369 **Fax:** (01768) 482608
Web: www.deepdalehall.co.uk **E-mail:** brown@deepdalehall.freeserve.co.uk

A 17th-century lakeland farmhouse situated on a working hill farm with stunning mountain views. Miles of unspoilt walks from your doorstep, both high mountain ascents or delightful lakeside ambles. Log fires, oak beams and breakfast cooked on the Aga, all add to the warm, friendly atmosphere. Within walking distance of Lake Ullswater with its steamer cruises, boats and many other activities. Access is by a scenic quarter mile driveway from the main road and there is ample parking.

Bed & Breakfast per night: double room from £40.00–£45.00

Bedrooms: 1 double, 1 family
Bathrooms: 1 en-suite, 1 private
Parking: 4 spaces
Open: March–November

28 Elm House

◆◆◆◆ Silver Award

Pooley Bridge, Penrith, Cumbria CA10 2NH **Tel:** (01768) 486334 **Fax:** (01768) 486851
Web: www.elmhouse.demon.co.uk **E-mail:** b&b@elmhouse.demon.co.uk

A short stroll form Lake Ullswater, just five miles from the M6, Elm House makes the perfect base from which to explore the Lake District, Eden Valley or Borders. Numerous outdoor and water-based activities are available locally. Alternatively, take a cruise on Ullswater and enjoy the breathtaking, panoramic views this area is renowned for. Your friendly hosts, Kate and Nigel, are always very willing to help you make the most of your stay.

Bed & Breakfast per night: single occupancy from £25.00–£28.00; double room from £38.00–£47.00

Bedrooms: 4 double, 1 twin
Bathrooms: 4 en-suite, 1 private
Parking: 5 spaces
Cards accepted: Mastercard, Visa, Switch/Delta

29 Tymparon Hall

◆◆◆◆

Newbiggin, Stainton, Penrith, Cumbria CA11 0HS **Tel:** (01768) 483236 **Fax:** (01768) 483236
Web: www.tymparon.freeserve.co.uk **E-mail:** margaret@tymparon.freeserve.co.uk

Tymparon Hall is easy to find, close to Lake Ullswater and M6 junction 40. A perfect location for the Lakes, Eden Valley, Hadrian's Wall and the Borders. The secluded 18th-century farmhouse in peaceful surroundings is found on the fringe of a quiet village. Enjoy comfortable, spacious accommodation, personal service and good food. Home cooked three-course dinners available most evenings. Relax in the cosy lounge with a real fire on chilly evenings. Many tourist attractions within easy reach.

Bed & Breakfast per night: single occupancy from £23.00–£35.00; double room from £46.00–£50.00
Dinner, Bed & Breakfast per person, per night: £35.00–£37.00
Evening meal: 1830 (last bookings 1430)

Bedrooms: 1 double, 1 twin, 1 family
Bathrooms: 2 en-suite, 1 private
Parking: extensive
Open: March–November

30 The Black Swan Inn   ◆◆◆◆

Culgaith, Penrith, Cumbria CA10 1QW **Tel:** (01768) 88223 **Fax:** (01768) 88223
Web: www.blackswanculgaith.co.uk **E-mail:** info@blackswanculgaith.co.uk

Chris and Dawn Pollard invite you to their inn which is situated in the Eden Valley, seven miles west of Appleby and close to the River Eden and the Settle to Carlisle Railway. The Black Swan is a traditional 17th-century Cumbrian inn with oak beams, an open fire in winter and a beer garden for summer. You will find the finest quality in food, real ale and accommodation. Shooting, fishing, golf, swimming and walking are all to hand.

Bed & Breakfast per night: single occupancy from £35.00–£45.00; double room from £50.00–£70.00
Dinner, Bed & Breakfast per person, per night: £35.00–£45.00
Lunch available: 1200–1430 (summer); 1200–1400 (winter)

Evening meal: 1800 (last orders 2100)
Bedrooms: 4 double, 3 twin
Bathrooms: 6 en-suite, 1 shared
Parking: 12 spaces
Cards accepted: Mastercard, Visa, Switch/Delta, Visa Electron, Solo

31 Lands Farm   ◆◆◆◆ Silver Award

Westgate-in-Weardale, Bishop Auckland, County Durham DL13 1SN **Tel:** (01388) 517210 **Fax:** (01388) 517210

A high standard of accommodation in this peaceful stone-built farmhouse, situated in unspoilt Weardale. Relax in the conservatory overlooking the well-maintained garden and listen to the trickle of Swinhope Burn as is meanders by. Lands Farm is an ideal base for touring Durham City, Beamish Museum, Hadrian's Wall, the Lake District and the market towns of Hexham, Barnard Castle and Alston, which are all close by. The surrounding countryside is a delight for walkers and cyclists.

Bed & Breakfast per night: single occupancy £28.00; double room £46.00

Bedrooms: 1 double, 1 family
Bathrooms: 2 en-suite
Parking: 3 spaces

32 Appleby Manor Country House Hotel   ★★★ Silver Award

Roman Road, Appleby-in-Westmorland, Cumbria CA16 6JB **Tel:** (017683) 51571 or (017683) 51570 **Fax:** (017683) 52888
Web: www.applebymanor.co.uk **E-mail:** reception@applebymanor.co.uk

Probably the most relaxing and friendly hotel you'll choose. Set amidst breathtaking beauty, you'll find spotlessly clean bedrooms; satellite television and video films; sunny conservatory and terraces; magnificent lounges; log fires; a splendid indoor leisure club with small pool, jacuzzi, steam room, sauna and sunbed; and great food in the award-winning restaurant. With an 18-hole golf course, the mountains and valleys of the Lake District, and the Yorkshire Dales and North Pennine Fells close by, you're certain to enjoy yourselves.

Bed & Breakfast per night: double room from £104.00–£122.00
Dinner, Bed & Breakfast per person, per night: £69.00–£72.00 (min 2 nights)
Lunch available: 1100–1500
Evening meal: 1900 (last orders 2100)

Bedrooms: 13 double, 8 twin, 1 triple, 8 family
Bathrooms: 30 en-suite
Parking: 51 spaces
Cards accepted: Mastercard, Visa, Switch/Delta, Amex, Diners, Eurocard, JCB, Maestro, Visa Electron

At-a-glance symbols are explained on the flap inside the back cover

33 Old Rectory Hotel   ◆◆◆◆

Torver, Coniston, Cumbria LA21 8AX **Tel:** (01539) 441353 **Fax:** (01539) 441156
E-mail: enquiries@theoldrectoryhotel.com

The house, built in 1868, is set in three acres of gardens and woodland in the midst of rolling farmland beneath Coniston Old Man and close to the tranquil shores of Coniston Water. We have individually designed, light and airy bedrooms and have a lovely conservatory dining room, with panoramic views, where you can enjoy our imaginative home cooking. We offer a peaceful setting, an opportunity to unwind and an ideal base from which to explore.

Bed & Breakfast per night: double room from £40.00–£70.00
Dinner, Bed & Breakfast per person, per night: £38.00–£53.00
Evening meal: 1930

Bedrooms: 6 double, 2 twin, 1 family
Bathrooms: 9 en-suite
Parking: 10 spaces
Cards accepted: Mastercard, Visa, Switch/Delta, Amex, Diners, Eurocard, JCB, Maestro, Visa Electron

34 Wheelgate Country Guesthouse   ◆◆◆◆◆ Silver Award

Little Arrow, Coniston, Cumbria LA21 8AU **Tel:** (01539) 441418 **Fax:** (01539) 441114
Web: www.wheelgate.co.uk **E-mail:** wheelgate@conistoncottages.co.uk

A delightful 17th-century country house with a warm, relaxed atmosphere in a peaceful rural location, close to the heart of Lakeland. The house features exquisite individually-styled bedrooms and an enchanting oak-beamed lounge with log fire. Breakfasts are delicious, comprising an extensive buffet of cereals/fruits followed by a hearty grill. Free leisure club facilities are provided. Quality service is guaranteed - a perfect and unforgettable experience. Smoking restricted to the bar.

Bed & Breakfast per night: single room from £25.00–£30.00; double room from £48.00–£60.00

Bedrooms: 2 single, 3 double
Bathrooms: 5 en-suite
Parking: 5 spaces
Open: March–November
Cards accepted: Mastercard, Visa

35 Thwaite Cottage   ◆◆◆◆

Waterhead, Coniston, Cumbria LA21 8AJ **Tel:** (01539) 441367
Web: www.thwaitcot.freeserve.co.uk **E-mail:** m@thwaitcot.freeserve.co.uk

Thwaite Cottage is a beautiful oak-beamed 17th-century cottage set in peaceful wooded gardens a quarter of a mile from Coniston near the head of the lake. We have three charming guest bedrooms: one double en-suite, one double with private bathroom and one double/twin with private bathroom. There is a panelled sitting room with log fire in winter. A perfect base for fell walking, water sports, mountain biking or just exploring this lovely region. Non-smoking.

Bed & Breakfast per night: double room from £42.00–£48.00

Bedrooms: 2 double, 1 twin
Bathrooms: 1 en-suite, 2 private
Parking: 4 spaces

36 The Drunken Duck Inn
◆◆◆◆ Silver Award

Barngates, Ambleside, Cumbria LA22 0NG **Tel:** (015394) 36347 **Fax:** (015394) 36781
Web: www.drunkenduckinn.co.uk **E-mail:** info@drunkenduckinn.co.uk

Situated in 60 acres, at a crossroads in the middle of nothing but magnificent scenery. Although set apart it is literally within minutes of most of what Lakeland has to offer. Award-winning accommodation and food. Visit Barngates Brewery and sample the three real ales brewed on site. Family run for over 25 years, we know how to look after our guests.

Bed & Breakfast per night: double room from £80.00–£140.00
Lunch available: 1200–1430
Evening meal: 1800 (last orders 2100)

Bedrooms: 8 double, 1 twin
Bathrooms: 9 en-suite
Parking: 60 spaces
Cards accepted: Mastercard, Visa, Switch/Delta, Amex, JCB

37 Riverside Hotel
◆◆◆◆

Under Loughrigg, Nr. Rothay Bridge, Ambleside, Cumbria LA22 9LJ **Tel:** (01539) 432395 **Fax:** (01539) 432440
Web: www.riverside-at-ambleside.co.uk **E-mail:** info@riverside-at-ambleside.co.uk

Set in beautiful gardens, Riverside is a stylish Victorian country house that provides high quality bed & breakfast in a wonderful rural location – yet within ten minutes' walk from the centre of Ambleside. All of our bedrooms have en-suite facilities, some with spa baths, and all have either river, fell or garden views. Riverside is situated in the heart of the Lake District and is the perfect location for a peaceful and relaxing holiday.

Bed & Breakfast per night: single occupancy from £25.00–£40.00; double room from £50.00–£80.00

Bedrooms: 5 double, 1 twin, 1 family
Bathrooms: 5 en-suite
Parking: 15 spaces
Cards accepted: Mastercard, Visa

38 The Old Vicarage
◆◆◆◆

Vicarage Road, Ambleside, Cumbria LA22 9DH **Tel:** (015394) 33364 **Fax:** (015394) 34734
Web: www.oldvicarageambleside.co.uk **E-mail:** the.old.vicarage@kencomp.net

Tucked quietly away in its own grounds in the centre of one of the finest walking areas of the British Isles, the Old Vicarage at Ambleside in the beautiful English Lake District is an elegant Victorian residence, offering pleasant accommodation and a warm welcome. All the bedrooms have a television, alarm/clock radio, hairdryer, mini fridge, private bath/shower and toilet. There is ample parking within the grounds and pets are welcome.

Bed & Breakfast per night: double room from £60.00–£90.00

Bedrooms: 7 double, 1 twin, 1 triple, 1 family
Bathrooms: 10 en-suite
Parking: 12 spaces
Cards accepted: Mastercard, Visa, Switch/Delta, Eurocard, JCB, Maestro

39 Ambleside Lodge

♦♦♦♦ Silver Award

Rothay Road, Ambleside, Cumbria LA22 0EJ **Tel:** (015394) 31681 **Fax:** (015394) 34547
Web: www.ambleside-lodge.com **E-mail:** hmd@ambleside-lodge.com

Ambleside Lodge is an elegant Lakeland home situated just a minute's walk from the village centre and 3–4 minutes' stroll from Lake Windermere. Set in 2.5 acres of peaceful grounds, Ambleside Lodge provides a fine blend of high quality accommodation and excellent value for money. The Lodge offers a choice of beautifully furnished double rooms, king-size four-posters with jacuzzi spa baths and complimentary private leisure club facilities.

Bed & Breakfast per night: single room from £35.00–£60.00; double room from £60.00–£145.00

Bedrooms: 1 single, 16 double, 1 twin
Bathrooms: 18 en-suite
Parking: 25 spaces
Cards accepted: Mastercard, Visa, Switch/Delta, Amex, Eurocard, Solo

40 Lakeshore House

♦♦♦♦♦ Gold Award

Ecclerigg, Windermere, Cumbria LA23 1LJ **Tel:** (015394) 33202 **Fax:** (015394) 33213
Web: www.lakedistrict.uk.com **E-mail:** lakeshore@lakedistrict.uk.com

Cumbria Tourist Board 'Best Bed & Breakfast' 2001. Many hotels on Windermere have lake views, but few can match Lakeshore House for sheer proximity. Lakeshore provides the highest standard of bed & breakfast with guests own private access. Breakfast is served in Lakeshore's 45ft long carpeted conservatory which features a magnificent swimming pool and overlooks the ornamental terraces to the lake shore. Three exquisitely furnished en-suite bedrooms with private balconies, leather armchairs and footstalls, television, video, CD, flowers, decanter of sherry, oversized towels, bathrobes and telephones/modem facility. Simply the 'best view in England'.

Bed & Breakfast per night: single occupancy from £75.00–£112.00; double room from £130.00–£170.00

Bedrooms: 3 double/twin
Bathrooms: 3 en-suite
Parking: 6 spaces
Cards accepted: Mastercard, Visa, Switch/Delta, JCB, Maestro, Visa Electron, Solo

41 Cedar Manor Hotel

★★ Silver Award

Ambleside Road, Windermere, Cumbria LA23 1AX **Tel:** (015394) 43192 **Fax:** (015394) 45970
Web: www.cedarmanor.co.uk **E-mail:** cedarmanor@fsbdial.co.uk

Situated close to Windermere village and the lake, Cedar Manor Hotel is a haven for food lovers and those who enjoy the good things in life. Personally run by Lynn and Martin Hadley, the hotel has won many awards for food and service over the past twelve years. For those who like to work off the calories gained in the restaurant we have facilities at the nearby Spinnaker Club for their enjoyment.

Bed & Breakfast per night: single occupancy from £30.00–£60.00; double room from £60.00–£90.00
Dinner, Bed & Breakfast per person, per night: £34.00–£65.00
Lunch available: 1230–1500, Wednesday–Sunday

Evening meal: 1930 (last orders 2030)
Bedrooms: 9 double, 3 twin
Bathrooms: 12 en-suite
Parking: 16 spaces
Cards accepted: Mastercard, Visa

42 Belsfield House

4 Belsfield Terrace, Kendal Road, Bowness-on-Windermere, Windermere, Cumbria LA23 3EQ **Tel:** (015394) 45823

Belsfield House is a charming Victorian house situated in the very heart of Bowness and only one minute's walk from the beautiful Lake Windermere. It is an exceptionally well-appointed guest house offering a high degree of comfort, value for money and, most important of all, a warm, friendly atmosphere. Our guests have free access to the Burnside Leisure Complex including swimming pool, sauna, jacuzzi, gym and steam room - an excellent way to unwind after a busy day exploring the nooks and crannies of the Lake District.

Bed & Breakfast per night: single room from £24.00–£28.00; double room from £52.00–£56.00 (min 2 nights)

Bedrooms: 2 single, 3 double, 3 triple, 1 family
Bathrooms: 9 en-suite
Parking: 9 spaces

43 Lindeth Fell Country House Hotel   ★★ Gold Award

Windermere, Cumbria LA23 3JP **Tel:** (015394) 43286 or (015394) 44287 **Fax:** (015394) 47455
Web: www.lindethfell.co.uk **E-mail:** kennedy@lindethfell.co.uk

'Beautifully situated'. In a magnificent garden setting above Lake Windermere, Lindeth Fell offers brilliant lake views, peaceful surroundings and superb modern English cooking (AA Rosette and RAC Merits) - at highly competitive prices. Lawns are laid for croquet and putting, and Windermere Golf Club is one mile away. Good fishing is available free and interesting walks start from the door. Call for a brochure from the resident owners. Special breaks available in low season.

Bed & Breakfast per night: single room from £40.00–£69.00; double room from £80.00–£138.00
Dinner, Bed & Breakfast per person, per night: £55.00–£89.00
Lunch available: 1230–1400
Evening meal: 1930 (last orders 2030)

Bedrooms: 2 single, 5 double, 5 twin, 2 triple
Bathrooms: 14 en-suite
Parking: 20 spaces
Cards accepted: Mastercard, Visa, Switch/Delta, Eurocard

44 Linthwaite House Hotel   ★★★ Gold Award

Crook Road, Windermere, Cumbria LA23 3JA **Tel:** (015394) 88600 **Fax:** (015394) 88601
Web: www.linthwaite.com **E-mail:** admin@linthwaite.com

Country house hotel, 20 minutes from the M6, situated in 14 acres of peaceful hilltop grounds, overlooking Lake Windermere and with breathtaking sunsets. The 26 rooms have en-suite bathrooms, satellite television, radio, telephone and tea/coffee making facilities. The AA 2 Rosette restaurant serves modern British food using local produce complemented by fine wines. There is a tarn for fly-fishing, croquet, golf practice hole and free use of nearby leisure spa. Romantic breaks feature a king-size double bed with canopy, champagne, chocolates and flowers. English Tourist Board 'Hotel of the Year' 1994. ⌁ Category 3

Bed & Breakfast per night: single room from £85.00–£115.00; double room from £180.00–£260.00
Dinner, Bed & Breakfast per person, per night: £59.00–£169.00 (min 2 nights)
Lunch available: 1230–1330

Evening meal: 1915 (last orders 2045)
Bedrooms: 1 single, 21 double, 4 twin
Bathrooms: 26 en-suite
Parking: 30 spaces
Cards accepted: Mastercard, Visa, Switch/Delta, Amex, Diners, Solo

45 Gilpin Lodge Country House Hotel and Restaurant ★★★ Gold Award

Crook Road, Windermere, Cumbria LA23 3NE **Tel:** (015394) 88818 **Fax:** (015394) 88058
Web: www.gilpin-lodge.co.uk **E-mail:** hotel@gilpin-lodge.co.uk

A friendly, elegant, relaxing hotel in 20 tranqil acres of woodland, moors and delightful country gardens, 12 miles from the M6 and 2 miles from Lake Windermere. Opposite Windermere golf course, the hotel offers golf-inclusive breaks. Sumptuous bedrooms – many with split-level sitting areas and four-poster beds; special bathrooms – some with jacuzzi baths; exquisite cuisine (AA 3 Rosettes). Free use of nearby leisure club. Year-round 'Great Little Escapes'. A Pride of Britain hotel.

Bed & Breakfast per night: single occupancy from £80.00–£105.00; double room from £90.00–£210.00
Dinner, Bed & Breakfast per person, per night: £65.00–£125.00
Lunch available: 1200–1430

Evening meal: 1900 (last orders 2100)
Bedrooms: 9 double, 5 twin
Bathrooms: 14 en-suite **Parking:** 40 spaces
Cards accepted: Mastercard, Visa, Switch/Delta, Amex, Diners, Eurocard, JCB, Maestro, Visa Elect

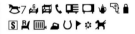

46 Tullythwaite House ◆◆◆◆ Silver Award

Underbarrow, Kendal, Cumbria LA8 8BB **Tel:** (015395) 68397

Tullythwaite House, a Grade II listed Regency house, is set in one acre of flower-filled gardens in the beautiful and tranquil Lyth Valley. Our bedrooms have lovely views, en-suite bathrooms, fresh flowers and antiques. Breakfast is served in the elegant dining room overlooking the unspoilt countryside. Dinner is optional, but we are renowned for excellent home cooking. Foremost a family home, the warmest of welcomes is assured. Winner of the Cumbria Tourist Board 'Bed & Breakfast of the Year' Award 1997.

Bed & Breakfast per night: single occupancy from £25.00–£27.00; double room £50.00
Dinner, Bed & Breakfast per person, per night: £40.00–£42.00
Evening meal: 1930

Bedrooms: 2 double, 1 twin
Bathrooms: 3 en-suite
Parking: 8 spaces
Open: March–November

47 Blaven Homestay ◆◆◆◆◆ Silver Award

Blaven, Middleshaw, Old Hutton, Kendal, Cumbria LA8 0LZ **Tel:** (01539) 734894 **Fax:** (01539) 727447
Web: www.blavenhomestay.co.uk **E-mail:** blaven@greenarrow.demon.co.uk

Friendly, informal hosts, Jan and Barry offer a warm welcome to guests visiting their delightfully situated 18th-century Lakeland home. Blaven has recently been sympathetically restored with considerable focus on luxury and convenience. The guest rooms are very special. Memorable breakfasts and stunning dinners ensure that a stay at Blaven is a pleasure not to be missed when visiting the Lakes or Dales. Both National Parks and junctions 36/37 of the M6 are a 15 minute drive away.

Bed & Breakfast per night: single occupancy from £39.95–£45.95; double room from £59.90–£71.90
Dinner, Bed & Breakfast per person, per night: £49.90–£61.90
Evening meal: 1900 (last bookings 1730)

Bedrooms: 1 double, 1 family
Bathrooms: 2 en-suite
Parking: 4 spaces
Cards accepted: Mastercard, Visa

48 Mayfields

3 Mayfield Terrace, Kents Bank Road, Grange-over-Sands, Cumbria LA11 7DW **Tel:** (01539) 534730
Web: www.accommodata.co.uk/010699.htm

Mayfields is a deceptively spacious, charming, small guest house, highly recommended for the warmth of welcome and exceedingly good home cooking. Situated on the fringe of Grange-over-Sands, adjacent to open countryside, ideally situated for exploring the Lakes, Dales, Cartmel and Furness peninsulas and the magnificent 12th-century Cartmel Priory. Mayfields' bedrooms are very well appointed and individually furnished and the residents' lounge is a cosy room with colour television and a lovely piano. A non-smoking establishment.

Bed & Breakfast per night: single room £25.00; double room £50.00
Dinner, Bed & Breakfast per person, per night: £37.00
Lunch available: 1230–1300 (Sundays)
Evening meal: 1830

Bedrooms: 1 single, 1 double, 1 twin
Bathrooms: 2 en-suite, 1 shared
Parking: 3 spaces
Open: all year except Christmas

Piel Island

Just offshore from Barrow in Furness is Piel Island, a small rocky outcrop in the sea surmounted by the brooding ruins of a castle. Tiny and unimportant it may be, but it still has its ferry service, pub – even its own king.

The island has a colourful history. It is separated from the mainland yet remains fairly accessible, so making it a useful haven in troubled times. From the 14th century it was the centre of a lively smuggling trade largely orchestrated by the monks of Furness Abbey. They built the impressive castle as a fortified warehouse to keep their cargoes safe from raiders, and to keep the King's customs men at bay.

The island's most historic moment arrived in June 1487, when Lambert Simnel, pretender to the English throne, landed at Piel with 8,000 men. Simnel was an impostor, a baker's son claiming to be the Earl of Warwick (then imprisoned in the Tower of London) who, backed by Margaret of Burgundy, gathered a force of German mercenaries and Irish recruits, intending to take the throne by force. Leaving Piel, he set off across Furness towards London, but was defeated at the Battle of Stoke on June 16th. In contrast, the 18th century brought more prosperous and settled times to the island, with Piel's busy harbour servicing Furness's thriving shipping and iron industries. The island's pub and its few houses were built at this time.

The Ship Inn continues to flourish, a useful watering-hole for sailors and day trippers from the mainland. The landlord is traditionally known as the 'King of Piel', a reference, it is supposed, to Lambert Simnel's claim to the throne. Anyone who sits in a particular old wooden chair in the pub, becomes a 'Knight of Piel', and must carry out certain gallant duties – such as buying everyone a drink, being a moderate smoker, a lover of the opposite sex, and generally of good character. If shipwrecked, a Knight of Piel has the right to free board and lodging in the pub.

The ferry from Roa runs from April to October, 11am–5pm, weather permitting (telephone in advance: 01229 835809), making the island an easy day trip. Facilities are minimal (the island has neither electricity nor telephone) but for those wishing to stay longer, camping is permitted anywhere on the island by arrangement, on arrival, with the Ship Inn.

49 Clare House

★ Silver Award

Park Road, Grange-over-Sands, Cumbria LA11 7HQ **Tel:** (01539) 533026 **Fax:** (01539) 534253
E-mail: ajread@clarehouse.fsbusiness.co.uk

We offer rest and relaxation, a garden to sit in, a promenade to stroll along, wonderful views across the Bay from our family-run hotel and delightful meals for which we hold an AA rosette. If this is what you seek, we would be pleased to hear from you. We offer four-day breaks or weekly stays at advantageous terms.

Dinner, Bed & Breakfast per person, per night: £52.50–£55.00
Evening meal: 1845 (last orders 1915)

Bedrooms: 3 single, 4 double, 10 twin
Bathrooms: 16 en-suite, 1 shared
Parking: 16 spaces
Open: March–November
Cards accepted: Mastercard, Visa, Switch/Delta

50 Capernwray House

◆◆◆◆ Silver Award

Borrans Lane, Capernwray, Carnforth, Lancashire LA6 1AE **Tel:** (01524) 732363 **Fax:** (01524) 732363
Web: www.capernwrayhouse.com **or** www.smoothhound.co.uk/hotels/capernwr.html **E-mail:** thesmiths@capernwrayhouse.com

Beautiful country house set in 18 acres of rolling countryside. Tastefully decorated throughout. Our bedrooms have all the usual en-suite 'trappings' plus many other 'little touches' to make your stay more comfortable. Guest lounge with television, books and magazines to while away the evenings after your day in the Lakes, Dales, Lancaster or bird reserves – the list of nearby attractions is endless. An ideal stop-over for the North or South. No smoking. Dinner by arrangement. Warm welcome guaranteed. Phone for brochure.

Bed & Breakfast per night: single room from £22.00–£30.00; double room from £45.00–£50.00
Dinner, Bed & Breakfast per person, per night: £34.50–£42.50

Bedrooms: 1 single, 2 double, 1 twin
Bathrooms: 3 en-suite
Parking: 6 spaces
Cards accepted: Mastercard, Visa, Switch/Delta, Eurocard, JCB, Maestro, Visa Electron, Solo

51 Rookhurst Country House

◆◆◆◆◆ Silver Award

West End, Gayle, Hawes, North Yorkshire DL8 3RT **Tel:** (01969) 667454 **Fax:** (01969) 667128
Web: www.rookhurst.co.uk **E-mail:** rookhurst@lineone.net

At Wensleydale's heart, Rookhurst fronts the Pennine Way, ten minutes' walk from Hawes. With 17th, 18th and 19th-century architectures, the hotel offers contrasting styles and a varied content of four-poster beds, antique furniture, porcelain and needlework. Memories are jogged with set dinner menus containing such evocative dishes as beef casseroles with dumplings and apple crumbles, while dry-cure bacon, free-range eggs, our local butcher's sausages, along with Judith's home-made breads, set you up for the day!

Bed & Breakfast per night: double room from £70.00–£110.00
Dinner, Bed & Breakfast per person, per night: £62.50–£70.00 (2 persons sharing)
Evening meal: 1930

Bedrooms: 4 double, 1 twin
Bathrooms: 4 en-suite, 1 private
Parking: 6 spaces
Cards accepted: Mastercard, Visa, Switch/Delta, Visa Electron, Solo

52 | Heron's Lee   ◆◆◆◆ Silver Award

Thornton, Berwick-upon-Tweed, TD15 2LP **Tel:** (01289) 382000 **Fax:** (01289) 382000
Web: www.northumbandb.co.uk **E-mail:** john_burton@btconnect.com

This peaceful countryside setting is four miles west of the historic walled town of Berwick-upon-Tweed. Guests can enjoy the warm welcome and panoramic views from the large conservatory. Here in the Scottish Borders a wealth of abbeys and castles, and the Rivers Tweed and Till wind through unspoilt rolling hills and valleys. Holy Island, the Farnes and St Abbs Head are within easy reach and are noted for their historic interest and abundance of bird life. Brochure available.

Bed & Breakfast per night: single occupancy from £23.00–£33.00; double room from £46.00–£56.00	**Bedrooms:** 1 double, 1 twin
	Bathrooms: 1 en-suite, 1 private
	Parking: 2 spaces
Dinner, Bed & Breakfast per person, per night: £38.00–£48.00	**Open:** all year except Christmas

53 | Tillmouth Park Country House Hotel   ★★★ Silver Award

Cornhill-on-Tweed, Northumberland TD12 4UU **Tel:** (01890) 882255 **Fax:** (01890) 882540
Web: www.tillmouthpark.co.uk **E-mail:** reception@tillmouthpark.f9.co.uk

This secluded country mansion is set in 15 acres of mature parkland gardens. Tillmouth Park boasts 14 fully appointed en-suite bedrooms which are spacious and individually styled with period and antique furniture, an award-winning wood-panelled restaurant, an informal bistro and a well-stocked bar. A perfect venue for golf, fishing and shooting – the hotel is ideally situated for peace and tranquillity. It offers exceptional hospitality, comfort and service. Helicopter landing pad on site.

Bed & Breakfast per night: single room from £90.00–£125.00; double room from £130.00–£170.00	**Evening meal:** 1900 (last orders 2100)
	Bedrooms: 1 single, 6 double, 6 twin, 1 triple
	Bathrooms: 14 en-suite
Dinner, Bed & Breakfast per person, per night: £83.00–£103.00 (min 2 nights, 2 sharing)	**Parking:** 50 spaces
Lunch available: 1200–1900	**Cards accepted:** Mastercard, Visa, Switch/Delta, Amex, Diners, Maestro, Solo

54 | The Estate House   ◆◆◆◆ Silver Award

Ford, Berwick-upon-Tweed, Northumberland TD15 2PX **Tel:** (01890) 820668 **Fax:** (01890) 820672
E-mail: theestatehouse@supanet.com

The Estate House, an elegant Edwardian home, is located in Ford Village in the heart of Northumberland's 'Secret Kingdom'. Although it is ideally situated for a wide range of visitor attractions, its tranquil setting, in an acre of garden, also makes it an ideal place to retreat to. The spacious accommodation includes a residents' lounge and dining room looking towards the Cheviots. Evening meals are available, with vegetarian food a speciality.

Bed & Breakfast per night: single occupancy from £23.00–£25.00; double room from £46.00–£50.00	**Bedrooms:** 2 double (1 can also be a family room), 1 twin
	Bathrooms: 1 en-suite, 1 shared
Dinner, Bed & Breakfast per person, per night: £32.00–£35.00	**Parking:** unlimited space

At-a-glance symbols are explained on the flap inside the back cover

55 Katerina's Guest House

◆◆◆◆ Silver Award

Sun Buildings, High Street, Rothbury, Northumberland NE65 7TQ **Tel:** (01669)620691
Web: www.katerinasguesthouse.co.uk **E-mail:** cath@katerinasguesthouse.co.uk

Charming, old, family-run guest house, close to all amenities of pretty Rothbury Village. Beautiful rooms, all en-suite, four-poster beds, television and tasteful decor. Ideal central point to explore unspoilt Northumberland hills, coastline, castles, Hadrian's Wall and Scottish Borders. Wide choice of breakfast and (if required) licensed evening menus – sample our 'whisky porridge' or 'steak Katerina'. We also cater for special dietary requirements. Warm welcome assured! No smoking.

Bed & Breakfast per night: single occupancy £30.00; double room from £44.00–£46.00
Evening meal: 1900 (last orders 2000)

Bedrooms: 3 double
Bathrooms: 3 en-suite

Chillingham White Cattle

Many visitors to Chillingham, Northumberland, come to see its splendid castle (tel: 01668 215359), set imposingly above the River Till, and complete with dungeons, torture chambers and a spine-tingling assortment of lurid ghost stories. But also at Chillingham is a 600 acre (240 hectare) park, managed separately from the castle, which for over 700 years has been home to a herd of wild white cattle, now the only pure-bred herd of its type in the world.

The 40 or so animals that roam freely within the confines of the walled park are thought to be descendants of the wild oxen which inhabited Britain in prehistoric times. Too savage to be tamed, they wandered at will across vast tracts of land foraging for food. In the 13th century, Chillingham Park was enclosed by a wall and a herd of these cattle confined within it. Because of their aggressive natures, they were quite safe from cattle thieves, and remained here, undisturbed, through seven centuries.

The cows are creamy white with long, black-tipped horns. The herd is ruled by a 'king' bull, which sires all the calves, until challenged by a rival male. The competing bulls attack each other head to head in a series of short 'rounds' until one is deemed victorious, and allowed to take his place as king. Calves are born away from the herd and are kept hidden by their mothers in hollows in the bracken. If touched by human hand they are abandoned and will certainly die.

Because the cattle are so wild, it is impossible to assist them in any way if they are ill, injured or having calving difficulties. Even in hard winters when food is scarce, they will eat only meadow hay, refusing other food even when the alternative is starvation. In the severe winter of 1947, 20 of Chillingham's 33 animals died and it was feared that the breed might become extinct. Gradually the numbers increased to previous levels, but, as a precaution, a reserve herd was established in Scotland.

Once the private property of the Lords Tankerville of Chillingham Castle, the herd is now owned by the Chillingham Wild Cattle Association, which allows viewings of the cattle in the company of a warden (tel: 01668 215250 for details of viewing times; not advisable for visitors with walking difficulties). Binoculars are recommended as it is not always possible to approach these fascinating beasts.

56 Silverton Lodge

◆◆◆◆ Silver Award

Silverton Lane, Rothbury, Morpeth, Northumberland NE65 7RJ **Tel:** (01669) 620144 **Fax:** (01669) 621920
Web: www.silvertonlodge.co.uk **E-mail:** info@silvertonlodge.co.uk

Bruce and Jeannette look forward to welcoming you to our former school house, Silverton Lodge, Rothbury. For your comfort we have provided a guest lounge full of books, radio, CD player, text television and video. Breakfast is a civilised, unhurried occasion and evening meals are available by arrangement. We are close to Cragside, and central in Northumberland for walking or touring, Alnwick, Newcastle and all other attractions. "A friendly, welcoming house – those little extras making all the difference."

Bed & Breakfast per night: double room from £44.00–£46.00
Dinner, Bed & Breakfast per person, per night: £35.00–£36.00

Bedrooms: 1 double, 1 twin
Bathrooms: 1 en-suite, 1 private
Parking: 4 spaces

57 Lee Farm

◆◆◆◆ Gold Award

Near Rothbury, Longframlington, Morpeth, Northumberland NE65 8JQ **Tel:** (01665) 570257 **Fax:** (01665) 570257
Web: www.leefarm.co.uk **E-mail:** enqs@leefarm.co.uk

Relax, unwind and take time to explore Northumberland's many attractions from our comfortable Georgian farmhouse, set in beautiful countryside near Rothbury. We offer a warm welcome, spacious en-suite bedrooms with television, hospitality tray, hairdryer and electric blankets. Our guest lounge has a log fire which complements full central heating. Delicious farmhouse breakfasts are served using local produce. Ample off-road parking. The Lee offers bed & breakfast accommodation to the very highest standard. Winner of the Pride of Northumbria 'Bed & Breakfast of the Year' Award 2001.

Bed & Breakfast per night: single occupancy from £30.00–£32.00; double room from £45.00–£46.00

Bedrooms: 1 double, 1 twin, 1 family
Bathrooms: 2 en-suite, 1 private
Parking: 4 spaces
Open: all year except Christmas

58 Swarland Old Hall

◆◆◆◆ Silver Award

Swarland, Morpeth, Northumberland NE65 9HU **Tel:** (01670) 787642
Web: www.swarlandoldhall.com **E-mail:** proctor@swarlandoldhall.fsnet.co.uk

This wonderful Grade II listed Georgian farmhouse is full of character and charm, surrounded by the Northumberland countryside with breathtaking views over the Coquet Valley. An ideal base for touring, walking, golfing and also to explore the magnificent coast, castles and countryside, as well as visiting the Scottish Borders. All rooms are furnished to a very high standard with window seats to admire the views. Colour television and hospitality tray in all rooms. Full colour brochure available on request.

Bed & Breakfast per night: single occupancy £30.00; double room £44.00

Bedrooms: 1 double, 1 twin, 1 family
Bathrooms: 2 en-suite, 1 private
Parking: 10 spaces
Open: all year except Christmas

59 Matfen High House ◆◆◆◆

Matfen, Newcastle upon Tyne, NE20 0RG **Tel:** (01661) 886592 **Fax:** (01661) 886592
Web: www.s-h-systems.co.uk/hotels/matfen.html **E-mail:** struan@struan.enterprise-plc.com

Spacious stone farmhouse dating from 1735, rural location one mile north of Hadrian's Wall. Comfortable en-suite rooms, pets by arrangement. Stable available. !8-hole golf course two miles. Good walking, cycling, riding. Pubs and restaurants nearby. Ideal for Hadrian's Wall, Kielder Water, Northumberland National Park, Beamish Museum, Alnwick, Warkworth, Dunstanburgh, Bamburgh, Holy Island and Farnes. Nearby picturesque towns of Corbridge and Hexham. Shopping at Gateshead Metro-Centre. Newcastle airport 12 miles, Corbridge railway station 7 miles.

Bed & Breakfast per night: single occupancy £25.00; double room £50.00	**Bedrooms:** 1 double, 1 twin **Bathrooms:** 2 en-suite **Parking:** 6 spaces	

60 Rose Hill Farm Bed and Breakfast ◆◆◆◆ Silver Award

Rose Hill Farm, Eastgate-in-Weardale, Bishop Auckland, County Durham DL13 2LB **Tel:** (01388) 517209 **Fax:** (01388) 517209
Web: www.rosehillfarmholidays.co.uk **E-mail:** june@rosehillfarm.fsnet.co.uk

Converted from former barns, this spacious accommodation enjoys panoramic views of Weardale from its large gardens. There are five en-suite bedrooms, two of which are in the ground floor annexe. The residents' lounge has a traditional stove in its centrepiece inglenook fireplace. An excellent base from which to explore or walk in the Durham Dales and north Pennines. Beamish Museum, Durham City, Hexham and Barnard Castle are within easy driving distance.

Bed & Breakfast per night: single occupancy £30.00; double room from £45.00–£50.00 **Dinner, Bed & Breakfast per person, per night:** £35.00–£42.50 **Evening meal:** 1800 (last orders 2030)	**Bedrooms:** 2 double, 1 twin, 2 family **Bathrooms:** 5 en-suite **Parking:** 6 spaces	

61 Brunswick House ◆◆◆◆

55 Market Place, Middleton-in-Teesdale, Barnard Castle, County Durham DL12 0QH **Tel:** (01833) 640393 **Fax:** (01833) 640393
Web: www.brunswickhouse.net **E-mail:** enquiries@brunswickhouse.net

Situated in unspoilt Teesdale, our guest house provides the perfect centre for those seeking to enjoy the delights of unspoilt countryside, quiet roads, flower-filled meadows and gentle strolls through the breathtaking scenery of the North Pennines. Our reputation is built on outstanding home cooking using, wherever possible, only fresh and local produce. The house, dating from 1760, retains great charm with beamed ceilings and original fireplaces, thoughtfully combined with all modern comforts.

Bed & Breakfast per night: single occupancy from £24.00–£32.00; double room from £40.00–£48.00 **Dinner, Bed & Breakfast per person, per night:** £34.00–£41.00 **Evening meal:** 1930 (last bookings 1900)	**Bedrooms:** 3 double, 2 twin **Bathrooms:** 5 en-suite **Parking:** 5 spaces **Cards accepted:** Mastercard, Visa, Switch/Delta, Amex, Diners, Eurocard, JCB, Maestro, Visa Elect	

62 The Rose Garden ◆◆◆◆

20 Hilda Place, Saltburn-by-the-Sea, Cleveland TS12 1BP **Tel:** (01287) 622947 **Fax:** (01287) 622947
Web: www.therosegarden.co.uk **E-mail:** enquiries@therosegarden.co.uk

Situated by the sea, on the edge of the North Yorkshire Moors, this is splendid walking country. The Rose Garden is a gracious Victorian terraced house with excellent amenities. The speciality is a substantial breakfast using local free-range/organic produce where possible and with interesting home-made jams and marmalades. Vegetarian and continental breakfasts can also be provided.

Bed & Breakfast per night: double room
£50.00

Bedrooms: 2 double, 1 twin
Bathrooms: 2 en-suite, 1 private
Parking: 3 spaces
Open: February–December

63 Manor House Farm ◆◆◆◆

Ingleby Greenhow, Great Ayton, North Yorkshire TS9 6RB **Tel:** (01642) 722384
E-mail: mbloom@globalnet.co.uk

A charming old farm (part c1760) set idyllically in 168 acres of parkland and woodland at the foot of the Cleveland Hills in the North York Moors National Park. Wildlife surrounds the farmhouse. The environment is tranquil and secluded, and the accommodation is warm and welcoming. Guests have their own entrance, dining room and lounge with library. Evening dinners are prepared meticulously and the hosts are proud of their reputation for fine food and wines. Brochure available.

Dinner, Bed & Breakfast per person, per night: £43.50–£50.00 (min 2 sharing)
Evening meal: 1900 (last bookings 1600)

Bedrooms: 1 double, 2 twin
Bathrooms: 1 en-suite, 2 private
Parking: 66 spaces
Cards accepted: Mastercard, Visa, Switch/Delta, Eurocard, JCB, Maestro, Visa Electron, Solo

64 Postgate Farm ◆◆◆◆

Glaisdale, Whitby, North Yorkshire YO21 2PZ **Tel:** (01947) 897353 **Fax:** (01947) 897353
E-mail: j-m.thompson.bandb@talk21.com

17th-century south-facing farmhouse with many historical features including a witch post. Situated in the peaceful Esk Valley, inland from Whitby, within national park. Magnificent moorland views – a walkers' paradise. Ten miles to the coast and close to steam railway and 'Heartbeat' country. The centrally heated accommodation comprises guests' lounge, dining room and kitchen with fridge and microwave. Patio/garden and BBQ, games room, laundry and drying facilities. Bedrooms are all en-suite with television, courtesy tray, hairdryer and clock radio. Also newly converted Four Star studio flat which sleeps 2/4.

Bed & Breakfast per night: single
occupancy from £25.00–£40.00; double room
from £35.00–£50.00

Bedrooms: 2 double, 1 twin
Bathrooms: 3 en-suite
Parking: 4 spaces

65 Broom House ◆◆◆◆

Broom House Lane, Egton Bridge, Whitby, North Yorkshire YO21 1XD **Tel:** (01947) 895279 **Fax:** (01947) 895657
Web: www.egton-bridge.co.uk **E-mail:** welcome@BroomHouseEgtonBridge.freeserve.co.uk

Broom House – an excellent place to stay. We provide comfortable en-suite rooms in old country farmhouse style, log fires in public rooms in winter, first class meals prepared by our resident chef and an idyllic setting with views over the Esk Valley. Egton Bridge is considered to be one of the prettiest villages in Yorkshire, situated in Eskdale with many fascinating corners to explore. A peaceful haven located within beautiful countryside yet close to Whitby and the east coast. Visit our website.

Bed & Breakfast per night: single occupancy £26.00; double room from £43.00–£47.00
Dinner, Bed & Breakfast per person, per night: £34.45
Evening meal: 1900 (last orders 2000)

Bedrooms: 4 double, 1 twin, 1 triple
Bathrooms: 6 en-suite
Parking: 6 spaces

66 Brookwood Farm ◆◆◆◆ Silver Award

Beck Hole, Whitby, North Yorkshire YO22 5LE **Tel:** (01947) 896402
Web: www.brookwoodfarm.co.uk

A Grade II listed farmhouse, situated in the wooded moorland valley of Beckhole, Brookwood Farm is a romantic place to stay. It is ideally located for local walks through woods and over moors or for a ride on the old steam trains running from Grosmont to Pickering. We feel we have captured the timeless tranquillity of the countryside without sacrificing 21st-century luxuries. Our three bedrooms are very individual and have a romantic peaceful mood.

Bed & Breakfast per night: single occupancy from £35.00–£40.00; double room from £50.00–£55.00

Bedrooms: 3 double
Bathrooms: 3 en-suite
Parking: 3 spaces

67 Stakesby Manor ★★ Silver Award

Manor Close, High Stakesby, Whitby, North Yorkshire YO21 1HL **Tel:** (01947) 602773 **Fax:** (01947) 602140
Web: www.stakesby-manor.co.uk **E-mail:** relax@stakesby-manor.co.uk

A tastefully converted Georgian manor house, set in its own grounds, with views of surrounding moorland. Approximately one mile from the town centre. The oak-panelled dining room serves excellent food and has an open fire during winter. There are 13 en-suite bedrooms with television, telephone and tea/coffee making facilities. A well stocked bar and relaxing coffee lounge. There is also a function room for weddings and conference facilities for up to 96 people.

Bed & Breakfast per night: single occupancy £59.00; double room from £78.00–£84.00
Dinner, Bed & Breakfast per person, per night: £48.00–£56.00 (min 2 nights, 2 sharing)
Evening meal: 1900 (last orders 2130)

Bedrooms: 10 double, 3 twin
Bathrooms: 13 en-suite
Parking: 40 spaces
Cards accepted: Mastercard, Visa, Switch/Delta, Amex

68   High Blakey House ◆◆◆◆

Blakey Ridge, Kirkbymoorside, York, North Yorkshire YO62 7LQ   **Tel:** (01751) 417186
Web: freespace.virgin.net/highblakey.house   **E-mail:** highblakey.house@virgin.net

Walk or drive around four valleys from our door. Picture windows overlook Rosedale. Comfortable rooms with king-size beds and television and video player. Spacious lounge/diner with television, maps, books and video library. Light refreshments are permanently available, packed lunches can be prepared and the historic Lion Inn is opposite. There are many local attractions including castles, museums and the coast. Clothes-drying facilities, cot, high chair, garage kennel for pets, parking spaces and a pleasant smoking area are available. Peace, comfort and a warm welcome await you.

Bed & Breakfast per night: single occupancy from £25.00–£29.00; double room from £46.00–£54.00

Bedrooms: 1 double, 2 triple
Bathrooms: 1 en-suite, 1 shared
Parking: 3 spaces

69   Helm ◆◆◆◆ Gold Award

Askrigg, Leyburn, North Yorkshire DL8 3JF   **Tel:** (01969) 650443   **Fax:** (01969) 650443
Web: www.helmyorkshire.com   **E-mail:** holiday@helmyorkshire.com

Idyllically situated with 'the finest view in Wensleydale'. Experience the comfort, peace and quiet of this 17th-century hillside Dales farmhouse. Each charmingly furnished bedroom has en-suite facilities and many special little touches. Period furniture, oak beams and log fires create the ideal atmosphere in which to relax and share the owner's passion for really good food. Helm offers a superb choice of breakfasts, home-made bread and preserves, exceptionally good dinners and an inspired selection of wines. Totally non-smoking.

Bed & Breakfast per night: double room from £64.00–£78.00
Dinner, Bed & Breakfast per person, per night: £51.50–£58.50 (min 2 sharing)
Evening meal: 1900

Bedrooms: 2 double, 1 twin
Bathrooms: 3 en-suite
Parking: 5 spaces
Cards accepted: Mastercard, Visa, Switch/Delta, Eurocard, JCB, Maestro, Visa Electron, Solo

70   Fellside ◆◆◆◆

Thornton Rust, Leyburn, North Yorkshire DL8 3AP   **Tel:** (01969) 663504   **Fax:** (01969) 663965
Web: www.wensleydale.org/accommodation/fellside   **E-mail:** harvey@plwmp.freeserve.co.uk

Situated by a small Dales village with panoramic views of Wensleydale. A warm and friendly welome awaits for a relaxing stay. Fellside is a modern stone house with ample private parking. Many attractions are close by, including Aysgarth Falls, Bolton Castle, Askrigg, Hardraw Scar and Semerwater. Two guest bedrooms offer either a double en-suite or twin with private bathroom. Both bedrooms are comfortably furnished and there is a residents' lounge where meals are taken.

Bed & Breakfast per night: double/twin room from £48.00–£54.00
Dinner, Bed & Breakfast per person, per night: £36.00–£42.00

Bedrooms: 1 double, 1 twin
Bathrooms: 1 en-suite, 1 private
Parking: 6 spaces

71 Stow House Hotel ◆◆◆◆

Aysgarth Falls, Aysgarth, Leyburn, North Yorkshire DL8 3SR **Tel:** (01969) 663635
Web: www.wensleydale.org **or** www.yorkshirevisitor.co.uk **E-mail:** davidpeterburton@aol.com

Delightful former Victorian vicarage in private grounds, a short walk from Aysgarth Falls, a series of three spectacular waterfalls along the River Ure. Elevated position offers breathtaking views over Wensleydale and Bishopdale. Panoramic walks and drives from the door, an ideal location for exploring all the Yorkshire Dales and surrounding picturesque villages and ancient castles. Bedrooms individually decorated with every comfort. Delicious home-cooked food of the highest standard. Tennis and croquet lawns in season.

Bed & Breakfast per night: single occupancy from £32.00–£40.00; double room from £64.00–£70.00
Dinner, Bed & Breakfast per person, per night: £41.00–£52.50
Evening meal: 1930

Bedrooms: 5 double, 4 twin
Bathrooms: 9 en-suite
Parking: 10 spaces
Cards accepted: Mastercard, Visa, Switch/Delta

Yorkshire Dales Barns

The beauty of the Yorkshire Dales derives in large part from the natural magnificence of the landscape: nature generously gave this central stretch of the Pennine chain dramatic limestone outcrops and clear, fast-running rivers. But man too has added to the splendour of the Dales. The trees may have been cleared long ago, but in their stead on the lower slopes came hay-meadows full of as many as 40 species of herb, bounded by drystone walls of simple beauty. In the northern Dales such as Swaledale and Arkengarthdale, almost every field has its own barn, each one adding to the glorious impression these valleys create.

These barns – it is estimated that there are over a thousand in Swaledale and Arkengarthdale alone – are a sign of a vanishing form of agriculture. In the 17th, 18th and 19th centuries, when most of these barns were built, farms were small and numerous. Many who tended the land also worked in the local lead and coal mines, and so had little time to devote to farming. The summer harvest of the hay crop was the most labour-intensive time of year, and the hard-pressed farmers evolved an agricultural system which allowed a more even spread of work. They built their barns – almost all using the drystone method of construction with stones sloping outwards to take the rain away – in the fields where the hay was growing. Storing the hay in the nearby barns was therefore a simple task. Since the cows spent the winter in the same barn as their foodstuff, it was easy

both to feed the cattle and to fertilise the same field with their manure. The quid pro quo was that the farmer had to walk to each of his barns in the winter months – not too arduous if there were only a few barns on the round.

Modern employment practices and the quest for efficiency have meant that farms are now few and large. This no longer fits in with the traditional system, and many outlying field barns have become redundant. In Swaledale and Arkengarthdale a conservation scheme run by the national park has saved countless from dereliction; some are still used by their owners while others have found new life as 'bunkhouse barns'. These offer basic accommodation to walkers and are often on or near long-distance footpaths. At Hazel Brow, Low Row, visitors may go inside a traditional Dales barn as part of the open farm scheme (tel: 01748 886224 for more details).

72 Jasmine House

 ◆◆◆◆◆ Silver Award

Market Place, Middleham, Leyburn, North Yorkshire DL8 4NU **Tel:** (01969) 622858
Web: www.jasminehouse.net **E-mail:** enquiries@jasminehouse.net

Situated in the heart of Wensleydale, this beautiful Georgian Grade II listed building overlooks the Medieval market place of Middleham, within 500 yards of Richard III's historic castle. A small residence with the ambience of a bygone era offers exquisite individually styled accommodation, a relaxed romantic atmosphere, excellent dining, open fires and complimentary sherry. Couple this with a thriving race horse industry, stunning scenery and walking from the doorstep and you have a unique holiday destination for the discerning traveller.

Bed & Breakfast per night: single occupancy from £59.00–£69.00; double room from £78.00– £98.00
Dinner, Bed & Breakfast per person, per night: £60.00–£70.00
Evening meal: 1900 (last orders 2000)

Bedrooms: 2 double, 1 twin, 1 family
Bathrooms: 3 en-suite, 1 private
Cards accepted: Mastercard, Visa, Switch/Delta

73 Yore View

◆◆◆◆

Leyburn Road, Middleham, Leyburn, North Yorkshire DL8 4PL **Tel:** (01969) 622987
E-mail: yore_view@hotmail.com

Middleham is surrounded by beautiful dales, famous for race horse training and the castle ruins, home of Richard III. With numerous restaurants and bars all serving superb food, we keep their menus for you to choose from. Yore View, a former 1921 picture house, is situated 200 metres from Middleham centre. Individually furnished to a high standard, our bedrooms have every modern facility. We provide private parking and a warm welcome always awaits you. Free brochure.

Bed & Breakfast per night: single occupancy from £30.00–£40.00; double room from £44.00–£50.00

Bedrooms: 2 double, 1 family
Bathrooms: 2 en-suite, 1 private
Parking: 5 spaces

74 Little Holtby

◆◆◆◆ Silver Award

Leeming Bar, Northallerton, North Yorkshire DL7 9LH **Tel:** (01609) 748762 **Fax:** (01609) 748822
E-mail: littleholtby@yahoo.co.uk

Today's discerning traveller is looking for somewhere special, where the warmth of welcome and attention to comfort will remain a treasured memory. Beams, polished wood floors and antiques all add to the charm of an old farmhouse. All the spacious, period bedrooms have glorious views. One of the double bedrooms has a four-poster bed. Generous country breakfasts with local organic and free range produce, Aga-cooked. Our aim is to give our guests the best. Treat yourself to a really memorable stay.

Bed & Breakfast per night: single occupancy from £25.00–£30.00; double room from £45.00–£50.00
Dinner, Bed & Breakfast per person, per night: £35.00
Evening meal: 1930 (last orders 2100)

Bedrooms: 2 double, 1 twin
Bathrooms: 1 en-suite, 1 shared
Parking: 10 spaces

75 Laskill Grange (formerly Laskill Farm) ◆◆◆◆

Hawnby, Nr Helmsley, York, North Yorkshire YO62 5NB **Tel:** (01439) 798268 **Fax:** (01439) 798498
Web: www.laskillfarm.co.uk **E-mail:** suesmith@laskillfarm.fsnet.co.uk

A delightful country farmhouse with a beautiful one acre garden and lake with ducks and swans. We offer complete relaxation in our lovely en-suite rooms. Emphasis is placed on comfort and food, as characterised on the BBC 'Holiday' programme. Lots to do and see - a walkers' paradise. 'A jewel in the North Yorkshire Moors'. York and the coast are only 40 minutes' drive away.

Bed & Breakfast per night: single room from £29.50–£30.50; double room from £57.00–£60.00
Dinner, Bed & Breakfast per person, per night: £42.00–£43.50
Evening meal: 1900

Bedrooms: 1 single, 3 double, 2 twin
Bathrooms: 5 en-suite, 1 private
Parking: 10 spaces
Cards accepted: Mastercard, Visa, Switch/Delta, Visa Electron

76 Rawcliffe House Farm ◆◆◆◆

Stape, Pickering, North Yorkshire YO18 8JA **Tel:** (01751) 473292 **Fax:** (01751) 473766
Web: www.yorkshireaccommodation.com **E-mail:** sheilarh@yahoo.com

We are 'Somewhere Special' and our guests are special people who deserve the best service and accommodation in a fantastic rural location. We offer charming, en-suite ground floor rooms with every convenience in the idyllic and spectacular North Yorkshire Moors National Park. Peace and tranquillity plus friendly hosts who will always do their best. Extensive choice of breakfast menu. Optional home cooked evening meal with fresh local produce. Easy access to the coast and York. Highly recommended. Self-catering also available – see entry on page 81.

Bed & Breakfast per night: single occupancy from £30.50–£33.50; double room from £51.00–£57.00
Dinner, Bed & Breakfast per person, per night: £38.50 (min 2 nights, 2 sharing)
Evening meal: 1830

Bedrooms: 2 double, 1 twin
Bathrooms: 3 en-suite
Parking: 10 spaces
Open: January–November
Cards accepted: Mastercard, Visa

77 The Cornmill ◆◆◆◆ Silver Award

Kirby Mills, Kirkbymoorside, York, North Yorkshire YO62 6NP **Tel:** (01751) 432000 **Fax:** (01751) 432300
Web: www.kirbymills.demon.co.uk **E-mail:** cornmill@kirbymills.demon.co.uk

2001 Finalist, Yorkshire Tourist Board White Rose Awards for Tourism. This restored 18th-century Watermill and Victorian Farmhouse provides tranquil, luxurious accommodation on the River Dove. Large bedrooms with en-suite baths and/or powerful showers, fluffy towels, king-size beds, themed four-poster rooms, guest lounge, honesty bar, wood-burning stove and bootroom are in the Farmhouse. Our famous sumptuous breakfasts and pre-booked group dinners are served in the Mill with glass viewing panel over the millrace. Near golf, horse riding, abbeys, castles, coast and the North York Moors. Wheelchair friendly. French spoken. ⋏ Category 3

Bed & Breakfast per night: double room from £50.00–£65.00
Dinner, Bed & Breakfast per person, per night: £50.00–£57.50 (groups of 4+, pre-booked)
Evening meal: 1900

Bedrooms: 3 double, 2 twin
Bathrooms: 5 en-suite
Parking: 8 spaces
Open: Easter–October
Cards accepted: Mastercard, Visa

78 Burr Bank

 ◆◆◆◆◆ Gold Award

Cropton, Pickering, North Yorkshire YO18 8HL **Tel:** (01751) 417777 or 0776 884 2233 **Fax:** (01751) 417789
Web: www.burrbank.com **E-mail:** bandb@burrbank.com

Winner of Yorkshire's 'Guest Accommodation of the Year 2000'. A quarter mile from the village and set in 80 acres, with wonderful views over Cropton Forest and Moors. Comfortable, spacious ground-floor accommodation and personal attention. An interesting, peaceful holiday with easy access to the coast, Moors, Wolds and York. Much to do and see using Burr Bank as your home for a while. We hope you enjoy our part of Yorkshire as much as we do. No smoking.

Bed & Breakfast per night: single occupancy £27.00; double room £54.00
Dinner, Bed & Breakfast per person, per night: £43.00
Evening meal: 1900

Bedrooms: 1 double, 1 twin
Bathrooms: 2 en-suite
Parking: 10 spaces

79 Old Manse

◆◆◆◆

Middleton Road, Pickering, North Yorkshire YO18 8AL **Tel:** (01751) 476484 **Fax:** (01751) 477124

The Old Manse, once an Edwardian vicarage, has 2.5 acres of mature gardens and orchard and on-site parking. Friendly hospitality and excellent home-cooked breakfast and dinner awaits all our guests. North Yorkshire steam railway and the town centre is only four minutes' walk away – the moors and national parks are a few minutes' drive away. Scarborough, Whitby and Filey offer many attractions for those who enjoy the sea and coast. The market towns of Malton, Kirbymoorside, Helmsley and Pickering hold weekly street markets.

Bed & Breakfast per night: single room from £23.00–£28.00; double room from £44.00–£94.00
Dinner, Bed & Breakfast per person, per night: £34.00–£40.00

Bedrooms: 1 single, 6 double, 1 twin, 2 triple
Bathrooms: 10 en-suite
Parking: 10 spaces

80 Harmony Country Lodge

◆◆◆◆

80 Limestone Road, Burniston, Scarborough, North Yorkshire YO13 0DG **Tel:** 0800 298 5841 or 07967 157689 **Fax:** (01723) 870276
Web: www.spiderweb.co.uk/Harmony **E-mail:** harmonylodge@cwcom.net

Unique in design and three miles from Scarborough, Harmony offers a peaceful and relaxing smoke-free retreat within 1.5 acres of private grounds. Set in an elevated position with superb 360 degree panoramic views of the sea and National Park. The rooms, including the attractive dining room, guest lounge and conservatory, are tastefully decorated with attention to detail and all have superb views. You can spoil yourself with a relaxing fragrant massage during your stay.

Bed & Breakfast per night: single room from £23.50–£30.00; double room from £47.00–£59.00
Dinner, Bed & Breakfast per person, per night: £38.50–£45.00
Evening meal: 1830

Bedrooms: 2 single, 4 double, 1 twin, 1 family
Bathrooms: 5 en-suite, 1 shared
Parking: 11 spaces

81 The Alexander Hotel

33 Burniston Road, Scarborough, North Yorkshire Y011 6PG **Tel:** (01723) 363178 **Fax:** (01723) 354821
Web: www.atesto.freeserve.co.uk **E-mail:** alex@atesto.freeserve.co.uk

Somewhere Special, 100% non-smoking, detached hotel, close to Peasholm Park and all North Bay amenities. Warm and caring welcome, excellent food from resident chef, attractive dining room with separate tables and extensive service. All rooms are quality en-suite. No family rooms. Licensed cocktail bar. Off-road guest parking. 'Arrive as guests, leave as friends'.

Bed & Breakfast per night: single room from £24.50–£27.50; double room from £49.00–£55.00
Dinner, Bed & Breakfast per person, per night: £34.00–£38.00
Evening meal: 1800 (last orders 1900)

Bedrooms: 1 single, 8 double, 2 twin
Bathrooms: 11 en-suite
Parking: 13 spaces
Open: March–November
Cards accepted: Mastercard, Visa, Switch/Delta

82 Mallard Grange   ◆◆◆◆◆ Silver Award

Aldfield, nr Fountains Abbey, Ripon, North Yorkshire HG4 3BE **Tel:** (01765) 620242
E-mail: Mallard.Grange@btinternet.com

Rambling, 16th-century farmhouse full of character and charm in glorious countryside near Fountains Abbey. Offering superb quality and comfort, spacious rooms furnished with care and some lovely antique pieces. En-suite bedrooms have large comfortable beds, warm towels, colour television, hair dryer and refreshments tray. Delicious breakfasts! Pretty walled garden. Safe parking. Ideally placed for Harrogate, York, Yorkshire Dales, North York Moors and a wealth of historic houses, castles and gardens. Excellent evening meals locally.

Bed & Breakfast per night: single occupancy from £35.00–£60.00; double room from £55.00–£60.00

Bedrooms: 2 double, 2 twin
Bathrooms: 4 en-suite
Parking: 4 spaces

83 Oldstead Grange   ◆◆◆◆◆ Gold Award

Oldstead, Coxwold, York, North Yorkshire YO61 4BJ **Tel:** (01347) 868634
Web: www.yorkshireuk.com **E-mail:** oldsteadgrange@yorkshireuk.com

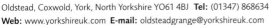

Oldstead Grange blends traditional 17th-century features with superb comfort and luxury in a beautiful and quiet situation amidst our fields, woods and valleys near Byland Abbey in the North York Moors National Park. Spacious en-suite bedrooms with really comfortable king-size beds, colour television, warm towels and robes, fresh flowers and home-made chocolates and biscuits. Special four-poster suite. Breakfast choice of freshly prepared traditional and specialty dishes. Renowned eating places in local picturesque villages. Colour brochure.

Bed & Breakfast per night: double room from £56.00–£76.00

Bedrooms: 1 double, 1 twin, 1 family
Bathrooms: 3 en-suite
Parking: 3 spaces
Cards accepted: Mastercard, Visa, Delta, Eurocard

84 Daleside

East End, Ampleforth, York YO62 4DA **Tel:** (01439) 788266

Daleside, listed for its cruck beams and oak panelling, is the oldest house in this charming stone village. The house has recently been sympathetically restored, including the two en-suite guest rooms overlooking the garden to the south. There is antique furniture throughout, with a splendid half-tester double bed in one of the guest rooms. There are two good inns within easy walking distance, excellent restaurants within a few miles and the beautiful unspoilt countryside offers excellent walking. Private parking for three cars.

Bed & Breakfast per night: single occupancy from £31.50–£35.50; double room from £55.00–£63.00

Bedrooms: 1 double, 1 twin
Bathrooms: 2 en-suite
Parking: 3 spaces
Open: all year except Christmas and New Year

85 Sproxton Hall

Sproxton, Helmsley, North Yorkshire YO62 5EQ **Tel:** (01439) 770225 **Fax:** (01439) 771373
Web: www.sproxtonhall.co.uk **E-mail:** info@sproxtonhall.demon.co.uk

Relax in the tranquil atmosphere and comfort of our 17th-century Grade II listed farmhouse. Magnificent views over idyllic countryside on a 300 acre working farm, one mile south of the market town of Helmsley. Lovingly and tastefully furnished, giving the cosy elegance of a country home. Restful, oak-beamed drawing room with log fire. Enjoy a hearty breakfast in a most attractive dining room. Extremely comfortable, centrally heated double and twin bedrooms. En-suite or private bathrooms, tea making facilities, remote control colour television. Delightful country garden to relax in. No smoking.

Bed & Breakfast per night: double room from £50.00–£60.00

Bedrooms: 1 double, 2 twin
Bathrooms: 2 en-suite, 1 private
Parking: 10 spaces
Cards accepted: Mastercard, Visa, Eurocard

86 Shallowdale House

◆◆◆◆◆ Silver Award

West End, Ampleforth, York, North Yorkshire YO62 4DY **Tel:** (01439) 788325 **Fax:** (01439) 788885
Web: www.shallowdalehouse.demon.co.uk **E-mail:** stay@shallowdalehouse.demon.co.uk

Shallowdale House is stunningly situated, in extensive hillside gardens, on the southern edge of the North York Moors National Park (20 miles north of York). Phillip Gill and Anton van der Horst have carefully created a distinctively elegant and restful place to stay, where good food matters and the service is always friendly and attentive. All the rooms enjoy exceptional panoramic views of gorgeous countryside and this is an excellent base for exploring a beautiful area.

Bed & Breakfast per night: single occupancy from £45.00–£55.00; double room from £65.00–£80.00
Dinner, Bed & Breakfast per person, per night: £55.00–£62.50
Evening meal: 1930 (last bookings 1200)

Bedrooms: 2 double, 1 twin
Bathrooms: 2 en-suite, 1 private
Parking: 3 spaces
Cards accepted: Mastercard, Visa, Delta

87 The Old Vicarage

◆◆◆◆ Silver Award

Market Place, Easingwold, York, North Yorkshire YO61 3AL **Tel:** (01347) 821015 **Fax:** (01347) 823465
E-mail: kirman@oldvic-easingwold.freeserve.co.uk

Standing in the market square, yet surrounded by half an acre of gardens with croquet lawn and ample parking, our 18th-century home provides a tranquil haven easily accessible to York, the Moors and Dales. Tastefully furnished, well-appointed bedrooms are complemented with patchwork quilts and little unexpected extra touches. A traditional English breakfast using local produce is served in the east-facing dining room and the drawing room, with its grand piano, is exclusively for guests' enjoyment.

Bed & Breakfast per night: double room from £55.00–£65.00

Bedrooms: 3 double, 1 twin
Bathrooms: 4 en-suite
Parking: 5 spaces
Open: All year except January and December

---

88 The Granary

◆◆◆◆

Stearsby, York, North Yorkshire YO61 4SA **Tel:** (01347) 888652 **Fax:** (01347) 888652
E-mail: robertturl@thegranary.org.uk

An 18th-century converted farm granary situated in the hamlet of Stearsby, nestling in the Howardian Hills close to Castle Howard and approximately 12 miles from York. Surrounded by beautiful woodlands and set in a lovely one acre garden. Ideally located for visiting York, the Yorkshire Dales and of course James Herriot country! The Granary offers private en-suite bedrooms with their own sitting rooms in the Barn Annexe and we have a heated swimming pool.

Bed & Breakfast per night: single occupancy £30.00; double room £50.00

Bedrooms: 3 double
Bathrooms: 3 en-suite
Parking: 6 spaces

---

89 Ascot House Hotel

★★ Silver Award

53 Kings Road, Harrogate, North Yorkshire HG1 5HJ **Tel:** (01423) 531005 **Fax:** (01423) 503523
Web: www.ascothouse.com **E-mail:** admin@ascothouse.com

A delightful, family-run hotel within easy walking distance of Harrogate's renowned shops and gardens. Relax over a drink in our comfortable lounge bar before dining in our elegant restaurant. Enjoy quality cuisine - and a great selection of wines! All 19 bedrooms are individually furnished and have en-suite facilities, telephone, television, radio/alarm, hairdryer, electric blankets and tea and coffee making facilities. Plan your days out using our large collection of brochures about local attractions - we'll be pleased to advise! Car park. Major credit cards welcome.

Bed & Breakfast per night: single room from £53.00–£63.00; double room from £78.00–£98.00
Dinner, Bed & Breakfast per person, per night: £51.00–£56.00 (min 2 nights in double/twin room)
Evening meal: 1900 (last orders 2030)

Bedrooms: 4 single, 7 double, 7 twin, 1 triple
Bathrooms: 19 en-suite
Parking: 14 spaces
Cards accepted: Mastercard, Visa, Switch/Delta, Amex, Diners, Eurocard

---

90 Franklin View   ◆◆◆◆

19 Grove Road, Harrogate, North Yorkshire HG1 5EW **Tel:** (01423) 541388 **Fax:** (01423) 547872
Web: www.franklinview.com **E-mail:** jennifer@franklinview.com

An ideally situated Edwardian house overlooking a beautiful tree-lined street, only six minutes' walk from the town and conference centre. The accommodation has been tastefully refurbished with quality and comfort being the main criteria. Traditional English breakfasts are freshly cooked to order. We have plenty of alternatives to offer those wishing for something lighter. Guests enjoy the relaxed and informal atmosphere, with many returning annually. Private parking off street.

Bed & Breakfast per night: single occupancy from £35.00–£40.00; double room from £48.00–£55.00

Bedrooms: 1 double, 2 twin
Bathrooms: 3 en-suite
Parking: 3 spaces

91 Ascot House   ◆◆◆◆

80 East Parade, York YO31 7YH **Tel:** (01904) 426826 **Fax:** (01904) 431077
Web: www.ascothouseyork.com **E-mail:** j&k@ascot-house-york.demon.co.uk

Ascot House is a family-run 15 bedroomed Victorian villa built in 1869, with en-suite rooms of character – many having four poster or canopy beds. There is a spacious lounge for residents to relax in and delicious traditional English or vegetarian breakfasts are served in the dining room. The historic city centre and York Minster are 15 minutes' walk away and it is only an hours' drive to the Dales, the Moors or the beautiful Yorkshire coast. Residential licence, sauna and private enclosed car park.

Bed & Breakfast per night: single room from £22.00–£46.00; double room from £44.00–£60.00

Bedrooms: 1 single, 8 double, 3 twin, 2 triple, 1 family
Bathrooms: 12 en-suite, 1 private, 1 shared
Parking: 12 spaces
Cards accepted: Mastercard, Visa, Switch/Delta, Diners, Eurocard, JCB, Maestro, Visa Electron

92 Holmwood House Hotel   ◆◆◆◆

112–114 Holgate Road, York YO2 4BB **Tel:** (01904) 626183 **Fax:** (01904) 670899
Web: www.holmwoodhousehotel.co.uk **E-mail:** holmwood.house@dial.pipex.com

Close to the city walls, an elegant listed Victorian town house offering a feeling of home with a touch of luxury. All the en-suite bedrooms are different in size and decoration, some with four-poster beds and one has a spa bath. All rooms are non-smoking and air conditioned rooms are available. Imaginative breakfasts are served to the sound of gentle classical music. There is an inviting sitting room with an open fire. Car park. On the A59. Why not take a look at our web-site?

Bed & Breakfast per night: single occupancy from £50.00–£80.00; double room from £65.00–£110.00
Gourmet breaks with Meltons Restaurant, per person, per night: £55.00–£85.00 (min 2 nights, 2 sharing)

Bedrooms: 10 double, 3 twin, 1 triple
Bathrooms: 14 en-suite
Parking: 9 spaces
Cards accepted: Mastercard, Visa, Switch/Delta, Solo

93 The Hazelwood

◆◆◆◆ Silver Award

24–25 Portland Street, York YO31 7EH **Tel:** (01904) 626548 **Fax:** (01904) 628032
Web: www.thehazelwoodyork.com **E-mail:** reservations@thehazelwoodyork.com

Luxury and elegance in the very heart of York. The Hazelwood is situated in an extremely quiet residential area only 400 yards from York Minster and has its own car park. The bedrooms in our elegant Victorian townhouse are individually styled and are fitted to the highest standards using designer fabrics. We offer a wide choice of high quality breakfasts, including vegetarian, ranging from traditional English to croissants and Danish pastries. We operate a non-smoking policy throughout.

Bed & Breakfast per night: single room from £40.00–£85.00; double room from £75.00–£95.00

Bedrooms: 1 single, 7 double, 4 twin, 2 triple
Bathrooms: 14 en-suite
Parking: 10 spaces
Cards accepted: Mastercard, Visa, Switch/Delta, Eurocard, JCB, Visa Electron, Solo

94 Bay Court Hotel

◆◆◆◆

35a Sands Lane, Bridlington, East Riding of Yorkshire YO15 2JG **Tel:** (01262) 676288
Web: www.baycourt.co.uk **E-mail:** bay.court@virgin.net

The Bay Court is a small high quality licensed hotel, catering for discerning guests who expect tasteful accommodation, delicious food, a relaxing informal environment and friendly service. We are opposite the quiet north beach and are within easy walking distance to the harbour, nearby cliffs and delightful countryside. Our south-facing sun patio and gardens have lovely sea views and offer you a haven to relax and enjoy the surroundings – at the same time as enjoying light refreshments from our tea room or a drink from the bar.

Bed & Breakfast per night: single room £25.00; double room from £50.00–£56.00
Dinner, Bed & Breakfast per person, per night: £34.00–£37.00
Lunch available: light snacks throughout the day
Evening meal: 1800 (last orders 1900)

Bedrooms: 2 single, 3 double, 2 twin
Bathrooms: 5 en-suite, 2 private
Parking: 5 spaces
Open: March–October
Cards accepted: Mastercard, Visa

95 Manor House Hotel

★★★ Silver Award

Ribby Hall Village, Ribby Road, Wrea Green, Nr Blackpool, Lancashire PR4 2PR **Tel:** (01772) 688000 **Fax:** (01772) 688036
Web: www.mhhotel.co.uk **E-mail:** themanorhousehotel@ribbyhall.co.uk

Newly opened in June 2001, the Manor House Hotel offers luxury spacious accommodation in the heart of the Fylde countryside, yet less than ten miles from Blackpool and Lytham St Annes. Located in the award winning Ribby Hall Village, the Manor House nestles amidst relaxing grounds and landscaped gardens overlooking an ornamental lake and fountain. Comprising 28 sumptuous apartments, including two penthouse suites, The Manor House is ideal for business executives, couples or friends seeking something special.

Bed & Breakfast per night: single occupancy from £65.00–£115.00; double room from £95.00–£160.00
Dinner, Bed & Breakfast per person, per night: £66.50 (double occupancy) – £84.00 (single occupancy)

Bedrooms: 23 double, 4 twin, 2 family
Bathrooms: 29 en-suite
Parking: 50 spaces
Cards accepted: Mastercard, Visa, Switch/Delta, Amex

96 Northcote Manor

★★★ Gold Award

Northcote Road, Langho, Blackburn, Lancashire BB6 8BE **Tel:** (01254) 240555 **Fax:** (01254) 246568
Web: www.northcotemanor.com **E-mail:** admin@northcotemanor.com

Northcote Manor is a privately owned, 14 bedroom country house hotel situated in the beautiful Ribble Valley in the heart of north-west England. In the capable hands of Craig Bancroft and award-winning chef Nigel Haworth, the Manor is best known for its excellent restaurant and friendly hospitality, awarded a Michelin Star and, in 1999, an independent hotel of the year award. Gourmet one-night breaks available from £160 per couple which include champagne, a five-course gourmet dinner and stunning Lancashire breakfast.

Bed & Breakfast per night: single occupancy from £100.00–£120.00; double room from £130.00–£150.00
Lunch available: 1200–1330
Evening meal: 1900 (last orders 2130)

Bedrooms: 10 double, 4 twin
Bathrooms: 14 en-suite
Parking: 50 spaces
Cards accepted: Mastercard, Visa, Switch/Delta, Amex, Visa Electron

97 Ponden House

◆◆◆◆

Stanbury, Nr Haworth, Keighley, West Yorkshire BD22 0HR **Tel:** (01535) 644154
Web: www.pondenhouse.co.uk **E-mail:** brenda.taylor@pondenhouse.co.uk

Ponden House, built on the site of the 16th-century 'old house and barn', offers comfort and tranquillity in a secluded historical setting. Local craftsmen and women have blended local materials with traditional skills and imaginative design; old and new come together to provide a unique atmosphere. Food is home cooked, stylish and imaginative. With views down to the reservoir and across to the moors, Ponden House is the perfect base for long walks, gentle strolls or visiting local towns and villages.

Bed & Breakfast per night: single occupancy from £25.00–£30.00; double room from £46.00
Dinner, Bed & Breakfast per person, per night: from £36.00
Evening meal: 1900

Bedrooms: 3 double/twin
Bathrooms: 2 en-suite, 1 shared
Parking: 5 spaces

98 Five Rise Locks Hotel

◆◆◆◆ Silver Award

Beck Lane, Bingley, West Yorkshire BD16 4DD **Tel:** (01274) 565296 **Fax:** (01274) 568828
E-mail: 101731.2134@compuserve.com

Built for a wealthy Victorian mill owner, the house stands in mature gardens overlooking the Aire valley, yet is only a few minutes' walk away from the Five Rise Locks and Bingley town centre. Each bedroom has a unique view and has been individually designed and furnished. The restaurant is open for lunch and dinner offering imaginative dishes and a well-chosen wine list, in elegant, yet comfortable, surroundings. Experience Haworth, Esholt village, steam trains, museums and tranquil, vast open spaces.

Bed & Breakfast per night: single room from £45.00–£55.00; double room from £65.00–£75.00
Dinner, Bed & Breakfast per person, per night: £45.00–£50.00 (min 2 nights, 2 sharing)
Evening meal: 1800 (last orders 2100)

Bedrooms: 1 single, 5 double, 3 twin
Bathrooms: 9 en-suite
Parking: 15 spaces
Cards accepted: Mastercard, Visa, Switch/Delta, Eurocard, JCB, Maestro, Visa Electron, Solo

99 Glebe Farm

Bolton Percy, York, North Yorkshire YO23 7AL **Tel:** (01904) 744228

An elegant family-run Victorian farmhouse on a working farm. Offering excellent accommodation within easy reach of York city. The Moors, Dales and coast can be reached within an hour. Self-contained en-suite annexe, conservatory, garden and ample parking. The farm is in a quiet village with an exceptional 15th-century church. Bolton Percy is four miles from Tadcaster and nine miles from York.

Bed & Breakfast per night: single occupancy from £22.00–£24.00; double room from £44.00–£48.00	**Bedrooms:** 1 twin **Bathrooms:** 1 en-suite **Parking:** 2 spaces **Open:** April–November	

Wakefield Rhubarb

In spring, supermarkets throughout the country are stocked with a crop which was once the pride of many a cottage garden and is now undergoing something of a renaissance in restaurant popularity – rhubarb. The chances are that the succulent pink stalks which end up in your shopping basket were pulled from a plant growing somewhere near Wakefield, for this is where a large proportion of the country's rhubarb is grown.

A hundred years ago an area stretching between Wakefield, Leeds and Morley, often known as the 'rhubarb triangle', was the world centre of rhubarb growing. At the height of its popularity in the 1930s over 4,000 acres were under cultivation. Today that figure is only 750 acres, but Wakefield still prides itself on being the country's rhubarb capital. The national rhubarb collection is kept just north of 'the triangle' at the Harlow Carr Botanic Gardens, near Harrogate, and consists of 150 or so different varieties.

Although regarded as one of the most English of desserts, rhubarb probably originated in China, where it has been used for medicinal purposes for almost 5,000 years. Its purgative properties are well-known, but it has also been claimed as a miracle cure for a whole variety of other ailments, from poisonous animal bites to venereal disease. It only took off as a culinary delicacy in England in the early 19th century.

Rhubarb is technically a vegetable rather than a fruit in that, like celery, the stalks of the plant are consumed. The first, tender shoots of the spring have the sweetest flavour and so the practice has developed of covering the plants in winter and surrounding them with warm straw to 'force' them into early growth. Much of Wakefield's rhubarb is grown in forcing sheds, now artificially heated to bring the crops to fruition as early as Christmas. Some growers still insist on picking by candle light to ensure maximum darkness for the crop. It is possible to arrange group tours of the rhubarb growing areas and forcing sheds by calling 01924 305841. The dedicated horticulturalist may inspect the national rhubarb collection at Harlow Carr Gardens (tel: 01423 565418) while the acres of plants growing to the north of Wakefield, fleshy leaves dark, glossy and shoulder-high by late spring, are visible for all to see.

100 The Manor Country House   ◆◆◆◆

Acaster Malbis, York YO23 2UL **Tel:** (01904) 706723 **Fax:** (01904) 700737
Web: www.manorhse.co.uk **E-mail:** manorhouse@selcom.co.uk

Family-run manor house in rural tranquillity, with private lake, set in five and a half acres of beautiful mature grounds on the banks of the River Ouse. Fish in the lake, cycle or walk. Close to racecourse and only a 10 minute car journey from the city – or take the leisurely river bus (Easter to October). Conveniently situated to take advantage of the Dales, Moors, Wolds and splendid coastline. Cosy lounge and licensed lounge bar with open fire. Conservatory breakfast room with Aga-cooked food.

Bed & Breakfast per night: single room from £45.00–£60.00; double room from £64.00–£84.00

Bedrooms: 1 single, 4 double, 3 twin, 2 family rooms
Bathrooms: 10 en-suite
Parking: 15 spaces
Cards accepted: Mastercard, Visa, Switch/Delta, Eurocard

101 Cornerstones   ◆◆◆◆

230 Washway Road, Sale, Cheshire M33 4RA **Tel:** (0161) 283 6909 **Fax:** (0161) 283 6909
E-mail: toncasey@aol.com

Cornerstones is located on the main A56 road into the city centre. The building is Victorian – built by Sir William Cunliff Brooks, Lord of the Manor. A total refurbishment was carried out in 1985, reproducing the splendour of the Victorian era. Brookland Metro station is less than five minutes' walk away, and on the fifteen minute journey into the city you will pass Manchester United Football Club, Lancashire County Cricket Club and the G-Mex. At your journey's end you will find an abundance of shops, theatres, museums and art galleries.

Bed & Breakfast per night: single room from £25.00–£35.00; double room from £45.00–£50.00
Dinner, Bed & Breakfast per person, per night: £40.00–£50.00
Evening meal: 1930

Bedrooms: 3 single, 3 double, 3 twin
Bathrooms: 5 en-suite, 2 rooms with private shower, 1 shared
Parking: 10 spaces
Cards accepted: Mastercard, Visa, JCB

102 Tankersley Manor Hotel   ★★★ Silver Award

Church Lane, Upper Tankersley, Tankersley, Barnsley, South Yorkshire S75 3DQ **Tel:** (01226) 744700 **Fax:** (01226) 745405
Web: www.marstonhotels.com **E-mail:** tankersley@marstonhotels.com

Built around a former 17th-century residence, Tankersley Manor is set in an elevated position backing on to the edge of the National Park and woodland. The hotel offers 70 bedrooms, each with a character of its own. Many retain original features like exposed beams and windowsills of Yorkshire stone and all have private bathrooms. Guests can enjoy the finest food in the oak beamed split-level restaurant or relax in the hotel's own country pub with open log fires.

Bed & Breakfast per night: single occupancy from £94.00–£105.00; double room from £117.00–£139.00
Dinner, Bed & Breakfast per person, per night: £50.00–£62.50 (min 2 nights)
Evening meal: 1900 (last orders 2145)

Bedrooms: 40 double, 25 twin, 4 four-poster suites
Bathrooms: 69 en-suite
Parking: 400 spaces
Cards accepted: Mastercard, Visa, Switch/Delta, Amex, Diners, Eurocard, JCB, Maestro, Visa Electron

At-a-glance symbols are explained on the flap inside the back cover

103 Whitley Hall Hotel

★★★ Silver Award

Elliott Lane, Grenoside, Sheffield S35 8NR **Tel:** (0114) 245 4444 **Fax:** (0114) 245 5414
Web: www.whitleyhall.com **E-mail:** reservations@whitleyhall.com

Whitley Hall dates from the 16th century and is a lovely country house standing in its own thirty acres of gardens, woodland and lakes. Privately owned as a hotel for over 30 years, we offer accommodation, food and service of the highest quality and in the best English tradition. This popular country hotel is ideally situated between the Yorkshire Dales and Derbyshire Peak District and only a few minutes from Sheffield's theatres, sports facilities and magnificent Meadowhall shopping complex.

Bed & Breakfast per night: single room from £77.00–£87.00; double room from £98.00–£108.00
Dinner, Bed & Breakfast per person, per night: £72.00–£110.00
Lunch available: 1145–1345

Evening meal: 1900 (last orders 2130)
Bedrooms: 2 single, 12 double, 4 twin, 1 family
Bathrooms: 19 en-suite
Parking: 100 spaces
Cards accepted: Mastercard, Visa, Switch/Delta, Amex, Diners, Visa Electron, Solo

104 Forest Pines Hotel, Golf Course and Spa

★★★★ Silver Award

Ermine Street, Broughton, Brigg, Scunthorpe, North Lincolnshire DN20 0AQ **Tel:** (01652) 650770 **Fax:** (01652) 650495
Web: www.forestpines.co.uk **E-mail:** enquiries@forestpines.co.uk

Superbly located for all business and pleasure needs. Nestling amid an idyllic landscape of wooded parkland, the hotel is a haven for those who enjoy being pampered. Easily accessible from the motorway system, Lincoln, Hull and York are within easy reach. International cuisine is served in the elegant Beech Tree Restaurant. Extensive table d'hôte and à la carte menus are available daily. For more casual dining, the Garden Room is open all day, every day. Forest Pines, a 27 hole championship golf course provides the perfect venue for golfing breaks. The luxurious leisure club and beauty spa make this an ideal venue for a relaxed break.

Bed & Breakfast per night: single occupancy from £70.00–£90.00; double room from £90.00–£100.00
Dinner, Bed & Breakfast per person, per night: £68.00–£123.00
Lunch available: 1200–1400

Evening meal: 1900 (last orders 2200)
Bedrooms: 46 double, 40 twin
Bathrooms: 86 en-suite
Parking: 300 spaces
Cards accepted: Mastercard, Visa, Switch/Delta, Amex, Diners, Visa Electron

105 Prospect Farm

◆◆◆◆

Waltham Road, Brigsley, Grimsby, North East Lincolnshire DN37 0RQ **Tel:** (01472) 826491 **Fax:** (01472) 826491

Prospect Farm is a charming country house set in 40 acres of grassland with horses and sheep grazing. It is within easy reach of Grimsby/Cleethorpes, Louth and Humberside airport. The rooms are tastefully furnished and the 'Snug' is available to guests and has an open coal fire. The Aga-cooked breakfasts will set you up for the day! Accommodation comprises two double rooms (one en-suite) and one single. Holiday cottages are also available – see entry on page 84.

Bed & Breakfast per night: single room £25.00; double room from £45.00–£50.00

Bedrooms: 1 single, 2 double
Bathrooms: 1 en-suite, 1 private, 1 shared
Parking: 6 spaces

106 Grove House

Holme Street, Tarvin, Cheshire CH3 8EQ **Tel:** (01829) 740893 **Fax:** (01829) 741769

♦♦♦♦

A warm welcome awaits you in a relaxing, spacious, comfortable home with a long-established Cheshire family. Ideal situation for Chester, Oulton Park, North Wales, Liverpool, the Potteries and Manchester Airport (where guests can be met by prior arrangement). Hosts happy to help with sight-seeing suggestions. Attractive walled garden, listed trees and ample off-road parking. Traditional English breakfast served in family dining room. In winter an open coal fire burns in the elegant drawing room. Excellent evening meals available within two miles. North West Tourist Board 'Place to Stay' Award and runner-up for B&B of the Year. AA 'Landlady of the Year' finalist 2001.

| **Bed & Breakfast per night:** single room from £30.00–£40.00; double room from £60.00–£70.00 | **Bedrooms:** 1 single, 1 double, 1 twin
Bathrooms: 2 en-suite, 1 private
Parking: 8 spaces |  |

Cheshire Salt

Everyone knows that coal – in the main – comes from the North, while tin comes from Cornwall, but what about salt? The answer is the Cheshire Plain, that area of flat, fertile farmland between Chester and Macclesfield. Most of us may not know, for example, that one mine at Winsford supplies all the salt used to clear snow and ice from the United Kingdom's roads. But the Romans, those industrious plunderers of England's natural resources, knew all about the estimated 400 billion tons of salt lying beneath the rich soil – and they were here almost 2,000 years ago to tap the wealth of the area. Indeed the Latin name for Middlewich, 'Salinae', can be roughly translated as 'saltworks'.

The Cheshire Plain, 200 million years ago, was at the bottom of a shallow, salty sea. As the water evaporated, the salt formed into vast deposits of solid sodium chloride – or rock salt. Water flowing through this layer of rock salt reaches the surface as brine, and it was these brine springs that attracted the Romans.

In the 17th century, coal began to be used to evaporate the brine in large iron pans, and the efficiency of salt production was hugely improved. The biggest headache then became transport, of coal to the works and salt from them. To this end the navigable stretch of the River Weaver was extended to Winsford, and the Trent and Mersey Canal completed in 1777, allowing salt works to open at Northwich, Middlewich, Wheelock and Lawton. Larger, deeper salt beds were soon discovered, and by the late 19th century over 1 million tons of white salt were sailing down the Weaver Navigation each year.

Workers clogs and mine bucket at the Lion Salt Works

Today there are three commercial plants producing white salt for a range of uses (from food storage to soap and plastic manufacture). These (and others) adopted the 'vacuum evaporation process' at the turn of the century, but one, the Lion Salt Works at Marston, near Northwich, stuck with the traditional 'open pan' system of evaporation, largely unchanged since Roman times. In 1986 it eventually closed, but the local council bought the fascinating site, now open to the public in the afternoons (tel: 01606 41823). Together with the Salt Museum in the old Northwich Workhouse (tel: 01606 41331), it makes an intriguing exploration of Cheshire's industrial past – although perhaps the most fascinating site of all is the Anderton Boat Lift, a vast monument to the engineering achievements of the Victorian era. For over a century this 'wonder of the waterways' just north of Northwich, built in 1875, hauled boats from the Weaver Navigation up 50ft (15m) and into the Trent and Mersey Canal above. Closed in 1982, the Boat Lift may yet work again if a local restoration group is successful.

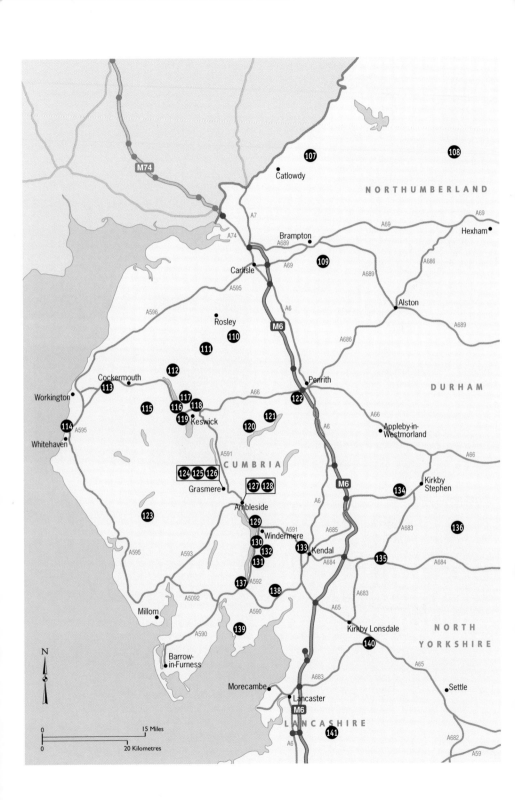

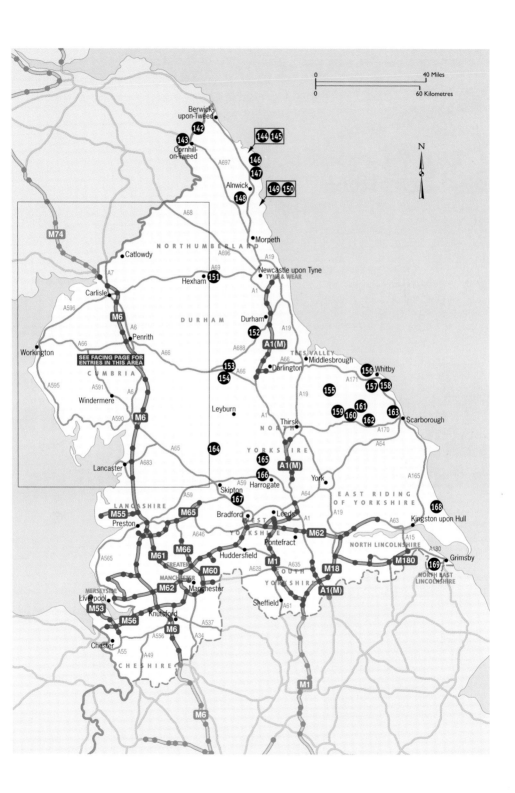

107 Saughs Farm Cottages ★ ★ ★ ★

Bailey, Newcastleton, Roxburghshire **Web:** www.skylarkcottages.co.uk
Contact: Mrs J Gray, Saughs Farm, Bailey, Newcastleton, Roxburghshire TD9 0TT
Tel: (016977) 48000 or (016977) 48346 **Fax:** (016977) 48180 **E-mail:** skylark@onholiday.co.uk

Superb character cottages on conservation farm. Unspoiled landscape, panoramic views, high quality furnishings. Every cottage has a wood-burning stove, central heating and its own patio. Stylish, warm, cosy and welcoming, they are perfect for any time of year. You can bring your horse or dog by arrangement, there is stabling and riding on the farm and good walking and cycling. There are forest tracks and bridleways and fishing and golfing within six miles. Visit the Lake District, Hadrian's Wall or Solway Coast. Carlisle 40 minutes, Edinburgh two hours.

Low season per week: £245.00–£350.00
High season per week: £325.00–£450.00
(plus supplement at Christmas and New Year)
Short breaks: from £150.00–£250.00

3 cottages: sleeping 4–8 people

108 Conheath Cottage ★ ★ ★ ★

Bellingham, Hexham, Northumberland **Web:** www.conheath.co.uk
Contact: Mrs Z Riddle, Blakelaw Farm, Bellingham, Hexham, Northumberland NE48 2EF
Tel: (01434) 220250 **Fax:** (01434) 220250 **E-mail:** stay@conheath.co.uk

Conheath is a quiet semi-detached cottage set in picturesque open countryside. Stunning views. One and a half miles out of the village of Bellingham. It is furnished to a very high standard. Centrally heated, with coal for an open fire. The garden is private with furniture and a gas BBQ. Towels and linen are provided. A welcome pack awaits in the fridge. Children most welcome. Regret no pets. Beautiful indoor heated swimming pool available for guests.

Low season per week: £170.00–£250.00
High season per week: £280.00–£350.00

1 cottage: sleeping 5 people + cot

109 Tottergill Farm ★ ★ ★ ★ – ★ ★ ★ ★ ★

Castle Carrock, Brampton, Cumbria **Web:** www.tottergill.demon.co.uk
Contact: Tottergill Farm, Castle Carrock, Brampton, Cumbria CA8 9DP
Tel: (01228) 670615 or (07785) 996950 **Fax:** (01228) 670727 **E-mail:** alison@tottergill.demon.co.uk

Five beautiful self-catering holiday cottages in an idyllic setting, with fantastic panoramic views over the Solway Plain. Walking from your doorstep. Excellent location for visiting the Lake District, the Roman Wall, Southern Scotland, Northumberland and North Yorkshire. The cottages are of the highest standard, very well equipped, fully centrally heated, log-burning stoves with free logs. All linen and towels included in price. Pets welcome. Cottages sleep three, four or eight. Groups of up to 23 catered for.

Low season per week: from £216.00
High season per week: max £703.00
Short breaks: from £144.00–£468.00

5 cottages: sleeping 3–8 people

110 Monkhouse Hill

★ ★ ★ ★ – ★ ★ ★ ★ ★

Sebergham, Nr Caldbeck, Cumbria **Web:** www.monkhousehill.co.uk
Contact: Mrs J Collard, Monkhouse Hill, Sebergham, Nr Caldbeck, Cumbria CA5 7HW
Tel: (016974) 76254 **Fax:** (016974) 76254 **E-mail:** cottages@monkhousehill.co.uk

Award-winning cottage holidays at an imaginatively converted Cumbrian hill farm, nestling in the unspoilt splendour of North Lakeland. Spacious family cottages, oozing character, with oak beams, exposed stonework and impressive first floor living areas. Romantic cottages for couples, with four-posters, log fires and complimentary champagne. Free membership of the exclusive North Lakes Hotel Leisure Club with swimming pool, fitness suite etc. Home-cooked and vegetarian meals delivered. Please see owners' website for more information. ⟨ **Category 2**

Low season per week: £235.00–£680.00
High season per week: £335.00–£1560.00
Short breaks: from £165.00–£1036.00

9 cottages: sleeping 2–14 people
Cards accepted: Mastercard, Visa, Switch/Delta

111 Manor Cottage

★ ★ ★ ★

Fellside, Caldbeck, Wigton, Cumbria
Contact: Mrs A Wade, Manor Cottage, Caldbeck, Wigton, Cumbria CA7 8HA
Tel: (016974) 78214 **E-mail:** walterwade@tiscali.co.uk

The converted barn nestles in the Caldbeck Fells, an unspoilt corner of the Lake District National Park. Retaining its original pine beams and old hay loft (now the upper lounge), it has magnificent views to the distant Pennines. The picturesque village of Caldbeck is only two miles away and there are good places to eat locally. The accommodation provides a spacious lounge, double bedroom, well equipped oak fitted kitchen and shower room with toilet.

Low season per week: £120.00–£180.00
High season per week: £220.00–£300.00
Short breaks: from £90.00–£120.00 (low season only)

1 cottage: sleeping 2/3 people
Open: all year except Christmas and New Year

112 Castle Hill Cottage

★ ★ ★ ★

Bassenthwaite, Keswick, Cumbria **Web:** www.cumbrian-cottages.co.uk
Contact: Cumbrian Cottages, 7 The Crescent, Carlisle CA1 1QW
Tel: (01228) 599960 **Fax:** (01228) 599970 **E-mail:** enquiries@cumbrian-cottages.co.uk

A newly refurbished, traditional Lakeland cottage providing comfortable accommmodation in a peaceful location. Castle Hill is centrally heated, with an open log fire, colour television and video in the living room. The kitchen/diner is equipped with an electric oven/hob, fridge and microwave. The utility room has a washing machine, dishwasher and tumble dryer. Three bedrooms, sleeping six guests, comprise one double, one twin and one bunk bedroom. Rear lawned garden with small patio. All heating, electricity and linen are included. Parking for three cars. Cot and payphone available. Castle Inn and Armathwaite Hall Hotel, with leisure club facilities, are within a short stroll.

Low season per week: £310.00–£420.00
High season per week: £470.00–£890.00
Short breaks: from £190.00

1 cottage: sleeping 6 people
Cards accepted: Mastercard, Visa, Switch/Delta

113 Swallow Barn Cottage ★ ★ ★ ★

Greysouthen, Cockermouth, Cumbria **Web:** www.swallowbarn.co.uk
Contact: Mr & Mrs R G James, 6 Evening Hill View, Brigham Road, Cockermouth, Cumbria CA13 0BB
Tel: (01900) 823016 **Fax:** (01900) 821446 **E-Mail:** swallowbarn@millenium-uk.net

Luxury converted barn built in 1827, tucked away at the end of the village of Greysouthen overlooking open fields. It has a private garden and parking for three cars. Warm and cosy, fully equipped to a very high standard and enhanced by the wood-burning stove, exposed beams and stone walls throughout. The ideal base to explore the beautiful lakes, fells and coast of unspoilt north west Cumbria with an abundance of birds and wildlife.

Low season per week: £295.00–£395.00
High season per week: £395.00–£495.00
Short breaks: from £170.00–£212.00

1 cottage: sleeping 4 people

114 Swallows Return and Owls Retreat ★ ★ ★ ★

Moresby, Whitehaven, Cumbria **Web:** www.cottageguide.co.uk/moresby
Contact: Mr and Mrs J W Moore, Moresby Hall Cottage, Moresby, Whitehaven, Cumbria CA28 6PJ
Tel: (01946) 64078

Converted 19th-century farm buildings – now beautifully appointed character cottages entirely managed by friendly Cumbrian owners living in same hamlet. Ten minutes' walk to quiet beach/coastal path. Close to all western lakes, St Bees, miniature railway, Muncaster Castle. Two miles to Georgian Whitehaven with its 250 listed buildings, Rum Story and Beacon attraction and interesting harbour/marina. Half mile to Rosehill Theatre, within two miles of golf course, swimming pool, sports centre. Easily accesible via rail/bus for people without vehicles. Free collection service. Good transport and cycle network.

Low season per week: from £180.00
High season per week: max £320.00

2 cottages: sleeping 4 + 1 people + cot

115 Brewery House ★ ★ ★ ★ ★

High Lorton, Cockermouth, Cumbria **Web:** www.cumbrian-cottages.co.uk
Contact: Cumbrian Cottages, 7 The Crescent, Carlisle CA1 1QW
Tel: (01228) 599960 **Fax:** (01228) 599970 **E-mail:** enquiries@cumbrian-cottages.co.uk

Built in the 1830s on the banks of Boonbeck, this unusual property has been converted to the highest standard, whilst retaining beautiful exposed timbers, stone and slate. Fully fitted kitchen with dishwasher, washer/dryer, microwave, electric cooker and fridge/freezer. The spacious lounge, with exposed beams, multi-fuel stove, colour television, video and hi-fi, leads to a patio with seating for six. Separate dining room. Four bedrooms, sleeping up to seven (master twin bedroom with en-suite, one twin, one single and one double bedroom). Luxury bathroom. All linen, towels, electric and fuel included. Parking for two cars. Unsuitable for toddlers.

Low season per week: £400.00–£550.00
High season per week: £590.00–£1350.00
Short breaks: from £375.00

1 cottage: sleeping 7 people
Cards accepted: Mastercard, Visa, Switch/Delta

Entries are cross referenced by number to the maps on pages 60–61

116 Coledale House ★ ★ ★ ★

Braithwaite, Keswick, Cumbria **Web:** www.cumbrian-cottages.co.uk
Contact: Cumbrian Cottages, 7 The Crescent, Carlisle CA1 1QW
Tel: (01228) 599960 **Fax:** (01228) 599970 **E-mail:** enquiries@cumbrian-cottages.co.uk

Coledale House enjoys an elevated position with superb views to Grisedale Pike and is located in the popular village of Braithwaite. Two pubs, a restaurant and store are all within five minutes' walk and the house is only two miles from Keswick with its many attractions. Two double bedrooms – one with en-suite shower room, and one bunk bedroom – sleep six guests. The remainder of the property comprises of bathroom, store room with washer/dryer, lounge/diner with colour television, video and coal-effect fire, kitchen with electric oven, fridge/freezer, microwave and dishwasher. Two car parking spaces. All electric and linen included.

Low season per week: £250.00–£350.00
High season per week: £390.00–£610.00
Short breaks: from £140.00

1 cottage: sleeping 6 people
Cards accepted: Mastercard, Visa, Switch/Delta

117 Apartment 1, Oakfield House ★ ★ ★ ★

Underskiddaw, Keswick, Cumbria **Web:** www.cumbrian-cottages.co.uk
Contact: Cumbrian Cottages Limited, 7 The Crescent, Carlisle CA1 1QW
Tel: (01228) 599960 **Fax:** (01228) 599970 **E-mail:** enquiries@cumbrian-cottages.co.uk

Oakfield House, which was built in 1850, has an idyllic situation which commands majestic and panoramic views towards the Helvellyn Range, Borrowdale and Derwentwater. Having recently undergone extensive modernisation, the interior has been separated into four spacious apartments. Apartment 1 is on the ground floor and has large picture windows, an open marble fireplace, a sofabed, television and video and a fully-fitted, luxury kitchen/dining room/conservatory with glorious views. The two bedrooms (one double, one twin) are both en-suite and on the lower ground floor. Payphone and cot available.

Low season per week: £310.00–£420.00
High season per week: £470.00–£890.00
Short breaks: from £180.00

1 apartment: sleeping 4–6 people
Cards accepted: Mastercard, Visa, Switch/Delta

118 Underscar ★ ★ ★ ★ ★

Keswick, Cumbria **Web:** www.heartofthelakes.co.uk
Contact: Heart of the Lakes, Fisherbeck Hill, Old Lake Road, Ambleside, Cumbria LA22 0DH
Tel: (015394) 32321 **Fax:** (015394) 33251 **E-mail:** contactus@heartofthelakes.co.uk

Underscar offers a small number of exclusive holiday homes that occasionally become available for rental and which will appeal to discerning clients looking for something rather special. Properties sleep 2–4+2, or 6+2 in one, two or three bedrooms. Two bathrooms, one en-suite to the main bedroom. Award-winning designers have introduced a feeling of originality and style. All properties have use of the on-site health spa. No pets. Non-smoking. Nearest shops in Keswick, one mile.

Low season per week: from £550.00
High season per week: max £1590.00

25 mews-style houses: sleeping 2–8 people
Cards accepted: Mastercard, Visa, Switch/Delta

119 Drystones ★★★★

Keswick, Cumbria **Web:** www.cumbrian-cottages.co.uk
Contact: Cumbrian Cottages, 7 The Crescent, Carlisle CA1 1QW
Tel: (01228) 599960 **Fax:** (01228) 599970 **E-mail:** enquiries@cumbrian-cottages.co.uk

Drystones is a newly-built three storey, four bedroomed, two bathroomed townhouse sleeping eight guests. Comfortably furnished and centrally heated, it provides cosy accommodation comprising: lounge with colour television/video and CD hi-fi, with double doors leading to the dining room; fully-fitted kitchen with oven/hob, freezer, microwave, fridge, dishwasher and washer/dryer; on the first floor a double bedroom with television, twin bedroom and bathroom; on the second floor a double bedroom, twin bedroom and shower room. All electric/gas and linen included. Cot, highchair and payphone available. Parking for one car.

Low season per week: £370.00–£490.00
High season per week: £550.00–£1150.00
Short breaks: from £220.00

1 cottage: sleeping 8 people
Cards accepted: Mastercard, Visa, Switch/Delta

120 Lookin How ★★★★★

Dockray, Penrith, Cumbria **Web:** www.cumbrian-cottages.co.uk
Contact: Cumbrian Cottages, 7 The Crescent, Carlisle CA1 1QW
Tel: (01228) 599960 **Fax:** (01228) 599970 **E-mail:** enquiries@cumbrian-cottages.co.uk

A superior, spacious, detached cottage in an idyllic, rural location. Lookin How is centrally heated throughout, with an open log fire and colour television in the lounge. A beamed dining room with seating for ten leads to a conservatory overlooking the garden with views to Aira Beck. Well equipped kitchen with dishwasher, washing machine, gas cooker, microwave, fridge/freezer. Four bedrooms comprising one double on first floor, two twin bedrooms (one of which is on first floor) and a single bedroom with Z-bed. Also shower room, bathroom and drying room with tumble dryer. Parking for four cars. Landscaped lawned garden leading to Aira Beck.

Low season per week: £370.00–£490.00
High season per week: £550.00–£1150.00
Short breaks: from £240.00

1 cottage: sleeping 7/8 people
Cards accepted: Mastercard, Visa, Switch/Delta

121 Lakefield ★★★★

Watermillock, Ullswater, Penrith, Cumbria **Web:** www.heartofthelakes.co.uk
Contact: Heart of the Lakes, Fisherbeck Mill, Old Lake Road, Ambleside, Cumbria LA22 0DH
Tel: (015394) 32321 **Fax:** (015394) 33251 **E-mail:** contactus@heartofthelakes.co.uk

A large, detached bungalow set on the shores of Ullswater with 500 yards of private lake frontage and with stunning lake and mountain views. Four bedrooms (two doubles, one twin, one child's twin) and two bathrooms. This property offers substanital accommodation and even has its own sundeck verandah which is built over the water. Most main windows have lake views. Plenty of private parking. Nearest shops are in Glenridding which is about four miles away. No pets. Leisure membership included.

Low season per week: from £583.00
High season per week: max £1688.00

1 bungalow: sleeping 8 people
Cards accepted: Mastercard, Visa, Switch/Delta

Entries are cross referenced by number to the maps on pages 60–61

122 Tirril Farm Cottages ★ ★ ★ ★

Tirril, Penrith, Cumbria
Contact: Mr D Owens, Tirril View, Tirril, Penrith, Cumbria CA10 2JE
Tel: (01768) 864767 **Fax:** (01768) 864767 **E-mail:** tirril.farmcottages@btopenworld.com

Opened in 2001, these attractive barn conversions are well positioned in a quiet courtyard offering 4 Star accommodation. Ranging in size from bedsit to four bedroomed, some enjoying outstanding views of the Fells, this is an ideal location for visiting the Lakes and Eden Valley. The village of Tirril offers a pub/restaurant and is located three miles from junction 40 of the M6 and two miles from Ullswater.

Low season per week: £100.00–£400.00
High season per week: £190.00–£800.00
Short breaks: from £100.00–£400.00

5 cottages: sleeping 2–10 people

123 Bridge End Farm Cottages ★ ★ ★ ★ – ★ ★ ★ ★ ★

Boot, Eskdale, Cumbria **Web:** www.selectcottages.com
Contact: Select Cottages, Office No 1, Unit 11, Lansdown Industrial Estate, Gloucester Road, Cheltenham, Gloucestershire GL51 8PL
Tel: 08700 735328 or 08700 SELECT **Fax:** 08700 735328 **E-mail:** greg@selectcottages.com

Winner of the 2000 'Cumbria for Excellence' and 'Self Catering Holiday of the Year' Award. Twice 'England for Excellence' Silver Award winners. Gorgeous, romatic Grade II listed cottages full of charm and character in a glorious setting in the beautiful Eskdale Valley, nestling beneath mighty Scafell and beside the tumbling William Beck in the picturesque hamlet of Boot with its traditional cosy inns and superb walks from the doorstep. Open all year. Cottages sleep two to nine guests.

Low season per week: £250.00–£500.00
High season per week: £475.00–£1180.00
Short breaks: from £155.00–£385.00 (winter low season only)

7 cottages: sleeping 2–9 people
Cards accepted: Mastercard, Visa, Switch/Delta

124 2 Michael's Fold ★ ★ ★ ★

Grasmere, Ambleside, Cumbria **Web:** www.grasmerevillage.demon.co.uk
Contact: Mr P Nelson, Undercrag, Easedale Road, Grasmere, Ambleside, Cumbria LA22 9QD
Tel: (01539) 435301 (daytime) or (01539) 435349 (evenings) **E-mail:** paul@grasmerevillage.demon.co.uk

A gracious country home on the settlement of the Shepherd Michael (as immortalised by William Wordsworth). Set in two acres of mature gardens, the house enjoys an elevated position, ten minutes' walk from the village. Fully-equipped kitchen, spacious lounge with open fire, colour television, VCR and CD player. Original pieces abound, complemented by quality soft furnishings. A terrace with barbecue for al fresco dining, table tennis room and badminton provide a house for all seasons.

Low season per week: £345.00–£430.00
High season per week: £455.00–£620.00
Short breaks: from £250.00–£295.00 (low season only)

1 house: sleeping 2–6 people

125 Coachmans Cottage   ★ ★ ★ ★

Ryelands, Grasmere, Ambleside, Cumbria **Web:** www.heartofthelakes.co.uk
Contact: Heart of the Lakes, Fisherbeck Hill, Old Lake Road, Ambleside, Cumbria LA22 0DH
Tel: (015394) 32321 **Fax:** (015394) 33251 **E-mail:** contactus@heartofthelakes.co.uk

Converted from an old coach house, this delightful cottage is situated in peaceful surroundings with views over nearby fields and hills. Built of Lakeland stone and with its own enclosed garden, the accommodation is all at first floor level. Light and sunny L-shaped sitting/dining room. Two en-suite bedrooms, one double and one twin. Well-equipped kitchen. Private parking. No pets. Non smoking. Village shops in Grasmere are within a few hundred yards. Leisure club membership included.

Low season per week: from £265.00
High season per week: max £673.00
Short breaks: from £175.00–£565.00

1 cottage: sleeping 4 people
Cards accepted: Mastercard, Visa, Switch/Delta

126 Dove Holme   ★ ★ ★ ★

Town End, Grasmere, Ambleside, Cumbria **Web:** www.cumbrian-cottages.co.uk
Contact: Cumbrian Cottages, 7 The Crescent, Carlisle CA1 1QW
Tel: (01228) 599960 **Fax:** (01228) 599970 **E-mail:** enquiries@cumbrian-cottages.co.uk

A 'story book' Lakeland cottage with modern comforts. Situated on the fringe of this popular Lakeland village, with an abundance of delightful walks straight from your doorstep. The centrally heated accommodation comprises a lounge with wood burner, television/video and CD player. Kitchen/dining with oven/hob, fridge, washer/dryer, microwave and seating for four. Upstairs are two pretty bedrooms – a double and bunk bedroom, both furnished to a high standard. Bathroom with overbath shower. All heating and linen provided. Parking in nearby car park with permit provided. Cot available.

Low season per week: £240.00–£330.00
High season per week: £370.00–£530.00
Short breaks: from £150.00

1 cottage: sleeping 4 people
Cards accepted: Mastercard, Visa, Switch/Delta

127 The Grove Cottages   ★ ★ ★ ★ – ★ ★ ★ ★ ★

Stockghyll Lane, Ambleside, Cumbria
Contact: Mrs Z Thompson, The Grove Farm, Stockghyll Lane, Ambleside, Cumbria LA22 9LG
Tel: (015394) 33074 **Fax:** (015394) 31881

Three beautiful, traditional cottages set in over 200 acres of Stockghyll Valley with views to the Langdale Pikes and Old Man of Coniston. Just over one mile from Ambleside shops and restaurants. Wonderful walks from your doorstep. A warm welcome.

Low season per week: £215.00–£350.00
High season per week: £250.00–£495.00
Short breaks: from £120.00–£240.00

3 cottages: sleeping 2–6 people

128 Loughrigg Suite

★ ★ ★ ★ ★

Ambleside, Cumbria **Web:** www.heartofthelakes.co.uk
Contact: Heart of the Lakes, Fisherbeck Hill, Old Lake Road, Ambleside, Cumbria LA22 0DH
Tel: (015394) 32321 **Fax:** (015394) 33251 **E-mail:** contactus@heartofthelakes.co.uk

This newly-prepared, luxury apartment is situated within a magnificent Victorian mansion, formerly the Ambleside Vicarage. Reached via either stairs or lift, this property has panoramic views over the countryside. Most attractive sitting/dining room, modern well-equipped kitchen, two bedrooms – one en-suite double room and one single room. Separate shower room. No pets. Non smokers. Shops and village amenities half a mile away. Shared use of tennis court and grounds. Leisure club membership included.

Low season per week: from £305.00
High season per week: max £490.00
Short breaks: from £208.00–£411.00

1 apartment: sleeping 2/3 people
Cards accepted: Mastercard, Visa, Switch/Delta

129 Hodge Howe

★ ★ ★ ★ ★

Windermere, Cumbria **Web:** www.heartofthelakes.co.uk
Contact: Heart of the Lakes, Fisherbeck Mill, Old Lake Road, Ambleside, Cumbria LA22 0DH
Tel: (015394) 32321 **Fax:** (015394) 33251 **E-mail:** contactus@heartofthelakes.co.uk

Delightfully renovated cottage only 300 yards from Lake Windermere in a lovely, peaceful, woodland setting. Cosy sitting room with log-burning stove. Newly fitted, gallery-style kitchen leads to dining room with its floor-to-ceiling windows and access to the courtyard garden. Three bedrooms – double room with en-suite, a further double and a twin. Separate bathroom. Courtyard garden has table and chairs. Ample parking. Non-smoking. Local shops and pub, 2–3 miles. Leisure club membership included.

Low season per week: from £303.00
High season per week: max £716.00
Short breaks: from £208.00–£601.00

1 cottage: sleeping 6 people
Cards accepted: Mastercard, Visa, Switch/Delta

130 Glebe Holme

★ ★ ★ ★

Glebe Road, Bowness-on-Windermere, Cumbria **Web:** www.cumbrian-cottages.co.uk
Contact: Cumbrian Cottages, 7 The Crescent, Carlisle CA1 1QW
Tel: (01228) 599960 **Fax:** (01228) 599970 **E-mail:** enquiries@cumbrian-cottages.co.uk

Close to Lake Windermere, this beautifully restored property is perfectly located in a central position. This ideal family holiday home is all on one level and comprises: cosy lounge with real-flame gas fire, television/video and feature window; a kitchen which is equipped with electric oven, gas hob, dishwasher and microwave, and leads to the utility room with fridge/freezer, washer/dryer and garden furniture storage; conservatory; luxury bathroom; three pretty double bedrooms. A separate shower room completes the accommodation. All electric/gas and linen included. Garage and secluded garden.

Low season per week: £310.00–£420.00
High season per week: £470.00–£890.00
Short breaks: from £200.00

1 bungalow: sleeping 6 people
Cards accepted: Mastercard, Visa, Switch/Delta

131 1 Meadowcroft ★ ★ ★ ★

Storrs Park, Bowness-on-Windermere, Cumbria **Web:** www.cumbrian-cottages.co.uk
Contact: Cumbrian Cottages, 7 The Crescent, Carlisle CA1 1QW
Tel: (01228) 599960 **Fax:** (01228) 599970 **E-mail:** enquiries@cumbrian-cottages.co.uk

Formerly a gentleman's residence, these luxurious apartments stand in private grounds surrounded by delightful formal gardens, complete with all-weather tennis court. Apartment number one is centrally heated and includes a magnificent drawing room leading to private patio. The dining area and fully fitted, open-plan kitchen is equipped with an oven, microwave, dishwasher, washer/dryer, fridge and freezer. The three bedrooms, consisting of two doubles and one twin, are all en-suite. The basement area has a fully equipped sauna and gym. Indulge in luxury in one of the most sought-after parts of southern Lakeland.

Low season per week: £400.00–£550.00
High season per week: £590.00–£1350.00
Short breaks: from £180.00

1 apartment: sleeping 6 people
Cards accepted: Mastercard, Visa, Switch/Delta

132 Gavel Cottage ★ ★ ★ ★

Storrs Park, Bowness-on-Windermere, Cumbria **Web:** www.screetons.co.uk
Contact: Screetons, 25 Bridgegate, Howden, Goole, East Yorkshire DN14 7AA
Tel: (01430) 431201 **Fax:** (01430) 432114 **E-mail:** howden@screetons.co.uk

A secluded period cottage situated south of the village, close to the marina. Full of character and tastefully furnished, Gavel Cottage offers a comfortable holiday retreat situated in a quiet location overlooking its own private grounds. The fully equipped accommodation has gas central heating and comprises entrance hall, open plan living area including cosy lounge with open fire, dining area and kitchen, two bedrooms, bathroom, gardens and summer house. Membership of Burnside Leisure Complex is included.

Low season per week: £195.00–£270.00
High season per week: £270.00–£440.00
Short breaks: from £175.00

1 cottage: sleeping 4 people

133 Hylands ★ ★ ★ ★

Brigsteer Road, Kendal, Cumbria **Web:** www.hylands-lakedistrict.co.uk
Contact: Simon Lambeth, 5 Stable Close, Finmere, Buckingham MK18 4AD
Tel: (01280) 848779 **Fax:** (01280) 847519 **E-mail:** simonlambeth@aol.com

On the edge of the Lake District, this classic period property, built in the Arts & Crafts style, is set in two to three acres of mature gardens. The main house – which forms part of the property shown – has many original features including an oak-panelled hall with snooker table and piano. Situated one mile from Kendal town centre, it is convenient for local shops and restaurants and is an ideal base from which to explore the Lakes.

Low season per week: from £450.00
High season per week: max £1250.00

1 house: sleeping 10/11 people

134 Coldbeck Cottage

★ ★ ★ ★

Ravenstonedale, Kirkby Stephen, Cumbria

Contact: Mrs S Cannon, Coldbeck House, Ravenstonedale, Kirkby Stephen, Cumbria CA17 4LW
Tel: (015396) 23230 **Fax:** (015396) 23230 **E-mail:** david.cannon@coldbeck.demon.co.uk

Spacious, comfortable, en-suite accommodation in centrally heated cottage adjacent to owner's home. French windows give level access to two acre garden, for croquet or al fresco meals. A multi-fuel stove cheers cooler days. A nine-hole fun golf course, tennis and good accessible local pubs for your refreshment. Ravenstonedale, an unspoilt village in the Upper Eden Valley, has good road links to Lakes and Dales. Walks from the door to Howgills and Smardale Nature Reserve. Settle/Carlisle railway four miles. ♿ **Category 2**

Low season per week: from £350.00
High season per week: max £400.00
Short breaks: from £70.00–£350.00 (low season only)

1 cottage: sleeping 6 people + cot

🐴 ⛳ ✎ 🖥 🎰 ☉ 📺 ❄ 🖳
DW 🍴 📺 🍳 📻 🍷 📻 ✂
🗒 🚗 ❀ 🐕 ◎

Lady Anne Clifford and Her Monuments

'They that shall be of thee shall build the old waste places' reads the quotation (from Isaiah 58:12) above the door of Outhgill church near Kirkby Stephen. The message, carved at the instigation of Lady Anne Clifford who restored the church in the 17th century, was one which she took to heart. When at the age of 60 she inherited lands in Cumberland, Westmorland and Yorkshire, she embarked upon a frenzy of building, repairs and restoration with a near-religious zeal.

Her enthusiasm was engendered by long years of frustration. She was just 15 in 1605 when her father died and, as his only surviving child, she confidently expected to inherit his extensive northern estates. Instead she found they had been left to his brother and nephew, and she immediately began a long and fruitless campaign to regain her inheritance. In 1643, however, her cousin Henry died without heir, and the estates, at long last, passed to her as his only legitimate successor.

Neglect and the Civil War had taken their toll on her many castles. Those of Appleby, Skipton, Brough, Brougham (shown here), Pendragon and Barden Tower had all fallen into decay, but during the next two decades Lady Anne restored them to their original splendour. She also repaired churches at Skipton, Brough, Brougham and Appleby and built almshouses and monuments, a display of wealth not altogether wise in the puritan atmosphere of Commonwealth England.

To celebrate the restoration of her inheritance Lady Anne commissioned a remarkable painting – depicting herself and all the major characters from her eventful life. Known as the Great Picture, this now hangs in the keep of Appleby Castle (tel: 017683 51402). Also in the town she built the St Anne's almshouses and the white pillars at either end of the main street, while her tomb and that of her beloved mother, Margaret, Countess of Cumberland, lie in St Lawrence's church. On the road to Brougham is the Countess Pillar marking the spot where Lady Anne last saw her mother alive.

Skipton Castle, lovingly restored by Lady Anne, remains one of the most complete and best preserved medieval castles in England (tel: 01756 792442). But, despite all her efforts, Barden Tower and the castles of Pendragon, Brough and Brougham are all ruins once more. (Details from Kirkby Stephen Tourist Information Office, tel: 017683 71199). A 100 mile (160km) walk, Lady Anne's Way, takes in all the buildings and monuments associated with this redoubtable lady.

135 Oakdene Country House ★★★★

Garsdale Road, Sedbergh, Cumbria **Web:** www.meetforworkorleisure.co.uk
Contact: Oakdene Country House, Garsdale Road, Sedbergh, Cumbria LA10 5JN
Tel: (015396) 20280 **Fax:** (015396) 21501 **E-mail:** oakdene@compuserve.com

A Victorian mill owner's house in a tranquil setting in the Yorkshire Dales National Park. Two sitting rooms, both with open fires, large dining room, kitchen and six bedrooms. Half an acre of garden, including a Victorian ornamental pond with ducks and views of fields and fells all round. The perfect place for a party, gathering or reunion. Book for three, four or seven nights. Quality catering available if you choose.

Low season per week: from £1120.00
High season per week: from £1540.00
Short breaks: from £672.00–£924.00
(3–4 nights throughout the year)

1 house: sleeping 14+ people
Cards accepted: Mastercard, Visa, Switch/ Delta, JCB, Solo, Maestro, Visa Electron

136 Turfy Gill Hall ★★★★

Skeugh Head, Angram, Richmond, North Yorkshire **Web:** www.turfygill.com
Contact: Turfy Gill Hall, Skeugh Head, Angram, Richmond, North Yorkshire DL11 6DT
Tel: (01748) 886369 **Fax:** (01748) 886593 **E-mail:** info@turfygill.com

First floor luxury accommodation providing stunning views of upper Swaledale. Everything is provided for your comfort, from warm towels in the bathroom to touch lights by your bedside. A fully equipped kitchen/dining room contains all that two people are likely to require for an extended stay. A laundry service is available if required and full central heating is included in the price. Parking is right by your front door.

Low season per week: £200.00–£250.00
High season per week: £300.00–£355.00
Short breaks: from £40.00–£60.00 daily

1 apartment: sleeping 2 people

137 The Barn ★★★★

Finsthwaite, Cumbria **Web:** www.cumbrian-cottages.co.uk
Contact: Cumbrian Cottages, 7 The Crescent, Carlisle CA1 1QW
Tel: (01228) 599960 **Fax:** (01228) 599970 **E-mail:** enquiries@cumbrian-cottages.co.uk

This beautifully converted 17th-century barn enjoys forest and meadow views. A footpath provides a five minute walk to Lake Windermere. A wealth of character, with many original features, and delightful, individually furnished rooms comprising: large fitted kitchen/diner with oven/hob, fridge and diswasher, leading to utility room for washer/dryer and freezer. An elegant, beamed lounge has television/video, CD player, wood-burning stove and patio doors. Upstairs, the galleried landing leads to four bedrooms: master double with en-suite, further double and two twin bedrooms. A separate shower room completes the accommodation. All electric/oil, towels and linen provided. Parking for two cars.

Low season per week: £470.00–£650.00
High season per week: £670.00–£1550.00
Short breaks: from £350.00

1 cottage: sleeping 8 people
Cards accepted: Mastercard, Visa, Switch/Delta

138 Swimmers Farm ★ ★ ★ ★ ★

Witherslack, Cumbria **Web:** www.cumbrian-cottages.co.uk
Contact: Cumbrian Cottages, 7 The Crescent, Carlisle CA1 1QW
Tel: (01228) 599960 **Fax:** (01228) 599970 **E-mail:** enquiries@cumbrian-cottages.co.uk

A welcoming atmosphere surrounds this attractive 17th-century building, with its flagged floors, ancient beams, Aga and four-poster bed. Centrally heated, the accommodation offers a magnificent kitchen/diner, fridge, microwave, television and dishwasher. The utility room houses a washer/dryer and separate fridge/freezer. The beamed lounge has a CD player, open fire and patio doors, while the snug/second sitting room has a further television and video. Five bedrooms comprise one twin, one single, one gothic-style double, one double and one master double with en-suite and four-poster. Primary bathroom with shower cubicle and a separate shower room. All oil, electric and linen included.

Low season per week: £510.00–£720.00
High season per week: £740.00–£1690.00
Short breaks: from £380.00

1 cottage: sleeping 9 people
Cards accepted: Mastercard, Visa, Switch/Delta

139 Grange End Cottage ★ ★ ★ ★

Cark in Cartmel, near Cartmel, Cumbria **Web:** www.holidaycottagescumbria.com
Contact: Mr B T Colling, 7 Rushside Road, Cheadle Hulme, Stockport, Cheshire SK8 6NW
Tel: (0161) 485 7015 **Fax:** (0161) 355 6346 **E-mail:** ibex32@aol.com

The 'cosiest' cottage. Grange End, originally a Georgian barn, is now a holiday home just oozing character and charm. Step back in time, yet luxuriate in all the comforts and conveniences of a modern well-equipped home. Situated in a secluded position in the heart of the rural village of Cark in Cartmel, two minutes' walk from the local pub, four minutes from a coastal route railway station and just ten minutes' drive from Lake Windermere.

Low season per week: £220.00–£390.00
High season per week: £390.00–£495.00
Short breaks: from £100.00–£180.00

1 cottage: sleeping 6 people

140 Riverside Cottage ★ ★ ★ ★ ★

Burton-in-Lonsdale, North Yorkshire
Contact: Ms P Leverton
Tel: (01274) 560542

A delightful cottage nestling on the banks of the river Greta. Approched along a private lane, the cottage enjoys a peaceful, tranquil position. Magnificent views of Ingleborough mountain and with the benefit of fishing from the pleasant rear garden. Furnished, equipped and maintained to high standards, tastefully decorated with co-ordinated furnishings. Ideal for touring the Yorkshire Dales, Lake District, Trough of Bowland and coast. Close to the Three Peaks and Ingleton Waterfall walks. Excellent pubs and restaurants in the area.

Low season per week: £195.00–£235.00
High season per week: £240.00–£350.00
Short breaks: subject to availability upon request

1 cottage: sleeping 2 people

141 Higher Lee ★ ★ ★ ★

Abbeystead, Lancaster, Lancashire
Contact: Mrs S T Entwistle, Lentworth Farm, Abbeystead, Lancaster, Lancashire LA2 9BE
Tel: (01524) 791287

A perfect English country house set in two acres of delightful walled gardens, providing privacy amd peaceful seclusion. This beautiful house, dating from 16/1, has open fireplaces and wooden floors. Complemented by traditional-style furniture and fabrics. Sleeps ten. Booking through Hoseasons (01502) 501515, Ref E1977.

Low season per week: £601.00–£601.00
High season per week: £727.00–£1227.00
Short breaks: from £339.00–£810.00

1 house: sleeping 8 adults + 2 children

142 Boathouse Cottage ★ ★ ★ ★

Norham, Berwick-upon-Tweed **Web:** www.boathouse.ntb.org.uk
Contact: Mrs S Dalgety, The Columns, Norham, Berwick-upon-Tweed TD15 2JZ
Tel: (01289) 382300 **Fax:** (01289) 382334 **E-mail:** alexdalgety@compuserve.com

This riverside cottage, overlooking Tweed and beyond, was thoughtfully modernised with comfort in mind. Visitors will appreciate the spacious open-plan kitchen and other features designed for their enjoyment. At the end of a quiet lane and barely half a mile from Norham village, with its castle, pubs and shops. From the private garden, walk straight onto riverbank or countryside footpaths, or take the easy road or train access to Edinburgh, Durham and many Borders attractions.

Low season per week: £250.00–£340.00
High season per week: £340.00–£450.00
Short breaks: from £150.00

1 cottage: sleeping 6 people

143 The Stables ★ ★ ★ ★

Cornhill-on-Tweed, Northumberland **Web:** www.thestables.cornhill.btinternet.co.uk
Contact: Mrs M Buckle, Tor Cottage, Cornhill-on-Tweed, Northumberland TD12 4QA
Tel: (01890) 882390 **Fax:** (01890) 883778 **E-mail:** david.buckle@btinternet.com

Peaceful, single storey cottage adjacent to owner's 1840s house, three acre garden, mill pond, views across neighbouring fields. Accommodation: large lounge/dining room with patio doors, kitchen with microwave, fridge, washer/dryer, bathroom with shower. One double bedroom, one twin bedroom. Electricity, heating, linen inclusive. Two car parking. Village with pub/hotel, shop and post office – five minute walk. Good walking, golf, horse riding and bird watching. Coldstream one mile. Berwick-upon-Tweed 12 miles.

Low season per week: £205.00–£235.00
High season per week: £290.00–£375.00
Short breaks: details upon request

1 cottage: sleeping 4 people
Open: March–December

144 Brockburn ★ ★ ★ ★

Monkshouses, Seahouses, Northumberland
Contact: Mrs P Thompson, Highfield House, Woodhill Farm, Ponteland, Newcastle upon Tyne NE20 0JA
Tel: (01661) 860165

With over 700 years of history, this house is full of character. Although thoroughly refurbished, it still retains much of its original charm and cosy features, including a log fire. Brockburn's intimate yet spacious feel offers accommodation suitable for couples or families. With direct access to miles of beautiful sandy beaches, a games room for indoor days and sit-down kitchen table, it is the perfect retreat for year-round getting away from it all!

Low season per week: £350.00–£600.00
High season per week: £600.00–£850.00
Short breaks: from £300.00 (low season only)

1 house: sleeping 2–9 people

145 Springhill Farm Cottages ★ ★ ★ ★

Bamburgh, Northumberland **Web:** www.springhill-farm.co.uk
Contact: Mrs J Gregory, Springhill Farmhouse, Seahouses, Northumberland NE68 7UR
Tel: (01665) 720351 **Fax:** (01665) 721820 **E-mail:** jygregory@aol.com

A tranquil setting, glorious coastline with miles of golden beaches and superb country views are just three reasons to come to Springhill and Copywell Cottages. For those exploring beautiful Northumberland and the Scottish Borders, or those who just want to relax, our cottages offer you value for money, quality and comfort. Within a 50 mile radius you will find countless castles, historic houses, gardens, market towns and much more.

Low season per week: £180.00–£190.00
High season per week: £210.00–£430.00
Short breaks: from £80.00–£145.00 (low season only)

2 cottages: sleeping 4/5 people

146 Link House Farm ★ ★ ★ ★

Newton-by-the-Sea, Alnwick, Northumberland
Contact: Mrs J Hellmann, The Granary, Link House Farm, Newton-by-the-Sea, Alnwick, Northumberland NE66 3DF
Tel: (01665) 576820 **Fax:** (01665) 576820 **E-mail:** jayne.hellman@talk21.com

A group of five individual holiday cottages, skillfully created from the quality conversion of old stone-built farm buildings. Situated on a farm in the village of Newton-by-the-Sea, only yards from National Trust sand dunes and sandy beaches at Beadnell Bay. Each cottage completely self-contained with own garden/sitting area. All furnished, decorated and equipped to high standard. Excellent for bird watching. Also children's payground and grass area. Local pubs half a mile. Shops in the next village which is just two miles away.

Low season per week: £220.00–£600.00
High season per week: £300.00–£910.00
Short breaks: from £110.00–£330.00 (low season only)

5 houses and cottages: sleeping 2–10 people

147 Dairy Cottage   ★ ★ ★ ★

Dunstan Steads, Embleton, Alnwick, Northumberland **Web:** www.ntb.org.uk
Contact: Mrs Tiernan, St Andrew's House, College Place, Berwick-upon-Tweed TD15 1DA
Tel: (01289) 309826 **E-mail:** ktiernan@waitrose.com

Converted from an old dairy, this charming stone cottage is superbly located on the Northumbrian Heritage Coast. It takes just five minutes to walk from the cottage to Embleton Bay – a spectacular sandy beach overlooked by the dramatic ruins of Dunstanburgh Castle. The accommodation is spacious, cosy and comfortable for year-round holidays, with all modern facilities and central heating. Local attractions include: local links golf course, coast and country walking, birdwatching, sailboarding, castles and country houses.

Low season per week: £200.00–£300.00
High season per week: £360.00–£450.00
Short breaks: max £160.00 (November–March only)

1 cottage: sleeping 4 people

148 The Pele Tower   ★ ★ ★ ★ ★

Whitton, Rothbury, Northumberland **Web:** www.thepeletower.com
Contact: Mr & Mrs J D Malia, The Pele Tower, Whitton, Rothbury, Northumberland NE65 7RL
Tel: (01669) 620410 **Fax:** (01669) 621006 **E-mail:** davidmalia@aol.com

A luxurious 19th-century wing of a Northumbrian pele tower (with 14th-century origins). Sleeps four. Bathroom with whirlpool bath and shower, separate WC. Superb large kitchen with facilities too numerous to mention! Great thought has been given to the lounge/dining room to provide a most relaxing ambience. Facilities include a wood-burning stove, digital satellite television, music centre, telephone, playstation 2, mountain bikes and much more! Secluded, yet only half a mile from Rothbury. Regret no pets or smoking.

Low season per week: from £220.00
High season per week: max £575.00
Short breaks: from £120.00–£160.00 (low season only)

1 apartment: sleeping 4 people
Cards accepted: Mastercard, Visa

149 The Loft   ★ ★ ★ ★

Morwick Road, Warkworth, Morpeth, Northumberland
Contact: Mrs M Wraith, Albion House, 21 Morwick Road, Warkworth, Morpeth, Northumberland NE65 0TG
Tel: (01665) 711389 **E-mail:** mariewraith@hotmail.com

The Loft is a 700 sq ft Scandinavian-style open plan living space, beautifully converted from a detached stone-built hayloft, with views over open fields in an Area of Outstanding Natural Beauty. Located on the edge of historic Warkworth village, it offers a relaxing, superbly equipped base for country and coastal walks, with Northumberland's castles, great houses, National Park, Hadrian's Wall and offshore islands in easy distance. A free 24 hour laundry service is available for guests. No pets, no smoking. Unsuitable for children.

Low season per week: max £275.00
High season per week: max £350.00

1 studio flat: sleeping 2 people
Open: end-May–October

150 Marina Cottage ★ ★ ★ ★

The Wynd, Amble-by-the-Sea, Morpeth, Northumberland
Contact: Mr D Black, Marina Cottage, The Wynd, Amble-by-the-Sea, Morpeth, Northumberland NE65 0HH
Tel: (01665) 711019 **E-mail:** mangotree@supanet.com

Luxury accommodation on one level, with patio doors leading to garden. Kitchen equipped with microwave, washing machine etc. Amble centre shops easily accessible. Large bedroom with double bed and further bedroom with twin beds. Colour television/video and music centre. Alnwick eight miles. Fine attractions, including gardens, castles, golf, farms and islands. The National Park is a half hour's drive away, with some of the finest scenery in England complementing our unspoilt beaches. A well-behaved pet is welcome.

Low season per week: £210.00–£230.00	**1 bungalow:** sleeping 4 people	
High season per week: £298.00–£330.00	**Open:** April–October	
Short breaks: from £95.00–£120.00		

151 Sammy's Place ★ ★ ★ ★ ★

St Wilfred's Road, Hexham, Northumberland **Web:** www.sammyshideaways.com
Contact: Mr R McKechnie, Dilston House, Corbridge, Northumberland NE45 5RH
Tel: (01434) 633653 **Fax:** (01434) 634640 **E-mail:** roger@dilstonhouse.freeserve.co.uk

Self-catering in the heart of Hexham – Hadrian's Wall country. Beautifully appointed, two bedroom en-suite ground floor apartment. Within two minutes' walk of the Abbey, theatre, market, shops, pubs, restaurants and bus station, with the railway station three quarters of a mile away. Perfect base from which to visit Hadrian's Wall, rural Northumberland, North Pennines and the Newcastle night life, which is only 30 minutes by train. Car not essential, public transport excellent.

Low season per week: from £250.00	**1 apartment:** sleeping 4 people	
High season per week: max £450.00		

152 Five Gables Cottage ★ ★ ★ ★

Binchester, Bishop Auckland, County Durham **Web:** www.fivegables.co.uk
Contact: Mr & Mrs P&J Weston, Five Gables, Binchester, Bishop Auckland, County Durham DL14 8AT
Tel: (01388) 608204 **Fax:** (01388) 663092 **E-mail:** cottage@fivegables.co.uk

Quiet, comfortable, Victorian miner's cottage (circa 1860) with country views, opposite owners' guest house at edge of village. Completely refurbished for five guests to sleep in two bedrooms. Modern fully equipped kitchen, central heating etc. Lawn, gardens and parking to the front and side. Small shops and Post Office one mile. Ideal centre for Durham World Heritage Site, Beamish and all tourist attractions in North Yorkshire and Northumbria. One and a half hours from York and the Lake District.

Low season per week: £200.00–£250.00	**1 cottage:** sleeping 5 people	
High season per week: £250.00–£300.00	**Cards accepted:** Mastercard, Visa,	
Short breaks: from £130.00–£150.00 (low season only)	Switch/Delta	

153 Boot and Shoe Cottage ★★★★

Wycliffe, Barnard Castle, County Durham **Web:** www.bootandshoecottage.co.uk
Contact: Mrs R Peat, Waterside Cottage, Wycliffe, Barnard Castle, County Durham DL12 9TR
Tel: (01833) 627200 **Fax:** (01833) 627200 **E-mail:** info@bootandshoecottage.co.uk

This historic cottage, once used by a cobbler and as a pub, is in an idyllic setting on the south bank of the River Tees. Beautifully restored, with an open fire, antique furniture and all 'mod cons', the cottage provides the perfect location for a relaxing holiday in peaceful and scenic surroundings. Ideally situated for exploring Barnard Castle and Teesdale, Yorkshire Dales, North Pennines AONB, Durham and York. Trout fishing is also available.

Low season per week: £275.00–£300.00
High season per week: £320.00–£340.00
Short breaks: from £170.00

1 cottage: sleeping 4 people

154 Dyson House Barn ★★★★

Newsham, Richmond, North Yorkshire **Web:** www.cottageguide.co.uk/dysonhousebarn
Contact: Mr and Mrs R Clarkson, Dyson House, Newsham, Richmond, North Yorkshire DL11 7QP
Tel: (01833) 627365 or (07714)445405

Converted from a stone barn, stable and granary, in open countryside, this large well-appointed cottage retains many original features. Between Richmond and Barnard Castle, it makes an ideal base for touring Swaledale, Teesdale and North Yokshire. Beautifully decorated and furnished throughout, the spacious, well-equipped accommodation includes a twin bedroom and full shower room on the ground floor. Children and small pets welcome. Two public houses/restaurants within short walking distance. Full colour brochure available on request.

Low season per week: £205.00–£420.00
High season per week: £295.00–£420.00
Short breaks: from £120.00 (low season only)

1 cottage: sleeping 6 people

155 Ingleby Manor ★★★★

Ingleby Greenhow, Great Ayton, North Yorkshire **Web:** www.inglebymanor.co.uk
Contact: Mrs C Bianco, Ingleby Manor, Ingleby Greenhow, Great Ayton, North Yorkshire TS9 6RB
Tel: (01642) 722170 **Fax:** (01642) 722170 **E-mail:** christine@inglebymanor.co.uk

Built by a courtier of Henry VIII, listed Grade II* by English Heritage, and set in 50 peaceful acres of formal gardens and woodland with trout stream and wild deer, Ingleby Manor provides a unique base in the National Park for exploring the moors, coast, York and Durham. The fascinating spacious apartments, carefully furnished with antiques and all mod cons, have beautiful views of the 1000ft-high Cleveland Hills. Individual attention, high standards and a warm welcome assured.

Low season per week: £221.00–£342.00
High season per week: £347.00–£617.00
Short breaks: from £111.00–£338.00

4 apartments: sleeping 3–6 people
Cards accepted: Mastercard, Visa, Switch/Delta

156 Fayvan Holiday Apartments   ★ ★ ★ ★

West Cliff, Whitby, North Yorkshire
Contact: Fayvan Holiday Apartments, 43 Crescent Avenue, West Cliff, Whitby, North Yorkshire YO21 3EQ
Tel: (01947) 604813 **Fax:** (01947) 604813

An elegant Victorian residence containing superior apartments on the West Cliff with side-sea views over the Royal Crescent Gardens to the sea. We are a non-smoking establishment with apartments which are beautifully appointed with particular attention given to furniture and fittings and with a wealth of facilities. You will find a welcoming atmosphere and high standards of service for all our guests.

Low season per week: £195.00–£320.00
High season per week: £435.00–£485.00
Short breaks: from £75.00–£235.00 (low season only)

3 apartments: sleeping 5 people
Cards accepted: Mastercard, Visa, Eurocard

Wade's Causeway

Wade, legend has it, was a giant, a Saxon King who lived in Mulgrave Castle, Lythe. Legend also decrees that he lies buried near by, stretched out between two standing stones a mile or so apart, the one near Goldsborough, the other at East Barnby. His giantess wife, Bell, kept cows at Pickering Castle and so had to cross 20 miles (32km) of moorland each day to milk them. To make things easier, Wade built her a footpath. He scooped out earth, creating the Hole of Horcum near Saltersgate, and what was left over he threw across the moors, making Blakey Topping or, some say, Roseberry Topping. Bell helped in the construction work by carrying stones for the surface in her apron, dropping some now and then and leaving great mounds dotted about the moors.

Wade's Causeway is, if the truth be told, Britain's best-preserved stretch of Roman road. Under the governorship of Agricola, the Romans built a network of roads and forts north of York in about 80AD. One of these roads ran 25 miles (40km) north from Malton, entering the North York Moors at Cawthorne, north of Pickering, where four camps were built in about 100AD, and running on across to a signal station and landing point on the coast at Goldsborough. After the Romans left, the road lay uncared for on the bleak and boggy moor, with heather gradually creeping over it, until it was rediscovered in 1914. A section about 1¼ miles (2km) long was cleared.

Like any other Roman road, or stratum (from which our word 'street' derives), Wade's Causeway was constructed with a foundation of large stones that were then covered with pebbles or gravel. About 16ft (4.8m) wide, it is cambered, allowing drainage into gutters at either side. The gravel top-surface is lost, but foundation slabs, some kerb stones and a few drainage culverts at the northern end survive. Only a century ago most of our roads were unsurfaced tracks, so it is nothing but amazing, and a tribute to the engineering skills of the Romans, that a length of road constructed some 2,000 years ago should have survived in such remarkably good condition.

Wade's Causeway is on Wheeldale Moor, south-west of the village of Goathland, parallel to and west of Wheeldale Beck. It is best approached either from Goathland (it is close to Wheeldale Lodge Youth Hostel, 2 miles (3.2km) south of the village) or from the minor road between Stape and Egton Bridge at National Grid ref. SE 805 975.

157 Bennison House Farm ★ ★ ★ ★

Sneaton, Whitby, North Yorkshire
Contact: Mr & Mrs R G Thompson, Bennison House Farm, Sneaton, Whitby, North Yorkshire YO22 5HS
Tel: (01947) 820292

Bennison Farmhouse is on a working dairy farm, standing in an elevated position. This spacious detached farmhouse has been renovated to a high standard. The house has a large secluded garden and is half a mile from the village of Sneaton. It is surrounded by open countryside and is only three miles from Whitby, ideally situated for Moors, Dales and coast. The house sleeps six plus a cot.

Low season per week: £190.00–£225.00 **High season per week:** max £425.00 **Short breaks:** from £45.00–£60.00	**1 house:** sleeping 6 people	

158 Inglenook ★ ★ ★ ★

Fylingthorpe, Whitby, North Yorkshire   **Web:** www.inglenook-cottage.co.uk
Contact: Mrs L Abbott, 7 Goodwood Grove, York YO24 1ER
Tel: (01904) 622059 (daytime) or (01904) 700164 (evenings) **Fax:** (01904) 622059

Delightful Victorian cottage enjoying a private south-facing garden beside open fields. Family friendly. Three bedrooms, king-size with en-suite. Double and two adult single. Family bathroom. Spacious yet cosy lounge with wood-burning stove for chillier winter evenings (logs available). Forget the car – seconds from beautiful countryside and minutes from the beach. Idyllic retreat. Local attractions – horseriding, riding over beaches, old coastguard station, National Trust Visitor Centre. Sorry no pets.

Low season per week: £250.00–£350.00 **High season per week:** £350.00–£480.00 **Short breaks:** from £120.00–£150.00	**1 cottage:** sleeping 6 people	

159 Gales House Farm ★ ★ ★ ★

Kirkby Lane, Gillamoor, York   **Web:** www.gillamoor.com
Contact: Mr D Ward, Gales House Farm, Kirkby Lane, Gillamoor, York YO62 7HT
Tel: (01751) 431258 **Fax:** (01750) 650741 **E-mail:** cottages@gillamoor.com

These excellent cottages have a reputation for one of the most bookable properties in the area. In the 'Yorkshire Cottage of the Year' they were the runner-up in 1998, winners in 1999 and finalists in 2001. The accommodation is first class, attention to detail spot on, and housekeeping at its best. The cottage gardens are a delight and so relaxing. It's a stroll to the village with spectacular views over the moors. Good pub/restaurants for eating out.

Low season per week: £184.00–£295.00 **High season per week:** £198.00–£454.00 **Short breaks:** from £98.00–£158.00 (November–March only)	**3 cottages:** sleeping 2–4 people **Cards accepted:** Mastercard, Visa	

160 Beech Farm Cottages

★ ★ ★ ★ – ★ ★ ★ ★ ★

Wrelton, Pickering, North Yorkshire **Web:** www.beechfarm.com
Contact: Beech Farm Cottages, Wrelton, Pickering, North Yorkshire YO18 8PG
Tel: (01751) 476612 **Fax:** (01751) 475032 **E-mail:** holiday@beechfarm.com

As winners of the 'Holiday Cottage of the Year' awards from both English and Yorkshire Tourist Boards, quality is assured. Set in a tranquil village on the edge of the moors national park, the eight stone cottages surround a pretty courtyard and back onto fields. They are all outstandingly well furnished and equipped. Heated indoor pool, sauna, children's play area. Central heating, double glazing. Central location for exploring moors, coast, York etc. Brochure available. Yorkshire Tourist Board 'White Rose Awards for Tourism' 2001 Winner.

Low season per week: £285.00–£695.00
High season per week: £295.00–£1500.00
Short breaks: from £145.00–£350.00

8 cottages: sleeping 2–10 people
Cards accepted: Mastercard, Visa

161 Rawcliffe House Farm

★ ★ ★ ★

Stape, Pickering, North Yorkshire **Web:** www.yorkshireaccommodation.com
Contact: Mr and Mrs D Allsopp, Rawcliffe House Farm, Stape, Pickering, North Yorkshire YO18 8JA
Tel: (01751) 473292 **Fax:** (01751) 473766 **E-mail:** sheilarh@yahoo.com

Come and stay 'Somewhere Special'. Spacious, comfortable and superbly equipped cottages in a fantastic rural location. Our stone barns have been converted into charming and luxurious cottages with every convenience. Enjoy the idyllic and spectacular North Yorkshire Moors with easy access to the coast and York. Large landscaped area with loads of space. Adventure play area for children. Peace and tranquillity, plus friendly hosts who will always do their best. Highly recommended. Disabled facilities. See also our serviced accommodation on page 48. **Category 2**

Low season per week: from £125.00
High season per week: max £620.00
Short breaks: from £100.00 (low season only)

3 cottages: sleeping 2–7 people + cot

162 East Kingthorpe House

★ ★ ★ ★

Whitby Road, Thornton Dale, Pickering, North Yorkshire **Web:** www.kingthorpe.freeservers.com
Contact: Mr and Mrs G Abbott, Buckthorn, Malton Road, Pickering, North Yorkshire YO18 8EA
Tel: (01751) 473848 **E-mail:** geoffabbott@supanet.com

Luxuriously spacious Victorian farmhouse enjoying private grounds with sweeping views over North Yorkshire Moors National Parkland, the Vale of Pickering and Yorkshire Wolds beyond. A lovely area for scenic walks/drives. Two lounges, fully equipped kitchen, stone-flagged dining room, five bedrooms, four shower/bathrooms. Quality furnishings. Central heating plus open fires in authentic marble period fireplace. Wheelchair accessible. Centrally located for York, Castle Howard, Flamingoland Theme Park, Pickering's Steam Railway, East Coast resorts, "Herriot', 'Heartbeat' and 'Harry Potter' country.

Low season per week: £495.00–£895.00
High season per week: £955.00–£1260.00

1 house: sleeping 10/11 people
Cards accepted: Mastercard, Visa

163 Barmoor Farmhouse Holiday Cottages   ★ ★ ★ ★

Scalby, Scarborough, North Yorkshire
Contact: Mr D A Sharp, 16 Throxenby Lane, Newby, Scarborough, North Yorkshire YO12 5HW
Tel: (01723) 363256

Located in glorious Yorkshire countryside with stunning panoramic views over rolling meadowland, the sea and Scarborough Castle. Stylishly decorated, our cottages have en-suite facilities, beamed ceilings, mahogany floors and full central heating. Jasmine and Rose Cottages each have a four-poster bed in the master bedroom, and Lavendar Cottage is designed to accommodate disabled guests with assistance. An intoxicating mixture of countryside. Moorland and sea beckons, and a warm welcome awaits you.

Low season per week: £180.00–£307.00
High season per week: £396.00–£585.00
Short breaks: from £117.00–£200.00 (low season only, min 3 nights)

5 cottages: sleeping 2–7 people

164 Fold Farm Cottages   ★ ★ ★ ★

Kettlewell, Skipton, North Yorkshire **Web:** www.foldfarm.co.uk
Contact: Mrs B Lambert, Fold Farm, Kettlewell, Skipton, North Yorkshire BD23 5RH
Tel: (01756) 760886 **Fax:** (01756) 760464 **E-mail:** fold.farm@lineone.net

Converted from an 18th-century barn, these four delightful, oak-beamed cottages are situated beside the village stream and are within easy walking distance of all the village amenities – pubs, shops, church etc. The cottages are well equipped and have coal fires, dishwashers, complete well-fitted kitchens, and there is ample parking. Kettlewell nestles in the Upper Wharfedale Valley and is an ideal centre for walking and sightseeing.

Low season per week: from 150.00
High season per week: max £420.00

4 cottages: sleeping 2–5 people
Cards accepted: Mastercard, Visa, Switch/Delta

165 Sawley Arms Cottages   ★ ★ ★ ★

Sawley, Fountains Abbey, Ripon, North Yorkshire
Contact: Mrs J Hawes, Sawley Arms and Holiday Cottages, Sawley, Fountains Abbey, Ripon, North Yorkshire HG4 3EQ
Tel: (01765) 620642

Luxury cottages in the award-winning garden of a country inn and restaurant. In a number of guides for wining and dining. Very comfortable, spacious and tastefully furnished to a high standard, with pleasant views over gardens and surrounding open fields. Close to Fountains Abbey in an Area of Outstanding Natural Beauty. Harrogate is ten miles away and Ripon six miles. Non-smoking accommodation. Sorry, no pets or children. Two cottages, each sleeping two people. Open all year round.

Low season per week: from £230.00
High season per week: from £330.00
Short breaks: from £170.00

2 cottages: sleeping 2 people

166 Mount Pleasant Farm Holiday Cottages ★ ★ ★ ★

Skipton Road, Killinghall, Harrogate North Yorkshire
Contact: Mrs L Prest, Mount Pleasant Farm, Skipton Road, Killinghall, Harrogate, North Yorkshire HG3 2BU
Tel: (01423) 504694

These converted farm buildings, situated just two miles from the spa town of Harrogate, are immaculately maintained and fully equipped and sleep from three to six people. Set in rolling countryside, they are ideal for exploring the Dales and nearby historic points of interest such as Bolton and Fountains Abbey and the ancient cities of York and Ripon. With a family pub/restaurant only 200 yards away, the cottages are suitable for couples and families alike.

Low season per week: £180.00–£230.00
High season per week: £260.00–£365.00

2 cottages and 1 bungalow: sleeping 3–6 people

Salts Mill

A marvel of its age and pre-eminent among Bradford's textile mills until its closure in the 1980s, Salts Mill was built in 1853 by Titus Salt for his worsted manufacturing business. Now the vast Italianate-style mill is a Grade II listed building, still surrounded by the terraced sandstone houses and community buildings of the village that the visionary Salt planned to cater for his workers' every need. In 1987 it was bought by locally-born Jonathan Silver and since then has been undergoing creative but sympathetic restoration. It is now home to several businesses (employing some 1,400 people in fields such as electronics and manufacturing) and a clutch of cultural enterprises. Of the latter, the most notable are the galleries devoted to the work of artist David Hockney, another of Bradford's sons, a schoolmate of Jonathan Silver and a regular visitor to the mill.

The 1853 Gallery, on the ground floor of the main spinning block, was the first of the three Hockney galleries to open. On its walls hang 350 original works, a permanent exhibition of cartoons, prints, paintings and computer-generated images from Hockney's childhood years to recent times. Here, too, a bookshop displays its wares not on conventional shelves but on tables, chairs and other pieces of furniture, between vases of flowers and local pottery. The mood is set for browsing with strains of Hockney's favourite pieces of music, often from opera, playing in the background. A second gallery is to be found in an old wool-sorting room, next to Salts Diner on the second floor. This is an experimental space and exhibitions change regularly: the past few years have, for example, seen pictures of Hockney's dachshunds and his opera sets. The third and newest gallery, above the Diner, is a more intimate space, displaying images that have a particular meaning for David Hockney personally.

Apart from the galleries, Salts Mill has some fairly upmarket shops, whose goods range from contemporary furniture and high-quality household objects to top designer label clothes. The civilised, relaxed atmosphere that pervades the galleries carries through to Salts Diner, where you can pick up a newspaper to read while you enjoy good, reasonably priced food and drink. Salts Mill (tel: 01274 531163, fax 01274 531184) is open daily 10am–6pm, admission free. Frequent trains link Saltaire with Bradford and Leeds.

167 Westwood Lodge, Ilkley Moor ★ ★ ★ ★

Wells Road, Ilkley, West Yorkshire **Web:** www.westwoodlodge.co.uk
Contact: Westwood Lodge, Wells Road, Ilkley, West Yorkshire LS29 9JF
Tel: (01943) 433430 **Fax:** (01943) 433431 **E-mail:** welcome@westwoodlodge.co.uk

Charming, spacious yet cosy, well equipped, historic cottages and apartments in the grounds of Westwood Lodge, on the very edge of the world famous Ilkley Moor. Peaceful, yet close to town. Ideal base for Dales and Brontë Country. Well equipped throughout, including microwave, video, CD etc. Free use of laundry, gym, sauna and spa in main house. Extensive gardens with play area. Welcome basket with crusty bread, jams, cheese, cake – even a bottle of chilled wine!

Low season per week: £295.00–£395.00
High season per week: £345.00–£595.00
Short breaks: from £177.00

6 cottages and apartments: sleeping 2–6 people
Cards accepted: Mastercard, Visa, Switch/Delta, JCB, Maestro, Visa Electron

168 Lilac Cottage ★ ★ ★ ★

Seaside Road, Aldbrough, East Yorkshire **Web:** www.aer96.dial.pipex.com/lilac-cottage
Contact: Mrs H Stubbs, 19 Seaside Road, Aldbrough, East Yorkshire HU11 4RX
Tel: (01964) 527645 **E-mail:** helen@seasideroad.freeserve.co.uk

Combining a good deal of charm and character with a pleasant and peaceful east Yorkshire village location, surrounded by open fields with no shortage of interesting walks. Cosy, comfortable and well equipped, the cottage sleeps up to four adults, plus cot, in two bedrooms. The living room features an open beamed ceiling, open brick fireplace, television and video. There is a private garden with patio and BBQ. The area is ideal for cycling, birdwatching etc, and visitors may, by arrangement, use the facilities of our recording studio.

Low season per week: from £170.00
High season per week: from £315.00
Short breaks: from £100.00

1 cottage: sleeping 4 people + cot

169 Prospect Farm Cottages ★ ★ ★ ★

Waltham Road, Brigsley, Grimsby, South Humberside **Web:** www.prospectfarm.co.uk
Contact: Mrs J Speight, Prospect Farm, Waltham Road, Brigsley, Grimsby, North East Lincolnshire DN37 0RQ
Tel: (01472) 826491 **Fax:** (01472) 826491 **E-mail:** prospectfarm@btclick.com

Prospect Farm is situated down a long leafy lane, which opens up into a large expanse of well-kept private grounds and pasture fields. We have ample, safe, illuminated parking. It is ideally situated for the Lincolnshire Wolds and the coast. We have a private, well-stocked fishing pond for guests. There are four luxury cottages set around a courtyard. Each cottage is fully equipped to cater for your every need. See also our serviced accommodation on page 58.

Low season per week: from £250.00
High season per week: max £360.00

4 cottages: sleeping 3–6 people

England's Heartland

► Kilpeck

At Kilpeck, eight miles (13km) south west of Hereford, is the tiny sandstone church of Sts Mary and David. Its size may be modest, but its stone-carvings are the most glorious example of the exuberant work of the 12th-century Herefordshire School of stonemasons. The south door in particular, long protected by a wooden porch, displays a magnificent array of carvings – of beasts, fishes, foliage, fruit – in an almost pristine state. Similar work may be found in churches at Fownhope and Rowlstone (both in Herefordshire) and at Ruardean in the Forest of Dean, all set in glorious countryside.

► Blue John

Near Castleton in Derbyshire, two cave systems, Treak Cliff Cavern (tel: 01433 620571) and Blue John Cavern (tel: 01433 620638), contain deposits of a rare blue-veined fluorspar found nowhere else. Known as blue john, it was mined extensively in the 18th century, but now only about half a ton is produced annually, mostly carved into small decorative items sold in Castleton's souvenir shops. Tours of the caverns provide an unusual insight into a unique Peak District industry, while the superb stalactites cannot fail to impress.

Away from the throng

From East Anglia's fertile plains to the rugged border country of the Welsh Marches, from the Home Counties' prosperous market towns to the dark, stone-built communities of the Peaks, the great swathe of counties that forms England's Heartland has it all. And for the most part you can have the elegance, the raw beauty, the culture and the history to yourself. Yes, the Peak District National Park is deservedly popular and yes, Stratford-upon-Avon is rightly a stop on most visitors' itineraries, but choose your moment wisely and even these can be enjoyed at a leisurely pace, the madding crowd left far behind.

In the steps of literary giants

Whatever your particular bent, there's ample opportunity to indulge it. Keen to follow in the footsteps of the famous? Try Lichfield, whose sons include three major figures from the 18th-century flowering of the arts: Joseph Addison, David Garrick and Dr Johnson. The last has his own museum, based in the house of his birth in Breadmarket Street. Other places of literary pilgrimage are D H Lawrence's Eastwood and Lord Byron's gothic Newstead Abbey (both Nottinghamshire, though at opposite ends of the social scale), Shaw's comfortable Corner in Ayot St Lawrence (Hertfordshire), A E Housman's much wilder Wenlock Edge (Shropshire) and Samuel Pepys' urbane Brampton (Cambridgeshire).

Lanes for walking, cycling or pootling

But if meandering lazily along English backwaters on a limpid afternoon is more your taste, consider a few of the following. Add a couple more ingredients – a half-decent road map and nothing to hurry back for – and you are guaranteed some perfect pootling. Almost anywhere away from the big towns will reward an adventurous spirit, but these are an eclectic assortment of suggested starting points. Try the warren of lanes switchbacking around the Golden Valley in the shadow of the Black Mountains, in Herefordshire. Or the northern reaches of the Cotswolds, where vistas stretch to the Malverns, the Vale of Evesham and Stratford-upon-Avon. There's the little-known but savagely beautiful countryside around the Clee Hills south and west of Bridgnorth, or the gentler, undulating farmland of Suffolk between Diss and Southwold. Norfolk's north coast offers sleepy villages – a pair are appropriately called Little and Great Snoring – and unspoilt coastline. And there are the Lincolnshire Wolds west of Louth, where few visitors discover the distinct charms of Bag Enderby or Normanby le Wold.

Striking out

But if the narrowest of lanes still has too much of the hurly-burly, swap the car for a pair of boots, the road atlas for a walking map. Strike out along the footpaths and bridleways. A good place to start is on one of England's many long-distance paths. Almost all have circular walks of anything from two to 20 miles (3–30km)

sharing their waymarks, so don't be put off by the "long-distance" element. Running down the western edge of the region, and criss-crossing in and out of Wales is Offa's Dyke Path, which roughly follows the route of the 8th-century earthwork constructed by the Mercian king to keep the Welsh at bay. Also oriented north–south, but stretching from Staffordshire to the Cotswolds, is the Heart of England Way. Rural in character for most of its length, it follows the Birmingham and Fazeley Canal to the east of the city, before dropping down to Chipping Campden (where it joins the Cotswold Way). Two more long-distance paths explore East Anglia's many sandy beaches. The first, the Peddars Way and Norfolk Coast Path, was, as its name suggests, once two separate routes. It starts in the flinty fields near Thetford and follows the course of a Roman road (the Peddars Way) till it reaches the coast near Holme. From here until Cromer – the Norfolk Coast Path – you will have as company the varied birdlife that throngs the dunes and marshes. Meanwhile, the Suffolk Coast Path between Lowestoft and Felixstowe involves a couple of ferries, and skirts the cliffs that once supported the lost medieval village of Dunwich.

Art for all

One highlight of the Suffolk Coast Path is Snape Maltings, home of the Aldeburgh Festival (June), devoted in part to the music of Sir Benjamin Britten. The welcome proliferation of literary and musical festivals ensures a huge number of events, catering for every taste. By way of a small sample, you can now choose your venue from: Cheltenham (jazz in April, music – and cricket – in July, literature in October), Chelmsford Cathedral (jazz, classical and art exhibitions, May), Solihull (folk music, May), Thaxted (classical and jazz, weekends in June and July), Ludlow (music, drama and dance, June), Warwick and Leamington Spa (classical music, July), Ledbury (poetry, July), Oundle (organ recitals, July), Buxton (opera, July), Three Choirs Festival (August) and Ross-on-Wye (dance, comedy and theatre, August).

Narrow streets and imposing townhouses

Such events are frequently based in attractive, historical market towns, the sort of town that specialises in medieval higgledy-piggledyness, Elizabethan and Jacobean sturdiness, Georgian elegance or a combination of these and countless other architectural styles. Some are well-known, others less so. Tewkesbury, for example, is a fine medieval town that has long been blessed by – and suffered from – its position at the confluence of the rivers Severn and Avon. A magnificent row of 15th-century shops and the memorably named House of the Nodding Gables are a couple of venerable survivors of the regular flooding. Bewdley is a thoroughly gracious former river port higher up the Severn. Since 1798, the centrepiece has been Thomas Telford's elegant bridge, but as well as the myriad streets ideal for strolling, there is a station on the scenic Severn Valley Railway. Bromyard, by contrast, has a

► Birmingham Pre-Raphaelites

Birmingham's City Museum and Art Gallery (tel: 0121 303 2834) houses the largest (and arguably finest) collection of Pre-Raphaelite art in the world, including Holman Hunt's *The Last of England, The Blind Girl* by Millais and Rossetti's *Beata Beatrix*, together with a vast number of other paintings, drawings and crafts. Nearby Wightwick Manor, just outside Wolverhampton (tel: 01902 761108) is entirely furnished and decorated by some of the most prominent Pre-Raphaelite artists, while in Birmingham Cathedral may be found some superb stained-glass designed by Edward Burne-Jones, a native of the city.

► Westonbirt

Robert Holford was just 21 when he began the outstanding collection of tree specimens that now forms Westonbirt Arboretum. Almost 170 years later, visitors can see the spectacular culmination of his life's work. The arboretum covers 600 acres (240 hectares) of woodland with 17 miles (27km) of paths and 18,000 listed specimens of plants. Some 4,000 species flourish here, many as exotic as the Chilean firebush or the handkerchief tree, all arranged in a landscape of great beauty (tel: 01666 880220).

▶ Slimbridge

When the naturalist and painter Peter Scott founded the Wildfowl & Wetlands Trust at Slimbridge, Gloucestershire, in 1946, he operated from two derelict cottages and used wartime pill-boxes as hides. Today the organisation is internationally recognised for its research into wetland conservation and, at Slimbridge, offers visitors a superb opportunity to watch a vast range of birds. In winter up to 8,000 migrants fly in to the 800 acre (323 hectare) reserve, forming possibly the world's largest collection of ducks, geese and swans. Slimbridge is also the only place in Europe where all six species of flamingo can be seen!

▶ Dunmow Flitch

The once-common phrase 'to eat Dunmow bacon' means to live in conjugal bliss, and refers to an ancient custom still practised in Great Dunmow, near Bishop's Stortford in Essex. In order to win a flitch (or side) of bacon, a couple must prove that in the first twelve months and a day of their marriage they have not exchanged a word of anger, and certainly never repented of the day they wed. The trial, held every four years before a bewigged judge, is conducted with the utmost (mock) seriousness.

striking hill setting, two old coaching inns and a clutch of timber-framed houses, not to mention sweeping views from the nearby Bromyard Downs. Uppingham is crammed full of 17th-, 18th- and 19th-century buildings all made from the glorious, mellow Rutland stone of the area. Southwold has the pleasing air of a town ignored by most aspects of the 20th century. The Suffolk port enjoyed something of a renaissance when it became fashionable with Victorian holidaymakers, but otherwise just the right amount of nothing has entertained locals and visitors ever since the bustling medieval harbour silted up. Melton Mowbray's cattle market was established over 900 years ago. Not much in the town is quite as old, but 14th-century Anne of Cleves' House is now witnessing its eighth century.

Pies and produce

Melton's real fame derives from its associations with pork pies and Stilton cheese, both of which are still made and sold here. Bakewell, in Derbyshire, is synonymous with a delicious upside-down pudding, widely available in the area, but the town is also worth visiting for an agricultural show in August and its fine stone architecture. Heacham, in Norfolk, has long been the English headquarters of lavender growing; tours are available. Spalding, over the border into Lincolnshire, draws thousands in early May to its annual flower parade, while asparagus takes centre stage at the Fleece Inn at Bretforton in Worcestershire. The ancient pub, owned by the National Trust, runs an auction devoted to asparagus on the evening of the last Sunday in May.

Homes and gardens

The Trust owns and manages a vast range of properties throughout the region, from Mr Straw's House in Worksop – a modest hundred-year-old semi – to the working Theatre Royal in Bury St Edmunds. A random sample of other historic houses – most still privately owned – includes: Weston Park (Palladian mansion with gardens by 'Capability' Brown, Staffordshire); Eastnor Castle (Georgian castle with Gothic interiors, Ledbury, Herefordshire); Woburn Abbey (18th-century mansion with considerable art collection, Bedfordshire); Audley End (17th-century house with Adam touches, Essex); Stanford Hall (riverside William and Mary house with notable ballroom, Swinford, Leicestershire); Burghley House (Elizabethan palace with baroque interiors, Stamford, Lincolnshire); Kentwell Hall (Tudor mansion with garden maze, Long Melford, Suffolk); and Sulgrave Manor (ancestral home of George Washington, Northamptonshire). All these properties run special events of one form or another in high season.

Look East

The region's coastline runs from Essex to Lincolnshire. Essex has a mixture of lonely marsh and fine beach, while Suffolk alternates sand and shingle. Norfolk's golden shores, though, stretch for mile after mile, and Lincolnshire – after a marshy section around the Wash – boasts more excellent beaches.

Naturally, there are the famous seaside resorts, with their quintessentially English attractions and their cheerful brashness, but there is another side to the coastline. For a quieter maritime excursion try Frinton (Essex), Covehithe (Suffolk), Happisburgh – pronounced 'Haysborough' – Holkham and Hunstanton (all Norfolk) and Anderby Creek (Lincolnshire). Unique amongst east coast resorts, Hunstanton has the distinction of facing west. Watch the sun go down over the waves in the knowledge that no one else within 150 or so miles (240km) is doing the same...

Divine inspiration

And, of course, there are the region's countless churches. The medieval stone-carvers of Herefordshire honed their skills to perfection at Kilpeck. Distinctive round towers stand out against the gentle Norfolk landscape, as at Sedgeford. The warm, honey-coloured stone that characterises so many of the unsung Northamptonshire villages was used on consecrated ground, too; Brixworth is a marvellous Saxon church in an imposing setting. In Suffolk and northern Essex, the locally abundant flint was the main material in such opulent churches as Long Melford and Dedham, both villages of remarkable beauty aside from their churches.

Some useful contact numbers

Samuel Johnson Birthplace Museum, Lichfield (tel: 01543 264972)

D H Lawrence Birthplace, Eastwood (tel: 01773 763312)

Newstead Abbey, Newstead (tel: 01623 455900)

Shaw's Corner, Ayot St Lawrence (tel: 01438 820307)

Cheltenham International Jazz Festival (tel: 01242 237377)

Cheltenham Festival of Literature (tel: 01242 521621)

Cheltenham International Festival of Music (tel: 01242 521621)

Thaxted Festival (tel: 01371 831421)

Warwick and Leamington Festival (tel: 01926 496277)

Ledbury Poetry Festival (tel: 01531 634156)

Oundle International Festival (tel: 01832 272026)

Buxton Festival (tel: 01298 70395)

Three Choirs Festival (tel: 01905 616200)

Ross-on-Wye Festival (tel: 01594 544446)

Bakewell Agricultural Show (tel: 01629 812736)

Norfolk Lavender, Heacham (tel: 01485 570384)

Spalding Flower Parade (tel: 01775 724843)

Fleece Inn, Bretforton (tel: 01386 831173)

Mr Straw's House, Worksop (tel: 01909 482380)

Theatre Royal, Bury St Edmunds (tel: 01284 755127)

Weston Park, Shifnal (tel: 01952 852100)

Eastnor Castle, Ledbury (tel: 01531 633160)

Woburn Abbey (tel: 01525 290666)

Audley End (tel: 01799 522399)

Stanford Hall, Swinford (tel: 01788 860250)

Burghley House, Stamford (tel: 01780 752451)

Kentwell Hall, Long Melford (tel: 01787 310207)

Sulgrave Manor (tel: 01295 760205)

► The Malvern Hills

Looking from the east, the Malverns, rising from the Severn Plain near Worcester, seem to belie their modest height. What they lack in altitude, however, they more than make up for in beauty and the panoramas they offer. On a clear day the views from the top stretch to far-distant horizons. The best way to explore these glorious hills – they stretch roughly 8 miles (13km) in a north–south direction – is on foot, but several roads cross the Malverns affording magnificent views for the less mobile.

► Bakewell Puddings

The story of Bakewell's famous puddings is one of triumph over adversity. In 1860 a cook at the White Horse Inn (now the Rutland Arms) preparing a strawberry tart for some dignitaries mistakenly placed egg mixture intended for the pastry base on top of the jam. The resulting 'disaster' was nevertheless cooked up and promptly declared a culinary masterpiece. The puddings (those in the know never call them 'tarts') have been served in the town ever since.

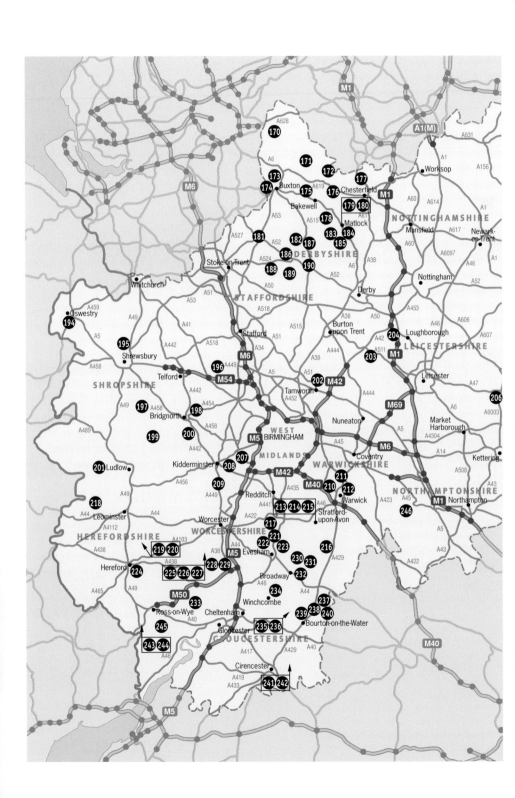

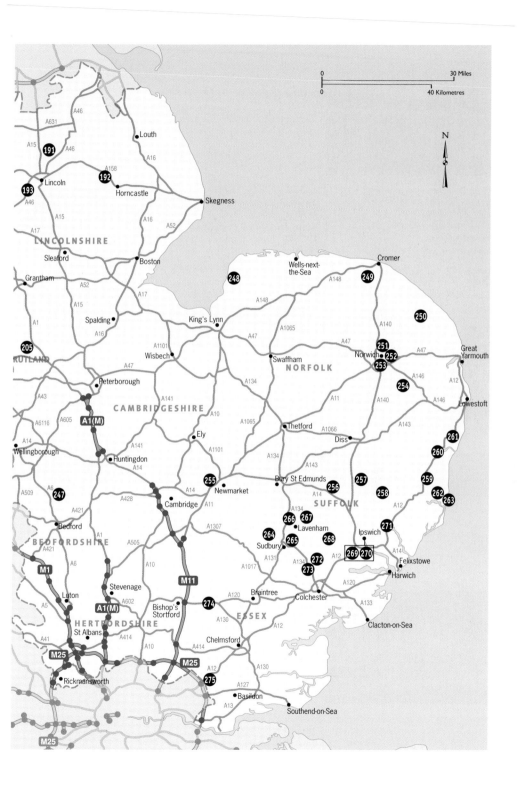

170 Wind in the Willows Hotel   ★★ Silver Award

Derbyshire Level, off Sheffield Road (A57), Glossop, Derbyshire SK13 7PT **Tel:** (01457) 868001 **Fax:** (01457) 853354
Web: www.windinthewillows.co.uk **E-mail:** info@windinthewillows.co.uk

The Wind in the Willows is a family-owned, early Victorian country house hotel set in five acres, amidst unspoilt views of the Peak District National Park, nestling in the heather-clad hills of the Pennines. The 12 traditionally styled en-suite bedrooms, oak-panelled rooms, open log fires, antiques, conference rooms and adjacent golf course ensure a memorable stay. The dining room offers fine English home cooking, all freshly prepared.

Bed & Breakfast per night: single occupancy from £75.00–£95.00; double room from £99.00–£121.00
Dinner, Bed & Breakfast per person, per night: £74.50–£117.00
Evening meal: 1900–2100

Bedrooms: 9 double, 3 twin
Bathrooms: 12 en-suite
Parking: 20 spaces
Cards accepted: Mastercard, Visa, Switch/Delta, Amex, Diners, Eurocard, Visa Electron, Solo

171 Underleigh House   ◆◆◆◆◆ Silver Award

Edale Road, Hope, Hope Valley, Derbyshire S33 6RF **Tel:** (01433) 621372 or (01433) 621324 **Fax:** (01433) 621324
Web: www.underleighhouse.co.uk **E-mail:** Underleigh.House@btinternet.com

A stunning, tranquil setting and delightful garden set the scene for this charming extended cottage and barn conversion (dating from 1873). Nestling under Lose Hill, one mile from Hope village centre, Underleigh is in the heart of magnificent walking country. Each room is furnished to a high standard with many thoughtful extras included. Delicious breakfasts in the flag-stoned dining hall feature local and homemade specialities. The welcoming beamed lounge offers log fires on chilly evenings.

Bed & Breakfast per night: single occupancy from £33.00–£46.00; double room from £60.00–£66.00

Bedrooms: 4 double, 2 twin
Bathrooms: 6 en-suite
Parking: 10 spaces
Cards accepted: Mastercard, Visa, Switch/Delta, Maestro, Solo

172 The Plough Inn   ◆◆◆◆

Leadmill Bridge, Hathersage, Hope Valley, Derbyshire S32 1BA **Tel:** (01433) 650319 or (01433) 650180 **Fax:** (01433) 651049

Situated in nine acres of grounds, the 16th-century Plough Inn has recently been restored to give visitors every modern facility and comfort. It is an idyllic location close to the meandering River Derwent and surrounded by magnificent countryside. Cosy and tastefully decorated, the inn provides an ideal environment in which to unwind or visit the many heritage sites of the Peak District National Park. Food at The Plough Inn is a real star attraction.

Bed & Breakfast per night: single occupancy from £49.50–£69.50; double room from £69.50–£99.50 (min 2 nights at weekends)
Lunch available: 1130–1430
Evening meal: 1800 (last orders 2130)

Bedrooms: 2 double, 1 triple
Bathrooms: 3 en-suite
Parking: 50 spaces
Cards accepted: Mastercard, Visa, Switch/Delta, Eurocard, Maestro, Visa Electron, Solo

173 Barms Farm

 ◆◆◆◆ Silver Award

Fairfield, Buxton, Derbyshire SK17 7HW **Tel:** (01298) 77723 **Fax:** (01298) 78692
Web: www.highpeak.co.uk/barmsfarm **E-mail:** barmsfarm@highpeak.co.uk

Superb farmhouse accommodation, furnished to a high standard throughout, offering three luxurious en-suite rooms. Romantic king-size 'seventh heaven' brass bedsteads draped in quality bed linen adorn extensively equipped rooms. Choice of freshly cooked breakfasts served in the dining room at separate tables before a busy day exploring the surrounding Peaks and Dales. Genuine country hospitality and a warm welcome awaits, courtesy of the Naden family. Sorry - No smoking - No pets.

Bed & Breakfast per night: double room from £48.00–£55.00

Bedrooms: 3 double
Bathrooms: 3 en-suite
Parking: 4 spaces
Open: all year except Christmas
Cards accepted: Mastercard, Visa

174 Grendon Guesthouse

◆◆◆◆◆ Silver Award

Bishops Lane, Buxton, Derbyshire SK17 6UN **Tel:** (01298) 78831 **Fax:** (01298) 79257
Web: www.grendonguesthouse.co.uk

A warm welcome awaits you at our beautiful Edwardian home with far-reaching hill views, within one mile of Buxton's historic centre. Our very spacious bed-sitting rooms provide the ultimate in comfort, with king-size beds, lounge chairs, luxury en-suites and a superb four-poster bedroom. Delicious breakfasts include all the favourites plus fresh fruit salad and home-made bread. Evening meals available. Remembered and revisited by many for our unsurpassed location and quality. A *Which?* recommended hotel.

Bed & Breakfast per night: single occupancy £33.00–£45.00; double room from £48.00–£66.00
Evening meal: by arrangement

Bedrooms: 2 double, 1 twin
Bathrooms: 3 en-suite
Parking: 4 spaces
Cards accepted: Mastercard, Visa, Switch/Delta, Eurocard

175 Cressbrook Hall

 ◆◆◆◆

Cressbrook, Buxton, Derbyshire SK17 8SY **Tel:** (01298) 871289 or 0800 3583003 **Fax:** (01298) 871845
Web: www.cressbrookhall.co.uk **E-mail:** stay@cressbrookhall.co.uk

A period piece with pedigree! Cressbrook Hall is a fine William IV residence, built 1835 and enjoying a spectacular hillside location. The formal gardens designed by Edward Kemp are currently under restoration. Self-catering cottages, together with elegant serviced accommodation in the Hall are available for weekends or longer visits and ideal for reunions, management training/team building and special family celebrations. Hall 'home catering' gives you more free time to enjoy this idyllic place. Accommodation which is decidedly, delightfully different! ⭡ Category 3

Bed & Breakfast per night: single occupancy from £50.00–£65.00; double room from £75.00–£105.00

Bedrooms: 1 double, 1 twin, 1 triple
Bathrooms: 3 en-suite
Parking: 10 spaces
Cards accepted: Mastercard, Visa, Switch/Delta, Eurocard, Maestro, Solo

176 The Old School House

School Lane, Baslow, Bakewell, Derbyshire DE45 1RZ **Tel:** (01246) 582488 **Fax:** (01246) 583323
E-mail: yvonnewright@talk21.com

This beautifully restored Victorian house offers you a luxurious and cosseted retreat, situated in the heart of Baslow. All rooms are individually furnished with every modern amenity. After relaxing slumbers, wake to birdsong, tranquillity and a hearty breakfast. On the doorstep, gritstone edges, heatherclad moorlands, limestone dales and tumbling waterfalls beckon walkers and nature lovers alike. Nearby Chatsworth, Haddon Hall, Bakewell and a host of other attractions along with an abundance of delightful eating places.

Bed & Breakfast per night: single occupancy from £35.00–£58.00; double room from £70.00–£80.00

Bedrooms: 2 double, 1 twin
Bathrooms: 2 en-suite, 1 private
Parking: 4 spaces

Eyam and the Plague

The village of Eyam (pronounced 'Eem'), 800ft (240m) up in the Derbyshire hills, is like many another in the Peaks: pretty old stone buildings against a backdrop of wild, mountainous terrain. But Eyam has a dark past which singles it out from any other village in the country, a tale of shared human misery which, though experienced over 300 years ago, has never been forgotten.

In September 1665, George Viccars, a journeyman tailor lodging in a cottage near the church, opened a parcel of cloth sent from London where bubonic plague was then raging. Within four days he was dead, his body marked with the tell-tale purple rings which characterised the disease. Plague had descended on Eyam, and, though many must have been tempted to flee, the young rector of Eyam, William Mompesson, realising that this would immediately spread the disease, persuaded the whole village to make a courageous act of self-sacrifice. Eyam was sealed off from the outside world: no one could enter it, and no one could leave. The Lord of the Manor, the Earl of Devonshire, arranged for vital supplies to be left at isolated spots around the village boundary, such as Mompesson's Well, and money, dipped in vinegar to

disinfect it, was returned as payment. Eyam paid dearly for its bravery: out of an estimated population of 350, some 250 died, almost three in every four villagers. The self-imposed quarantine lasted a year, before the plague finally ran its course in October 1666.

Today, it is hard to imagine the horror which once pervaded Eyam's quiet streets, but there are many reminders. Viccars' lodging (now called Plague Cottage) still stands, as do many other houses where victims died, now marked by neatly painted signs. In the churchyard are the graves of plague victims, including that of Mompesson's wife, Katherine. In a field about half a mile from the village, just off the Grindleford Road, are the Riley Graves, poignant memorials to a father, three sons and three daughters, all of whom died in the space of eight days in August 1666. Mompesson took to preaching in a limestone cavern known as Cucklet Church, where on the last Sunday in August, an annual commemorative service is held. An exhibition in Eyam church recounts the full story of the plague year. Information on Eyam is available from Bakewell's Tourist Information Centre (tel: 01629 813227).

177 Millbrook

 ◆◆◆◆ Silver Award

Furnace Lane, Monkwood, Barlow, Dronfield S18 7SY **Tel:** (01142) 890253 or (07831) 398373 **Fax:** (01142) 891365

Millbrook is spacious and comfortably furnished, having en-suite facilities with drinks tray, colour television, hairdryer, alarm radio, trouser press and guests' lounge. Attention is paid to detail making your stay as enjoyable and comfortable as possible. Situated down a quiet country lane surrounded by lovely countryside with many walks, yet within easy reach of Sheffield and Chesterfield, we are on the edge of the Peak District, with Chatsworth House and Haddon Hall close by. Many nearby hostelries serve good pub food.

Bed & Breakfast per night: single occupancy £30.00; double room £50.00

Bedrooms: 1 double, 1 twin
Bathrooms: 2 en-suite
Parking: 8 spaces
Open: all year except Christmas and New Year

178 Hawthorn Cottage

 ◆◆◆◆ Silver Award

Well Street, Elton, Matlock, Derbyshire DE4 2BY **Tel:** (01629) 650372

Tucked away in a picturesque corner of a conservation village, our cosy 17th-century cottage offers a luxurious self-contained private suite. Situated on the ground floor with double en-suite and lounge/dining room, complete with mini fridge, television, video, clock radio, hairdryer etc. Secluded sunny patios and garden with glorious views over miles of open countryside. Hearty breakfasts and a warm welcome. Ideally placed for the Peak District and Derbyshire Dales. Ten minutes from Chatsworth House and Haddon Hall.

Bed & Breakfast per night: single occupancy £30.00; double room from £44.00–£48.00

Bedrooms: 1 double
Bathrooms: 1 en-suite
Parking: 1 space

179 Sheriff Lodge

◆◆◆◆

51 Dimple Road, Matlock, Derbyshire DE4 3JX **Tel:** (01629) 760760 **Fax:** (01629) 760860
Web: www.sherifflodge.co.uk **E-mail:** kate@sherifflodge.co.uk

An Edwardian 'gentleman's residence' in the heart of the Derbyshire Dales, Sheriff Lodge offers luxurious accommodation and a thoroughly warm welcome. All our named rooms (Mousehole, Dray, Loft and Nest) offer an en-suite 'heritage' bath or shower and have access to sattelite television. Within easy reach are a multitude of activities – walking in the Peak District, Chatsworth House, Haddon Hall, Bakewell (for the pudding) and Matlock Bath. You can be assured of a very enjoyable stay.

Bed & Breakfast per night: single occupancy from £36.50–£39.00; double room from £55.00–£60.00 (min 2 nights during summer and at weekends)

Bedrooms: 2 double, 2 twin
Bathrooms: 4 en-suite
Parking: 6 spaces
Cards accepted: Mastercard, Visa, Switch/Delta

At-a-glance symbols are explained on the flap inside the back cover

180 Riber Hall

★★★ Silver Award

Matlock, Derbyshire DE4 5JU **Tel:** (01629) 582795 **Fax:** (01629) 580475
Web: www.riber-hall.co.uk **E-mail:** info@riber-hall.co.uk

Renowned historic country manor house set in tranquil rolling Derbyshire hills. Gourmet cuisine – AA two rosettes. Many stately homes nearby including Chatsworth. Recommended by all major guides. Two day breaks available. M1 exit 28, twenty minutes.

Bed & Breakfast per night: single occupancy from £97.00–£112.00; double room from £127.00–£170.00
Dinner, Bed & Breakfast per person, per night: £100.00–£125.00
Lunch available: 1200–1330 (last orders)

Evening meal: 1900 (last orders 2130)
Bedrooms: 12 double, 2 twin
Bathrooms: 14 en-suite
Parking: 50 spaces
Cards accepted: Mastercard, Visa, Switch/Delta, Amex, Diners, Eurocard, JCB

181 Beechfields Victorian Guest House

◆◆◆◆

Park Road, Leek, Staffordshire ST13 8JS **Tel:** (01538) 372825
Web: www.beech-fields.fsnet.co.uk **E-mail:** judith@beech-fields.fsnet.co.uk

A peaceful, comfortable Victorian house, set amidst beautiful and secluded gardens. Guests' own lounge. En-suite pine bedrooms with television, tea/coffee making facilities etc. Delicious traditional breakfasts served in the pine dining room. The market town of Leek is a short stroll through Brough Park and has many inns and restaurants offering a wide choice of meals. Beechfields is an ideal place to relax, or as a base from which to explore the Peak District, Potteries and surrounding beautiful countryside and villages. Winner of Staffordhire Tourism's 'Best Staffordshire Breakfast' Award 2001/2202.

Bed & Breakfast per night: single occupancy £28.00; double room £44.00

Bedrooms: 3 double/twin
Bathrooms: 3 en-suite
Parking: 7 spaces

182 Stanshope Hall

◆◆◆◆

Stanshope, Ashbourne, Derbyshire DE6 2AD **Tel:** (01335) 310278 **Fax:** (01335) 310470
Web: www.stanshope.demon.co.uk **E-mail:** naomi@stanshope.demon.co.uk

Seven miles from Ashbourne, between Dovedale and the Manifold Valley in the southern Peak District, Stanshope Hall offers peace and quiet, comfortable licensed en-suite accommodation and home cooking. The rooms have been decorated by theatre artists and the result is a mixture of the theatrical, the humorous and the indulgent. Fruit and vegetables served at dinner are, whenever possible, from our own kitchen garden.

Bed & Breakfast per night: single occupancy from £25.00–£40.00; double room from £50.00–£80.00
Dinner, Bed & Breakfast per person, per night: £46.00–£61.00
Evening meal: 1900 (last orders 2000)

Bedrooms: 2 double, 1 twin
Bathrooms: 3 en-suite
Parking: 3 spaces
Cards accepted: Mastercard, Visa, Switch/Delta, Solo

Entries are cross referenced by number to the maps on pages 90–91

183 Eastas Gate   ◆◆◆◆

18 Main Street, Middleton, Matlock, Derbyshire DE4 4LQ **Tel:** (01629) 822790
E-mail: eastasgate@hotmail.com

Eastas Gate is a limestone house built around 1650, lying at the edge of a village within a conservation area. It has mature gardens and uninterrupted views over the surrounding countryside. Great care has been taken to create a peaceful and calm atmosphere, with guest accommodation limited to two en-suite rooms – ensuring personal attention at all times. There is a separate guest lounge. All rooms have period furniture and are centrally heated. Ample off-road parking.

Bed & Breakfast per night: single occupancy £25.00; double room £50.00
Dinner, Bed & Breakfast per person, per night: £35.50
Evening meal: 1800 (last orders 1930)

Bedrooms: 2 double/twin
Bathrooms: 2 en-suite
Parking: 6 spaces

184 Hodgkinson's Hotel   ◆◆◆◆

150 South Parade, Matlock Bath, Matlock, Derbyshire DE4 3NR **Tel:** (01629) 582170 **Fax:** (01629) 584891
Web: www.hodgkinsons-hotel.co.uk **E-mail:** enquiries@hodgkinsons-hotel.co.uk

A Grade II listed Georgian hotel dating from 1770, situated in the heart of the historic spa town of Matlock Bath. The town is ideally situated for exploring the natural beauty of the Peak District and a host of historic houses, including Chatsworth. Beautifully restored, most of our seven en-suite rooms overlook the steep wooded slopes of the River Derwent and all are individually decorated and furnished with antiques. Our intimate candlelit restaurant offers the best of Peak local produce imaginatively prepared by our Italian chef proprietor.

Bed & Breakfast per night: single room from £38.00–£55.00; double room from £69.00–£95.00
Dinner, Bed & Breakfast per person, per night: £49.50–£54.50 (min 2 nights)
Evening meal: 1930 (last orders 2100)

Bedrooms: 1 single, 5 double, 1 twin
Bathrooms: 7 en-suite
Parking: 5 spaces
Cards accepted: Mastercard, Visa, Switch/Delta, Amex

185 Old Lock Up   ◆◆◆◆◆ Gold Award

North End, Wirksworth, Derby, Derbyshire DE4 4FG **Tel:** (01629) 826272 or (01629) 826929 **Fax:** (01629) 826272
Web: www.theoldlockup.co.uk **E-mail:** wheeler@theoldlockup.co.uk

The first to stay here were murderers and malcontents. Now you can share their experience in the luxury of a restored Victorian magistrate's house and police station with Gothic chapel. The manor is in the Derbyshire Peak District National Park, a treasury of history and atmosphere. Historically unique luxury accommodation, blending Victorian charm and heritage with modern day comfort. Excellent cuisine, open fires, double airbath, antique beds and secure parking. As featured on national television. Heart of England Tourist Board B&B of the Year Award 2000.

Bed & Breakfast per night: single occupancy from £40.00–£60.00; double room from £70.00–£100.00
Dinner, Bed & Breakfast per person, per night: £60.00–£80.00
Evening meal: 1700 (last orders 2000)

Bedrooms: 3 double, 1 twin
Bathrooms: 4 en-suite
Parking: 6 spaces

186 Lee House Farm

♦♦♦♦ Silver Award

Leek Road, Waterhouses, Stoke-on-Trent, Staffordshire ST10 3HW **Tel:** (01538) 308439

A charming 18th-century house in the centre of a picturesque village in the Peak District National Park. Lee House is full of character: all bedrooms are non-smoking, centrally heated and en-suite, with colour television and tea/coffee making facilities. Ideally situated for walking and cycling in the Manifold Valley, visiting stately homes, touring the Staffordshire Moorlands, the Peak District and the famous Potteries. Waterhouses is midway between Leek and Ashbourne on the A523. 6 miles from Alton Towers.

Bed & Breakfast per night: double room from £40.00–£50.00

Bedrooms: 2 double, 1 twin
Bathrooms: 3 en-suite
Parking: 4 spaces

187 Thorpe Cottage

♦♦♦♦

Thorpe, Ashbourne, Derbyshire DE6 2AW **Tel:** (01335) 350466 or (07711) 217475 **Fax:** (01335) 350217
Web: www.thorpecottage.fsworld.co.uk **E-mail:** thorpecottage@aol.com

Thorpe and Daisy Cottage. Within a short walking distance of Dovedale, this stone-built listed cottage is ideally situated for visiting the wonderful attractions of the Peak District. Recently established and refurbished, the owner offers a warm welcome and comfortable rooms with bathrooms. The home-made daily fresh muffins are a much appreciated addition to the more traditional and plentiful English breakfast. The uneaten ones get packed up for elevenses!

Bed & Breakfast per night: single room from £20.00–£30.00; double room from £40.00–£60.00
Dinner, Bed & Breakfast per person, per night: £32.50–£45.00

Bedrooms: 1 single, 3 double, 1 twin, 1 family
Bathrooms: 2 en-suite, 2 shared
Parking: 7 spaces

188 Bank House

♦♦♦♦♦ Gold Award

Farley Road, Oakamoor, Stoke-on-Trent, Staffordshire ST10 3BD **Tel:** (01538) 702810 **Fax:** (01538) 702810
Web: www.smoothhound.co.uk/hotels/bank.html **E-mail:** john.orme@dial.pipex.com

A luxurious, elegant and peaceful licensed country home offering the highest standards of food and comfort, a third of a mile south of the village. Each en-suite or private-bath bedroom has a beautiful view of the picturesque Churnet Valley, England's little Rhineland. Within the Staffordshire Moorlands, next to the National Park, one mile from Alton Towers, and amidst superb countryside for walking, it is also convenient for visiting the Potteries, Derbyshire Dales, numerous great houses, gardens and other attractions. We offer discounts for stays of more than three nights.

Bed & Breakfast per night: single occupancy from £45.00–£54.00; double room from £60.00–£78.00

Bedrooms: 1 double, 2 twin
Bathrooms: 2 en-suite, 1 private
Parking: 8 spaces
Cards accepted: Mastercard, Visa, Diners, Eurocard

189 Manor House Farm   ◆◆◆◆

Prestwood, Denstone, Uttoxeter, Staffordshire ST14 5DD **Tel:** (01889) 590415 **Fax:** (01335) 342198
Web: www.4posteraccom.com **E-mail:** cm_ball@yahoo.co.uk

An oak-panelled, four-postered Tudor retreat, two miles from Alton Towers. An enchanting, rambling farmhouse, the kind of time capsule you can't simulate. Oak timbers, stone, tapestry drapes, curios, pewter and books galore. There are georgous lawned grounds, full of bird song. A summerhouse, tennis and croquet. Rare breed cattle graze peacefully. Rooms have majestic four-poster beds and great views. Chris and Margaret are busy, informal people and the attitude here is 'stay as friends'.

Bed & Breakfast per night: single occupancy from £26.00–£28.00; double room from £40.00–£50.00

Bedrooms: 2 double, 1 family
Bathrooms: 3 en-suite
Parking: 6 spaces
Cards accepted: Mastercard, Visa

---

190 Omnia Somnia   ◆◆◆◆◆ Gold Award

The Coach House, The Firs, Ashbourne, Derbyshire DE6 1HF **Tel:** (01335) 300145 or 07773 460795 **Fax:** (01335) 300958
E-mail: omnia.somnia@talk21.com

A private house, formerly a Victorian coach house, nestling amongst mature trees in a quiet location near Ashbourne town centre. Our rooms are very different, each one special in its own way: Oriens – a room with every facility and many, many pictures, and the superb bathroom has a bath big enough for two! Occidens – enter into your own sitting room, then climb the stairs to a romantic hideaway bedroom. Meridies – a sumptuous, panelled room with a hand-crafted, fully draped four-poster bed.

Bed & Breakfast per night: single occupancy from £50.00–£60.00; double room from £70.00–£80.00
Dinner, Bed & Breakfast per person, per night: £56.00–£61.00
Evening meal: from 1900

Bedrooms: 3 double
Bathrooms: 3 en-suite
Parking: 3 spaces
Cards accepted: Mastercard, Visa, Switch/Delta, JCB, Solo

191 Honeyholes   ◆◆◆◆

South Farm, Hackthorn, Lincoln, Lincolnshire LN2 3PW **Tel:** (01673) 861838 **Fax:** (01673) 861868
E-mail: DGreen8234@aol.com

Step free from the stresses of life and enjoy the relaxing atmosphere of our Edwardian farmhouse. Stroll through the cottage-style gardens or unwind by a flickering open fire on cooler days. Rediscover the tastes of home cooking and baking, using local produce when possible. Centrally located for exploring Lincolnshire. Go racing at Market Rasen. Local golf, fishing and horse riding. Explore cathedral, castles and country houses, five minutes from county showground and Hemswell antique centre.

Bed & Breakfast per night: single occupancy from £20.00–£25.00; double room from £38.00–£44.00
Dinner, Bed & Breakfast per person, per night: £31.00–£34.00 (min 2 nights, 2 sharing)

Bedrooms: 2 double, 1 twin
Bathrooms: 1 en-suite, 2 shared
Parking: 6 spaces

192 Baumber Park ◆◆◆◆

Baumber, Horncastle, Lincolnshire LN9 5NE **Tel:** (01507) 578235 or 07977 722776 **Fax:** (01507) 578417
Web: www.tuckedup.com/baumberpark.html

Spacious, elegant farmhouse of character in pastoral setting on a working farm. Large gardens, wildlife pond, grass tennis court. Fine bedrooms with lovely views. Guest lounge, period furniture, log fires and books. Close to the Lincolnshire Wolds, this rolling countryside is little known and quite unspoilt. The bridleways and lanes are ideal for walking, cycling or riding – and stabling is available. Woodhall Spa's championship golf course is nearby. Aviation heritage, historic Lincoln, interesting market towns and antique shops. Peace, relaxation and a warm welcome.

Bed & Breakfast per night: single
occupancy £22.50–£35.00; double room
£45.00–£50.00
**Dinner, Bed & Breakfast per person, per
night:** £30.00–£45.00 (min 3 nights)
Evening meal: by arrangement

Bedrooms: 1 double, 1 twin
Bathrooms: 1 en-suite, 1 private
Parking: 4 spaces

193 Damon's Motel ◆◆◆◆

997 Doddington Road, Lincoln, LN6 3SE **Tel:** (01522) 887733 **Fax:** (01522) 887734

Damon's is a beautiful, superior-grade motel, conveniently situated on the Lincoln by-pass. All rooms have either a king-size double bed, or two single beds, all with en-suite double bed. Each room has satellite television, tea/coffee making facilities, direct dial telephone and hairdryer. Enjoy the indoor family swimming pool, gym and solarium. The motel is adjacent to the celebrated Damon's American Restaurant and Lounge Bar which serves food from breakfast through to dinner. **Category 3**

Bed & Breakfast per night: single
occupancy from £49.25–£52.25; double room
from £55.00–£58.00

Bedrooms: 27 double, 20 twin, 18 family
Bathrooms: 47 en-suite
Parking: 47 spaces
Cards accepted: Mastercard, Visa, Switch/Delta,
Amex, Diners

194 Sweeney Hall Hotel ★★ Silver Award

Morda, Oswestry, Shropshire SY10 9EU **Tel:** (01691) 652450 **Fax:** (01691) 668023
Web: www.sweeneyhall.co.uk **E-mail:** enquiries@sweeneyhall.co.uk

'A real find'. 'Nothing is too much trouble'. An impressive Georgian country house with extensive grounds. Individually furnished en-suite bedrooms. Excellent local reputation for food. Wonderful warm atmosphere, relaxed and informal, yet with professional service. Come and try us for yourself.

Bed & Breakfast per night: single
occupancy from £52.50–£57.25; double room
from £69.50–£77.25
**Dinner, Bed & Breakfast per person, per
night:** £45.00–£73.50
Evening meal: 1900 (last orders 2130)

Bedrooms: 5 double, 4 twin
Bathrooms: 9 en-suite
Parking: 45 spaces
Cards accepted: Mastercard, Visa, Switch/Delta,
Amex

195 The Old Vicarage

Leaton, Shrewsbury SY4 3AP **Tel:** (01939) 290989 **Fax:** (01939) 290989
Web: www.oldvicleaton.com **E-mail:** m-j@oldvicleaton.com

Enjoy a relaxing break at The Old Vicarage which nestles in beautiful open countryside only four miles from medieval Shrewsbury. The house, set in five acres, was built in 1859 in high Victorian style with handsome Minton floor tiles, stone mullions and period furnishings throughout. Large en-suite bedrooms with Emperor and King-size beds, television, radio and refreshments. Traditional home cooking from an extensive breakfast menu. Ideally situated for Shropshire's many attractions and spectacular countryside.

Bed & Breakfast per night: single room £25.00; double room £44.00

Bedrooms: 2 double/twin
Bathrooms: 2 en-suite
Parking: 6 spaces
Cards accepted: Mastercard, Visa, Switch/Delta

The Shropshire Hills

The 'Shropshire Alps' and 'Little Switzerland' are not altogether fanciful names for that dramatically hilly part of the county sandwiched between the Welsh border and the River Severn. Here, ancient earth movements have tilted up great layers of different rock strata, each now forming its own ridge of hills stretching in a roughly south-westerly to north-easterly direction.

Most easterly of the ridges are the Clee Hills, formed of rich red sandstone, topped with basalt, and consisting of two separate ridges, Brown Clee Hill (1,792ft, 546m) and Titterstone Clee Hill (1,749ft, 533m). To their west the River Corve flows through a gentle wooded valley, before the land rises again to Wenlock Edge, a well-defined and steep-sided ridge of limestone flanked with trees. West of the Edge the hump of Caer Caradoc (1,506ft, 459m) dominates the Caradoc Hills around Church Stretton, and beyond rises the forbidding plateau of the Long Mynd (1,696ft, 517m). This 10 mile (16km) ridge of moorland, composed of heather-covered grit and shale, is a favourite launch point for gliders, and also some of the best walking country in Shropshire. An ancient path of unknown age, the Port Way, runs the entire length of the crest, commanding magnificent views of the Wrekin (1,335ft, 407m), which protrudes dramatically from the Shropshire Plain, its volcanic rocks the oldest in England. The eastern flank of the Long Mynd is eroded by streams into a series of deep ravines, of which the popular Carding

Mill Valley (shown above) is considered the most beautiful; two others are Callow Hollow and Ashes Hollow. Westward again are the Stiperstones, a sombre rocky outcrop where devils are believed to gather on Midwinter Night and, at 1,731ft (528m), a dramatic vantage point.

Aside from its superb scenery the area is rich in other attractions, with appealing towns, such as Shrewsbury, Bridgnorth, Bewdley and Ludlow all within easy reach. It boasts a string of impressive castles and fortified manors (Ludlow, Clun and Stokesay are three of many), some fine ecclesiastical ruins (Buildwas and Wenlock), and a fascinating industrial heritage (Ironbridge). At the heart of the hills is Church Stretton, an appealing little town which became something of a land-locked resort in the 19th century, a perfect base, then and now, from which to explore the slopes. Contact Church Stretton Tourist Information Centre (tel: 01694 723133, Easter–September only) for details of sights and walks (guided hikes are available) throughout the region.

196 The Blackladies

♦♦♦♦♦ Gold Award

Kiddemore Green Road, Brewood, Stafford ST19 9BH **Tel:** (01902) 850210 **Fax:** (01902) 851782

The Blackladies is a fine Grade II* listed Tudor house set in five acres. Formerly a Benedictine Priory and now a much-loved family home, Blackladies offers large en-suite bedrooms, individually furnished to a high standard. All rooms have colour television, clock/radio, hairdryer, trouser press and tea/coffee making facilities. Brewood is three miles away and the M5 and M6 motorways six miles. Weston Park and Ironbridge Museums are a short distance. Free range eggs served at breakfast. Four-poster honeymoon suite available. Non-smoking. A warm welcome awaits you.

Bed & Breakfast per night: single occupancy from £32.00–£35.00; double room from £58.00–£65.00

Bedrooms: 2 double, 2 twin, 1 family
Bathrooms: 5 en-suite
Parking: 10 spaces

197 The Wenlock Edge Inn

♦♦♦♦ Silver Award

Hilltop, Wenlock Edge, Much Wenlock, Shropshire TF13 6DJ **Tel:** (01746) 785678 **Fax:** (01746) 785285
Web: www.wenlockedgeinn.co.uk **E-mail:** info@wenlockedgeinn.co.uk

Situated in a peaceful location on Wenlock Edge – an Area of Outstanding Natural Beauty. Run by two generations of the Waring family for the last 18 years, the atmosphere of the inn is informal and friendly. Guests can relax in the comfort and cosiness of Silver Award-winning rooms and enjoy wholesome country cooking with fresh local produce and organic bread for breakfast. Chosen as 'Pub of the Year' 2002 by the Good Pub Guide.

Bed & Breakfast per night: single occupancy from £43.00–£48.00; double room from £63.00–£80.00
Lunch available: 1200–1400 Tuesday–Sunday
Evening meal: 1900 (last orders 2100)

Bedrooms: 2 double, 1 twin
Bathrooms: 3 en-suite
Parking: 40 spaces
Cards accepted: Mastercard, Visa, Switch/Delta, Amex, JCB, Visa Electron, Solo

198 Old Vicarage Hotel

★★★ Gold Award

Worfield, Bridgnorth, Shropshire WV15 5JZ **Tel:** (01746) 716497 **Fax:** (01746) 716552
Web: www.oldvicarageworfield.com **E-mail:** admin@the-old-vicarage.demon.co.uk

An Edwardian vicarage set in two acres of grounds on the edge of a conservation village in glorious Shropshire countryside, close to Ironbridge Gorge, Severn Valley Railway and Welsh border towns. With an award-winning (AA 3 Rosettes) dining room and cellar, the Old Vicarage is personally run by David and Sarah Blakstad. Two-night leisure breaks available at any time of the year. ♿ **Category 2**

Bed & Breakfast per night: single occupancy from £75.00–£110.00; double room from £115.00–£175.00
Dinner, Bed & Breakfast per person, per night: £75.00–£107.50 (min 2 nights)
Lunch available: 1200–1400

Evening meal: 1900 (last orders 2100)
Bedrooms: 8 double, 5 twin, 1 triple
Bathrooms: 14 en-suite
Parking: 30 spaces
Cards accepted: Mastercard, Visa, Switch/Delta, Amex, Visa Electron

Entries are cross referenced by number to the maps on pages 90–91

199 Earnstrey Hill House   ◆◆◆◆

Abdon, Craven Arms, Shropshire SY7 9HU **Tel:** (01746) 712579 **Fax:** (01746) 712631
E-mail: hugh.scurfield@smwh.org.uk

A comfortable, warm, spacious, stone and brick-built family house, 1200 feet up Brown Clee Hill. Superb views westwards towards the Long Mynd and Wales. We keep horses, dogs, rare-breed Shropshire sheep and free-range hens on our 11 acres. Wonderful walking country, and experienced walking hosts will help plan or guide if required.

Bed & Breakfast per night: single occupancy from £20.00–£25.00; double room from £40.00–£50.00

Bedrooms: 1 double, 2 twin
Bathrooms: 1 en-suite, 1 shared
Parking: 6 spaces
Open: all year except Christmas

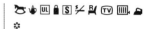

200 Bulls Head Inn   ◆◆◆◆

Chelmarsh, Bridgnorth, Shropshire WV16 6BA **Tel:** (01746) 861469 **Fax:** (01746) 862646
Web: www.virtual-shropshire.co.uk/bulls-head-inn **E-mail:** dave@bullshead.fsnet.co.uk

Charming 17th-century Inn in the village of Chelmarsh with views over the Severn valley offering excellent accommodation. Four miles from historic Bridgnorth and set in the beautiful Shropshire countryside. All bedrooms are individually and tastefully furnished (one with a four-poster bed). There are ground floor bedrooms/apartments situated around the well-stocked, pretty beer garden that are equipped for people with disabilities. There is a choice of delightfully furnished cottages for self-catering breaks. Ideally located to explore the many places of interest. **⋔ Category 3**

Bed & Breakfast per night: single room from £33.00–£46.00; double room from £48.00–£70.00
Lunch available: 1200–1400
Evening meal: 1900 (last orders 2130)

Bedrooms: 1 single, 4 double, 1 twin, 2 triple
Bathrooms: 8 en-suite
Parking: 50 spaces
Cards accepted: Mastercard, Visa, Switch/Delta, Solo

201 The Brakes   ◆◆◆◆

Downton, Ludlow, Shropshire SY8 2LF **Tel:** (01584) 856485 **Fax:** (01584) 856485

In the heart of beautiful rolling countryside, only five miles from the historic town of Ludlow, The Brakes offers delightful accommodation with excellent cuisine. A period farmhouse, tastefully furnished, with central heating throughout, standing in three acres of grounds with a beautiful garden. Bedrooms are en-suite, with TV, and there is a charming lounge with a log fire for chilly evenings. Licensed; dinner at 19.15. Excellent walking country, including Offa's Dyke and the Long Mynd. Golf, riding and fishing available. Steeped in history, with many places of interest nearby.

Bed & Breakfast per night: single occupancy from £33.00–£40.00; double room from £56.00–£65.00
Dinner, Bed & Breakfast per person, per night: from £47.00
Evening meal: 1915 (last orders 2015)

Bedrooms: 1 double, 2 twin
Bathrooms: 3 en-suite
Parking: 8 spaces
Open: March–October

202 Oak Tree Farm

 ◆◆◆◆◆ **Gold Award**

Hints Road, Hopwas, Tamworth, Staffordshire B78 3AA **Tel:** (01827) 56807 or 07836 387887 **Fax:** (01827) 56807

A country farmhouse with river frontage. Maintained to luxurious standards. Large, warm and welcoming bedrooms, all en-suite, with all comforts provided – sofas, courtesy tray, trouser press, hairdryer, iron, mineral water, telephone and modem link etc. Set in the pretty village of Hopwas, between the River Tame and the Fazely Canal, Oak Tree Farm offers tranquil surroundings, but is very convenient for Tamworth, Lichfield, NEC and the airport. Indoor heated swimming pool and steam room.

Bed & Breakfast per night: single occupancy from £57.00–£90.00; double room from £75.00–£100.00

Bedrooms: 3 double, 1 twin, 2 triple
Bathrooms: 6 en-suite
Parking: 10 spaces
Cards accepted: Mastercard, Visa, Switch/Delta, Amex, Eurocard

203 Church Lane Farm House

◆◆◆◆

Ravenstone, Leicestershire LE67 2AE **Tel:** (01530) 810536 or (01530) 811299 **Fax:** (01530) 811299
Web: www.ravenstone-guesthouse.co.uk **E-mail:** annthorne@ravenstone-guesthouse.co.uk

Queen Anne farmhouse situated in the Domesday village of Ravenstone in the National Forest between the M1 (22) and M42 (13). It is an interior designers' and artists' home with antiques in the bedrooms and throughout the house. Evening meals, featuring locally produced meat and traditional dry-cured English bacon, are served in a gracious beamed dining room – try our speciality Leicester lamb roast or local traditionally cooked venison. Special diets are available. Full residents' bar. Enjoy our tranquil water garden. Secure yard parking. Guest airport parking. Ideal for business or vacation.

Bed & Breakfast per night: single occupancy from £25.00–£32.50; double room from £49.50–£63.00
Evening meal: by arrangement

Bedrooms: 2 double, 1 twin
Bathrooms: 3 en-suite
Parking: 10 spaces
Cards accepted: Mastercard, Visa

204 The Grange Courtyard

◆◆◆◆

The Grange, Forest Street, Shepshed, Loughborough, Leicestershire LE12 9DA **Tel:** (01509) 600189 **Fax:** (01509) 600189
Web: www.thegrangecourtyard.co.uk **E-mail:** linda.lawrence@thegrangecourtyard.co.uk

The converted outbuildings of this Grade II listed, 11th-century farmhouse provide individually designed rooms with beamed ceilings, en-suite bathrooms, telephone, internet access, tele-video, residents' lounge and kitchen area, plus tranquil gardens, secure parking and staff on duty 24 hours. The Grange is licensed and can provide evening meals. Shepshed is surrounded by the beautiful Charnwood Forest, yet is just a mile from the M1 and only 10 minutes' drive from East Midlands Airport and Donington Park racetrack.

Bed & Breakfast per night: single occupancy £55.00; double room £65.00

Bedrooms: 7 double, 2 twin
Bathrooms: 9 en-suite
Parking: 18 spaces
Cards accepted: Mastercard, Visa, Switch/Delta, JCB, Maestro, Visa Electron

Entries are cross referenced by number to the maps on pages 90–91

205 Barnsdale Lodge Hotel

★★★ Silver Award

The Avenue, Exton, Oakham, Leicestershire LE15 8AH **Tel:** (01572) 724678 **Fax:** (01572) 724961

Set in the heart of Rutland's beautiful countryside overlooking Rutland Water, this 17th-century farmhouse welcomes you with luxury and warmth. Traditional English fayre, using fresh, locally-grown produce, is served in an Edwardian dining room. International wines complement the menues. Afternoon tea, elevenses and buttery lunches are available in the conservatory. Our 45 en-suite bedrooms are filled with antique furniture. The ideal retreat from everyday life. Come and discover the tranquillity of Rutland.

Bed & Breakfast per night: single room £69.00; double room £89.00
Dinner, Bed & Breakfast per person, per night: £69.00 (min 2 nights)
Lunch available: 1215–1415
Evening meal: 1900 (last orders 2145)

Bedrooms: 8 single, 27 double, 8 twin, 2 triple
Bathrooms: 45 en-suite
Parking: 220 spaces
Cards accepted: Mastercard, Visa, Switch/Delta, Amex, Diners, Eurocard

206 Lake Isle Hotel

★★ Silver Award

16 High Street East, Uppingham, Oakham, Leicestershire LE15 9PZ **Tel:** (01572) 822951 **Fax:** (01572) 824400

The personal touch we provide will make your stay extra special, starting with a decanter of sherry, home-made biscuits and fresh fruit in your room. Our AA 2 Rosette restaurant menues, changed weekly, offer fresh produce and a list of over 300 wines, with special 'Wine Dinners' held throughout the year. Whirlpool baths and cottage suites are available. The shops of this sleepy market town surround us, yet we are within a short drive of Rutland Water, Burghley House and many pretty villages.

Bed & Breakfast per night: single room from £45.00–£62.00; double room from £65.00–£85.00
Dinner, Bed & Breakfast per person, per night: £54.00–£60.00
Lunch available: 1200–1400

Evening meal: 1930 (last orders 2130)
Bedrooms: 1 single, 9 double, 2 twin
Bathrooms: 12 en-suite
Parking: 7 spaces
Cards accepted: Mastercard, Visa, Amex, Diners

207 St. Elizabeth's Cottage

◆◆◆◆

Woodman Lane, Clent, Stourbridge, West Midlands DY9 9PX **Tel:** (01562) 883883 **Fax:** (01562) 885034
E-mail: st_elizabeth_cot@btconnect.com

A beautiful country cottage in a tranquil setting, with six acres of landscaped garden plus outdoor heated swimming pool. Lovely country walks. Accommodation includes television in all rooms, plus tea/coffee making facilities. Residents' lounge available. Plenty of pubs and restaurants nearby. Easy access to the M5, M6, M42 and M40. 25 minutes from the NEC and Birmingham Airport. Destinations within easy reach include the Symphony Hall and Convention Centre in Birmingham, the Black Country Museum, Dudley, Stourbridge, Crystal factories and the Severn Valley Railway. No smoking. Pets welcome. Open all year.

Bed & Breakfast per night: single occupancy from £28.00–£30.00; double room from £55.00–£60.00

Bedrooms: 2 double, 1 twin
Bathrooms: 3 en-suite
Parking: plenty

208 Brockencote Hall

★ ★ ★ Gold Award

Chaddesley Corbett, Kidderminster, Worcestershire DY10 4PY **Tel:** (01562) 777876 **Fax:** (01562) 777872
Web: www.brockencotehall.com **E-mail:** info@brockencotehall.com

Nestling in the heart of the Worcestershire countryside, Brockencote Hall is set in seventy acres of private parkland with its own lake. It is the perfect place for relaxation. Proprietors Alison and Joseph Petitjean have created a charming Gallic oasis in the heart of England, combining traditional French comfort and friendliness with superb French cuisine. The hotel offers a choice of seventeen magnificent en-suite bedrooms, including one that has been especially designed to make stays comfortable for disabled guests.

Bed & Breakfast per night: single occupancy from £110.00–£130.00; double room from £135.00–£170.00
Dinner, Bed & Breakfast per person, per night: £87.50–£112.50 (min 2 sharing)
Lunch available: 1200–1330

Evening meal: 1900 (last orders 2130)
Bedrooms: 13 double, 3 twin, 1 triple
Bathrooms: 17 en-suite
Parking: 50 spaces
Cards accepted: Mastercard, Visa, Switch/Delta, Amex, Diners, Eurocard

209 Yew Tree House

◆ ◆ ◆ ◆ Silver Award

Norchard, Crossway Green, Hartlebury, Kidderminster, Worcestershire DY13 9SN **Tel:** (01299) 250921 **Fax:** (01299) 253472
Web: www.yewtreeworcester.co.uk **E-mail:** paul@knightp.swinternet.co.uk

An elegant Georgian farmhouse and 'cider house' cottage, both with a wealth of beams and shrouded in history. Built in 1754, stepping over the threshold of Yew Tree House is a fascinating mix of elegance and atmosphere. Peacefully tucked away but convenient to all motorway systems and sightseeing. Beautifully appointed en-suite rooms with television and hospitality tray. Tennis on-site by arrangement. Golf course and many good eating establishments nearby. Splendid breakfasts are provided.

Bed & Breakfast per night: single occupancy from £30.00–£35.00; double room from £50.00–£55.00

Bedrooms: 2 double, 2 twin, 1 family
Bathrooms: 5 en-suite
Parking: 7 spaces

210 Northleigh House

◆ ◆ ◆ ◆ Silver Award

Five Ways Road, Hatton, Warwick, Warwickshire CV35 7HZ **Tel:** (01926) 484203 or 07774 101894 **Fax:** (01926) 484006
Web: www.northleigh.co.uk

A personal welcome, the individually-designed rooms with colour co-ordinated furnishings, en-suite bathrooms, television, fridge, kettle and many thoughtful extras make this the perfect hide-away in rural Warwickshire. A full English breakfast is freshly cooked to suit guests' individual tastes. There are some excellent country pubs nearby, as well as the historic towns of Stratford-upon-Avon and Warwick, and the exhibition centres. Please call Sylvia Fenwick for brochures. No smoking. Visit our website for more information.

Bed & Breakfast per night: single room from £36.00–£43.00; double room from £52.00–£62.00

Bedrooms: 1 single, 5 double, 1 twin
Bathrooms: 7 en-suite
Parking: 8 spaces
Open: All year except January and December
Cards accepted: Mastercard, Visa

211 Victoria Lodge Hotel ◆◆◆◆

180 Warwick Road, Kenilworth, Warwickshire CV8 1HU **Tel:** (01926) 512020 **Fax:** (01926) 858703
Web: www.victorialodgehotel.co.uk **E-mail:** info@victorialodgehotel.co.uk

Victoria Lodge is a family-run hotel providing luxurious accommodation for those who appreciate the finer things in life and enjoy being looked after with care and courtesy. All the highly appointed bedrooms are en-suite. We have our own car park and a Victorian walled garden for guests' use. From its central Kenilworth location, the hotel is ideally situated for touring Shakespeare country and the Cotswolds. Victoria Lodge is a no smoking hotel.

Bed & Breakfast per night: single room from £40.00–£48.00; double room £59.00

Bedrooms: 1 single, 7 double, 1 twin
Bathrooms: 9 en-suite
Parking: 11 spaces
Cards accepted: Mastercard, Visa, Switch/Delta, Amex, Eurocard, JCB

212 Forth House ◆◆◆◆ Silver Award

44 High Street, Warwick CV34 4AX **Tel:** (01926) 401512 **Fax:** (01926) 490809
Web: www.forthhouseuk.co.uk **E-mail:** info@forthhouseuk.co.uk

Our rambling pre-Georgian family home, within the old town walls of Warwick, provides two peaceful guest suites hidden away at the back of the house. One ground floor suite opens onto the garden, whilst the other overlooks it. Both have private sitting and dining rooms. Warwick Castle is two minutes' walk away, as are the museums and restaurants. Breakfasts, English or continental, are at times agreed with our guests. Ideal location for holiday or business visits.

Bed & Breakfast per night: single occupancy from £40.00–£48.00; double room from £60.00–£70.00

Bedrooms: 1 double, 1 twin
Bathrooms: 2 en-suite
Parking: 1 space
Cards accepted: Mastercard, Visa, Switch/Delta

213 Stratford Victoria ★★★★ Silver Award

Arden Street, Stratford-upon-Avon, Warwickshire CV37 6QQ **Tel:** (01789) 271000 **Fax:** (01789) 271001
Web: www.marstonhotels.com **E-mail:** stratfordvictoria@marstonhotels.com

The Stratford Victoria provides all the facilities one would expect in a superior hotel. For special occasions the hotel has four-poster rooms and a luxurious suite. With ample free parking, the hotel is just a few minutes' walk to the town centre and its many attractions. All guests can enjoy free use of Stratford Manor's Leisure Centre during their stay or use our gymnasium and relax in our large whirlpool spa or our beauty salon.

Bed & Breakfast per night: single room from £105.00–£125.00; double room from £139.00–£179.00
Dinner, Bed & Breakfast per person, per night: £72.50–£92.50 (min 2 nights)
Lunch available: 1200–1400

Evening meal: 1800 (last orders 2145)
Bedrooms: 10 single, 47 double, 40 twin/family, 5 suites **Bathrooms:** 102 en-suite
Parking: 102 spaces
Cards accepted: Mastercard, Visa, Switch/Delta, Amex, Diners, Eurocard

At-a-glance symbols are explained on the flap inside the back cover

214 Payton Hotel

◆◆◆◆ Silver Award

6 John Street, Stratford-upon-Avon, Warwickshire CV37 6UB **Tel:** (01789) 266442 **Fax:** (01789) 294410
Web: www.payton.co.uk **E-mail:** info@payton.co.uk

Situated in the centre of Stratford-upon-Avon in a quiet exclusive location, yet only three minutes' walk to both the theatre and Shakespeare's birthplace. Experience the delights of a stay in this charming listed Georgian house where the caring proprietors – Peter and Brenda Wardle – will warmly welcome you. Tasteful, individually-furnished, cosy bedrooms include a king-size bed and a four-poster room. An excellent four-course breakfast is served until 10am at weekends. Special dietary requirements are welcomed.

Bed & Breakfast per night: single occupancy from £35.00–£60.00; double room from £56.00–£70.00 (min 2 nights Friday and Saturday)

Bedrooms: 3 double, 2 twin
Bathrooms: 4 en-suite, 1 room with private shower
Parking: 3 spaces
Cards accepted: Mastercard, Visa, Switch/Delta, Amex, Eurocard, JCB, Solo

---

Packwood Yew Garden

There is something rather surreal about the famous yew garden at Packwood House. On the manicured green lawn, smooth and flat as a billiard table, immaculately clipped yew bushes stand to attention. Seen from a distance they are strangely people-like, resembling a gathering of hooded figures, poised waiting, listening, ready to hurry off about their business. It is no wonder that a human symbolism has been attributed to them; the arrangement of 100 trees with its single large yew, 'the Master', standing atop a mound, surrounded by a 'multitude' of others, is said to represent the Sermon on the Mount. Further refinements to the scheme include a row of twelve on a raised terrace called 'the Apostles'.

Whether the original designer of the garden intended such a scheme is unknown, for references to the Sermon on the Mount idea do not appear in documents until the late 19th century, some 200 years after the first trees were planted. All that is known about the origins of the yew garden is that John Fetherston, who inherited Packwood in 1634, laid out at least part of it between 1650 and 1670, but it is possible that many of the trees were planted some time later.

It was probably John Fetherston's father, another John, who began the fine timber-framed mansion which still forms the core of the present house. Though less famous than the garden, this too is of considerable interest. During the course of the Fetherston family's ownership the original Tudor building underwent considerable alterations, in particular the addition of fine stables and outbuildings in the 1670s. Packwood left the Fetherston family in 1869 and was eventually bought by Alfred Ash, a wealthy industrialist, in 1905. Ash's son, Graham Baron Ash, lavished meticulous care on it, restoring it to match his vision of the perfect Tudor mansion. He was a punctiliously correct and obsessively tidy man who kept everything, including the gardens, in perfect order. The restoration of his house became his passion – until he tired of it and bought a moated castle in Sussex. Donating Packwood to the National Trust, he hoped it would be kept forever as he created it, and so it has been. It remains the kind of museum piece it always was in his lifetime, a perfect monument to the Tudor age. Packwood House (tel: 01564 782024) is 2 miles (3km) east of Hockley Heath on the A3400.

  Entries are cross referenced by number to the maps on pages 90–91

215 Hill House   ◆◆◆◆

Hampton Lucy, Warwick CV35 8AU **Tel:** (01789) 840329 **Fax:** (01789) 840329
Web: www.stratford-upon-avon.co.uk/hillhouse.htm **E-mail:** eliz_hunter@hotmail.com

Set in over two acres of its own grounds, this charming Georgian country house overlooks the Avon Valley. It offers a wonderfully peaceful stay in rural surroundings, with magnificent country views on all sides. Yet it is only eight minutes by car from both Stratford-upon-Avon and Warwick Castle and 30 minutes from Birmingham's NEC. This spacious accommodation is traditionally furnished to suit the period quality of this elegant home. A warm welcome is assured.

Bed & Breakfast per night: single room from £30.00–£35.00; double room from £45.00–£50.00

Bedrooms: 1 single/double, 1 twin/family
Bathrooms: 2 private
Parking: ample

---

216 Folly Farm Cottage   ◆◆◆◆ Gold Award

Ilmington, Nr Stratford-upon-Avon, Warwickshire CV36 4LJ **Tel:** (01608) 682425 **Fax:** (01608) 682425
Web: www.follyfarm.co.uk

A large country cottage in a delightful, undiscovered and quiet Cotswold village, with country pubs and pretty cottages. Within easy reach of Stratford-upon-Avon and Warwick. Offering outstanding B&B accommodation for that special occasion. Romantic en-suite double or four-poster rooms, with television, video, free video library and hospitality tray. As an added luxury, breakfast may be served in your room overlooking the pretty cottage gardens or in our new dining room. Luxury honeymoon self-catering apartment suite with double whirlpool bath also available.

Bed & Breakfast per night: double room from £56.00–£80.00

Bedrooms: 3 double
Bathrooms: 3 en-suite
Parking: 8 spaces

---

217 The Cottage Apartment   ◆◆◆◆

The Cottage, Gooms Hill, Abbots Morton Manor, Abbots Morton, Worcestershire WR7 4LT **Tel:** (01386) 792783 **Fax:** (01386) 792783

Whatever you seek from your holiday can be found right here. Our beautifully-appointed apartment is in the grounds of an old timber-framed cottage built c1455. It is set in a picturesque village steeped in history and surrounded by breathtaking countryside, pubs, walks and places of historical interest. Stratford, the Cotswolds and motorways are all within a 20 minute drive. A quality self-service continental breakfast is provided in the apartment. Reflexology and Indian head massage are available on site. Private swimming pool, horse riding, golf and more are close by.

Bed & Breakfast per night: single occupancy from £25.00–£30.00; double room from £40.00–£50.00

Bedrooms: 1 double
Bathrooms: 1 en-suite
Parking: 12 spaces

At-a-glance symbols are explained on the flap inside the back cover   **109**

218 The Paddock

◆◆◆◆ Gold Award

Shobdon, Leominster, Herefordshire HR6 9NQ **Tel:** (01568) 708176 **Fax:** (01568) 708829
E-mail: thepaddock@talk21.com

Situated in idyllic countryside bordering Wales, The Paddock offers a warm welcome, wonderful service and delightful en-suite accommodation. All the well-equipped rooms are on the ground floor and include a mechanical ventilation system and underfloor central heating. Guests have their own entrance, a comfortable lounge with satellite television, and a large garden and patio. We serve a substantial breakfast and offer a delicious three-course dinner. Visit The Paddock for a truly relaxing break. 🛧 **Category 3**

Bed & Breakfast per night: single occupancy from £32.00–£35.00; double room from £44.00–£48.00
Dinner, Bed & Breakfast per person, per night: £37.00–£50.00
Evening meal: by arrangement

Bedrooms: 4 double, 1 twin
Bathrooms: 5 en-suite
Parking: 10 spaces

219 The Steppes

◆◆◆◆◆ Silver Award

Ullingswick, Hereford HR1 3JG **Tel:** (01432) 820424 **Fax:** (01432) 820042
Web: www.steppeshotel.fsbusiness.co.uk **E-mail:** bookings@steppeshotel.fsbusiness.co.uk

This award-winning country house hotel with an intimate atmosphere abounds in antique furniture, inglenook fireplaces, oak beams and flag-stoned floors. The old dairy now houses a magnificent cobbled bar with Dickensian atmosphere, and a restored timber-framed barn and converted stable accommodate six large luxury en-suite bedrooms. Outstanding cordon bleu cuisine is served by candle light, and highly praised breakfasts come with an imaginative selection.

Bed & Breakfast per night: single occupancy £45.00–£50.00; double room from £80.00–£90.00
Dinner, Bed & Breakfast per person, per night: £66.00–£72.00
Evening meal: 1930 (last orders 2030)

Bedrooms: 5 double, 1 twin
Bathrooms: 6 en-suite
Parking: 8 spaces
Open: All year except January and December
Cards accepted: Mastercard, Visa, Switch/Delta, Amex, Eurocard

220 Felton House

◆◆◆◆ Gold Award

Felton, Hereford HR1 3PH **Tel:** (01432) 820366 **Fax:** (01432) 820366
Web: www.smoothhound.co.uk/hotels/felton.html **or** www.bandherefordshire.co.uk **E-mail:** bandb@ereal.net

Felton House is truly somewhere very special where you can relax on arrival with refreshments in the library, drawing room, conservatory or in the tranquil four-acre gardens. Eat an excellent evening meal in a local inn, then sleep in a historic bed and awake refreshed to enjoy, in a superb Victorian dining room, the breakfast you have chosen from a wide selection of Herefordshire and vegetarian dishes. The highest levels of quality, hospitality and service just 20 minutes by car from Hereford, Leominster, Bromyard and Ledbury. See our website for more information. Winner Herefordshire Best Breakfast 2001.

Bed & Breakfast per night: single room £25.00; double room £50.00

Bedrooms: 1 single, 2 double, 1 twin
Bathrooms: 2 en-suite, 2 private
Parking: 6 spaces

221 Bredon View Guest House

◆◆◆◆ Silver Award

Village Street, Harvington, Evesham, Worcestershire WR11 5NQ **Tel:** (01386) 871484 **Fax:** (01386) 871484
Web: www.bredonview.heartuk.net **E-mail:** b.v.circa1898@bushinternet.com

Bredon View is a Victorian house set in the heart of the 'Blossom Valley' – the fruit growing area of the Vale of Evesham. The spring blossom is a wonderful sight and attracts many visitors. Our en-suite bedrooms – one twin and two double, of which one has a four-poster bed – are tastefully decorated and equipped with hospitality tray, combi television, clock/radio, hairdryer and iron. We have a comfortable guest lounge and secure parking.

Bed & Breakfast per night: double room from £40.00–£50.00

Bedrooms: 2 double, 1 twin
Bathrooms: 3 en-suite
Parking: 3 spaces

222 Wood Norton Hall and Conference Centre

★★★★ Gold Award

Evesham, Worcestershire WR11 4YB **Tel:** (01386) 420007 **Fax:** (01386) 420190
Web: www.woodnortonhall.co.uk **E-mail:** woodnortonhall.info@bbc.co.uk

Overlooking the Vale of Evesham, this Grade II listed hotel is set in 170 acres of gardens and grounds. There are a number of special leisure breaks available and the hotel is perfectly situated to explore the Cotswolds, as well as being centrally located between Cheltenham and Stratford-upon-Avon. The Hall itself boasts many original features, including beautiful ornate oak panelling throughout, and Le Duc's Restaurant has earned an outstanding reputation together with 2 AA Rosettes.

Bed & Breakfast per night: single occupancy from £95.00–£160.00; double room from £145.00–£240.00
Dinner, Bed & Breakfast per person, per night: from £132.00
Lunch available: 1200–1400

Evening meal: 1900 (last orders 2200)
Bedrooms: 45 double/ twin
Bathrooms: 45 en-suite
Parking: 250 spaces
Cards accepted: Mastercard, Visa, Switch/Delta, Amex, Diners

223 The Mill at Harvington

★★ Silver Award

Anchor Lane, Harvington, Evesham, Worcestershire WR11 8PA **Tel:** (01386) 870688 **Fax:** (01386) 870688

Friendly, owner-run hotel, sensitively converted from a beautiful Georgian house and former baking mill. Situated on the banks of the River Avon in acres of private parkland, our hotel offers peace, tranquillity and a view over the garden and river towards the morning sun from every bedroom. Find gentle elegance without formality, good food without fussiness (AA 2 Rosettes), and friendly staff who will help you relax immediately.

Bed & Breakfast per night: single occupancy from £66.00–£85.00; double room from £99.00–£149.00
Dinner, Bed & Breakfast per person, per night: £55.00–£78.00 (min 2 nights)
Lunch available: 1200–1400

Evening meal: 1900 (last orders 2045)
Bedrooms: 16 double, 5 twin
Bathrooms: 21 en-suite **Parking:** 45 spaces
Cards accepted: Mastercard, Visa, Switch/Delta, Amex, Diners, JCB, Maestro, Visa Electron, Solo

224 Montgomery House ◆◆◆◆

12 St Owen Street, Hereford, HR1 2PL **Tel:** (01432) 351454 **Fax:** (01432) 344463
E-mail: lizforbes@lineone.net

Montgomery House – discreet comfort in the heart of Hereford. Elegant accommodation in a Grade II listed Georgian town house. Close to the Cathedral and town centre, with many restaurants, pubs, bars and cafés within walking distance. Two double en-suite rooms. Huge, comfortable beds with Egyptian cotton sheets and blankets. Fine toiletries, hospitality trays offering a selection of teas and cafetiere coffee. Sandwich menu and picnic lunches available. Full English breakfast includes award-winning local produce or continental alternative. Non-smoking. Open all year. Off-street parking.

Bed & Breakfast per night: single occupancy from £40.00–£45.00; double room from £50.00–£55.00

Bedrooms: 2 double
Bathrooms: 2 en-suite
Parking: 2 spaces

---

225 Wyche Keep Country House ◆◆◆◆ Silver Award

22 Wyche Road, Malvern, Worcestershire WR14 4EG **Tel:** (01684) 567018 **Fax:** (01684) 892304
Web: www.jks.org/wychekeep **E-mail:** wychekeep@aol.com

Wyche Keep is a stunning arts and crafts-style house, perched high on the Malvern Hills, built by the family of Sir Stanley Baldwin, Prime Minister, to enjoy the spectacular sixty-mile views, and having a long history of elegant entertaining. Three large luxury double suites, including a four-poster. Traditional English cooking is a speciality and guests can savour memorable four-course candlelit dinners. Fully licensed. Magical setting with private parking. A no smoking establishment.

Bed & Breakfast per night: single occupancy from £40.00–£45.00; double room from £60.00–£70.00
Dinner, Bed & Breakfast per person, per night: £50.00–£55.00
Evening meal: 1930 (last orders 2000)

Bedrooms: 1 double, 2 twin
Bathrooms: 3 en-suite
Parking: 6 spaces

---

226 Colwall Park ★★★ Silver Award

Colwall, Malvern, Worcestershire WR13 6QG **Tel:** (01684) 540000 **Fax:** (01684) 540847
Web: www.colwall.com **E-mail:** hotel@colwall.com

Situated on the sunny western slopes of the beautiful Malvern Hills, the hotel provides an ideal setting for a relaxing break in unspoilt countryside on the edge of the Cotswolds. Winner of the Courtesy and Care Award for 1999/2000, Colwall Park provides a country house style whilst situated in a rural village. The award-winning restaurant serves English cuisine at its best, using fresh ingredients. Cheltenham, Worcester, Hereford and Gloucester are all within 20 miles.

Bed & Breakfast per night: single room from £65.00–£80.00; double room from £110.00–£150.00
Dinner, Bed & Breakfast per person, per night: £69.95–£79.95 (min 2 nights)
Lunch available: 1200–1400
Evening meal: 1930 (last orders 2100)

Bedrooms: 3 single, 9 double, 7 twin, 2 triple, 2 family
Bathrooms: 23 en-suite
Parking: 40 spaces
Cards accepted: Mastercard, Visa, Switch/ Delta, Amex

Entries are cross referenced by number to the maps on pages 90–91

227 The Cottage in the Wood Hotel

★★★ Silver Award

Holywell Road, Malvern Wells, Malvern, Worcestershire WR14 4LG **Tel:** (01684) 575859 **Fax:** (01684) 560662
Web: www.cottageinthewood.co.uk **E-mail:** proprietor@cottageinthewood.co.uk

Stunningly set high on the Malvern Hills, looking across thirty miles of the Severn Plain to the horizon formed by the Cotswold Hills. Owned and run by the Pattin family for fourteen years, the aim is to provide a relaxing and peaceful base from which to tour this area of outstanding natural beauty. The restaurant provides exceptional food backed by an extensive wine list of over six hundred bins. The daily half board price is based on a minimum two-night stay, and the weekly price offers seven nights for the price of six. Special breaks all week, all year. AA 2 Rosettes.

Bed & Breakfast per night: single occupancy from £77.00–£87.00; double room from £95.00–£150.00
Dinner, Bed & Breakfast per person, per night: £63.00–£100.00 (min 2 nights, 2 sharing)
Lunch available: 1230–1400

Evening meal: 1900 (last orders 2100)
Bedrooms: 16 double, 4 twin
Bathrooms: 20 en-suite
Parking: 40 spaces
Cards accepted: Mastercard, Visa, Switch/ Delta, Amex, Eurocard, JCB, Visa Electron

228 Holdfast Cottage Hotel

★★ Silver Award

Marlbank Road, Little Malvern, Malvern, Worcestershire WR13 6NA **Tel:** (01684) 310288 **Fax:** (01684) 311117
Web: www.holdfast-cottage.co.uk **E-mail:** holdcothot@aol.com

Pretty wisteria-covered country house hotel, set in two acres of gardens and private woodland, tucked into the foot of the Malvern Hills. Highly recommended for its freshly-prepared menu which changes daily and uses the best local and seasonal produce. Delightful dining room and bar. Cosy lounge with log fire. Enchanting en-suite bedrooms are individually furnished. A personal welcome plus care and attention throughout your stay is assured by the resident proprietors.

Bed & Breakfast per night: single room £50.00; double room from £86.00–£92.00
Dinner, Bed & Breakfast per person, per night: £66.00 (min 2 nights)
Evening meal: 1900 (last orders 2100)

Bedrooms: 1 single, 5 double, 2 twin
Bathrooms: 8 en-suite
Parking: 20 spaces
Cards accepted: Mastercard, Visa, Switch/Delta, Visa Electron, Solo

229 Ryall House Farm

◆◆◆◆

Ryall, Upton-upon-Severn, Worcester WR8 0PL **Tel:** (01684) 592013 **Fax:** (01684) 592013

A warm and friendly welcome awaits you at this lovely Georgian farmhouse. The bedrooms have all recently been stylishly refurbished. All are en-suite with colour television, tea/coffee making facilities and with many extras provided. We are ideally situated in the quiet village of Ryall, just on the edge of Upton-on-Severn, within three miles of junction 1 of the M50 and junction 8 of the M5, and close to the Three Counties Showground.

Bed & Breakfast per night: single room £25.00; double room £45.00

Bedrooms: 1 single, 2 double
Bathrooms: 3 en-suite
Parking: 3 spaces

230 Myrtle House ◆◆◆◆

High Street, Mickleton, Chipping Campden, Gloucestershire GL55 6SA **Tel:** (01386) 430032 or 07971 938085
Web: www.myrtlehouse.co.uk **E-mail:** kate@myrtlehouse.co.uk

An elegant Georgian house conveniently situated in the village of Mickleton, on the edge of the Cotswolds and only 7 miles from Stratford-upon-Avon. Our 5 en-suite bedrooms are individually decorated and are non-smoking, although we allow smoking in the comfortable residents' lounge. We are the ideal base for Hidcote and Kiftsgate Gardens which are just 1.5 miles away. A full English breakfast with freshly baked croissants will set you up for a day of walking, cycling, touring or shopping.

Bed & Breakfast per night: single occupancy from £37.50; double room from £55.00–£75.00
Evening meal: by arrangement

Bedrooms: 2 double, 2 twin, 1 triple
Bathrooms: 5 en-suite
Parking: 3 spaces
Cards accepted: Mastercard, Visa, Switch/Delta, Eurocard, Visa Electron, Solo

---

231 Nineveh Farm ◆◆◆◆ Silver Award

Campden Road, Mickleton, Chipping Campden, Gloucestershire GL55 6PS **Tel:** (01386) 438923
Web: www.ninevehfarm.co.uk **E-mail:** stay@ninevehfarm.co.uk

A 200 year-old farmhouse (on a non-working farm), with flagstone floors, beams and antique furnishing. Log fire in winter in guest sitting room. One and a half acres of gardens surrounded by open countryside. Ideally situated for touring the Cotswolds and for visiting Stratford-upon-Avon. Evening meals available from pubs and restaurant in Mickleton village (10 minutes walk). Hidcote Manor Gardens close by. Other National Trust properties, golf and horse riding within a short drive. Free loan of bicycles.

Bed & Breakfast per night: double room from £50.00–£55.00

Bedrooms: 2 double, 2 twin, 1 family
Bathrooms: 5 en-suite
Parking: 6 spaces
Cards accepted: Mastercard, Visa, Switch/Delta

---

232 Dormy House ★★★ Silver Award

Willersey Hill, Broadway, Worcestershire WR12 7LF **Tel:** (01386) 852711 **Fax:** (01386) 858636
Web: www.dormyhouse.co.uk **E-mail:** reservations@dormyhouse.co.uk

The 17th-century Dormy House is ideally located for visiting the picturesque villages of the Cotswolds as well as Shakespeare's Stratford-upon-Avon. Enjoy the beautifully appointed rooms, superb restaurant and high standard of cuisine and service. Our croquet lawn, putting green, sauna/steam room, gym, games room and nature trail offer the chance to combine leisure with pleasure. Pamper yourself with a Classic Dormy Break midweek or weekends in the Heart of England.

Bed & Breakfast per night: single occupancy from £113.00; double room from £156.00–£205.00
Dinner, Bed & Breakfast per person, per night: £97.00–£118.00 (min 2 nights, 2 sharing)
Lunch available: bar meals 1200–1400 daily, restaurant 1200–1400 Sunday

Evening meal: 1900 (last orders 2130)
Bedrooms: 2 single, 14 double, 26 twin, 3 suites
Bathrooms: 49 en-suite
Parking: 90 spaces
Cards accepted: Mastercard, Visa, Switch/Delta, Amex, Diners, Eurocard, JCB, Maestro, Visa Elect

---

233 Three Ashes House

Ledbury Road, Newent, Gloucestershire GL18 1DE **Tel:** (01531) 820226 **Fax:** (01531) 820226
E-mail: jrichard.cockroft@tinyworld.co.uk

Three Ashes House offers excellent en-suite accommodation. Centrally heated throughout, and furnished and equipped to a high standard. All rooms have colour television, hairdryer, clock/radio and tea/coffee making facilities. There is ample private parking and a guest lounge. Three Ashes sits in three acres of grounds with views over open countryside. The Wye Valley, Forest of Dean and Malvern Hills are all within easy distance, making it an ideal centre for exploring and walking in west Gloucestershire and Herefordshire.

Bed & Breakfast per night: single room from £21.00–£25.00; double room from £40.00–£44.00

Bedrooms: 2 single, 2 double, 1 twin
Bathrooms: 4 en-suite, 1 private
Parking: 10 spaces

---

234 Isbourne Manor House ◆◆◆◆◆ Gold Award

Castle Street, Winchcombe, Cheltenham, Gloucestershire GL54 5JA **Tel:** (01242) 602281 **Fax:** (01242) 602281
Web: www.isbourne-manor.co.uk **E-mail:** felicity@isbourne-manor.co.uk

This beautiful listed house is quietly situated within attractive gardens which are bordered by the River Isbourne. We are adjacent to the lovely grounds of Sudeley Castle and only two minutes' walk away from both stunning Cotswold countryside and the centre of historic Winchcombe. All rooms are decorated and furnished to the highest standard, combining modern comfort with family antiques and beautiful fabrics. Guests have the sole use of two elegant reception rooms, private parking and garden.

Bed & Breakfast per night: double room from £60.00–£80.00

Bedrooms: 2 double, 1 twin
Bathrooms: 2 en-suite, 1 private
Parking: 5 spaces

---

235 Guiting Guesthouse ◆◆◆◆◆ Gold Award

Post Office Lane, Guiting Power, Cheltenham, Gloucestershire GL54 5TZ **Tel:** (01451) 850470 **Fax:** (01451) 850034
Web: www.freespace.virgin.net/guiting.guest_house/ **E-mail:** guiting@virgin.net

The house is a delightful and carefully-restored 16th-century Cotswold stone farmhouse. Everywhere there are exposed beams, inglenook fireplaces, open fires and polished solid elm floors from the Wychwood forest. Three rooms have four-poster beds and are en-suite, whilst the other room has totally private facilities. Television and generously-filled hospitality tray in each room. Access to the guesthouse is available at all times. Delicious evening meals, served by candle light, are prepared and presented by the hosts (with the exception of Sunday and Monday). 2 AA Egg Cups.

Bed & Breakfast per night: single occupancy £35.00; double room £58.00
Dinner, Bed & Breakfast per person, per night: £45.00–£47.00
Evening meal: 1845

Bedrooms: 3 double, 1 twin
Bathrooms: 3 en-suite, 1 private
Parking: 4 spaces
Cards accepted: Mastercard, Visa, Switch/Delta, Eurocard, JCB

At-a-glance symbols are explained on the flap inside the back cover

236 Tally Ho Guesthouse ◆◆◆◆

1 Tally Ho Lane, Guiting Power, Cheltenham, Gloucestershire GL54 5TY **Tel:** (01451) 850186
Web: www.cotswolds-bedandbreakfast.co.uk **E-mail:** tallyhobb@aol.com

In the heart of the north Cotswold countryside, family-run Tally Ho Guest House is waiting to welcome you. An idyllic location for visiting Cotswold attractions, touring and walking. Luxury furnished accommodation situated in the picturesque village of Guiting Power, with two local inns serving home-cooked evening meals. Luxurious en-suite rooms have super king/double and twin beds with television, well stocked hospitality tray etc. Large guest television lounge. Private parking. Open all year.

Bed & Breakfast per night: single occupancy from £25.00–£30.00; double room from £40.00–£50.00

Bedrooms: 2 double/twin
Bathrooms: 2 en-suite (showers)
Parking: 4 spaces

The Cotswolds

At the heart of England lie the Cotswolds. And at the very soul of the Cotswolds lies stone: oolitic limestone to be precise. This glorious, rich material, laid down beneath ancient seas, has formed the very essence of the area from the neolithic (New Stone Age) period until the present day. Our distant ancestors revered the strong, workable blocks they hewed from their quarries. They created circles of mystical importance – such as the Rollright Stones near Long Compton – and long barrows for their noble dead. Hetty Pegler's Tump, near Stroud, and Belas Knap, south of Winchcombe, are fine examples of the 70 or so within the Cotswolds.

Later generations have lived on, in and beside the stone. The Romans used it to construct majestic roads (much of the Foss Way, Ermin Way and Akeman Street are now quiet lanes ideal for unhurried exploration) that radiated from Corinium (Cirencester), then the second most important town in this outpost of empire. Now it offers quality shopping, convivial dining and, at the Corinium Museum, edification for the mind. Some Romans lived in style, as visitors to the museum and to Chedworth Roman villa, complete with central-heating system and mosaic floors, can see. The Saxons founded many of today's towns and villages. Winchcombe and Malmesbury, where part of the once-glorious abbey still stands, were important settlements with much of interest for the modern-day visitor.

But what we think of as quintessential Cotswolds – mellow honey-coloured cottages huddling round a grand church and with a perfect manor – owes most to medieval times. Almost every village has reminders of the period. A surprising number of buildings date back to the 13th, 14th and 15th centuries, when the region's prosperity, founded on the hardy Cotswold sheep, was at its height. Farmhouses became bigger and grander, and tithe barns – often a perfect fusion of grace and function, as at Great Coxwell, near Faringdon, and Bredon – were needed for storage. But most importantly, churches were enlarged or built anew on the grand scale. The best of these marvellous 'wool' churches includes Chipping Campden, Northleach, Cirencester (shown above), Fairford and Lechlade. A beautifully pinnacled tower, an especially fine collection of memorial brasses, a porch which is a stonemason's tour de force, the most complete medieval stained-glass in Britain, and a marvellous setting by the infant Thames, respectively, individual highlights.

237 Aston House

◆◆◆◆

Broadwell, Moreton-in-Marsh, Gloucestershire GL56 0TJ **Tel:** (01451) 830475 or 07773 452037 (mobile)
Web: www.netcomuk.co.uk/~nmfa/aston_house.html **E-mail:** fja@netcomuk.co.uk

Guests are welcomed to our home in this quiet village, just 1.5 miles from Stow-on-the-Wold and central for touring the Cotswold villages and surrounding towns. All rooms (one on the ground floor) are comfortably furnished and have tea/coffee making facilities, radio, colour television, armchairs and electric blankets for those colder nights. Bedtime drinks and biscuits are provided. Good English breakfast. No smoking. Pub within walking distance.

Bed & Breakfast per night: double room from £46.00–£50.00

Bedrooms: 2 double, 1 twin
Bathrooms: 2 en-suite, 1 private
Parking: 3 spaces
Open: All year except January and December

Then, in the 16th century, Henry VIII dissolved the monasteries and redistributed their wealth to his cronies' coffers. One result was the rise of the country house. If the area has the architecture of the modest cottage to a fine art, it is no surprise that on a larger canvas the results are even more stupendous. Owlpen Manor (near Dursley) and Chavenage House (near Tetbury) date from the Elizabethan era, while Chastleton House (recently acquired by the National Trust, near Moreton-in-the Marsh) and Stanway (north-east of Winchcombe) are both the epitome of Jacobean taste. Late 17th-century style lives on at Dyrham Park (another National Trust property, north of Bath). One of the most singular of all houses is Sezincote, at Bourton-on-the-Hill. This eye-opening extravaganza was remodelled in 1800 in Indian style, complete with dome, and was the inspiration for the Indianisation of the Brighton Pavilion.

Many of these magnificent properties are set off by sumptuous gardens, another Cotswold speciality. Two nestling together in the north of the region are Hidcote Manor, where the gardens are conceived as a series of separate outdoor rooms, and Kiftsgate Court, at its best in June when the myriad roses impart their heady scent to the summer breeze. Further south are the world-famous Arboretum at Westonbirt (best in late October for blazing autumnal shades), Barnsley House Garden for herbaceous borders to die for, and Painswick, where the Rococo garden is a magnet for those with a bent for horticultural history. If you're here on the Sunday on or following 19 September, you could join in the Clipping Ceremony, when the

congregation, holding hands, encircles the church. At Westbury Court (Westbury-on-Severn) is a 17th-century formal Dutch water garden.

In the late 19th century, William Morris, won over by the Cotswolds, set up home at Kelmscott Manor (occasionally open, near Bibury). An influential proponent of craftsmanship rather than the mass production of the Victorian age, he attracted like-minded artists and artisans to join him. The nearby village of Kelmscot has many reminders of the Arts and Crafts movement they began, while at Selsley the church is a monument to their achievements and to those of the allied Pre-Raphaelite Brotherhood.

For Morris, Bibury was 'the most beautiful village in England'. He may have been right, though many another Cotwold village would fancy its chances too. And so, beyond all the magnificent scenery that lies between them – the blustery tops of Cleeve and Bredon Hills, the ancient woodland near Sapperton, the Devil's Chimney (a rock pinnacle jutting out of Leckhampton Hill, near Cheltenham) – it is the villages that we love. Shaped by the centuries, carved out of the living stone, encrusted with the patina of time and a golden lichen, they are the embodiment of all that is right in the land. Spend a decade exploring them and there will be more to admire tomorrow. A list of ten, unscientifically selected, is: Bibury, Bourton-on-the-Water, Broadway, Burford, Castle Coombe, the Colns, the Duntisbournes, the Slaughters and Stanton.

The Cotswolds extend eastward into Oxfordshire – see feature on page 211.

238 Grapevine Hotel ★★★ Silver Award

Sheep Street, Stow-on-the-Wold, Gloucestershire GL54 1AU **Tel:** (01451) 830344 **Fax:** (01451) 832278
Web: www.vines.co.uk **E-mail:** enquiries@vines.co.uk

An historic 17th-century award-winning hotel in the antiques centre of the Cotswolds. The Grapevine has a country house feel, with each bedroom individually designed and furnished with antiques; rich warm fabrics complement the mellowed Cotswold stone. The romantic conservatory is home to the historic Hamburg vine, which canopies the restaurant and gives the hotel its name. Consistent, fine cuisine and excellent service have earned the hotel its AA Rosettes for the fourth consecutive year.

Bed & Breakfast per night: single occupancy from £73.50; double room from £110.00
Dinner, Bed & Breakfast per person, per night: from £64.00 (min 2 nights at weekends)
Lunch available: 1200–1430
Evening meal: 1900 (last orders 2130)

Bedrooms: 1 single, 7 double, 12 twin, 2 triple
Bathrooms: 22 en-suite
Parking: 23 spaces
Cards accepted: Mastercard, Visa, Amex, Diners, JCB

239 The Dial House Hotel ★★ Silver Award

The Chestnuts, Bourton-on-the-Water, Gloucestershire GL54 2AN **Tel:** (01451) 822244 **Fax:** (01451) 810126
Web: www.dialhousehotel.com **E-mail:** info@dialhousehotel.com

Built in 1698 of Cotswold stone, The Dial House is one of the oldest buildings in Bourton. Privately owned and run, the service is second to none. Beautifully furnished in traditional English country house style. All rooms are en-suite, some with antique four-poster beds. Dine in style in our award-winning restaurant, relax by the roaring log fire in winter or in our 1.5 acre garden in summer. Ample parking for residents.

Bed & Breakfast per night: single room from £45.00–£57.00; double room from £90.00–£114.00
Dinner, Bed & Breakfast per person, per night: £75.00 (min 2 nights)
Lunch available: 1200–1415
Evening meal: 1845 (last orders 2115)

Bedrooms: 1 single, 10 double/twin, 1 family room
Bathrooms: 12 en-suite
Parking: 15 spaces
Cards accepted: Mastercard, Visa, Switch/Delta, Eurocard, Visa Electron, Solo

240 Kings Head Inn and Restaurant ◆◆◆◆

The Green, Bledington, Oxford, Gloucestershire OX7 6XQ **Tel:** (01608) 658365 **Fax:** (01608) 658902
Web: www.kingsheadinn.net **E-mail:** kingshead@orr-ewing.com

History comes hot buttered at this quintessential 15th-century Cotswold inn which nestles on the village green, complete with brook and attendant ducks. The inn has always served as a hostelry and indeed Prince Rupert of the Rhine supposedly lodged here prior to the battle of Stow in 1642. To this day much of the medieval character remains with exposed stone walls, an inglenook fireplace, settles and pews. Delightful bedrooms complement with full facilities and thoughtful extras. Our award-winning restaurant offers bar fayre, table d'hôte and à la carte. Excellent value and ideal for exploring many attractions – Blenheim, Warwick, Stratford, Oxford etc.

Bed & Breakfast per night: single occupancy from £45.00–£75.00; double room from £60.00– £90.00
Lunch available: 1200–1400
Evening meal: 1900 (last orders 2200)

Bedrooms: 10 double, 2 twin
Bathrooms: 12 en-suite
Parking: 60 spaces
Cards accepted: Mastercard, Visa, Switch/Delta, Amex, Eurocard

241 The Swan Hotel

★★★ **Gold Award**

Bibury, Cirencester, Gloucestershire GL7 5NW **Tel:** (01285) 740695 **Fax:** (01285) 740473
Web: www.swanhotel.co.uk **E-mail:** swanhot1@swanhotel-cotswolds.co.uk

A luxurious hotel with cosy parlours, elegant dining room, sumptuous bedrooms (a few with four-poster beds) and lavish bathrooms (some with large jacuzzi baths). Our head chef, Shaun Naen, presents a regularly changing menu in a modern European style which is occasionally influenced by oriental cuisine. An ideal base for touring the Cotswolds, visiting Shakespeare's Stratford, Roman Bath, antiques in Burford and the Oxford colleges. Take pleasure in our private garden on the banks of the River Coln – enjoy the ambience or fish for your own trout. Licensed for weddings. Ideal venue for special occasions. **Category 3**

Bed & Breakfast per night: single occupancy from £125.00–£160.00; double room from £180.00–£260.00
Dinner, Bed & Breakfast per person, per night: £110.00–£150.00
Lunch available: 1200–1430

Evening meal: 1930 (last orders 2130)
Bedrooms: 15 double, 4 twin, 1 family
Bathrooms: 20 en-suite
Parking: 30 spaces
Cards accepted: Mastercard, Visa, Switch/Delta, Amex, Diners, Eurocard, JCB, Visa Electron, Solo

242 Coln Cottage

 ◆◆◆◆

Coln Court, Bibury, Cirencester, Gloucestershire GL7 5NL **Tel:** (01285) 740314 **Fax:** (01285) 740314

Converted from 17th-century listed buildings in the landscaped grounds of the owner's house, these character properties offer a unique blend of accommodation, and feature a deluxe en-suite room for bed and breakfast. Located in a conservation area in the renowned riverside village of Bibury, within easy walking distance of the village pub and two riverside hotels. Shops, the village store, Mill Museum and Trout Farm are easily accessible. Nearby attractions include Cotswold Water Park, racing, golf, fishing, riding, historic houses and gardens.

Bed & Breakfast per night: single occupancy from £40.00–£45.00; double room from £55.00–£65.00

Bedrooms: 1 double/twin
Bathrooms: 1 en-suite
Parking: 10 spaces

243 Walnut Tree Cottage Hotel

 ◆◆◆◆

Symonds Yat West, Ross-on-Wye, Herefordshire HR9 6BN **Tel:** (01600) 890828 **Fax:** (01600) 890828
Web: www.walnuttreehotel.co.uk **E-mail:** enquiries@walnuttreehotel.co.uk

A small, family-run, Wales Tourist Board 3-Star hotel, we offer peace and quiet in a relaxed, informal atmosphere. Stunning views of the Wye river and forest. Two lounges and a conservatory. Wood burning stove. Walks from our doorstep. We specialise in Italian-based cuisine, using mainly home-made organic and local produce whenever possible. All rooms are en-suite and furnished to a high standard. A non-smoking hotel.

Bed & Breakfast per night: single occupancy from £41.00–£45.00; double room from £62.00–£74.00
Dinner, Bed & Breakfast per person, per night: £52.00–£58.00
Evening meal: 1930 (last orders 2130)

Bedrooms: 3 double, 2 twin
Bathrooms: 5 en-suite
Parking: 12 spaces
Open: February–December
Cards accepted: Mastercard, Visa, Switch/Delta

244 Norton House

◆◆◆◆ Gold Award

Whitchurch, Ross-on-Wye, Herefordshire HR9 6DJ **Tel:** (01600) 890046 **Fax:** (01600) 890045
Web: www.norton-house.com **E-mail:** jackson@osconwhi.source.co.uk

A 17th-century Grade II listed former farmhouse, which has been beautifully renovated with pine shutters and doors, oak beams, flagstone floors and inglenook fireplaces. It oozes old fashioned charm but offers all the modern comfort our guests could wish for. Delicious Aga-cooked meals served by candle light make for a romantic escape. Situated in the beautiful Wye Valley, a short walk from the River Wye and a five minute drive from Yat Rock, making it an ideal touring centre.

Bed & Breakfast per night: single occupancy from £28.00–£32.00; double room from £44.00–£48.00
Dinner, Bed & Breakfast per person, per night: £34.00–£36.00
Evening meal: 1930

Bedrooms: 2 double, 1 twin
Bathrooms: 3 en-suite
Parking: 3 spaces

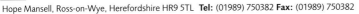

245 The Old Rectory

◆◆◆◆

Hope Mansell, Ross-on-Wye, Herefordshire HR9 5TL **Tel:** (01989) 750382 **Fax:** (01989) 750382
E-mail: rectory@mansell.wyenet.co.uk

An attractive Georgian house in peaceful surroundings in hills bordering the River Wye and the Forest of Dean, designated as an Area of Outstanding Natural Beauty. The house is surrounded by mature gardens, a small orchard and has an all-weather tennis court. The comfortable rooms have period furniture. A wealth of local information is provided and the library includes a wide selection of reference and general reading books for all ages. Families are welcomed.

Bed & Breakfast per night: single occupancy £24.50; double room £49.00

Bedrooms: 2 double, 1 twin
Bathrooms: 1 private, 1 shared
Parking: 4 spaces

246 The Old Coach House

◆◆◆◆ Silver Award

Lower Catesby, Daventry, Northamptonshire NN11 6LF **Tel:** (01327) 310390 **Fax:** (01327) 312220
Web: www.lowercatesby.co.uk **E-mail:** coachhouse@lowercatesby.co.uk

The Old Coach House is a former Victorian coach house – now an elegantly refurbished family home with south and west facing terraces, gardens, private lake, and lawn for croquet. Lying amidst beautiful open countryside, yet within 20 minutes of junction 16 (Northampton) of the M1 and junction 11 (Banbury) of the M40, and so convenient for Althorp, Stoneleigh, Silverstone or historic Warwick and Leamington Spa. A special place to relax in comfortable, spacious surroundings with idyllic views.

Bed & Breakfast per night: single occupancy from £35.00–£45.00; double room from £60.00–£70.00

Bedrooms: 1 double, 1 twin
Bathrooms: 1 en-suite, 1 private
Parking: ample

247 North End Barns
◆◆◆◆ Silver Award

North End Farm, Risley Road, Bletsoe, Bedford, Bedfordshire MK44 1QT **Tel:** (01234) 781320 **Fax:** (01234) 781320

North End Barns is on a working arable and sheep farm. A superb barn conversion in quiet north Bedfordshire countryside providing en-suite rooms with television and tea and coffee making facilities. Breakfast is served in the 16th-century farmhouse. Tennis court available along with miles of country walks. We are just off the main A6, north of Bedford, near the village of Bletsoe. There are several excellent pubs and restaurants in the area and lots of places of interest.

Bed & Breakfast per night: single occupancy from £25.00–£27.50; double room from £45.00–£50.00

Bedrooms: 4 twin
Bathrooms: 4 en-suite
Parking: 8 spaces
Cards accepted: Mastercard, Visa, Switch/Delta, Amex, Eurocard, JCB, Solo

248 The Grove
◆◆◆◆

Collins Lane, Heacham, King's Lynn, Norfolk PE31 7DZ **Tel:** (01485) 570513
Web: www.leisure.ic24.net/heacham/pictures/accommodation_01.htm **E-mail:** tm.shannon@virgin.net

The Grove is a charming, restored Victorian house located in the quiet seaside village of Heacham, two miles from Hunstanton. It is conveniently located for the beaches and Norfolk Lavender, as well as many other attractions such as Sandringham, RSPB nature reserves, Holkham Hall and several golf courses. You will feel welcome on your arrival, with refreshments in the guests' lounge or in the garden. Breakfasts are delicious, using eggs from our own hens.

Bed & Breakfast per night: double room from £50.00–£55.00 (min 2 nights, July and August)

Bedrooms: 3 double
Bathrooms: 2 en-suite, 1 private
Parking: 5 spaces

249 Felbrigg Lodge
◆◆◆◆◆ Gold Award

Aylmerton, Norfolk NR11 8RA **Tel:** (01263) 837588 **Fax:** (01263) 838012
Web: www.felbrigglodge.co.uk **E-mail:** info@felbrigglodge.co.uk

Set in beautiful countryside two miles from the coast, Felbrigg Lodge is hidden in eight acres of spectacular woodland gardens. Time has stood still since Edwardian ladies came here in their carriages to take tea and play croquet. Great care has been taken to preserve this atmosphere with large comfortable en-suite rooms all luxuriously decorated and with every facility. This is a true haven of peace and tranquillity. A nature lover's paradise. Delicious candlelit dinners and copious breakfast. Indoor heated pool and gym.

Bed & Breakfast per night: single occupancy from £60.00–£90.00; double room from £80.00–£110.00; suite £140.00
Dinner, Bed & Breakfast per person, per night: £66.50–£96.50
Lunch available: Packed lunches by arrangement

Evening meal: 1945
Bedrooms: 4 double
Bathrooms: 4 en-suite
Parking: 8 spaces
Cards accepted: Mastercard, Visa

250 Wayford Bridge Hotel

★★★ Silver Award

Wayford Bridge, Stalham, Norwich, NR12 9LL **Tel:** (01692) 582414 **Fax:** (01692) 581109
Web: www.wayford-bridge-hotel.co.uk **E-mail:** wayford-bridge-hotel@fsmail.net

The Wayford Bridge Hotel, dating in parts from the late 17th-century, is a family-run riverside hotel fronting on to the River Ant in the Norfolk Broads National Park. Set in acres of parkland and attractive gardens, the hotel has a unique location for a peaceful and relaxing stay. The hotel offers a choice of dining in either the Bistro or À la Carte Restaurant and has a comfortable lounge bar with an open log fire.

Bed & Breakfast per night: single room from £49.00–£55.00; double room from £65.00–£75.00
Dinner, Bed & Breakfast per person, per night: from £39.00–£47.00 (min 2 nights)
Evening meal: 1800 (last orders 2100)

Bedrooms: 1 single, 9 double, 2 twin
Bathrooms: 12 en-suite
Parking: 50 spaces
Cards accepted: Mastercard, Visa, Switch/Delta, Connect, Solo

Norfolk Lavender

The Romans used lavender daily. They used it as a healing agent and as an insect repellent, in massage oils and to scent their bath water. Indeed, the name of the genus to which all species of lavender belong, *Lavandula,* derives from the Latin word meaning 'for washing'. Whether the Romans brought lavender to England or whether it was already growing here is uncertain, but Roman soldiers settling here would certainly have planted it as part of their herbal first-aid kit. Similarly, lavender was grown for medicinal uses in medieval monastic gardens. The dried flowers were used in Tudor times to scent chests and closets and to keep bedbugs at bay. Its cleansing properties were particularly valued during the plague of 1665, when the street cries of lavender sellers were part of everyday urban life. Victorian women used lavender perfume lavishly to scent themselves, their linen and their clothes.

In Victorian days there were a number of famous lavender fields in the south of England but in the early years of this century the bushes were attacked by a deadly disease, shab, and very little has been commercially grown since. However,

Norfolk Lavender at Heacham in Norfolk (tel: 01485 570384), which was founded in 1932, still grows seven varieties of lavender – five for distilling and two for drying. The fields are harvested – mechanically – from about mid-July, roughly one third of the crop being used as flowers for potpourris and sachets, two thirds for distilling. The flowers for drying are packed loosely into sacks through which warm air is blown for several days. The flower heads are then removed from the stalks and sifted. The distilling process is an ancient one. Lavender's fragrance is contained in the oil stored in glands at the base of each floret and this oil is extracted by steam distillation. About 500lb (230kg) of flowers, stalks and all, are loaded into each still while one of the workers stands in it treading them down. Steam is then passed through the still and the mixture of steam and oil vapour passes to the condenser. The pure essential oil then collects in the separator and is drawn off, at the rate of about half a litre per still-load. The oil is matured for a year before being blended with other oils and fixatives.

251 Marriott Sprowston Manor Hotel & Country Club ★★★★ Silver Award

Sprowston Park, Wroxham Road, Norwich, Norfolk NR7 8RP **Tel:** (01603) 410871 **Fax:** (01603) 423911
Web: www.marriotthotels.com/nwigs **E-mail:** reservation.sprowstonmanor@whitbread.com

This beautiful 16th-century manor house is an idyllic retreat set in acres of mature parkland and combines the elegance and informality of the English country house with the warmest of welcomes and hospitality. Surrounded by an 18-hole golf course and boasting a large leisure club with poolside bar to relax and unwind. For the more active, visit the gym. Or, for the ultimate pampering, treat yourself in the award-winning La Fontanna Spa. At the end of the day dine in the AA Rosette Manor Restaurant.

Bed & Breakfast per night: double room from £120.00–£160.00
Dinner, Bed & Breakfast per person, per night: £150.00–£190.00 (min 2 nights)
Lunch available: 1230–1400

Bedrooms: 27 double, 48 twin, 3 family, 16 suites
Bathrooms: 94 en-suite
Parking: 120 spaces
Cards accepted: Mastercard, Visa, Switch/Delta, Amex, Diners, Eurocard

252 The Blue Boar Inn ◆◆◆◆

259 Wroxham Road, Sprowston, Norwich, NR7 8RL **Tel:** (01603) 426802 **Fax:** (01603) 487749
Web: blueboarnorwich.co.uk **E-mail:** blueboar102@hotmail.com

Just ten minutes from the medieval city of Norwich, with its 11th-century Cathedral and Castle, and a shopping centre which is in the top ten in England. The Norfolk Broads are 15 minutes away and beautiful beaches can be reached in 30 minutes. We are a friendly family pub/restaurant with five superb non-smoking, en-suite rooms. We have an enviable reputation for our food which is, in the main, home-cooked with fresh local produce.

Bed & Breakfast per night: single occupancy from £50.00–£60.00; double room from £60.00–£70.00
Lunch available: 1200–1400 weekdays, all day, Saturday and Sunday
Evening meal: 1800 (last orders 2100)

Bedrooms: 2 double, 2 twin, 1 family
Bathrooms: 4 en-suite, 1 private
Parking: 70 spaces
Cards accepted: Mastercard, Visa, Switch/Delta, Amex

253 Beeches Hotel & Victorian Gardens ★★★ Silver Award

2–6 Earlham Road, Norwich, Norfolk NR2 3DB **Tel:** (01603) 621167 **Fax:** (01603) 620151
Web: www.beeches.co.uk **E-mail:** reception@beeches.co.uk

'An oasis in the heart of Norwich' with access to three acres of English Heritage Victorian garden for our guests to enjoy, this hotel provides a peaceful retreat from the bustle of the city, which is just ten minutes' walk away. Three separate listed Victorian houses and a modern annexe have been tastefully refurbished and extended to offer high standards of comfort in a relaxed, informal setting. Non-smoking bedrooms are individually designed, enhancing their own character and charm. Our licensed rosette restaurant offers mouth-watering contemporary cuisine. The photograph shows Plantation House, which is part of the Beeches. 🅰 Category 2

Bed & Breakfast per night: single room from £59.00–£69.00; double room from £76.00–£94.00
Dinner, Bed & Breakfast per person, per night: £51.00–£60.00 (min 2 nights, 2 sharing)
Evening meal: 1830 (last orders 2100)

Bedrooms: 8 single, 28 double/twin
Bathrooms: 36 en-suite
Parking: 24 spaces
Cards accepted: Mastercard, Visa, Switch/Delta, Amex, Diners, Eurocard

254 The Old Vicarage

48 The Street, Brooke, Norwich, Norfolk NR15 1JU **Tel:** (01508) 558329

Situated in the award-winning village of Brooke in a peaceful and secluded situation with extensive gardens. Within seven miles of the centre of Norwich, on the B1332 Norwich–Bungay road, and within easy reach of the Suffolk heritage coast and Norfolk Broads. One large four-poster room with adjoining private bathroom and one twin bedroom with en-suite shower room. Private sitting room with television available for guests' use. We are a no smoking house. No children under 15 years.

Bed & Breakfast per night: double room £42.00
Dinner, Bed & Breakfast per person, per night: £35.50

Bedrooms: 1 double, 1 twin
Bathrooms: 1 private, 1 en-suite shower
Parking: 3 spaces

255 The Meadow House

2A High Street, Burwell, Cambridge, Cambridgeshire CB5 0HB **Tel:** (01638) 741926 or (01638) 741354 **Fax:** (01638) 743424
Web: www.themeadowhouse.co.uk **E-mail:** hilary@themeadowhouse.co.uk

The Meadow House, Burwell is an exceptional, modern property set in two acres of wooded grounds. King-size luxury beds, suite of rooms with balcony available. Large car park. No smoking. Close to Cambridge and Newmarket.

Bed & Breakfast per night: single occupancy from £25.00–£30.00; double room from £42.00–£45.00

Bedrooms: 1 double, 2 twin, 2 triple, 1 family
Bathrooms: 4 en-suite, 1 shared
Parking: 14 spaces

256 Red House Farm

Station Road, Haughley, Stowmarket, Suffolk IP14 3QP **Tel:** (01449) 673323 **Fax:** (01449) 675413
Web: www.farmstayanglia.co.uk **E-mail:** mary@noy1.fsnet.co.uk

A warm welcome and homely atmosphere await you at our attractive farmhouse which is situated just half a mile from the picturesque village of Haughley. The bedrooms are comfortably furnished and all have en-suite shower rooms. There is also a guest sitting room and separate dining room. Mid Suffolk is an ideal base for exploring East Anglia and there are excellent facilities in the area for horse riding, swimming, fishing, golfing, walking, cycling and birdwatching.

Bed & Breakfast per night: single room from £25.00–£30.00; double room from £45.00–£50.00

Bedrooms: 2 single, 1 double, 1 twin
Bathrooms: 4 en-suite
Parking: 3 spaces
Open: All year except Christmas

257 The Step House ◆◆◆◆

Hockey Hill, Wetheringsett, Stowmarket, Suffolk IP14 5PL **Tel:** (01449) 766476 **Fax:** (01449) 766476
E-mail: stephouse@talk21.com

Step House is a recently restored 15th-century timber-framed hall house. It is heavily beamed, with inglenook fireplaces. We offer two private suites, both with sitting rooms and bathrooms. We are located in the heart of Suffolk which is ideal for touring and exploring the Heritage Coast. Just half a mile off the A140. A warm welcome awaits our guests who can use our garden and lounge. There is ample car parking.

Bed & Breakfast per night: single occupancy £28.00; double room £50.00

Bedrooms: 1 double, 1 twin
Bathrooms: 2 en-suite
Parking: 6 spaces

258 The Cretingham Bell ◆◆◆◆ Silver Award

The Street, Cretingham, Woodbridge, Suffolk IP13 7BJ **Tel:** (01728) 685419 **Fax:** (01728) 685419

The Cretingham Bell is an oak-beamed Tudor manor house situated in the quiet village of Cretingham. Ideal for the traveller who enjoys a stay in a tranquil setting. We offer mainly traditional home-cooked dishes which can be eaten in the non-smoking restaurant or bar areas. The Bell is ideally positioned for many of Suffolk's varied attractions. Virginia and Vic offer you a welcome as warm as our log fires.

Bed & Breakfast per night: single occupancy £39.95; double room £58.75
Lunch available: 1200–1400
Evening meal: 1900 (last orders 2100)

Bedrooms: 2 double, 1 twin
Bathrooms: 3 en-suite
Parking: 25 spaces
Cards accepted: Mastercard, Visa, Switch/Delta, Eurocard, Visa Electron, Solo

259 Mile Hill Barn ◆◆◆◆◆ Gold Award

Main Road, Kelsale, Saxmundham, Suffolk IP17 2RG **Tel:** (01728) 668519
Web: www.abreakwithtradition.co.uk **E-mail:** richard@milehillbarn.freeserve.co.uk

Welcome to this superbly converted and characterful Suffolk oak barn. Three delightfully furnished ground floor en-suite rooms with colour television, beverage tray, individual access and private parking. Double and luxury super-king (or twin) all to ETC's highest accolade of 5 Diamonds and coveted Gold Award. Stroll in the grounds, relax in our enchanting walled garden or by the log fire in the beamed and vaulted lounge. Farmhouse-style Aga cooking using fresh local ingredients and home-made preserves for traditional breakfasts and candlelit dinners (October–March) in our cosy dining room. Central for Minsmere, Snape, Aldeburgh and Southwold. No smoking .

Bed & Breakfast per night: double room from £65.00–£85.00
Dinner, Bed & Breakfast per person, per night: £47.00–£50.00 (min 3 nights, Tuesday–Thursday, October–March only)
Evening meal: 1900 (last orders 1900)

Bedrooms: 3 double
Bathrooms: 3 en-suite
Parking: 12 spaces

260 The Old Vicarage ◆◆◆◆

Wenhaston, Halesworth, Suffolk IP19 9EG **Tel:** (01502) 478339 **Fax:** (01502) 478068
E-mail: theycock@aol.com

An attractive and comfortable house set in large grounds in the heart of the village, but very quiet and peaceful. Southwold is a ten minutes' drive away with all its attractions and Snape Maltings and Aldeburgh are within easy distance. The historic village of Dunwich is also nearby as is Minsmere RSPB. Two double bedrooms (one four-poster and one half-tester) with private bathrooms are available – both with television, hairdryer and courtesy tray.

Bed & Breakfast per night: single occupancy from £30.00–£35.00; double room from £50.00–£60.00

Bedrooms: 2 double
Bathrooms: 2 private
Parking: 6 spaces

261 Poplar Hall ◆◆◆◆

Frostenden Corner, Frostenden, Wangford, Suffolk NR34 7JA **Tel:** (01502) 578549
Web: www.southwold.co.uk/poplar-hall

An early 16th-century, thatched house set in lovely gardens and surrounded by gentle Suffolk countryside, yet only 3.5 miles from the delightful seaside town of Southwold. Poplar Hall offers luxury Bed & Breakfast in a beautifully furnished home with beams and inglenooks. Sumptuous breakfasts are served in a delightful dining room where guests enjoy fresh and local produce and home-made preserves, whilst watching the activity at the bird tables scattered around the garden. A haven of tranquillity. Self-catering also available – see entry on page 143.

Bed & Breakfast per night: single room £25.00; double room from £48.00– £58.00

Bedrooms: 1 single, 2 double
Bathrooms: 1 en-suite, 1 shared
Parking: 6 spaces

262 Field End Guest House ◆◆◆◆ Silver Award

1 Kings Road, Leiston, Suffolk IP16 4DA **Tel:** (01728) 833527 **Fax:** (01728) 833527
Web: www.fieldend-guesthouse.co.uk **E-mail:** pwright@fieldend-guesthouse.co.uk

A comfortable, newly refurbished Edwardian house, Field End is conveniently placed for touring the Heritage Coast from Woodbridge to Southwold – only three miles from RSPB Minsmere and Aldeburgh – five miles from Snape, home of the Aldeburgh Festival. Breakfast is taken in the private guest dining room/lounge which is available all day. Bedrooms are all beautifully appointed with a choice of en-suite or private bathroom. The house is fully centrally heated and double glazed ensuring a cosy and peaceful night.

Bed & Breakfast per night: single room from £28.00–£40.00; double room from £50.00–£55.00

Bedrooms: 2 single, 2 double, 1 twin, 1 family
Bathrooms: 1 en-suite, 5 private
Parking: 5 spaces

263 White Lion Hotel   ★★★ Silver Award

Market Cross Place, Aldeburgh, Suffolk IP15 5BJ **Tel:** (01728) 452720 **Fax:** (01728) 452986
Web: www.whitelion.co.uk **E-mail:** whitelionaldeburgh@btinternet.com

Located in the centre of Aldeburgh, an Edwardian fishing town on the Suffolk Heritage coast. Bedrooms overlook the beach where fresh fish is sold from traditional wooden huts lining the shore. The White Lion is Aldeburgh's oldest hotel, offering highest levels of quality and service. Bedrooms provide every comfort. Four-poster rooms are available for special occasions. Restaurant 1563, named after the year the hotel was built, is ideal for elegant dining with oak-panelled walls and a roaring log fire in winter.

Bed & Breakfast per night: single room from £72.00–£80.00; double room from £110.00–£150.00
Dinner, Bed & Breakfast per person, per night: £50.00–£87.00
Lunch available: 1230–1430

Evening meal: 1900 (last orders 2100)
Bedrooms: 4 single, 34 double/twin
Bathrooms: 38 en-suite
Parking: 15 spaces
Cards accepted: Mastercard, Visa, Switch/Delta, Amex

264 Embleton House   ◆◆◆◆ Silver Award

Melford Road, Cavendish, Sudbury, Suffolk CO10 8AA **Tel:** (01787) 280447 **Fax:** (01787) 282396
Web: www.smoothhound.co.uk/hotels/embleton **E-mail:** silverned@aol.com

A large family-run 1930's house, set well back from the road, within its own secluded gardens at the eastern edge of Cavendish. Enjoy one of our famous 'Suffolk breakfasts' with lots of local produce and home-made jellies, after a good night's sleep in one of our five spacious en-suite bedrooms, individually designed with comfort and relaxation in mind. Explore the treasures of South Suffolk, Constable Country and beyond – or simply relax.

Bed & Breakfast per night: single occupancy from £35.00–£45.00; double room from £55.00–£75.00

Bedrooms: 2 double, 2 twin, 1 family
Bathrooms: 5 en-suite
Parking: 6 spaces

265 Jasmine Cottage   ◆◆◆◆

The Heath, Lavenham Road, Great Waldingfield, Sudbury, Suffolk CO10 0RN **Tel:** (01787) 374665
E-mail: JasmineCottage-B-and-B.co.uk

Two delightful self-contained units situated in courtyard garden setting of this Grade II listed 17th-century thatched cottage. The accommodation has access all day. 'The Croft' is a thatched listed building. It is charmingly decorated with a double bed, en-suite facilities and dining area - a romantic place to stay. 'The Pavillion' is spacious and Scandinavian in style. It contains a luxury king-size bed, large bathroom with bath and shower and separate sitting/dining room - every comfort is provided for and an extra bed is available. Relax in the guests' garden and enjoy the use of the swimming pool. Private parking. Close to Lavenham. Magical.

Bed & Breakfast per night: double room from £38.50–£52.50

Bedrooms: 2 double
Bathrooms: 2 en-suite

266 The Red House   ◆◆◆◆

29 Bolton Street, Lavenham, Sudbury, Suffolk CO10 9RG **Tel:** (01787) 248074
Web: www.lavenham.co.uk/redhouse **E-mail:** redhouse@demon.co.uk

The Red House is a Victorian double-fronted town house and a most comfortable and friendly home. Situated in the heart of Lavenham, just a stone's throw from the Guildhall and Market Square. The three en-suite double bedrooms are attractively furnished and have tea and coffee making facilities. There is a pretty guest sitting room and a sunny country garden to relax in. Candlelit dinners can be arranged by prior notice and you can bring your own wine. For more information see our web-site or send us an e-mail.

Bed & Breakfast per night: double room from £50.00–£55.00 (min 2 nights at weekends)
Dinner, Bed & Breakfast per person, per night: £41.50
Evening meal: by arrangement

Bedrooms: 2 double, 1 twin
Bathrooms: 3 en-suite
Parking: 6 spaces
Open: All year except Christmas and January

267 The Old Convent   ◆◆◆◆

The Street, Kettlebaston, Ipswich IP7 7QA **Tel:** (01449) 741557
Web: www.kettlebaston.fsnet.co.uk **E-mail:** holidays@kettlebaston.fsnet.co.uk

A warm and friendly welcome awaits you at our Grade II listed 17th-century thatched house, situated within the tranquillity of a small Suffolk village. Our three bedrooms (one twin and two double), all have en-suite facilities; one with whirlpool bath. Hairdryer available on request. We are centrally situated to explore the many treasures of East Anglia, including Lavenham, Long Melford and Constable Country. Recently refurbished to a fine standard. Seasonal log fire. Guests' television/ video lounge. Colour brochure available.

Bed & Breakfast per night: single occupancy from £27.50–£45.00; double room from £50.00–£65.00

Bedrooms: 2 double, 1 twin
Bathrooms: 3 en-suite
Parking: 4 spaces

268 Weavers   ◆◆◆◆

25 High Street, Hadleigh, Ipswich, Suffolk IP7 5AG **Tel:** (01473) 827247 or (01473) 823185 **Fax:** (01473) 822805
Web: www.weaversrestaurant.co.uk **E-mail:** cyndymiles@aol.com

Weavers restaurant and bar offers the unbeatable combination of first class à la carte dining, the mellow ambience of our 500-year-old building and top quality service. Winter log fires, antique furnishings and luxury guest rooms make Weavers the perfect place for a relaxing break. Situated in the unspoilt market town of Hadleigh, in Constable country, with nearby tennis court, horseriding, summer pool, golf and country walks, Weavers is a really special experience.

Bed & Breakfast per night: double room from £55.00–£80.00
Dinner, Bed & Breakfast per person, per night: £47.50–£60.00
Evening meal: 1900 (last orders 2300)

Bedrooms: 3 double
Bathrooms: 3 en-suite
Parking: 3 spaces
Cards accepted: Mastercard, Visa, Switch/Delta, Eurocard, Visa Electron, Solo

269 Mockbeggars Hall Bed & Breakfast ◆◆◆◆ Silver Award

Paper Mill Lane, Claydon, Ipswich, IP6 0AH **Tel:** (01473) 830239 or (0770) 262 7770 **Fax:** (01473) 832989
Web: www.mockbeggars.co.uk **E-mail:** pru@mockbeggars.co.uk

A grand Grade II* listed Jacobean manor house set in rolling countryside, just north west of Ipswich. A warm welcome awaits our guests in this relaxing atmosphere. The spacious and comfortable bedrooms have antique and period furniture. Close to Constable Country and the Suffolk Coast. We offer yacht sailing and have a Complementary Therapy Centre on site. Brochures available.

Bed & Breakfast per night: single occupancy from £35.00–£42.00; double room from £45.00–£55.00

Bedrooms: 3 double, 1 twin, 1 family
Bathrooms: 5 en-suite
Parking: 10 spaces
Cards accepted: Mastercard, Visa, Switch/Delta, JCB, Solo

270 The Marlborough at Ipswich ★★★ Silver Award

Henley Road, Ipswich, Suffolk IP1 3SP **Tel:** (01473) 257677 **Fax:** (01473) 226927
E-mail: reception@themarlborough.co.uk

Privately owned by the Gough family for over 30 years, The Marlborough is a small hotel offering a friendly and relaxed atmosphere. Situated close to the beautiful Christchurch Park and just ten minutes' walk from the town centre. Our restaurant overlooks the floodlit garden and we are proud to boast an AA Rosette for food. All bedrooms are en-suite and tastefully furnished. Ideal base for exploring Constable country and Suffolk's coastline.

Bed & Breakfast per night: single room from £71.00; double room from £86.00–£93.00; £44.00 per person at weekends
Dinner, Bed & Breakfast per person, per night: £59.50
Lunch available: 1200–1400

Evening meal: 1930 (last orders 2130)
Bedrooms: 4 single, 13 double, 5 twin
Bathrooms: 22 en-suite
Parking: 60 spaces
Cards accepted: Mastercard, Visa, Switch/Delta, Amex, Diners

271 Seckford Hall Hotel ★★★ Silver Award

Woodbridge, Suffolk IP13 6NU **Tel:** (01394) 385678 **Fax:** (01394) 380610
Web: www.seckford.co.uk **E-mail:** reception@seckford.co.uk

A romantic Elizabethan mansion set in 32 acres of landscaped gardens and woodlands. Personally supervised by the owners, Seckford Hall is a haven of seclusion and tranquillity. Oak panelling, beamed ceilings, antique furniture, four-poster bedrooms, suites, leisure club with indoor pool, beauty salon, gym and spa bath and adjacent 18-hole golf course. Two restaurants featuring fresh lobster and game from local farms, extensive wine cellar. Picturesque Woodbridge with its tide mill, antique shops and yacht harbour is a short walk away. 'Constable Country' and Suffolk coast nearby.

Bed & Breakfast per night: single room from £79.00–£130.00; double room from £120.00–£170.00
Dinner, Bed & Breakfast per person, per night: £80.00–£105.00 (min 2 nights, 2 sharing)
Lunch available: 1200–1430
Evening meal: 1915 (last orders 2130)

Bedrooms: 3 single, 14 double, 10 twin, 1 triple, 4 family
Bathrooms: 32 en-suite
Parking: 102 spaces
Cards accepted: Mastercard, Visa, Switch/Delta, Amex, Diners, Eurocard, JCB

At-a-glance symbols are explained on the flap inside the back cover

272 The Angel Inn
◆◆◆◆ Silver Award

Polstead Street, Stoke-by-Nayland, Colchester CO6 4SA **Tel:** (01206) 263245 **Fax:** (01206) 263373
Web: www.angelhotel.com

A popular and busy 16th-century inn, situated in one of Suffolk's most interesting villages and surrounded by lovely countryside. The inn has been totally restored and refurbished whilst retaining such original features as exposed brickwork, beams, open fireplaces and a gallery overlooking the dining room. A high standard of individually decorated and furnished bedrooms are provided with modern en-suite facilities. The restaurant serves dishes as on the daily blackboard bar-meals menu. Both bars and restaurant are much frequented by local customers.

Bed & Breakfast per night: single occupancy £52.50; double room £67.50

Bedrooms: 5 double, 1 twin
Bathrooms: 6 en-suite
Parking: 25 spaces
Cards accepted: Mastercard, Visa, Switch/Delta

---

273 Gladwins Farm
◆◆◆◆

Harpers Hill, Nayland, Colchester, Suffolk CO6 4NU **Tel:** (01206) 262261 **Fax:** (01206) 263001
Web: www.gladwinsfarm.co.uk **E-mail:** gladwinsfarm@compuserve.com

Homely farmhouse B&B in a typical Suffolk farmhouse. Set in 22 acres of wooded grounds in the heart of Suffolk's beautiful rolling Constable Country, with marvellous views. Not far from the sea. Charming heritage villages to explore plus birdwatching and gardens. Heated indoor pool, sauna, steam room, tennis court, fishing, farm animals and childrens' playground. There are also charming cottages in converted Tudor buildings around the courtyard, sleeping from two to six. The new luxury cottage sleeps eight and has a four-poster bed.

Bed & Breakfast per night: single room £25.00; double room £60.00

Bedrooms: 1 single, 2 double
Bathrooms: 2 en-suite, 1 private
Parking: 14 spaces
Cards accepted: Mastercard, Visa, Switch/Delta, Visa Electron

---

274 Canfield Moat
◆◆◆◆◆ Silver Award

High Cross Lane West, Little Canfield, Dunmow, Essex CM6 1TD **Tel:** (01371) 872565 or 07811 165049 **Fax:** (01371) 876264
Web: www.canfieldmoat.co.uk **E-mail:** falk@canfieldmoat.co.uk

A peaceful Georgian rectory set among eight acres in the heart of the Essex countryside yet only ten minutes from the M11 and Stansted Airport and within easy reach of London, Cambridge, St Albans and 'Constable Country'. The large, elegant en-suite bedrooms are supplied with almost every conceivable luxury. Breakfasts include our own eggs and produce from our vegetable garden, and guests are welcome to use the tennis court, croquet lawn and, in season, heated outdoor swimming pool.

Bed & Breakfast per night: single occupancy from £35.00–£45.00; double room from £55.00–£65.00
Evening meal: 1930 (last orders 2100)

Bedrooms: 1 double, 1 twin
Bathrooms: 2 en-suite
Parking: 11 spaces

---

275 Marygreen Manor Hotel

★★★★ Silver Award

Pantheon Hotels & Leisure, London Road, Brentwood, Essex CM14 4NR **Tel:** (01277) 225252 **Fax:** (01277) 262809
Web: www.marygreenmanor.co.uk **E-mail:** info@marygreenmanor.co.uk

16th-century timber-framed building, visited by King Henry VIII. Original Tudor bedrooms with four-poster beds (3). Garden rooms overlook olde-worlde garden. AA Rosetted restaurant with offers extensive à la carte or fixed price menus complemented by comprehensive award-winning wine list. Lunch served from 1230–1430, dinner served from 1915–2215. Two minutes from J28 on the M25. Motorway links to the Channel Tunnel, Stansted, Gatwick and Heathrow Airports.

Bed & Breakfast per night: single occupancy from £135.50–£232.00; double room from £147.50–£244.00
Dinner, Bed & Breakfast per person, per night: £108.50–£160.00
Lunch available: 1230–1430

Evening meal: 1915 (last orders 2215)
Bedrooms: 26 double, 17 twin
Bathrooms: 43 en-suite
Parking: 100 spaces
Cards accepted: Mastercard, Visa, Switch/Delta, Amex, Diners

Audley End

At the Dissolution of the Monasteries in 1536, Henry VIII gave the Benedictine Abbey of Walden to Lord Audley, who built himself a distinguished house in the grounds. This passed to Lord Howard of Walden, who in 1603 was created 1st Earl of Suffolk. Rather than enlarge the existing building, the Earl (who later became Lord High Treasurer) decided to construct a house which befitted his elevated status. Indeed the plans were on such a vast scale that James I tellingly declared it 'too big for a king, but might do for the Lord Treasurer'. When completed, Audley End had two enormous courts, built around the ruins of the Benedictine Abbey, and was one of the largest houses in the land.

In the early 1720s, the 5th Earl, keen to leave his mark on the building, called in the services of the talented Sir John Vanbrugh, playwright, society figure and architect of both Castle Howard and Blenheim Palace. Vanbrugh recommended that the outer court should be demolished, and also substantially altered the rest of the house, although he ensured that the Jacobean flavour of the exterior, with its balustraded roof and many turrets, was retained.

After a short period of neglect, the strangely named Sir John Griffin Griffin was the next to shape the look of Audley End. Sir John commissioned Robert Adam who, like his predecessor Sir John Vanbrugh, kept the 17th-century façade but added many 18th-century devices to the interior, where his additions include the magnificent state rooms. Outside,

Lancelot 'Capability' Brown set about turning the park into the 18th-century ideal of the picturesque, with a Palladian bridge-cum-summerhouse, Temple of Victory, and the Temple of Concord (1781), from where there is a particularly fine vista.

Other highlights include the Jacobean Hall (largely untouched by Vanbrugh and Adam), some superb plaster ceilings, a chapel in the 'Strawberry Hill gothick' (highly ornate) style and some contemporary furniture and paintings. Some idea of the size of the earlier buildings can be gauged from the fact that Audley End is roughly half the size of its early 17th-century incarnation. The house (tel: 01799 522399) and its estate village of Audley End are 1 mile (1.6km) west of Saffron Walden.

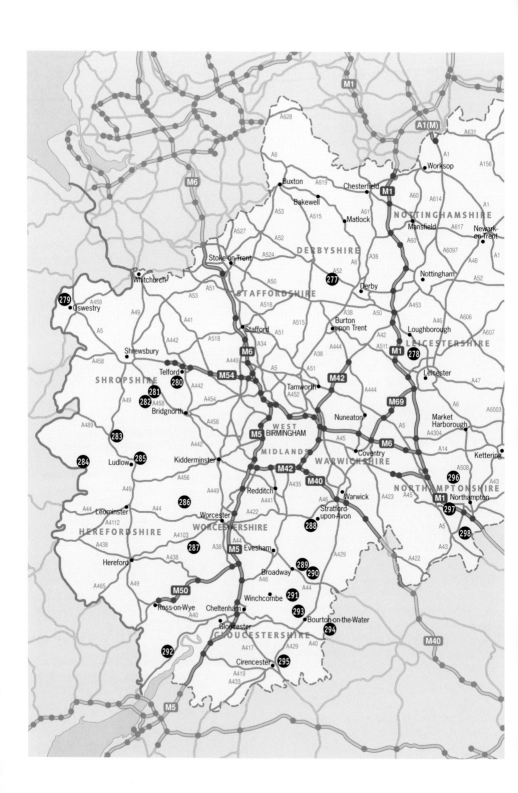

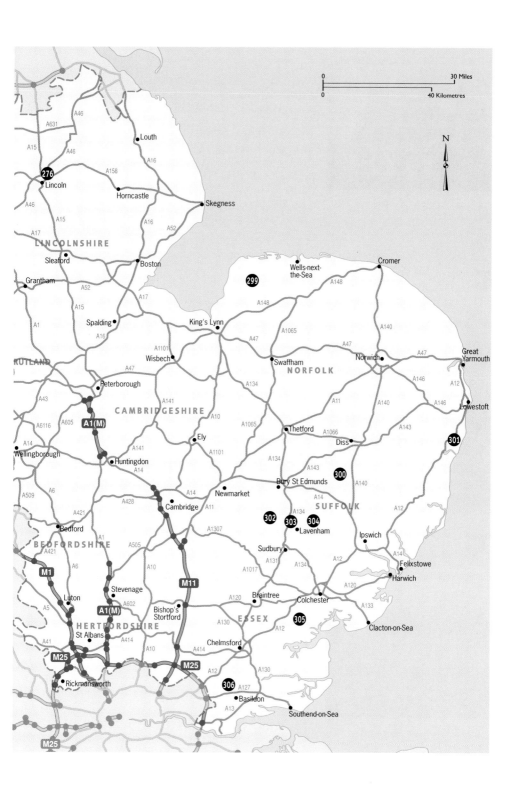

276 Howard Cottage ★★★★

Wragby Road, Lincoln
Contact: Mrs G Bateman, Wickens, High Street, Scampton, Lincoln LN1 2SE
Tel: (01522) 730811 **Fax:** (01522) 730027

A short walk from Lincoln's splendid medieval cathedral and historic Bailgate area, this beautifully restored and appointed Victorian cottage offers the perfect base for exploring this lesser-known county's numerous attractions. Fully appointed dining kitchen, including dishwasher, microwave etc. Twin and double bedrooms share a handy interconnecting dressing room. Cosy sitting room with two sofas and television/video. Walled patio garden and outside laundry room housing a washer/dryer. Welcome pack including a bottle of wine presented on arrival.

Low season per week: from £200.00
High season per week: max £300.00

1 cottage: sleeping 4 people

277 The Cottage ★★★★

Culland Mount Farm, Brailsford, Ashbourne, Derbyshire
Contact: Mrs C Phillips, Culland Mount Farm, Brailsford, Ashbourne, Derbyshire DE6 3BW
Tel: (01335) 360313 **Fax:** (01335) 360313 **E-mail:** carol@culland-mount.freeserve.co.uk

This beautiful, stylish, detached Victorian farmhouse is situated in a peaceful rural hamlet near the village of Brailsford – centre for local crafts. The self-catering wing of the farmhouse retains many original features, marble fireplace for log fires and large bay windows giving magnificent views over the surrounding countryside. Ideally situated for Ashbourne and the Peaks, Derby, Nottingham and Burton-on-Trent. Beds made up on arrival. Two bedrooms, one double, one twin, bed-settee downstairs. Bathroom with shower over bath. Large lounge/dining room. Modern kitchen with washing machine and dryer.

Low season per week: £150.00–£225.00
High season per week: £200.00–£320.00

1 apartment: sleeping 4 people

278 Kingfisher Cottage ★★★★

Barrow upon Soar, Loughborough, Leicestershire **Web:** www.AnEnglishCottage.com
Contact: Mr D Petty, 634 Pine Street, Philadelphia, PA 19106, USA
Tel: (1) 215 925-4648 **Fax:** (1) 215 925-2126 **E-mail:** nikkidavid@aol.com

Kingfisher Cottage was built as a mill worker's dwelling at 19th-century's end. Situated roadside in a quiet corner of Barrow upon Soar in Leicestershire, it backs on to the Grand Union Canal, separated from the waterside by a sizeable, mainly lawned garden. The location is convenient for shops, pubs, eating establishments, public transportation and the railway station – all only minutes' walk away. Recently extensively remodelled to accommodate up to six, the cottage has much to offer the most discerning visitor.

Low season per week: £400.00–£500.00
High season per week: £600.00–£600.00
Short breaks: from £190.00–£275.00

1 cottage: sleeping 4/6 people

279 Underhill House ★ ★ ★ ★

Oswestry, Shropshire
Contact: Mr G Hughes, Underhill House, Racecourse Road, Oswestry, Shropshire SY10 7PN
Tel: (01691) 661660 **Fax:** (01691) 656893 **E-mail:** info@underhillhouse.co.uk

These lovely cottages are the perfect base from which to explore Chester, The Marches, Wales and Offa's Dyke. Extremely comfortable, beautifully furnished, they are totally peaceful but only 15 minutes' walk away from Oswestry. An unending variety of all-age activites for both wet and dry weather will fully occupy everyone. Special touches include children's toys, fresh eggs, vegetables and herbs, home-produced lamb and comprehensive CD, video and book libraries.

Low season per week: £275.00–£450.00
High season per week: £375.00–£450.00

3 cottages: sleeping 2–6 people
Cards accepted: Mastercard, Visa, Switch/Delta

280 Bottom End Cottage ★ ★ ★ ★

Ironbridge, Telford, Shropshire **Web:** www.theironbridge.co.uk
Contact: Mr P A Ottley, 8 Ladywood, Ironbridge, Telford, Shropshire TF8 7JR
Tel: (01952) 883770 **E-mail:** bottomendcottage@btinternet.com

Tucked away on the edge of a wood against the great buttresses of the old railway station, the cottage affords wonderful views of the Ironbridge and Severn Gorge. The interior is charming and has many quality fixtures and fittings. Beautiful ornate tiling extends throughout the ground floor. The sitting room has period arts and crafts, oak furniture and an open log fire. There is a well equipped breakfast room/kitchen with a Rayburn gas-fired range. All the local museums are easily accessible. A truly unique retreat.

Low season per week: £200.00–£300.00
High season per week: £300.00–£450.00
Short breaks: from £100.00–£250.00 (when available)

1 cottage: sleeping 4–6 people
Cards accepted: by arrangement

281 No 1 & 2 Courtyard Cottages ★ ★ ★ ★

Lower Springs Farm, Kenley, Shrewsbury
Contact: Mrs A Gill, No 1 & 2 Courtyard Cottages, Lower Springs Farm, Kenley, Shrewsbury SY5 6PA
Tel: (01952) 510841 **Fax:** (01952) 510841

Two immaculate and very spacious newly converted barns appointed to the highest standards and with exposed oak beams. The farm is situated in the Kenley Valley, under Wenlock Edge with panoramic views, a large garden and stocked trout pools. The historic town of Much Wenlock is two miles away with a wealth of interesting shops, a market and many good pubs and restaurants. Local attractions include horse riding, golf, gardens and historic houses and castles.

Low season per week: from £150.00
High season per week: max £350.00

2 cottages: sleeping 2–4 people

282 Granary Cottage

★ ★ ★ ★

Church Preen, Church Stretton, Shropshire **Web:** www.lowerdayhouse.freeserve.co.uk
Contact: Mr & Mrs J Kirkwood, Lower Day House, Church Preen, Church Stretton, Shropshire SY6 7LH
Tel: (01694) 771521 **E-mail:** jim@lowerdayhouse.freeserve.co.uk

Part of an 18th-century farm courtyard and sited next to an oak-framed threshing barn, the cottage sleeps a family of four, is tastefully furnished and retains many of the original beams and features. With all-round magnificent views of Wenlock Edge, Granary Cottage is ideally suited for those seeking the real 'heart of the country' and is the perfect central location for visiting Ironbridge, the Long Mynd, Ludlow and the many fine local amenities.

Low season per week: £195.00–£225.00
High season per week: £225.00–£310.00
Short breaks: from £95.00 (October–April only)

1 cottage: sleeping 4 people

Cruck-framed Houses

The Midlands are particularly rich in timber-framed or, to use the popular term, half-timbered buildings – 'half-timbered' being a reference to the early medieval period when the timbers were formed by cutting logs in half. These buildings are classified as either box-frame construction or cruck construction. By far the more common type was box-frame, where jointed horizontal and vertical timbers formed a wall and either the panels were infilled or the whole wall was covered with some sort of cladding. In the cruck construction, the structure was supported by pairs of inclined, slightly curved timbers that normally met at the ridge of the roof and were tied by a collar or tie-beam, making an A shape. These timbers, called crucks or blades, were spaced at regular intervals along the building to take the weight of the roof and often of the walls too. Wherever possible crucks were cut from the trunk of one tree split along its length to get a symmetrical arch. Alternatively, they were taken from trees with a natural curve in the trunk and blades matched as closely as possible.

There were various forms of cruck construction, the most important being full cruck, base or truncated cruck, raised cruck and jointed cruck. Full crucks extend from ground level to the apex. Base or truncated begin on the ground but stop below the apex and are joined by a tie-beam or collar that supports the roof. Raised crucks start a few feet off the ground in a solid wall, and in jointed cruck construction the curving blade is jointed to a vertical post that begins on the ground.

Many crucks have been incorporated into larger buildings, hidden behind a cladding of stone or brick or plastered over, but where they are visible as the gable end they are an attractive and striking feature. Cruck-framing is particularly prevalent in the Midlands, the North and West (and is more or less entirely absent in East Anglia and the South-East, where box-framing predominates), and it is in Hereford & Worcester that the greatest concentration of cruck buildings is to be found. There are some fine examples in Weobley, unsurpassed for its black-and-white buildings. Explore its streets and you cannot fail to admire the skills of the 15th-, 16th- and 17th-century craftsmen. Other towns in the county worth visiting for their half-timbering are Eardisley, Eardisland, Pembridge and Dilwyn. Some excellent examples of cruck-framed buildings have been reconstructed at the Avoncroft Museum of Historic Buildings in Bromsgrove (tel: 01527 831886).

283 Orchard Cottage ★★★★

Strefford House, Strefford, Craven Arms, Shropshire
Contact: Mrs P Webb, Strefford House, Strefford, Craven Arms, Shropshire SY7 8DE
Tel: (01588) 673340 **Fax:** (01588) 673340 **E-mail:** webb.streffordhouse@virgin.net

This delightful, comfortable cottage stands beside the owner's house, facing an orchard of quince, plums and apples, with Wenlock Edge in the distance. It comprises two bedrooms, bathroom, sitting room with open fire, dining/kitchen opening on to garden, heating, television, video, music centre, microwave, washing machine and telephone. All linen is included. Strefford is a quiet hamlet in a conservation area, within easy reach of Ludlow and Church Stretton. Pets by arrangement. Our visitors' book is a joy to read!

Low season per week: from £185.00
High season per week: max £315.00
Short breaks: from £80.00 (low season only, min 2 nights)

1 cottage: sleeping 4 people

284 Weston Cottage ★★★★

Weston, Bucknell, Shropshire **Web:** www.westoncottage.co.uk
Contact: Mrs K Bevan, The Mews, 18 Keepers Lane, The Wergs, Wolverhampton, West Midlands WV6 8UA
Tel: (01902) 752442 **E-mail:** kbevan@allcomm.co.uk

Charming 18th-century beamed cottage, surrounded by meadows and wooded hillsides, in the quiet hamlet of Weston. The cottage sleeps four with two double bedrooms, bathroom, sitting room, dining room and fully equipped kitchen. Two open fires provide additional comfort and cheer on a chill evening. The peaceful, private garden overlooks the River Teme in a classified Area of Outstanding Natural Beauty. An ideal rural retreat for exploring the many attractions of Shropshire – zone of tranquillity.

Low season per week: £175.00–£220.00
High season per week: £260.00–£320.00
Short breaks: from £80.00–£120.00

1 cottage: sleeping 4 people

285 1 Whitcliffe Cottages ★★★★

Ludlow, Shropshire **Web:** www.periodpropertiesludlow.co.uk
Contact: Period Properties (Ludlow) Ltd, 9 Lower Broad Street, Ludlow, Shropshire SY8 1PQ
Tel: (01584) 877932 **Fax:** (01584) 879548 **E-mail:** bookings@periodpropertiesludlow.co.uk

Delightful detached Grade II listed tollgate cottage, five minutes' walk from Ludlow town centre. Enjoy beautiful medieval streets, atmospheric buildings, a fine castle and the largest number of Michelin-rated restaurants outside London. Tastefully furnished, with a wrought-iron bed, roll-top bath, separate shower, fully fitted limed-oak kitchen, whilst retaining the original range, quarry tiled floor and little latched doors. The secluded courtyard garden overlooks the town with views of the church and castle.

Low season per week: £310.00
High season per week: £375.00
Short breaks: from £60.00–£180.00 (1 night low season – 3 nights high season)

1 cottage: sleeping 2 people

286 Hopeway Cottage ★ ★ ★ ★ ★

The Village, Clifton upon Teme, Worcester **Web:** www.hopeway.co.uk
Contact: Mr & Mrs C&E White, Hope Wynd, The Village, Clifton upon Teme, Worcester, WR6 6EN
Tel: (01886) 812496 **Fax:** (01886) 812429 **E-mail:** countryways@hopeway.co.uk

A detached, timber-framed, single storey cottage in centuries-old village, set high above the river, within the beautiful Teme Valley. Furnished to excellent standards, it is welcoming, warm, comfortable and spotlessly clean. On the border of Herefordshire and Worcestershire, it is within easy access of picturesque villages, historical towns and ancient hills. Interesting visits, activities, walks and marvellous views abound. An area to discover and a place to unwind.

Low season per week: £220.00–£295.00
High season per week: £340.00–£395.00
Short breaks: from £100.00–£235.00 (low season, November–March only)

1 cottage: sleeping 4 people

287 The Cottages at Westwood House ★ ★ ★ ★

West Malvern, Worcestershire **Web:** www.oas.co.uk/ukcottages/westwood
Contact: The Cottages at Westwood House, Park Road, West Malvern, Worcestershire WR14 4DS
Tel: (01684) 892308 or (01684) 578004 **Fax:** (01684) 892882 or (01684) 578004 **E-mail:** DavidWrightTrans@cs.com

Offering only the high standards of a private home, the national award-winning cottages at Westwood House aim to provide the most elegant and best-equipped holiday accommodation in the Malvern Hills. There are three individual cottages – Coachmans and Ostlers, delightful conversions from the old family coach house, and Westwood Cottage, a charming Malvern stone cottage in its own garden. Within Westwood House itself is Butlers, a luxuriously appointed, self-contained ground floor flat.

Low season per week: £215.00–£350.00
High season per week: £285.00–£550.00

3 cottages and 1 apartment: sleeping 2–6 people

288 1 College Mews ★ ★ ★ ★

Stratford-upon-Avon, Warwickshire **Web:** www.alderminster99.freeserve.co.uk
Contact: Mr I R Reid, Inwood House, New Road, Alderminster, Stratford-upon-Avon, Warwickshire CV37 8PE
Tel: (01789) 450266 **Fax:** (01789) 450266 **E-mail:** ian@alderminster99.freeserve.co.uk

College Mews is a select development of apartments situated in the 'Old Town' area of Stratford. No 1 College Mews is a ground floor apartment with one double bedroom. There is a spacious sitting area with colour television and telephone. The kitchen is open plan onto the living room and is divided by a breakfast bar. The range of fitted cupboards are well stocked with cutlery and kitchen utensils. There is a gas hob and an electric oven, fridge and washer/dryer. Additional cooking facilities are provided by microwave. All bedlinen and towels are provided.

Low season per week: £260.00–£285.00
High season per week: £300.00–£350.00
Short breaks: from £48.00 per night (low season only, min 3 nights)

1 apartment: sleeping 2 people

289 Shepherd's Cottage ★ ★ ★ ★

Broad Campden, Chipping Campden, Gloucestershire **Web:** www.campdencottages.co.uk
Contact: Sheila Rolland, Folly Cottage, Paxford, Chipping Campden, Gloucestershire GL55 6XG
Tel: (01386) 593315 **Fax:** (01386) 593057 **E-mail:** campdencottages@btinternet.com

An exceptional cottage which has been lovingly renovated. Beautifully situated, tucked away at the bottom of a lane in a quiet, picturesque Cotswold village, one mile from Chippping Campden, in an Area of Outstanding Natural Beauty. Traditional pub in village serving food and real ale. Two double bedrooms. Shower room. Exposed beams, wood floors, oriental rugs, log fire. Enclosed garden. High quality fixtures and fittings. Not suitable for children under 12 (except babies) or dogs. Welcome tray with home-made cake and fresh flowers awaits your arrival.

Low season per week: £285.00–£340.00
High season per week: £350.00–£470.00

1 cottage: sleeping 2–4 people
Cards accepted: Mastercard, Visa, Switch/Delta

290 Fox Cottage ★ ★ ★ ★

Paxford, Chipping Campden, Gloucestershire **Web:** www.campdencottages.co.uk
Contact: Campden Cottages, Folly Cottage, Paxford, Chipping Campden, Gloucestershire GL55 6XG
Tel: (01386) 593315 **Fax:** (01386) 593057 **E-mail:** campdencottages@btinternet.com

Situated on a non-working farm in beautiful, peaceful Cotswold countryside. Single story stone barn conversion, forming one side of old brick courtyard. Spacious, sunny living area with exposed beams/rafters and log fire. High quality furnishings. Dishwasher, microwave, washer/dryer. Large double bedroom with en-suite bathroom. Double sofa bed in sitting room and ladder to loft platform, fun additional sleeping area for two teenage/adults (additional charge of £50.00 per week for use of either, £75.00 per week if both required). Pub in village recommended by Michael Winner as 'best pub food in country'.

Low season per week: £285.00–£340.00
High season per week: £350.00–£425.00

1 cottage: sleeping 2–4 people
Cards accepted: Mastercard, Visa, Switch/Delta

291 The Furrow ★ ★ ★ ★

Temple Guiting, Cheltenham, Gloucestershire
Contact: Mrs V Hughes, The Ploughmans Cottage, Temple Guiting, Cheltenham, Gloucestershire GL54 5RW
Tel: (01451) 850733 **Fax:** (01451) 850733

A delightful, honey coloured natural Cotswold stone cottage situated in the picturesque Windrush Valley, with views of open countryside and rolling hills. This deceptively spacious accommodation retains a cosy feeling, being tastefully furnished to an exceptional high standard and with thoughtful finishing touches. Temple Guiting, the 12th-century residence of the Knight Templars, offers the peace and tranquillity of an unspoilt village. An ideal base to walk quiet country lanes or tour the North Cotswolds.

Low season per week: £275.00–£300.00
High season per week: £300.00–£325.00
Short breaks: from £125.00–£200.00

1 cottage: sleeping 2 people

292 Cider Press Cottage ★ ★ ★ ★

Oldcroft, Lydney, Gloucestershire
Contact: Mr & Mrs S Hinton, 1 Westleigh Villa, St Swithens Road, Oldcroft, Lydney, Gloucestershire GL15 4NF
Tel: (01594) 510285 **Fax:** (01594) 510285

Situated in the Royal Forest of Dean, this superb cottage stands in four acres of ground bordering the forest. This comfortable cottage has a well equipped kitchen with dining area, downstairs double bedroom, shower room/WC , first-floor double bedroom, twin bedded room and bathroom/WC. Suitable for disabled people. A perfect location for visitors with pets. There is good fishing, riding and excellent walking and cycling opportunities nearby.
Category 2

Low season per week: £318.00
High season per week: £603.00

1 cottage: sleeping 6 people + cot

293 Magnolia Cottage Apartment ★ ★ ★ ★

Bourton-on-the-Water, Cheltenham, Gloucestershire **Web:** www.cottageguide.co.uk/magnolia
Contact: Magnolia Cottage, Lansdowne, Bourton-on-the-Water, Gloucestershire GL54 2AR
Tel: (01451) 821841 **Fax:** (01451) 821841 **E-mail:** kgrist@glos.businesslink.co.uk

Quality first-floor apartment, tastefully furnished. Sleeps four, in two twin-bedded rooms. Video, radio, dishwasher, microwave, freezer. Bathroom with shower. Carpeted throughout. Gas log-effect fire. Not suitable for children under ten. No pets. Non-smokers preferred. Available all year. SAE for brochure. Shops and restaurants within three minutes' easy walk. Terms available on request. All major cards accepted.

Low season per week: £250.00–£300.00
High season per week: £300.00–£350.00
Short breaks: from £145.00–£215.00 (min 3 nights)

1 apartment: sleeping 4 people
Cards accepted: Mastercard, Visa, Switch/Delta, Amex

294 Bruern Stable Cottages ★ ★ ★ ★ ★

Bruern, Chipping Norton, Oxfordshire **Web:** www.bruern.co.uk
Contact: Ms F Curtin, Red Brick House, Bruern, Chipping Norton, Oxfordshire OX7 6PY
Tel: (01993) 830415 **Fax:** (01993) 831750 **E-mail:** enquiries@bruern.co.uk

Sole winners of the English Tourism Council's 'England for Excellence' Award 1998. Bruern Stable Cottages contain every modern convenience that you would have in a contemporary city apartment, coupled with the open log fires, antiques and four-poster beds that you would find in a grand country house. There is a swimming pool, tennis court, games room and a children's play area. The gardens and interiors have been featured in The Sunday Times, Country Living, Condé Nast Traveller and The Lady.

Low season per week: £365.00–£786.00
High season per week: £744.00–£2012.00
Short breaks: from £255.00–£655.00

10 cottages: sleeping 2–8 people
Cards accepted: Mastercard, Visa, Switch/Delta

295 Glebe Farm Holiday Lets   ★ ★ ★ ★

Glebe Farm, Barnsley Road, Cirencester, Gloucestershire
Contact: Mrs P Handover, Glebe Farm, Barnsley Road, Cirencester, Gloucestershire GL7 5DY
Tel: (01285) 659226 **Fax:** (01285) 642622

Located in rural surroundings, but only three miles from Cirencester, these fine cottages have been converted to a very high standard, keeping the character with exposed beams and stone. One hour from Stratford-upon-Avon, Bath and Oxford, the cottages make an ideal base for touring the Cotswolds. Perfect for a quiet break in the country. All cottages are fully equipped with all mod cons, with gardens, patios and barbecues. Pets welcome.

Low season per week: £150.00–£275.00
High season per week: £230.00–£490.00
Short breaks: from £100.00–£210.00
(October–March only)

5 cottages: sleeping 2–6 people

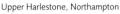

296 The Long Barn   ★ ★ ★ ★ ★

Upper Harlestone, Northampton
Contact: Mrs L Carter, Broombank, Upper Harlestone, Northampton NN7 4EL
Tel: (01604) 583237 **E-mail:** longbarn_uk@yahoo.co.uk

Set in beautiful terraced cottage gardens, with panoramic views overlooking unspoilt countryside, The Long Barn is the perfect choice for a peaceful and relaxing break. Creating a 'home from home' atmosphere, it comprises: sitting room/dining room, with beamed feature fireplace, fully equipped kitchen, a bright and cheerful bathroom with separate bath and shower cubicle. A master bedroom with impressive high ceiling and king-size bed and a second bedroom with two single beds.

Low season per week: £290.00–£340.00
High season per week: £340.00–£435.00
(all charges included)

1 cottage: sleeping 4 people

297 Brewer's Cottage   ★ ★ ★ ★

Flore, Northampton
Contact: Mrs A Loasby, The Old Baker's Arms, Kings Lane, Flore, Northampton NN7 4LQ
Tel: (01327) 349737 **Fax:** (01327) 349747

Brewer's Cottage is 'country Victorian' and has a large bedroom with double bed, bathroom, sitting room, a small kitchen and furnishings mainly from our family home. It is set within our own garden (which guests are invited to share with us), faces almost south and looks out over open farmland in the Nene Valley. Cars are parked within the garden behind double gates, in front of the cottage, away from the lane.

Low season per week: from £180.00
High season per week: from £200.00
Short breaks: from £140.00

1 cottage: sleeping 2 people

298 Vale Farm House   ★ ★ ★ ★

Ashton, Northampton

Contact: Mrs E Zanotto, Vale Farm House, Stoke Road, Ashton, Northampton NN7 2JN
Tel: (01604) 863697 **Fax:** (01604) 862859

Our fascinating guest annexe, set in extensive farm ground and riding stables, offers a billiard room with open fire, two large bedrooms and fully equipped kitchen. Home-grown produce, such as eggs, vegetables and meats are usually available. Bring your horse to our equestrian centre and explore the picturesque countryside around Salcey Forest. Pubs are nearby. Convenient for Silverstone, Stoke Bruene, Althorp, Castle Ashby and Stowe Gardens. Junction 15 of the M1 only five miles away.

Low season per week: £250.00–£300.00
High season per week: £350.00–£450.00
Short breaks: from £200.00–£250.00

1 cottage: sleeping 4–6 people

---

299 Courtyard Cottage and Norfolk House   ★ ★ ★ ★ ★

Docking, Norfolk

Contact: Tim & Liz Witley, 17 Peddars Way South, Ringstead, Norfolk PE36 5LF
Tel: (01485) 525341 **Fax:** (01485) 532715 **E-mail:** holidays@witleypress.co.uk

Situated in the village conservation area, these properties have been restored and totally refurbished to an excellent standard. They share a central courtyard garden and barbecue area. Tasteful décor and furnishings throughout create a seductive atmosphere of calm and comfort. Some bedrooms are en-suite, the others have a washbasin in each room. Comfortable seating and a log fire in the lounges; fully equipped kitchens; utility room. Also available, the *Rebecca Suite* (sleeps two, extra cost) and the *Long Hall*, a wonderful room available for a special occasion, with its own kitchen and cloakroom, seats up to ten for a dinner party. Shops, a restaurant and pubs – just a few minutes' walk!

Low season per week: Cottage £265.00–£360.00, House £295.00–£420.00
High season per week: Cottage £360.00–£520.00, House £380.00–£550.00

Winter breaks: (end October – end March) from £150.00 for 3 nights
1 cottage and 1 town house: sleeping 2–5 (+2) people

---

300 Coda Cottages   ★ ★ ★ ★

Poplar Farm, Dandy Corner, Cotton, Stowmarket, Suffolk **Web:** www.codacottages.co.uk
Contact: Mrs K Sida-Nicholls, Poplar Farm, Dandy Corner, Cotton, Stowmarket, Suffolk IP14 4QX
Tel: (01449) 780076 **Fax:** (01449) 780280 **E-mail:** codacottages@dandycorner.co.uk

A 17th-century barn with original features has been restored to three cottages set around a shared courtyard. They are surrounded by the owner's farmland in mid Suffolk. Each cottage has exposed beams, wooden floors, open brickwork and picture windows. They are all equipped to the highest standard with great attention to detail. The village of Cotton is ideally situated to many of Suffolk's attractions which include coastal and historic towns, houses and castles. **Category 2**

Low season per week: £140.00–£210.00
High season per week: £230.00–£320.00
Short breaks: from £77.00–£176.00

3 cottages: sleeping 2–3 people
Open: all year except February

---

301 Poplar Hall

Frostenden Corner, Frostenden, Wangford, Suffolk **Web:** www.southwold.ws/poplar-hall/
Contact: Mrs A L Garwood, Poplar Hall, Frostenden Corner, Frostenden, Wangford, Suffolk NR34 7JA
Tel: (01502) 578549

Poplar Hall Cottage and Poplar Hall Lofthouse are beautifully appointed and extremely well equipped. They both have large and attractive gardens with patios, gazebos and garden furniture. Parking is private and we welcome both children and pets. Frostenden Corner is only three and a half miles away from Southwold, the lovely country town by the sea. See also our serviced accommodation on page 126.

Low season per week: £180.00–£230.00
High season per week: £300.00–£400.00
Short breaks: from £120.00–£213.00 (low season only)

1 house and 1 cottage: sleeping 2–6 people

302 The Manse

★ ★ ★ ★ ★

The Green, Hartest, Bury St Edmunds, Suffolk **Web:** www.themanse.co.uk
Contact: Mrs E A Manning, Sturgeons Hall, The Green, Hartest, Bury St Edmunds, Suffolk IP29 4DH
Tel: (01284) 830690 **Fax:** (01284) 830228 **E-mail:** gig_manning@lineone.net

A beautifully appointed cottage in this quiet, charming village. Recently renovated to an extremely high standard with a most attractive enclosed garden and water feature. Beamed throughout, inglenook fireplace, fine furnishing and antiques. Listed pub with good food only 200 yards away. Situated close to Long Melford, Lavenham and Bury St Edmunds.

Low season per week: £450.00–£450.00
High season per week: £600.00–£600.00
Short breaks: from £275.00–£350.00 (weekends only)

1 cottage: sleeping 6 people

303 Lavenham Cottages

★ ★ ★ ★ ★

Market Place, Lavenham, Sudbury, Suffolk **Web:** www.lavenhamcottages.co.uk
Contact: Sheila Lane, Tile Barn, Hartest, Bury St. Edmunds, Suffolk IP29 4DN
Tel: (01284) 830771 **Fax:** (01284) 830771 **E-mail:** sheila@lavenhamcottages.co.uk

These award-winning cottages situated in the beautiful Market Place of this historic medieval town, were built in 1820 and have been recently renovated and refurbished to a very high standard. 37 and 38 have beautiful views of the National Trust's Guildhall and Market Place. 39 has pretty views of Market Lane and Church Street. Local amenities, shops, restaurants, inns, teashops, art and craft galleries are all within easy walking distance in the village.

Low season per week: £295.00–£395.00
High season per week: £400.00–£550.00

3 cottages: sleeping 4 people

304 Friar's Cottage ★ ★ ★ ★ ★

Bildeston, Ipswich, Suffolk **Web:** www.friarscottage.co.uk
Contact: Mrs P Sewell, 21 High Street, Bildeston, Ipswich, Suffolk IP7 7EX
Tel: (01449) 741108 **Fax:** (01449) 741108 **E-mail:** patricia@pmsewell.fsnet.co.uk

Beautifully restored part of Barons Hall, incorporating unique features such as crown posts, intricate oak work and beams. Located close to Lavenham, Long Melford – antiques centre of the East – and Dedham Vale. Impeccably furnished. Three double bedrooms, one en-suite, one communal. Large sitting room, dining hall, kitchen/breakfast room, all with open fires. Hand crafted units, fully equipped with washing machine, dishwasher, fridge/freezer, dryer, microwave. Centrally heated. Large, enclosed rear garden, two patios, bridge over stream. View on www.friarscottage.co.uk for tour of garden and inside property. Brochure available.

Low season per week: £300.00–£350.00
High season per week: £400.00–£500.00
Short breaks: from £200.00–£250.00

1 cottage: sleeping 6 people

305 The Tea House ★ ★ ★ ★

Layer Marney Tower, Colchester, Essex **Web:** www.layermarneytower.com
Contact: Mr N Charrington, Layer Marney Tower, Layer Marney, Colchester CO5 9US
Tel: (01206) 330784 **Fax:** (01206) 330784 **E-mail:** info@layermarneytower.com

The Tea House is an Edwardian folly, built in the grounds of Layer Marney Tower. With spectacular views of the Tudor Palace and the surrounding countryside, it offers the perfect location for a peaceful, rural break. Colchester, 'Constable Country' and the Abberton Reservoir are within easy reach. The Tea House has been renovated and equipped to the highest standards, with polished wood floors, original oak beams and wood-burning fire. It sleeps four in twin/double bedrooms.

Low season per week: £250.00–£340.00
High season per week: £340.00–£485.00
Short breaks: from £150.00

1 house: sleeping 4 people

306 The Pump House Apartment ★ ★ ★ ★ ★

Great Burstead, Billericay, Essex **Web:** www.thepumphouseapartment.co.uk
Contact: Mrs E R Bayliss, Pump House, Church Street, Great Burstead, Billericay, Essex CM11 2TR
Tel: (01277) 656579 **Fax:** (01277) 631160 **E-mail:** john.bayliss@willmottdixon.co.uk

Luxurious apartment on two floors and equipped to a very high standard. Ideal for visiting the south east and London. Options range from one bedroom/one bathroom, to three bedrooms/three bathrooms, all with two lounges, fully fitted kitchen/diner and air conditioning. The beautiful gardens have a summerhouse and barbeque facility. The outdoor swimming pool is heated to 80F May–September, with an all-year hot tub/gazebo. Special arrangements for children. Strictly no smoking. Brochure available.

Low season per week: £400.00–£800.00
High season per week: £525.00–£900.00
Short breaks: from £270.00–£540.00 (min 3 nights, short notice only)

1 apartment: sleeping 6 people
Cards accepted: Mastercard, Visa, Amex

England's
West Country

An unrivalled coastline

The very pace of life seems to slow as you head west. The counties of Cornwall, Devon, Dorset, Somerset and Wiltshire somehow conduct their various businesses at a more civilised speed. Wiltshire alone is land-locked, so perhaps the sea's proximity has a relaxing effect. The magnificent coastline certainly draws people, but its huge length – the South-West Coastal Path, hugging the foreshore from Minehead to Poole, is 613 miles (986km) long – ensures that even on the sunniest of days, many beaches remain uncrowded. As always, those further from car parks are the quietest, but have fewest facilities. The well-known resorts, such as Torquay, Newquay and Ilfracombe, cater for all tastes and depths of pocket. Quieter havens to consider include Ladram Bay (near Sidmouth), Soar (a tiny bay south west of Salcombe), Crinnis Beach (near St Austell), Pendower Beach (east of St Mawes), Portheras (west of St Ives), Lee Bay (near Ilfracombe) and St Audrie's Bay (just east of Watchet). Five minutes with a detailed map, especially of the superb southern coasts of Devon and Cornwall, will reveal countless other coves, bays and beaches, often with perfect sand.

Where the catch is landed

And if the weather is too cold for the beach, why not explore a Cornish or Devonian fishing village? These, as much a West Country speciality as Exmoor ponies or clotted cream, are one of the region's most engaging attractions. Some, such as Clovelly, on the northern coast of Devon, are justifiably famous. Cascading in picturesque manner down the cliffs into the sea and with a main 'street' too steep and too narrow for cars, it nevertheless copes admirably with its visitors. Others – some popular, some little-known – to explore include Port Isaac (on the North Cornish coast and also without cars), Helford, Looe (both East and West), Gorran Haven, Gunwalloe, Porthcurno (all on the southern coast of Cornwall) and Beer (on Devon's southern shores).

Perfect bases for exploration

As the sumptuous fishing villages are mainly in the extreme south-west, so the historic towns and cities tend to be further east in Somerset, Dorset and Wiltshire. Here you can choose from the incomparable cities of Salisbury, Bath and Wells, each with a magnificent range of secular and ecclesiastical architecture. Sherborne, too, has a glorious abbey and many fine buildings dating from the 16th and 17th centuries, as well as two castles, one in ruins, the other home to a range of art treasures. Shaftesbury is the setting for one of England's best-loved views – the steep, cobbled Gold Hill was famously used for a bread commercial – but has other intriguing nooks and crannies. Marlborough's broad High Street is lined with substantial 18th-century houses,

▶ Hawker's Morwenstow

Morwenstow, near Bude, was the home of Robert Stephen Hawker, a remarkable 19th-century parson and poet who left his whimsical mark upon the village. The vicarage chimneys are built to resemble the various churches with which he had been connected, while a capital on the village church displays the message 'This is the house of God' carved upside-down – for a celestial readership! High on the cliffs near by is a tiny driftwood hut, now owned by the National Trust, where, often in a fug of opium, he composed much of his poetry.

▶ Wookey Hole

Since the 15th century visitors have come to peer into the dark caverns and subterranean passages of Wookey Hole, near Wells. Today, dramatic electric lighting illuminates fantastic rock-formations and the glassy surface of an underground lake. There are a number of other attractions on offer too: paper-making demonstrations on the site of a 19th-century paper-mill; a collection of fairground art; a re-creation of Madame Tussaud's touring 'Cabinet of Curiosities'; and an exhibition of amusements from penny pier arcades (tel: 01749 672243).

yet is only a mile from Savernake, England's largest privately-owned forest, criss-crossed with footpaths. Ilchester dates from Roman times, but the town prospered in the medieval and Georgian periods; the houses round the green reveal the town's latter lineage. Looking further west, Salcombe, wonderfully situated on the Kingsbridge Estuary and enjoying the mildest of climates, became a resort in the 19th century. It has a gentle charm all its own, and is near Totnes, an appealing market town that has whole-heartedly embraced alternative culture. Just over the Tamar into Cornwall lies Launceston, a town of old-world character with two 16th-century bridges and a ruined medieval castle. Surrounded by unspoilt countryside, all make ideal bases for a long weekend's meandering.

Pasties, scrumpy and Yarg

An important part of a weekend away is to indulge in local specialities. The West Country has its fair share, with few visitors able to resist the cream tea. Clotted cream, the essential ingredient, is widely available throughout the region. Cornwall has its pasty, now eaten the length and breadth of the land, but nowhere as good, so they say, as in its home. Somerset's many orchards have long been given over to cider and the earthier, more potent scrumpy. Many farms still produce – and a couple of museums at Dowlish Wake and Bradford-on-Tone celebrate – the heady brews. The name of Cheddar is synonymous with cheese, but there are many more beside, from Cornish Yarg to Somerset Brie. And throughout, sold in market, shop, pub and restaurant, are fresh fish of the finest quality. The West Country is a piscivore's paradise!

Getting away from it all

Few places in the West Country have an urban feel. Bristol and Plymouth are cities redolent of their maritime history yet remaining close to their rural hinterlands. Elsewhere, the predominant mood is of the country, and visitors are spoilt for choice when it comes to walking territory. The three moors – Bodmin, Exmoor and Dartmoor – are all wild enough to have challenging routes suitable for the experienced hiker only, but on their gentler fringes are endless, easier options that reveal some of England's most sublime countryside. The national parks of Dartmoor and Exmoor have many suggestions for walks; outside these, areas particularly rewarding for exploration on foot include the Mendips in north Somerset, the Lizard in south west Cornwall, the Marlborough Downs in north east Wiltshire and the Quantock Hills just east of Exmoor. Thanks to the South-West Coastal Path, walking the coast is straightforward, though often strenuous. Other long-distance paths in the region include the Exe Valley Way (a 45 mile (72km) level route following the River Exe from Exmoor to its estuary); the West Devon Way, a shorter path that runs

► **Swindon, the Railway Town**

In the hundred years between 1830 and 1930, Swindon's population increased from 1,740 to 65,000. The reason was the arrival of the Great Western Railway (GWR) and the setting up of its manufacturing works in the town. The company built a 'railway village' to house its growing workforce: no. 34 Faringdon Road is now a museum (tel: 01793 466553) furnished as it might have been in the late 19th century. The company's hostel for male workers is now the GWR museum (tel: 01793 466555), displaying locomotives and railway memorabilia.

► **Chesil Beach**

One of the stranger natural phenomena of the South Coast, Chesil Beach is a 16 mile (26km) strip of shingle running from the Dorset village of Abbotsbury to the Isle of Portland. Fashioned entirely by the sea to a height of some 30–40ft (9–12m), the bank forms a thin barrier between the Fleet, the largest lagoon in Britain, and the sea. Barely disturbed by mankind, the Fleet supports as many as 150 species of seaweed, as well as abundant fish and water-fowl. (Chesil Beach Centre – tel: 01305 760579)

▶ Brunel's Bristol

The great engineer, Isambard Kingdom Brunel, was only 23 when he won a competition to design a bridge across the Avon Gorge at Bristol. This was the start of a long association with the city, one which produced its most famous landmarks.

Brunel, chief engineer for the Great Western Railway, designed its splendid neo-Tudor station, Temple Meads, now a Grade I listed building.

His great steam-ships SS *Great Western*, and SS *Great Britain* were built in Bristol: the latter, in the city docks, is now a museum (tel: 0117 926 0680).

▶ Lundy Island

Lundy is as remote an island as England has to offer and makes a magnificent day out from Ilfracombe and Bideford, both some 24 miles (38km) distant on the north Devon coast. The island, 3 miles (5km) long and never much more than half a mile (1km) wide, boasts some superb scenery, and there can be no better way of passing time here than strolling its gentle paths. The west coast is the highlight of the island: here Soay sheep and feral goats pick their way over stacks of granite tumbling hundreds of feet to the Atlantic while ravens wheel above.

along Dartmoor's western edge from Plymouth to Okehampton; the Two Moors Way, a magnificent and demanding path extending over 100 miles (160km) and linking Dartmoor and Exmoor; the Liberty Trail, following the route taken by the Monmouth Rebellion through south Somerset and west Dorset; and the Saints Way, a 37 mile (60km) coast to coast route across Cornwall from Padstow to Fowey. Public transport links with many of these longer paths, allowing them to be tackled in sections; most also have shorter, circular routes using part of their length. For the walker keen to get away from motor traffic, there is an alternative suggestion. The island of Lundy has a pub, church and shop, and just one small road within 12 miles (19km). But it does have spectacular cliff-top paths.

A celebration of words and music

Held annually in late May and early June, the Salisbury Festival presents both classical and jazz concerts, poetry and exhibitions, folk, circus and children's events. Further west, the Roman city of Bath hosts a festival of literature (February) and of music (May). The latter kicks off with opening-night celebrations featuring fireworks, and celebrates contemporary European jazz, early and classical music. On a smaller scale and at roughly the same time of year, Chard, in southern Somerset, promotes music in a variety of styles composed by women. Held over six weeks or so in July and August, the Dartington Festival gives a series of concerts devoted to opera, dance and classical music in the medieval Dartington Hall and gardens. It is aimed as much at those who wish to partake as to listen. Also in July is the Exeter Festival, when the broad-ranging programme may include classical music in the Gothic cathedral, opera and fireworks, lectures, comedy, jazz, theatre and fringe events.

Houses of substance

The region's historic houses range from the large-scale – such as Longleat and Wilton House, both in Wiltshire – to the more compact Coleridge Cottage at Nether Stowey, where the eponymous poet found inspiration for *The Rime of the Ancient Mariner*. Little has changed in the two centuries since Coleridge moved in. Other remarkable – and visitable – residences of the region include Great Chalfield Manor (near Melksham), a 15th-century house of mellow stone with a fine great hall, and Forde Abbey, a former monastery near Chard now also known for its gardens. Not far away, in the sleepy countryside near Beaminster, is the Tudor mansion of Parnham, renowned for its furniture workshop. By contrast, Bristol and Bath each preserve a magnificent 18th-century townhouse: Bristol's is appropriately called The Georgian House, while Bath's proudly proclaims its address – No. 1 Royal Crescent. The latter was once the home of the Duke of York who famously marched his men up and down hills. Devon, meanwhile, invites you to a couple of castles a little out of the ordinary. Castle Drogo, perched above the River Teign near Drewsteignton is the work of Edwin Lutyens, and was not completed until the 1930s. Of more authentic age for a castle is Bickleigh, though it is in reality more fortified manor house than full-blooded medieval castle. One of its attractions is a display of gadgets used by Second World War spies. It is best to turn up at Pencarrow, a Georgian family home near Bodmin, in late spring or early summer when no fewer than 692 separate species of rhododendron welcome visitors, whether of a botanical bent or not. Trerice, a few miles south east of Newquay, is a glorious Elizabethan house with unusual curved and scrolled gables. It is home to a remarkable collection of lawnmowers.

In search of St Hyacinth

Cornwall offers the church-hunter rich pickings. There are superb buildings – such as Launcells Church, inland from Bude, little altered since its completion in the 15th century. There are incomparable settings: the churches at St Anthony-in-Meneage on the Helford River and at St Just-in-Roseland are two of the best. And there are the wondrous names. Churches in Cornwall are dedicated to St Petroc, St Hyacinth, St Nonna, St Germans and St Winnow. Other consecrated buildings to seek out in the West Country include St Brannock's in Braunton and St Andrew's in Cullompton (both Devon), St Andrew's in Banwell (Somerset) and St Mary's in Lydiard Tregoze (near Swindon).

Some useful contact numbers

Perry's Cider Mills, Dowlish Wake, Ilminster (tel: 01460 52681)
Sheppy's Farmhouse Cider, Bradford-on-Tone, Taunton (tel: 01823 461233)
Dartmoor National Park (tel: 01822 890414)
Exmoor National Park (tel: 01398 323665)
Salisbury Festival (tel: 01722 323883)
Bath Literature Festival (tel: 01225 463362)
Bath International Music Festival (tel: 01225 463362)
Chard Festival of Women in Music (tel: 01460 66115)
Dartington International Summer School (tel: 01803 847077)
Exeter Festival (tel: 01392 265118)
Longleat, Warminster (tel: 01985 844400)
Wilton House, Wilton (tel: 01722 746720)
Coleridge Cottage, Nether Stowey (tel: 01278 732662)
Great Chalfield Manor, Melksham (tel: 01225 782239)
Forde Abbey, Chard (tel: 01460 220231)
Parnham, Beaminster (tel: 01308 862204)
The Georgian House, Bristol (tel: 0117 921 1362)
No. 1 Royal Crescent, Bath (tel: 01225 428126)
Castle Drogo, Drewsteignton (tel: 01647 433306)
Bickleigh Castle, Tiverton (tel: 01884 855363)
Pencarrow, Bodmin (tel: 01208 841369)
Trerice, Newquay (tel: 01637 875404)

▶ À la Ronde

À la Ronde, near Exmouth in Devon, was the brainchild of two cousins, Jane and Mary Parminter. They built it, in about 1796, in imitation of a church in Ravenna which they had admired on a grand tour of Europe. Though its exterior is extraordinary – it has 16 sides, diamond-shaped windows, and a conical roof – its interior is more bizarre still. The cousins decorated the rooms with feathers, shells, dried flowers, marbled paint, cut paper, sand, even seaweed and straw. These fragile decorations have recently been restored to their original condition (tel: 01395 265514).

▶ Dartmoor Longhouses

A defining feature of the longhouse is that humans and livestock lived under a single roof. This arrangement, common on the Continent, is very rare in England, and only occurs where it was vital to keep livestock warm and near at hand in harsh winter conditions. Around a hundred longhouses remain on Dartmoor: low, rectangular buildings, built between 1150 and 1700 from huge blocks of granite, often partly recessed into the hillside to maximise shelter.

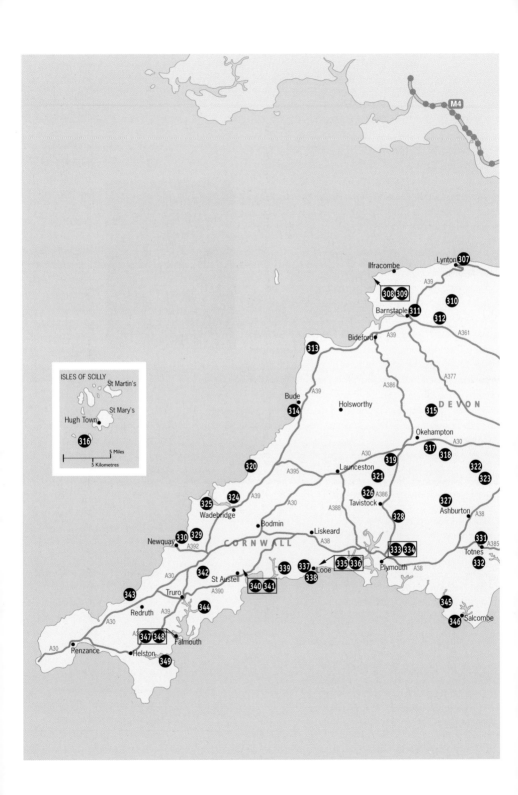

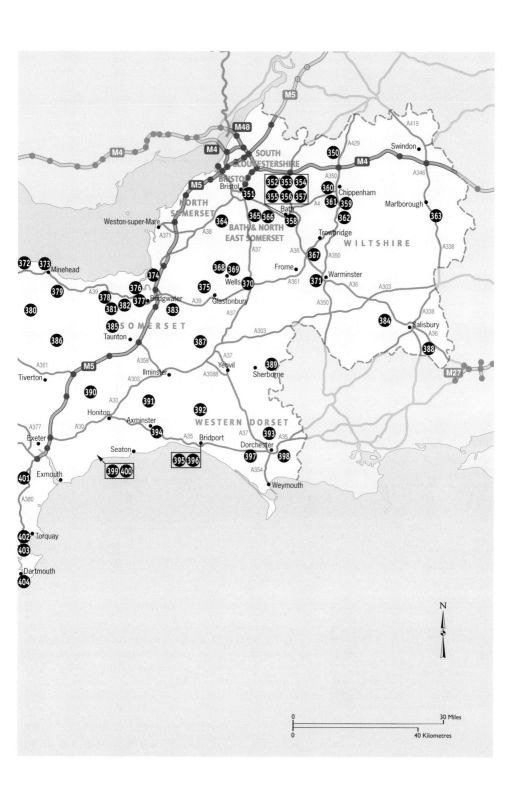

307 Kingford House

♦♦♦♦

Longmead, Lynton, Devon EX35 6DQ **Tel:** (01598) 752361

Nestling under Hollerday Hill, close to the 'Valley of Rocks'. All rooms are comfortably appointed to a high standard with colour television, clock radio, hairdryer and tea making facilities. Traditional home cooking, a choice of menu (changed daily) and selective wine list. Ideal situation for walkers, with the coastal path close by, or for touring Exmoor by car. Ample off-street parking available. Managed by resident, caring proprietors offering a warm welcome and relaxed, friendly atmosphere.

Bed & Breakfast per night: single room £21.50; double room £43.00
Dinner, Bed & Breakfast per person, per night: £35.00
Evening meal: 1900 (last bookings 1700)
Bedrooms: 2 single, 3 double, 1 twin

Bathrooms: 4 en-suite, 2 private
Parking: 8 spaces

308 Watersmeet Hotel

★★★ Silver Award

Mortehoe, Woolacombe, Devon EX34 7EB **Tel:** (01271) 870333 **Fax:** (01271) 870890
Web: www.watersmeethotel.co.uk **E-mail:** info@watersmeethotel.co.uk

Set on the National Trust Atlantic coastline with panoramic views of Hartland Point and Lundy Island, the three acres of garden enclose a lawn tennis court, an open air swimming pool and steps to the beach below. A superb indoor pool and spa is popular with everybody. Watersmeet offers the comfort and peace of a country house, and all the bedrooms, lounges and the octagonal restaurant overlook the sea. The Watersmeet offers a wine list to complement its national award-winning cuisine and service.

Bed & Breakfast per night: single room from £85.00–£125.00; double room from £125.00–£200.00
Dinner, Bed & Breakfast per person, per night: £75.00–£115.00
Lunch available: 1200–1400 (bar meals)
Evening meal: 1900 (last orders 2030)

Bedrooms: 1 single, 12 double, 8 twin, 2 triple
Bathrooms: 22 en-suite
Parking: 50 spaces
Open: All year except January
Cards accepted: Mastercard, Visa, Switch/Delta, Amex

309 Woolacombe Bay Hotel

★★★ Silver Award

Woolacombe, Devon EX34 7BN **Tel:** (01271) 870388 **Fax:** (01271) 870613
Web: www.woolacombe-bay-hotel.co.uk **E-mail:** woolacombe.bayhotel@btinternet.com

Set in six acres of quiet gardens gently leading to three miles of EC Blue Flag golden sands. Built in the halcyon days of the mid-1800s, the hotel has a relaxed style of comfort and good living. Guests can enjoy unlimited use of superb sporting facilities, or just relax with a good book in spacious lounges overlooking the Atlantic. The 'Hothouse' offers fitness, massage and beauty treatments. Superb cooking of traditional and French dishes. Shooting, fishing, horse-riding and boating available.

Bed & Breakfast per night: single occupancy from £50.00–£90.00; double room from £100.00–£180.00
Dinner, Bed & Breakfast per person, per night: £80.00–£120.00
Evening meal: 1930 (last orders 2100)

Bedrooms: 27 double, 11 twin, 5 triple, 22 family rooms **Bathrooms:** 65 en-suite
Parking: 150 spaces
Open: February–December
Cards accepted: Mastercard, Visa, Switch/Delta, Amex, Diners

310 Rockley Farmhouse

◆◆◆◆ Silver Award

Brayford, Nr Simonsbath, Exmoor, North Devon EX32 7QR **Tel:** (01598) 710429 **Fax:** (01598) 710429
Web: www.hicon.co.uk/rockley **E-mail:** rockley@hicon.co.uk

Red deer can often be seen grazing around our delightful farmhouse which is situated in spectacular seclusion within Exmoor National Park. Rockley, set in five peaceful acres, is an ideal base for coastal and moorland walks. A large stream-bordered garden offers a perfect retreat. We offer traditional, hearty breakfasts in lovely accommodation with a private guest lounge.

Bed & Breakfast per night: single occupancy £25.00; double room £50.00
Dinner, Bed & Breakfast per person, per night: £39.00
Evening meal: 1800

Bedrooms: 2 double, 1 twin
Bathrooms: 1 en-suite, 1 private (or family)
Parking: 8 spaces
Open: All year except Christmas

311 Bradiford Cottage

◆◆◆◆

Bradiford, Barnstaple, Devon EX31 4DP **Tel:** (01271) 345039 **Fax:** (01271) 345039
Web: www.humesfarm.co.uk **E-mail:** holidays@humesfarm.co.uk

The cottage is a creaky, lived-in, 17th-century converted farm building with good country taste. Along the flagstone passage there is a large, homely drawing room leading out to a secluded patio, the flower garden and the lawn which stretches up the hill. There is a bathroom with a huge bath under a sloping ceiling and a delightful main bedroom with wiggly walls. The village pub, swimming pools, sandy beaches and Exmoor are nearby.

Bed & Breakfast per night: single room from £18.00–£20.00; double room from £36.00–£40.00

Bedrooms: 1 single, 2 double, 1 twin
Bathrooms: 2 shared
Parking: 4 spaces

312 Huxtable Farm

◆◆◆◆ Silver Award

West Buckland, Barnstaple, Devon EX32 0SR **Tel:** (01598) 760254 **Fax:** (01598) 760254
Web: www.huxtablefarm.co.uk **E-mail:** jpayne@huxhilton.enterprise-plc.com

This beautiful Medieval Farmhouse (with oak panelling, beams, log fireplaces, uneven floors and low doorways!) situated in a secluded position within its 80 acres of rolling countryside and woodland, is an ideal hideaway for exploring North Devon, with Exmoor National Park and beautiful coastline close at hand. Tennis court, sauna, games room and farm walk with abundant wildlife and panoramic views. Enjoy a memorable candlelit dinner of farm/local produce served with a complimentary glass of home-made wine. A Devon cream tea awaits you!

Bed & Breakfast per night: single occupancy £35.00; double room from £50.00–£52.00
Dinner, Bed & Breakfast per person, per night: £41.00–£51.00
Evening meal: 1930 (last bookings 1730)

Bedrooms: 3 double, 1 triple, 2 family
Bathrooms: 5 en-suite, 1 private
Parking: 12 spaces
Open: All year except January and December
Cards accepted: Mastercard, Visa, Switch/Delta, JCB, Solo

313 Golden Park

Hartland, Bideford, Devon EX39 6EP **Tel:** (01237) 441254
E-mail: yeo@gopark.freeserve.co.uk

◆◆◆◆◆ Gold Award

17th-century farmhouse situated at the end of a private drive. All rooms are spacious, comfortable and tastefully decorated with lovely views of the old walled garden or the coast. This country house with its friendly atmosphere has an oak-beamed drawing room, dining room and garden room for guest use. Golden Park would make an ideal base for a relaxing and tranquil break in an area designated as an Area of Outstanding Natural Beauty.

Bed & Breakfast per night: single occupancy from £25.00–£27.00; double room from £40.00–£50.00

Bedrooms: 2 double, 1 twin
Bathrooms: 3 en-suite
Parking: 5 spaces

The South-West Coastal Path

'Poole 500 miles' reads the signpost pointing west along the Somerset coast at Minehead. In this daunting manner begins the South-West Coastal Path, a walk around England's 'toe' taking in some of the most magnificent coastal scenery in the land. The walk starts dramatically as it enters the Exmoor national park, hugging steep, wooded slopes that drop precipitously down to the sea, with stupendous views of the Welsh coast. Further on, the section of Devon coastline from Westward Ho! (the only British placename to include an exclamation mark) to the Cornish border is equally lovely as it passes the huddled village of Clovelly and the heights of Hartland Point with fine views of Lundy Island.

The Cornish Coast, both north and south, displays a stunning array of rocky promontories and soaring cliffs, interspersed with superb sandy beaches and fishing villages nestling in tiny coves. In general, the south coast, here and further on, is harder to negotiate than the north because of the many estuaries cutting into the lower-lying terrain, often requiring long detours inland.

The path re-enters Devon and, almost immediately, Plymouth, the largest city on its route. After rounding the wild promontories of Bolt Head and Prawle Point, it meanders through the gentler landscape of the 'Devon Riviera' and the seaside resorts of Paignton, Torquay, Teignmouth, and Dawlish. In Dorset, chalk cliffs run from Lyme Regis to Lulworth, interrupted by the long finger of shingle, Chesil Bank. The walk ends on a scenic high point as it negotiates the limestone heights of the Isle of Purbeck, an island in name only, for it remains firmly attached to the mainland.

As well as offering stunning scenery, the walk is rich in historical interest, from prehistoric hillforts in Dorset to Palmerston forts in Plymouth, or the abandoned village of Tyneham (Dorset) taken over by the army in 1943. In Cornwall, defunct engine houses and empty pilchard 'palaces' are relics of a rich industrial past.

The naturalist, as well as the historian, will find much of interest. The protruding coastline provides a landfall for migrating birds, while sub-tropical species of plants flourish in the mild climes of the south west. The Lizard, in particular, supports a unique flora, while army ranges at Lulworth, untouched by modern farming practices, have preserved a rare botanical habitat.

There are several guides to the South-West Coastal Path available, some suggesting shorter, circular walks and offering advice on accommodation, local attractions and other practical information.

314 The Falcon Hotel
★★★ Silver Award

Breakwater Road, Bude, Cornwall EX23 8SD **Tel:** (01288) 352005 **Fax:** (01288) 356359

Overlooking the famous Bude Canal, with beautiful walled gardens and yet only a short stroll from the beaches and shops, the Falcon has one of the finest settings in North Cornwall. Established in 1798, it still retains an old-world charm and atmosphere. The bedrooms are furnished to a very high standard, and have televisions with Teletext and Sky. Excellent local reputation for the quality of the food, both in the bar and candlelit restaurant.

Bed & Breakfast per night: single room from £42.00–£44.00; double room from £84.00–£88.00
Dinner, Bed & Breakfast per person, per night: £56.00–£58.00
Lunch available: 1200–1400
Evening meal: 1900 (last orders 2100)

Bedrooms: 7 single, 16 double, 6 twin
Bathrooms: 29 en-suite
Parking: 40 spaces
Cards accepted: Mastercard, Visa, Switch/Delta, Amex, Diners, Eurocard, Visa Electron, Solo

315 Lower Nichols Nymet Farm
◆◆◆◆ Silver Award

Lower Nichols Nymet, North Tawton, Devon EX20 2BW **Tel:** (01363) 82510 **Fax:** (01363) 82510
E-mail: pylefamlnn@aol.com

We offer a haven of comfort and rest on our farm that is set in rolling countryside in the centre of Devon. On holiday, food becomes important – we serve hearty and healthy breakfasts and candlelit dinners using local produce. Our elegantly furnished en-suite bedrooms have glorious views. There are many National Trust properties and other attractions to visit. This is a perfect base for exploring the beauties of the West Country. A no smoking establishment. Brochure available.

Bed & Breakfast per night: single occupancy £25.00; double room from £40.00–£45.00
Dinner, Bed & Breakfast per person, per night: £30.00–£32.50
Evening meal: 1830

Bedrooms: 1 double, 1 family
Bathrooms: 2 en-suite
Parking: 4 spaces
Open: March–October

316 Covean Cottage
◆◆◆◆

St Agnes, Isles of Scilly TR22 0PL **Tel:** (01720) 422620 **Fax:** (01720) 422620

Covean Cottage, on the peaceful island of St Agnes, is an old established business and now three generations of the family are working to make your holiday extra special. Very comfortable accommodation, good home-cooked food. Glorious sea views. An island paradise.

Bed & Breakfast per night: double room from £52.00–£64.00
Dinner, Bed & Breakfast per person, per night: £41.00–£47.00
Evening meal: 1800 (last orders 1900)

Bedrooms: 3 double, 1 twin
Bathrooms: 2 en-suite, 2 shared
Cards accepted: Mastercard, Visa, Switch/Delta, Amex

317 The Cleave House

Belstone, Okehampton, Devon EX20 1QY **Tel:** (01837) 840055
Web: www.caterham.force9.co.uk/cleavehouse.htm **E-mail:** natalie_aguilera@hotmail.com

Be enthralled by the special atmosphere, sweeping views and closeness to nature, of this unique Colonial-style Edwardian mansion, in eight acres of garden and paddocks, high on Dartmoor. The spacious rooms have polished wooden floors, period furniture and large, comfy beds. Breakfasts are lavish and varied with optional room service. Watching the sunset from the verandah, taking a moorland stroll to the waterfall or bathing in the river – will be joys to remember.

Bed & Breakfast per night: double room £60.00	**Bedrooms:** 3 double
Dinner, Bed & Breakfast per person, per night: £45.00	**Bathrooms:** 3 en-suite
	Parking: 10 spaces

318 Throwleigh Manor

Throwleigh, Okehampton, Devon EX20 2JF **Tel:** (01647) 231630 **Fax:** (01647) 231630
Web: www.throwleighmanor.com **E-mail:** info@throwleighmanor.com

A beautiful country house set in 12-acre grounds, within the idyllic, peaceful countryside of Dartmoor National Park – the perfect place to relax in a friendly, informal atmosphere. The rooms are individually and tastefully furnished and we are renowned for our excellent breakfasts. Guests can use the swimming pool and games room, walk in the gardens or take the woodland path to our private lake. We are superbly situated for walking or activity holidays and central to explore the whole of the West Country.

Bed & Breakfast per night: single room from £28.00–£38.00; double room from £40.00–£50.00	**Bedrooms:** 1 single, 1 double, 1 family
	Bathrooms: 1 en-suite, 2 private
	Parking: 10 spaces

319 The Knole Farm

◆◆◆◆ Silver Award

Bridestowe, Okehampton, Devon EX20 4HA **Tel:** (01837) 861241 **Fax:** (01837) 861241
Web: www.knolefarm-dartmoor-holiday.co.uk

This Victorian farm house sits on a small summit, offering wonderful views across Dartmoor, with miles of unspoilt upland walks. A warm welcome awaits you with a homely atmosphere and delicious home-cooked food. Spacious en-suite rooms with many extras for your comfort. On those cooler evenings, sit beside a cosy log fire and enjoy the peacefulness of our countryside where guests have been returning annually. An ideal base for touring the north and south coasts, with walking, pony-trekking, golfing, fishing and National Trust properties nearby. We are 30 minutes from Exeter, 29 miles from Plymouth and three miles from the A30.

Bed & Breakfast per night: double room from £42.00–£44.00	**Bedrooms:** 2 double, 2 twin/family
Dinner, Bed & Breakfast per person, per night: £30.00–£35.00	**Bathrooms:** 3 en-suite, 1 private
Evening meal: 1830 (last bookings 1500)	**Parking:** 4 spaces

320 Port William Inn

♦♦♦♦

Trebarwith Strand, Tintagel, Cornwall PL34 0HB **Tel:** (01840) 770230 **Fax:** (01840) 770936
E-mail: william@eurobell.co.uk

Probably the best located inn in Cornwall, romantically situated 50 yards from the sea, overlooking sea, beach and cliffs on the unspoilt north coast at Trebarwith Strand. All rooms are en-suite and overlook the sea. We are renowned for the quality of our home-cooked traditional fayre and local sea food, which also includes vegetarian alternatives. We have a good selection of real ales, including local brews.

Bed & Breakfast per night: single occupancy from £52.00–£58.00; double room from £69.00–£85.00
Lunch available: 1200–1430
Evening meal: 1800 (last orders 2130)

Bedrooms: 2 double, 1 twin, 1 triple, 2 family
Bathrooms: 6 en-suite
Parking: 50 spaces
Cards accepted: Mastercard, Visa, Switch/Delta, Amex, Eurocard

321 Tor Cottage

♦♦♦♦♦ Gold Award

Chillaton, Lifton, Devon PL16 0JE **Tel:** (01822) 860248 **Fax:** (01822) 860126
Web: www.torcottage.co.uk **E-mail:** info@torcottage.co.uk

Enjoy the ambience of this special place. A national winner of the English Tourist Board's 'England for Excellence' Award and holder of a Gold Award. 2002 'Guest Accommodation of the Year' Award for All England. Tor Cottage has a warm and relaxed atmosphere and nestles in its own private valley. Streamside setting, lovely gardens and 18 acres of wildlife hillsides. Peace, tranquillity and complete privacy in beautiful en-suite bedsitting rooms, each with a log fire and private garden/terrace. Superb traditional and vegetarian breakfasts. Heated pool (summer). Early booking advisable. 45 minute easy drive from the new Eden Project. Special winter breaks available.

Bed & Breakfast per night: single occupancy £89.00; double room £115.00 (min 2 nights); special winter/spring breaks 3 for 2 nights

Bedrooms: 3 double, 1 twin
Bathrooms: 4 en-suite
Parking: 8 spaces
Open: All year except Christmas and New Year
Cards accepted: Mastercard, Visa, Switch/Delta, Visa Electron

322 Moorcote Guest House

♦♦♦♦

Chagford Cross, Moretonhampstead, Devon TQ13 8LS **Tel:** (01647) 440966
E-mail: moorcote@smartone.co.uk

Overlooking the small town of Moretonhampstead, this Victorian house is set well back from the road in attractive gardens where guests are welcome to sit and relax at any time. The home is tastefully furnished, with most bedrooms benefitting from stunning views across Dartmoor and the surrounding countryside. The location makes an ideal base for those wishing to explore Dartmoor and the whole of glorious Devon. Ample parking is provided in the grounds.

Bed & Breakfast per night: double room from £38.00–£42.00

Bedrooms: 2 double, 1 twin, 2 family
Bathrooms: 4 en-suite, 1 private
Parking: 6 spaces
Open: March–October

323 Edgemoor Hotel

★★★ Silver Award

Haytor Road, Bovey Tracey, Devon TQ13 9LE **Tel:** (01626) 832466 **Fax:** (01626) 834760
Web: www.edgemoor.co.uk **E-mail:** edgemoor@btinternet.com

'Loaded with charm', this wisteria-clad country house hotel is personally run by resident proprietors Rod and Pat Day. With its beautiful gardens and lovely en-suite bedrooms (including some four-posters) the Edgemoor provides the ideal setting in which to unwind from the cares of modern life. Good food (AA 2 Rosettes), fine wines and beautiful countryside combine to help make your stay memorable and enjoyable.

Bed & Breakfast per night: single room from £52.50–£60.00; double room from £80.00–£100.00
Dinner, Bed & Breakfast per person, per night: £57.50–£70.00 (min 2 nights)
Lunch available: 1200–1400
Evening meal: 1900 (last orders 2100)

Bedrooms: 3 single, 9 double, 3 twin, 1 triple, 1 family
Bathrooms: 17 en-suite
Parking: 50 spaces
Cards accepted: Mastercard, Visa, Switch/Delta, Amex, Eurocard, JCB, Visa Electron

---

324 Kivells

◆◆◆◆

Chapel Amble, Wadebridge, Cornwall PL27 6EP **Tel:** (01208) 841755
Web: www.kivells.biz **E-mail:** hosegood@kivells.biz

Kivells is peacefully situated in lovely countryside, yet close to the market town of Wadebridge. The stunning north Cornwall coast is nearby and the Eden Project and Lanhydrock House (National Trust) are within easy reach. Guests enjoy a warm welcome and comfortable accommodation. Aga-cooked, wholesome breakfasts with home-made bread, scones and preserves. Evening meals on request – simple home-cooked food using our own produce when available. Alternatively, excellent food is served at nearby renowned pubs.

Bed & Breakfast per night: double room from £40.00–£48.00

Bedrooms: 2 double, 1 twin
Bathrooms: 1 en-suite, 1 shared
Parking: 5 spaces
Open: Easter–October

---

325 The Dower House

◆◆◆◆◆ Gold Award

Fentonluna Lane, Padstow, Cornwall PL28 8BA **Tel:** (01841) 532317 **Fax:** (01841) 532667
Web: www.padstow.uk.com/dowerhouse/ **E-mail:** dower@btinternet.com

As you step on to our terrace and smile at this beautiful old house, you'll glance to your right over the rooftops of old Padstow, and marvel at the magnificent view of the Camel Estuary and distant hills of Bodmin Moor. Paul and Patricia will greet and introduce you to their house. You will be delighted with the individually-decorated rooms and the care with which your breakfast is freshly prepared and presented in their elegant dining room.

Bed & Breakfast per night: single room from £44.00–£52.00; double room from £62.00–£92.00
Lunch available: 1200–1430
Evening meal: 1900 (last orders 1930)

Bedrooms: 1 single, 3 double, 2 twin
Bathrooms: 6 en-suite
Parking: 8 spaces
Open: March–November
Cards accepted: Mastercard, Visa, Switch/Delta, Eurocard

326 Colcharton Farm ◆◆◆◆

Gulworthy, Tavistock, Devon PL19 8HU **Tel:** (01822) 616435 **Fax:** (01822) 616435
Web: www.visit-dartmoor.co.uk **E-mail:** colchartonfarm@agriplus.net

Escape from town and city to Colcharton and enjoy unspoilt scenery. Peacefully situated in the beautiful Tamar Valley, with panoramic views of Dartmoor. Our modern farmhouse provides every comfort in tasteful surroundings. Victorian-style conservatory, charming garden and log fire. Good food a speciality. Easy to locate. Two miles west of the lovely historic town of Tavistock. Central for touring. Many National Trust properties, attractions, gardens, the Eden Project, golf and eating houses nearby.

Bed & Breakfast per night: single occupancy from £25.00–£30.00; double room from £40.00–£45.00
Dinner, Bed & Breakfast per person, per night: from £30.00
Evening meal: 1800 (last orders 2000)

Bedrooms: 2 double, 1 twin
Bathrooms: 3 en-suite
Parking: 6 spaces

327 The Forest Inn ◆◆◆◆

Hexworthy, Yelverton, Devon PL20 6SD **Tel:** (01364) 631211 **Fax:** (01364) 631515
Web: www.theforestinn.co.uk **E-mail:** info@theforestinn.co.uk

The Forest Inn is situated in the middle of Dartmoor and offers an atmosphere from a more relaxed era. There is an excellent restaurant plus an extensive range of bar meals, together with a selection of Devon beers and cider. Quench your thirst after the efforts of the day with a drink at the bar or relax on the chesterfields in the lounge, complete with log fire for winter evenings. Dogs and muddy boots welcome!

Bed & Breakfast per night: single room from £25.00–£33.00; double room from £44.00–£55.00
Dinner, Bed & Breakfast per person, per night: £39.50–£55.00
Lunch available: 1200–1400
Evening meal: 1900 (last orders 2100)

Bedrooms: 2 single, 5 double, 3 twin
Bathrooms: 7 en-suite, 3 private
Parking: 60 spaces
Open: February–December
Cards accepted: Mastercard, Visa, Switch/Delta

328 Harrabeer Country House Hotel ◆◆◆◆

Harrowbeer Lane, Yelverton, Devon PL20 6EA **Tel:** (01822) 853302 **Fax:** (01822) 853302
Web: www.harrabeer.co.uk **E-mail:** reception@harrabeer.co.uk

The Harrabeer Country House Hotel is set in its own secluded gardens. There are six bedrooms with en-suite or private facilities. Guests may relax in the lounge or enjoy a chat and a drink in the cosy bar (residential licence). The hotel has a friendly and relaxed atmosphere which offers a personal service, high standards of comfort and good food. Whatever the length of your stay, you are assured of a very warm welcome.

Bed & Breakfast per night: single occupancy from £30.00–£37.00; double room from £50.00–£57.00
Dinner, Bed & Breakfast per person, per night: £39.50–£51.50
Evening meal: 1930 (last bookings 1200)

Bedrooms: 4 double, 2 twin
Bathrooms: 4 en-suite, 2 private
Parking: 6 spaces
Open: all year except Christmas and New Year
Cards accepted: Mastercard, Visa, Switch/Delta

329 The Falcon Inn

◆◆◆◆

St Mawgan, Newquay, Cornwall TR8 4EP **Tel:** (01637) 860225 **Fax:** (01637) 860884
Web: www.falcon-inn.co.uk **E-mail:** enquiries@falconinn.net

A beautiful 16th-century inn, situated in a quiet village within a conservation area, only one mile from the coast, six miles from Padstow and 20 minutes from the Eden Project. Rooms are individually furnished to a high standard. We offer a varied menu, both lunchtimes and evenings, with local produce and fresh fish featured. A varied wine list, award-winning gardens and log fires in winter make The Falcon an ideal base for business or pleasure.

Bed & Breakfast per night: single room £20.00; double room from £48.00–£64.00
Lunch available: 1200–1400
Evening meal: 1830–2130 (Sunday 1900–2100)

Bedrooms: 1 single, 2 double, 1 twin
Bathrooms: 2 en-suite, 1 shared
Parking: 20 spaces
Cards accepted: Mastercard, Visa, Switch/Delta, Diners, JCB

330 The Harbour Hotel

◆◆◆◆

North Quay Hill, Newquay, Cornwall TR7 1HF **Tel:** (01637) 873040
Web: www.harbourhotel.co.uk **E-mail:** alan@harbourhotel.co.uk

Situated in one of the most enviable positions in the West Country and overlooking the picturesque harbour and beaches. All the bedrooms are individually decorated, are en-suite with showers and have their own balconies with uninterupted sea views. All are south-east facing and benefit from the sun for the majority of the day. This is a small, elegant, period building with a professional, yet so relaxed atmosphere. The town centre is five minutes' walk away.

Bed & Breakfast per night: single occupancy from £45.00–£55.00; double room from £80.00–£88.00
Evening meal: 1800 (last orders 2100)

Bedrooms: 5 double/twin, 1 family
Bathrooms: 6 en-suite
Parking: 7 spaces
Cards accepted: Mastercard, Visa, Amex

331 The Old Forge at Totnes

◆◆◆◆ Silver Award

Seymour Place, Totnes, Devon TQ9 5AY **Tel:** (01803) 862174 **Fax:** (01803) 865385

This beautiful 600-year-old building is a haven of comfort and relaxation, not far from the town centre. Rooms are delightfully co-ordinated, offering hairdryer, radio alarm, clocks, central heating, colour television, beverage tray, continental bedding and direct dial telephone. We also have ground floor rooms and a family cottage suite. Leisure lounge with whirlpool spa. Enjoy breakfast in the Tudor-style dining room which offers a wide choice of menu with vegetarian options. Four minutes' walk to the town centre, riverside, countryside and eating places. No smoking indoors. Extensive afternoon tea menu served in the walled tea garden or conservatory. Evening meals by prior arrangement.

Bed & Breakfast per night: single room from £42.00–£52.00; double room from £54.00–£74.00

Bedrooms: 1 single, 5 double, 2 twin, 2 family
Bathrooms: 9 en-suite, 1 private
Parking: 10 spaces
Cards accepted: Mastercard, Visa, Switch/Delta, Eurocard, JCB, Maestro, Visa Electron, Solo

332 Orchard House

 ◆◆◆◆◆ Silver Award

Horner, Halwell, Totnes, Devon TQ9 7LB **Tel:** (01548) 821448
Web: www.orchard-house-halwell.co.uk

Tucked away in a rural hamlet of the South Hams, between Totnes and Kingsbridge, Orchard House stands beneath an old cider orchard. It offers superb accommodation – all bedrooms are en-suite with beautiful furnishings. Breakfasts are ample and varied, with cereals, juice and fruit followed by a cooked platter using local produce. Also guests' own sitting and dining room furnished with antiques, with log fire in stone and slate hearth. Large garden and private parking.

Bed & Breakfast per night: single occupancy £32.00; double room from £40.00–£46.00

Bedrooms: 2 double, 1 triple
Bathrooms: 3 en-suite
Parking: 3 spaces
Open: March–October

333 Bowling Green Hotel

◆◆◆◆◆ Silver Award

9-10 Osborne Place, Lockyer Street, Plymouth, Devon PL1 2PU **Tel:** (01752) 209090 **Fax:** (01752) 209092
Web: www.smoothhound.co.uk/hotels/bowling.html

Situated in the historic naval city of Plymouth opposite the world famous 'Drake's Bowling Green', this elegant Georgian hotel has superbly appointed bedrooms offering all the modern facilities the traveller requires. With a full breakfast menu and friendly and efficient family staff, you can be sure of a memorable visit to Plymouth. The Bowling Green Hotel is centrally situated for the Barbican, Theatre Royal, leisure/conference centre and ferry port, with Dartmoor only a few miles away.

Bed & Breakfast per night: single room £40.00; double room from £54.00–£56.00

Bedrooms: 1 single, 8 double, 2 triple, 1 family
Bathrooms: 12 en-suite
Parking: 4 spaces
Cards accepted: Mastercard, Visa, Switch/Delta, Amex, Diners, Eurocard, Visa Electron, Solo

334 Berkeleys of St James

 ◆◆◆◆

4 St James Place East, The Hoe, Plymouth, Devon PL1 3AS **Tel:** (01752) 221654 **Fax:** (01752) 221654
Web: www.smoothhound.co.uk/hotels/berkely2.html

Elegant, non-smoking, Victorian guesthouse in a quiet square on Plymouth Hoe. An ideal location for visiting the historic Barbican or touring Devon and Cornwall. Luxury en-suite rooms. Excellent English breakfast menu serving free range and organic produce where possible. A comfortable and quiet stay assured.

Bed & Breakfast per night: single room from £28.00–£35.00; double room from £40.00–£50.00

Bedrooms: 1 single, 3 double, 1 triple
Bathrooms: 4 en-suite, 1 private
Parking: 3 spaces
Cards accepted: Mastercard, Visa, Switch/Delta, Eurocard, JCB, Maestro, Visa Electron, Solo

335 Coombe Farm Country House Hotel ◆◆◆◆

Widegates, near Looe, Cornwall PL13 1QN **Tel:** (01503) 240223 or (01503) 240329 **Fax:** (01503) 240895
Web: www.coombefarmhotel.co.uk **E-mail:** coombe_farm@hotmail.com

Relax in a tranquil setting of lawns, meadows, woods and streams, with superb views down a wooded valley to the sea. Enjoy warm, friendly hospitality in a house lovingly furnished with antiques and interesting objects. There are open log fires, an outdoor pool and a candlelit dining room in which we serve a four-course dinner every evening. Nearby are glorious walks and beaches, National Trust properties and the Eden Project.

Bed & Breakfast per night: double room from £72.00–£78.00
Dinner, Bed & Breakfast per person, per night: £53.50–£56.50

Bedrooms: 1 twin, 7 triple, 2 family
Bathrooms: 10 en-suite
Parking: 24 spaces
Open: March–November
Cards accepted: Mastercard, Visa, Switch/Delta, Amex, Eurocard

336 Bucklawren Farm ◆◆◆◆ Silver Award

St Martin-by-Looe, Looe, Cornwall PL13 1NZ **Tel:** (01503) 240738 **Fax:** (01503) 240481
Web: www.bucklawren.co.uk **E-mail:** bucklawren@compuserve.com

Enjoy a warm welcome at Bucklawren, an elegant farmhouse set in the Cornish countryside, only one mile from the beach and the South-West Coastal Path. The bedrooms are en-suite and individually decorated, with all the comforts you would expect. Enjoy a traditional farmhouse breakfast of local produce. We offer a candlelit dinner served in the Granary Restaurant which specialises in producing high quality food.

Bed & Breakfast per night: single occupancy from £25.00–£30.00; double room from £46.00–£50.00
Dinner, Bed & Breakfast per person, per night: £36.50–£38.50
Evening meal: 1800 (last orders 2000)

Bedrooms: 2 double, 2 twin, 2 family
Bathrooms: 6 en-suite
Parking: 6 spaces
Open: March–November
Cards accepted: Mastercard, Visa

337 Trenderway Farm ◆◆◆◆◆

Pelynt, Polperro, Cornwall PL13 2LY **Tel:** (01503) 272214 **Fax:** (01503) 272991
E-mail: trenderwayfarm@hotmail.com

Built in the late 16th century, this mixed working farm is set in peaceful, beautiful countryside at the head of the Polperro Valley. Bedrooms here are truly superb – with bathrooms as big as some hotel bedrooms – and are decorated with the flair of a professional interior designer. A hearty farmhouse breakfast is served in the sunny conservatory, using local produce. Although an evening meal is not provided, an excellent range of restaurants can be recommended. Totally no smoking.

Bed & Breakfast per night: double room from £60.00–£70.00

Bedrooms: 3 double, 1 twin
Bathrooms: 4 en-suite
Parking: 4 spaces
Open: All year except December

338 Fieldhead Hotel

★★ Silver Award

Portuan Road, Hannafore, West Looe, Looe, Cornwall PL13 2DR **Tel:** (01503) 262689 **Fax:** (01503) 264114
Web: www.fieldheadhotel.co.uk **E-mail:** field.head@virgin.net

Built in 1896, the hotel occupies a commanding site on West Looe, providing remarkable views across Looe Bay to Rame Head, Eddystone Lighthouse and the intriguing Looe Island. Set in one acre of landscaped tropical gardens with heated outdoor pool, the Fieldhead has 15 individually styled en-suite bedrooms, most with sea views, including four superior and two with balconies. Mainly fresh produce and locally caught seafood are served in the stylish restaurant. On-site private car park.

Bed & Breakfast per night: single room from £28.00–£60.00; double room from £56.00–£90.00
Dinner, Bed & Breakfast per person, per night: £50.00–£75.00
Sunday lunch available: 1230–1400
Evening meal: 1830 (last orders 2045)

Bedrooms: 1 single, 8 double, 3 twin, 1 triple, 2 family
Bathrooms: 15 en-suite
Parking: 15 spaces
Cards accepted: Mastercard, Visa, Switch/Delta, Amex, Solo

339 Lesquite

◆◆◆◆ Silver Award

Lansallos, Looe, Cornwall PL13 2QE **Tel:** (01503) 220315 **Fax:** (01503) 220137
E-mail: lesquite@farmersweekly.net

Nestling in its own secluded valley, Lesquite, dating from the 17th century, offers you quiet, friendly comfort. Our breakfast room has french doors opening onto a sunny patio overlooking our woodlands – a haven for wild life in all its forms, with paths for you to enjoy. The majestic Cornish coast with footpaths and secluded beaches is within 3.5 miles, whilst Fowey, Polperro, Looe, the Eden Project and Heligan are within easy reach.

Bed & Breakfast per night: double room from £48.00–£50.00

Bedrooms: 2 double, 1 twin
Bathrooms: 3 en-suite
Parking: 4 spaces

340 Cliff Head Hotel

★★★ Silver Award

Sea Road, Carlyon Bay, St Austell, Cornwall PL24 3RB **Tel:** (01726) 812345 **Fax:** (01726) 815511
Web: www.cliffheadhotel.com **E-mail:** cliffheadhotel@btconnect.com

The Cliff Head Hotel faces south, close to the beach, with sea views and cliff walks. Standing in its own extensive grounds of over two acres. Situated in the centre of the Cornish Riviera – ideally positioned for exploring Cornwall. We are the closest three-star hotel to the Eden Project (15 minutes). A friendly, caring staff create a warm and welcoming atmosphere. Accommodation is all en-suite, centrally heated and furnished to a very high standard. The hotel has a restaurant serving local fish and produce. There is a heated indoor swimming pool, sauna and fitness room. The hotel caters for weddings, large functions and conferences. Special rates for local golf courses are available.

Bed & Breakfast per night: single room from £54.00; double room from £90.00
Dinner, Bed & Breakfast per person, per night: £60.00–£69.00
Lunch available: 1200–1345
Evening meal: 1900 (last orders 2130)

Bedrooms: 19 single, 17 double, 15 twin, 8 triple
Bathrooms: 59 en-suite
Parking: 80 spaces
Cards accepted: Mastercard, Visa, Switch/Delta

341 Carlyon Bay Hotel

★★★★ Silver Award

Sea Road, Carlyon Bay, St Austell, Cornwall PL25 3RD **Tel:** (01726) 812304 **Fax:** (01726) 814938
Web: www.carlyonbay.co.uk **E-mail:** info@carlyonbay.co.uk

Set in 250 acres of exquisite grounds, including its own championship golf course, the Carlyon Bay Hotel is blessed with a setting that is unique and only 2 miles from the Eden Project. Renowned for its spectacular coastal views and outstanding hospitality, every comfort and luxury is catered for. From the magnificent indoor and outdoor heated swimming pools to the award-winning Bay View Restaurant. A relaxing, peaceful retreat or delightful family holiday, the Carlyon Bay Hotel combines the finest facilities with the warmest of West Country welcomes.

Bed & Breakfast per night: single room from £77.00–£98.00; double room from £78.00–£125.00
Dinner, Bed & Breakfast per person, per night: £90.00–£137.00

Bedrooms: 13 single, 16 double, 41 twin, 2 triple
Bathrooms: 72 en-suite
Parking: 74 spaces
Cards accepted: Mastercard, Visa, Switch/Delta, Amex, Diners

342 Bissick Old Mill

◆◆◆◆ Silver Award

Ladock, Truro, Cornwall TR2 4PG **Tel:** (01726) 882557 **Fax:** (01726) 884057

Bissick Old Mill is known to be 300 years old and continued as a flour mill until the mid-1960s. Its conversion has been sympathetically conceived to provide modern conveniences whilst maintaining its former character, including slate floors, natural stone walls and beamed ceilings. Our aim is to provide you with the perfect environment in which to relax and enjoy the beauty of Cornwall, all areas of which are readily accessible from our central location.

Bed & Breakfast per night: single room £39.95; double room from £54.40–£69.00
Dinner, Bed & Breakfast per person, per night: £46.50–£59.45
Evening meal: 1900 (last bookings 1200)

Bedrooms: 1 single, 3 double, 1 twin
Bathrooms: 5 en-suite
Parking: 9 spaces
Cards accepted: Mastercard, Visa, Switch/Delta, JCB

343 Aviary Court Hotel

★★ Silver Award

Marys Well, Illogan, Redruth, Cornwall TR16 4QZ **Tel:** (01209) 842256 **Fax:** (01209) 843744
E-mail: aviarycourt@connexions.co.uk

A charming 300-year-old Cornish country house set in two acres of secluded well-kept gardens with tennis court. An ideal touring location – the coast is five minutes away and St Ives Tate, Heligan Gardens, the Eden Project and St Michael's Mount are all within easy reach. Six well-equipped bedrooms with en-suite, tea/coffee making facilities, biscuits, mineral water, fresh fruit, telephone and a view of the gardens. The resident family proprietors ensure personal service, offering well-cooked varied food that uses as much Cornish produce as possible.

Bed & Breakfast per night: single occupancy from £43.00–£45.00; double room from £62.00–£65.00
Dinner, Bed & Breakfast per person, per night: £45.00–£46.50 (min 2 sharing)
Lunch available: 1230–1330 (Sunday only)
Evening meal: 1900 (last orders 2030)

Bedrooms: 4 double, 1 twin, 1 triple
Bathrooms: 6 en-suite
Parking: 25 spaces
Cards accepted: Mastercard, Visa, Switch/Delta, Solo

344 The Hundred House Hotel   ★★ Silver Award

Ruan Highlanes, Nr Truro, Cornwall TR2 5JR **Tel:** (01872) 501336 **Fax:** (01872) 501151
Web: www.hundredhousehotel.co.uk **E-mail:** eccles@hundredhousehotel.co.uk

Delightful 19th-century Cornish country house set in three acres of garden. Near St Mawes on the Fal estuary and surrounded by superb countryside and unspoilt sandy coves. It is now a charming small hotel, beautifully decorated and furnished like an elegant English home. Delicious candlelit dinners, Cornish cream teas, log fires and croquet on the lawn make a relaxing short break or a longer stay a memorable delight. Ideal for exploring Cornwall, viting the Eden Project or walking the coastal path. AA Rosette award for food.

Bed & Breakfast per night: single room from £45.50–£48.00; double room from £92.00–£96.00
Dinner, Bed & Breakfast per person, per night: £54.00–£75.00
Evening meal: 1930 (last orders 2000)

Bedrooms: 2 single, 4 double, 4 twin
Bathrooms: 10 en-suite
Parking: 15 spaces
Open: March–October
Cards accepted: Mastercard, Visa, Switch/Delta, Amex

345 Thurlestone Hotel   ★★★★ Gold Award

Thurlestone, Kingsbridge, Devon TQ7 3NN **Tel:** (01548) 560382 **Fax:** (01548) 561069
Web: www.thurlestone.co.uk **E-mail:** enquiries@thurlestone.co.uk

An intimate atmosphere, characteristic of grand establishments, distinguishes us from others due to our location on the Devon coast, in an area of outstanding natural beauty. Sixty seven en-suite bedrooms (includes five suites), well-furnished with every facility, including video in some rooms. A restaurant with a reputation for fine rosette food, superb wine and long-serving staff. Leisure activities include indoor swimming pool, spa bath, sauna, solarium, 9-hole championship golf course and tennis, squash and badminton courts as well as opportunities for walks and fishing. Please telephone for brochure.

Bed & Breakfast per night: single room from £65.00–£109.00; double room from £130.00–£210.00
Dinner, Bed & Breakfast per person, per night: £53.00–£141.00 (min 2 nights)
Lunch available: 1230–1400
Evening meal: 1930 (last orders 2100)

Bedrooms: 5 single, 18 double, 24 twin, 16 family, 5 suites
Bathrooms: 67 en-suite
Parking: 119 spaces
Cards accepted: Mastercard, Visa, Switch/Delta, Amex, Eurocard, JCB

346 Tides Reach Hotel   ★★★ Silver Award

South Sands, Salcombe, Devon TQ8 8LJ **Tel:** (01548) 843466 **Fax:** (01548) 843954
Web: www.tidesreach.com **E-mail:** info@tidesreach.com

Located on a tree-fringed sandy cove in an Area of Outstanding Natural Beauty where country meets the sea, with a glorious view across the Salcombe Estuary, you can relax in style in this beautifully furnished and decorated hotel. Pamper yourself in the superb leisure complex, extensively equipped and with a sunny tropical atmosphere. Award-winning creative cuisine (AA 2 Rosettes) served with courtesy and care in our garden-room restaurant.

Bed & Breakfast per night: single occupancy from £68.00–£98.00; double room from £126.00–£234.00
Dinner, Bed & Breakfast per person, per night: £80.00–£140.00
Evening meal: 1900 (last orders 2100)

Bedrooms: 17 double, 15 twin, 3 family
Bathrooms: 35 en-suite
Parking: 100 spaces
Open: All year except January and December
Cards accepted: Mastercard, Visa, Switch/Delta, Amex, Diners, Eurocard, JCB, Visa Electron, Solo

347 Dolvean Hotel

♦ ♦ ♦ ♦ ♦ Silver Award

50 Melvill Road, Falmouth, Cornwall TR11 4DQ **Tel:** (01326) 313658 **Fax:** (01326) 313995
Web: www.dolvean.co.uk **E-mail:** reservations@dolvean.co.uk

Historic Falmouth, with it's beautiful natural harbour and splendid Tudor castle, is one of Cornwall's finest locations for exploring the far south west. Experience the elegance and comfort of our Victorian home, where carefully chosen antiques, fine china and fascinating books create an ambience where you can relax and feel at home. Each bedroom has it's own character, with pretty pictures and lots of ribbons and lace – creating an atmosphere that makes every stay a special occasion.

Bed & Breakfast per night: single room from £30.00–£40.00; double room from £60.00–£80.00

Bedrooms: 3 single, 5 double, 2 twin
Bathrooms: 10 en-suite
Parking: 10 spaces
Cards accepted: Mastercard, Visa, Switch/Delta, Amex

The Lizard

If it's Britain's most southerly point you're after, then come to the Lizard (Land's End is the westernmost point). This small Cornish peninsula has much to interest the visitor besides its location, being especially rich both geologically and botanically. Like almost every part of the county, the Lizard also has many historical connections and a glorious coastline.

Opinions vary as to how it got its name: some claim it means high palace, others that it derives from a Celtic word for outcast. Both explanations are plausible, for the Lizard is a level moorland plateau about 200ft (61m) above sea level, almost cut off from the rest of the county. Much of the peninsula is formed of serpentine stone, a soft, easily-worked material used in local churches (and on sale in the shops of Lizard village). A farmer reputedly chanced upon its ornamental qualities when he erected some large rocks in his field as rubbing posts for his cows. He soon noticed that the 'polished' areas showed patterns resembling snakeskin, and colours ranging from grey-green to pink. Once Queen Victoria had chosen it for Osborne House its popularity was assured. In the church of St Winwalloe at Landewednack it can be seen alternated with granite. This, the most southerly church in Britain, is where the last sermon was preached in Cornish (1678).

Kynance Cove, owned by the National Trust, is typical of the majestic coastline of the Lizard. Its rocky outcrops enjoy some unlikely names, including Man-o'-War Rock, the Devil's Postbox, the Devil's

Bellows and Asparagus Island (where the plant grows wild). There are some intriguing caves (the Parlour and the Drawing Room), but take care not to be stranded by the incoming tide.

The flora of the Lizard is a botanist's delight. Here can be found plants too tender to grow outdoors elsewhere in the country (such as tamarisks and the Hottentot fig) and others which are unique to this corner of England, such as Cornish Heath. These plants have to be able to withstand the frequent onslaught of sea gales, something which countless local vessels have not managed. More shipwrecks have occurred here than almost anywhere else in the country. Off the eastern coast of the peninsula are the Manacles, a group of ferocious rocks extending over a couple of square miles. In 1770 parishioners of the nearby church of St Arkerveranus (in the village of St Deverne) redesigned the steeple as a landmark to warn passing ships. They may have been successful, but there are still over 400 victims of shipwrecks buried in the churchyard.

348 Green Lawns Hotel

★★★ Silver Award

Western Terrace, Falmouth, Cornwall TR11 4QJ **Tel:** (01326) 312734 or (01326) 312007 **Fax:** (01326) 211427
Web: www.greenlawnshotel.com **E-mail:** info@greenlawnshotel.com

Where can you relax in an elegant, centrally positioned, chateau-style hotel with views across a beautiful bay? The Green Lawns Hotel and the famous Garras restaurant! If you are looking for a holiday where high standards and personal attention are paramount, you will enjoy an excellent choice of imaginative cuisine from a table d' hôte or à la carte menu. All our guests enjoy free membership of the Garras Leisure Club with its magnificent indoor swimming pool. 'Britain in Bloom' winners for six years running.

Bed & Breakfast per night: single room from £55.00–£105.00; double room from £110.00–£150.00
Dinner, Bed & Breakfast per person, per night: £72.50–£122.50
Lunch available: 1200–1345
Evening meal: 1845 (last orders 2145)

Bedrooms: 6 single, 16 double, 9 twin, 2 triple, 6 family
Bathrooms: 39 en-suite
Parking: 60 spaces
Cards accepted: Mastercard, Visa, Switch/Delta, Amex, Diners, Eurocard

349 Tregildry Hotel

★★ Silver Award

Gillan, Manaccan, Helston, Cornwall TR12 6HG **Tel:** (01326) 231378 **Fax:** (01326) 231561
Web: www.tregildryhotel.co.uk **E-mail:** trgildry@globalnet.co.uk

An elegant small hotel with stunning sea views. Tucked away in an undiscovered corner of the Lizard Peninsula, this is for those seeking relaxed and stylish comfort in 'away from it all' surroundings. Large, light lounges with panoramic sea views have comfy sofas, fresh flowers and the latest books and magazines. The glamourous restaurant has won awards for cuisine and the pretty sea-view bedrooms are attractively decorated with colourful fabrics. Near coastal path walks and an ideal peaceful base for exploring Cornwall.

Dinner, Bed & Breakfast per person, per night: £65.00–£85.00
Evening meal: 1900 (last orders 2030)

Bedrooms: 1 single, 6 double, 3 twin
Bathrooms: 10 en-suite
Parking: 15 spaces
Open: March–October
Cards accepted: Mastercard, Visa, Switch/Delta, Eurocard, JCB

350 Bradfield Manor

♦♦♦♦♦ Silver Award

Hullavington, Chippenham, Wiltshire SN14 6EU **Tel:** (01666) 838000 **Fax:** (01666) 838200
Web: www.bradfieldmanor.co.uk **E-mail:** enquiries@bradfieldmanor.co.uk

A medieval hall house dating from 1425, Bradfield offers delightful rooms in a charming and historic setting. Situated close to Malmesbury, Bradfield is an ideal base for visiting Bath, Castle Combe and the Cotswolds. Our guest bedrooms are in a private wing and have king-size beds and lovely views over the surrounding countryside. There are several excellent pubs and restaurants nearby and you can enjoy an evening drink in our own cosy licensed bar.

Bed & Breakfast per night: single occupancy from £59.00–£69.00; double room from £79.00–£89.00

Bedrooms: 2 double, 1 twin
Bathrooms: 3 en-suite
Parking: unlimited
Cards accepted: Mastercard, Visa, Switch/Delta, Amex

351 Number 31

31 Royal York Crescent, Clifton, Bristol BS8 4JU **Tel:** (01179) 735330

Number 31 is part of a Grade II* listed building, superbly situated with stunning views from the balcony of the city and over to the countryside beyond. It has stylish interiors, charm and a warm hospitality. There is a prize-winning tranquil garden where guests may take breakfast. Ideally situated in Clifton village and with easy access to the city and the motorways.

Bed & Breakfast per night: double room from £65.00–£75.00

Bedrooms: 2 double/twin
Bathrooms: 1 shared
Parking: 1 space

352 Brompton House

Saint Johns Road, Bath BA2 6PT **Tel:** (01225) 420972 **Fax:** (01225) 420505
Web: www.bromptonhouse.co.uk **E-mail:** bromptonhouse@btinternet.com

A charming former Georgian rectory (1777) set in beautiful secluded gardens, Brompton House has been converted and extended with exquisite care and attractive furnishings and is only a few minutes' level walk from the city centre. All en-suite rooms are equipped with colour television, direct dial telephone, radio, hairdryer and tea/coffee-making facilities. A very friendly welcome is assured from the Selby family in a relaxing and informal atmosphere. Free private car park. Winter short breaks available. Strictly no smoking.

Bed & Breakfast per night: single room from £36.00–£55.00; double room from £60.00–£95.00

Bedrooms: 2 single, 9 double, 5 twin, 2 family rooms
Bathrooms: 18 en-suite
Parking: 18 spaces
Cards accepted: Mastercard, Visa, Switch/Delta, Amex

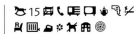

353 Roman City Guest House

18 Raby Place, Bathwick Hill, Bath BA2 4EH **Tel:** (01225) 463668 or (07899) 777953 **Fax:** (01225) 463668
Web: www.romancityguesthouse.co.uk **E-mail:** romancityguesthse@amserve.net

Enjoy any and every occasion in the peaceful surroundings of this beautifully restored house. Built in 1810 and retaining its many original features, character and charm. Tastefully decorated and furnished throughout. Relaxing en-suite bedrooms with four-poster beds and superb views. A full English breakfast served in an elegant dining room. A warm welcome and friendly atmosphere awaits you. Easy car parking and a five-minute walk to Bath Abbey. Truly a perfect setting for a perfect memory.

Bed & Breakfast per night: single room from £35.00–£50.00; double room from £50.00–£85.00

Bedrooms: 1 single, 2 double, 1 family
Bathrooms: 1 private, 2 shared
Parking: 4 spaces
Cards accepted: Mastercard, Visa, Switch/Delta

354 Walton Villa ♦♦♦♦

3 Newbridge Hill, Bath BA1 3PW **Tel:** (01225) 482792 **Fax:** (01225) 313093
Web: www.walton.izest.com **E-mail:** walton.villa@virgin.net

You will receive a warm and friendly welcome to our immaculate, non-smoking family-run bed and breakfast. Our en-suite bedrooms are delightfully decorated and furnished for your comfort, with colour television, hairdryer and complimentary hospitality tray. Our generous and delicious full English or vegetarian breakfasts are cooked to order and served in our elegant dining room. Situated one mile west of the city centre, we are convenient for exploring Roman and Georgian Bath and an ideal base for visiting Wells, Glastonbury, Stonehenge etc. Off-street parking available.

Bed & Breakfast per night: single room from £25.00–£40.00; double room from £45.00–£55.00

Bedrooms: 1 single, 2 double, 1 twin
Bathrooms: 3 en-suite, 1 private
Parking: 4 spaces
Cards accepted: Mastercard, Visa, Switch/Delta

355 The Ayrlington ♦♦♦♦♦ Silver Award

24/25 Pulteney Road, Bath BA2 4EZ **Tel:** (01225) 425495 **Fax:** (01225) 469029
Web: www.ayrlington.com **E-mail:** mail@ayrlington.com

A handsome Victorian house set in a splendid walled garden with exceptional views of the Abbey. Bath's centre and historic sites are just a five minute level stroll away. The elegant interior is a graceful blend of English and Asian antiques artwork and fine fabrics. All bedrooms have an individual theme and are beautifully furnished, some with four-poster beds and spa baths. The hotel has a residents bar, private parking and is entirely non-smoking.

Bed & Breakfast per night: single occupancy from £75.00–£145.00; double room from £90.00–£145.00

Bedrooms: 11 double, 1 twin
Bathrooms: 12 en-suite
Parking: 16 spaces
Cards accepted: Mastercard, Visa, Switch/Delta, Amex

356 Holly Lodge ♦♦♦♦♦ Silver Award

8 Upper Oldfield Park, Bath BA2 3JZ **Tel:** (01225) 424042 or (01225) 339187 **Fax:** (01225) 481138
Web: www.hollylodge.co.uk **E-mail:** stay@hollylodge.co.uk

This charming Victorian town house commands panoramic views of the city and is delightfully furnished with individually designed bedrooms, some with four-posters, and superb bathrooms. Elegant and stylish, it is owned and operated with meticulous attention to detail by George Hall. Superb breakfasts are enjoyed in the appealing breakfast room with yellow and green decor. Furnished with antiques, this immaculate establishment makes a pleasant base for touring Bath and the Cotswolds.

Bed & Breakfast per night: single room from £48.00–£55.00; double room from £79.00–£97.00

Bedrooms: 1 single, 4 double, 2 twin
Bathrooms: 7 en-suite
Parking: 8 spaces
Cards accepted: Mastercard, Visa, Switch/Delta, Amex, Diners, Eurocard, JCB, Maestro, Visa Elect

357 The Lansdown Grove Hotel

★ ★ ★ Silver Award

Lansdown Road, Bath BA1 5EH **Tel:** (01225) 483888 **Fax:** (01225) 483838
Web: www.marstonhotels.com **E-mail:** lansdown@marstonhotels.com

Grade II listed building enjoying breathtaking views over the Georgian part of the city and wooded hills beyond. 60 comfortable bedrooms with private bathroom, remote-controlled colour television with satellite channels, trouser press, hair dryer and hospitality tray. For those special occasions there are superior rooms and a four-poster suite. Excellent restaurant offering a varied menu, complemented by friendly and professional staff. Free car parking. Ten minute walk from the city centre.

Bed & Breakfast per night: single room from £94.00–£125.00; double room from £117.00–£179.00
Dinner, Bed & Breakfast per person, per night: £58.00–£72.50 (min 2 nights)
Evening meal: 1900 (last orders 2130)

Bedrooms: 8 single, 29 double, 7 twin, 4 triple
Bathrooms: 48 en-suite
Parking: 35 spaces
Cards accepted: Mastercard, Visa, Switch/Delta, Amex, Diners, Eurocard

358 Monkshill

◆ ◆ ◆ ◆ ◆ Gold Award

Shaft Road, Monkton Combe, Bath BA2 7HL **Tel:** (01225) 833028 **Fax:** (01225) 833028
Web: www.monkshill.com **E-mail:** monks.hill@virgin.net

Five minutes from the centre of Bath lies this secluded and very comfortable country residence, surrounded by its own peaceful gardens and enjoying far-reaching views over one of the most spectacularly beautiful parts of the Avon Valley. You can be assured of a warm welcome at Monkshill, where the emphasis is on luxurious comfort and complete relaxation. The drawing room, with its fine antiques and open log fire, is for the exclusive use of the guests and the spacious bedrooms enjoy fine views over the gardens and valley below. Monkshill is situated within a designated Area of Outstanding Natural Beauty.

Bed & Breakfast per night: single occupancy from £50.00–£65.00; double room from £65.00–£80.00

Bedrooms: 2 double, 1 twin
Bathrooms: 2 en-suite, 1 private
Parking: 6 spaces
Cards accepted: Mastercard, Visa, Switch/Delta, Eurocard, JCB, Maestro, Visa Electron, Solo

359 King John's Hunting Lodge

◆ ◆ ◆ ◆

21 Church Street, Lacock, Chippenham, Wiltshire SN15 2LB **Tel:** (01249) 730313 **Fax:** (01249) 730725

Romantic 13th-century guest house with Tudor tea rooms. King John's Hunting Lodge is the oldest house in this unspoilt medieval village and part of the lodge still has much of the original structure. Two bedrooms, both en-suite. The Kings' Room also has an adjoining twin-bedded room. Breakfast includes local farm produce and Margaret's home-made bread and jam.

Bed & Breakfast per night: single occupancy £45.00; double room from £75.00–£80.00
Lunch available: 1200–1500

Bedrooms: 2 double/twin/family
Bathrooms: 2 en-suite
Parking: 5 spaces
Open: all year except Christmas –mid January

360 Home Farm ◆◆◆◆

Harts Lane, Biddestone, Chippenham, Wiltshire SN14 7DQ **Tel:** (01249) 714475 or 07812 654693 **Fax:** (01249) 701488
E-mail: audrey.smith@homefarmbandb.co.uk

At Home Farm we welcome long and short stay visitors and business guests. A 17th-century farmhouse on a working farm, we are set in the picturesque village of Biddestone with its village greens and duck pond and two pubs just a stroll away. Breakfast is served in the oak-beamed dining room. Guests may use the garden or drawing room with log fire. Ample safe parking. We are well situated for easy M4 access and for visiting Bath, Castle Combe, Cotswolds, Cheddar etc.

Bed & Breakfast per night: single occupancy from £27.00–£32.00; double room from £45.00–£50.00

Bedrooms: 1 double, 1 triple, 1 family
Bathrooms: 2 en-suite, 1 private
Parking: 4 spaces

361 Heatherly Cottage ◆◆◆◆ Silver Award

Ladbrook Lane, Gastard, Corsham, Wiltshire SN13 9PE **Tel:** (01249) 701402 **Fax:** (01249) 701412
Web: www.smoothhound.co.uk/hotels/heather3.html **E-mail:** ladbrook1@aol.com

A 17th-century cottage in a quiet lane with two acres and views across open countryside. There is ample off-road parking and guests have a separate wing of the house with their own entrance and staircase. All rooms are en-suite (the larger double has a king-size bed) and all are equipped with colour television, clock/radio, tea/coffee tray and hairdryer. Close to Bath, Lacock, Castle Combe, Avebury, Stonehenge and National Trust properties. Restaurants nearby for good food.

Bed & Breakfast per night: single occupancy from £27.00–£30.00; double room from £46.00–£51.00

Bedrooms: 2 double, 1 twin
Bathrooms: 3 en-suite
Parking: 8 spaces

362 Springfield B&B ◆◆◆◆

403 The Spa, Melksham, Wiltshire SN12 6QL **Tel:** (01225) 703694 **Fax:** (01225) 703694

A family home in a 19th-century spa lodging house. Run by grandparents Janet and Peter. An historic house with relaxed atmosphere in Victorian gardens. A two-room luxury suite offers double or twin beds. Family room. Children welcome. Pretty and historic villages, towns and country parks within four to ten miles. Parking available. Use of garden. Tea/coffee maker, hairdryer, television lounge with small library if required. Visited by BBC. Quiet cul-de-sac location. Many returning guests. Daily/weekly special break terms.

Bed & Breakfast per night: single occupancy from £30.00–£36.00; double room from £46.00–£54.00

Bedrooms: 1 double/twin, 1 family
Bathrooms: 1 en-suite, 1 private
Parking: 3 spaces

363 Westcourt Bottom

◆◆◆◆

165 Westcourt, Burbage, Marlborough, Wiltshire SN8 3BW **Tel:** (01672) 810924
Web: www.westcourtbottom.co.uk **E-mail:** westcourt.b-and-b@virgin.net

A large 17th-century thatched cottage, five miles from Marlborough, set in quiet countryside. Half-timbered rooms and large interesting gardens with swimming pool offer a relaxed and informal atmosphere. Free range breakfasts with fresh juices and home-made bread. Sitting room with log fire and television for guests. Coffee, tea and biscuits in all rooms. Central for Stonehenge and Avebury, close to Savernake Forest, the Ridgeway, Kennet and Avon Canal. Excellent pub food nearby. Evening meals by arrangement.

Bed & Breakfast per night: single occupancy from £28.00–£30.00; double room from £46.00–£50.00

Bedrooms: 2 double, 1 twin
Bathrooms: 1 en-suite, 1 shared
Parking: ample

364 Butcombe Farm

◆◆◆◆

Aldwick Lane, Butcombe, Bristol BS40 7UW **Tel:** (01761) 462380 **Fax:** (01761) 462300
Web: www.butcombe-farm.demon.co.uk **E-mail:** info@butcombe-farm.demon.co.uk

Dating back to the late 14th century, Butcombe Farm is a beautiful manor house with individually decorated, en-suite bed and breakfast rooms. Set in several acres of field and woodland, amid the tranquil Somerset countryside, the fantastic views combine perfectly with our excellent facilities. Winter weekend offers available. Activities include fly fishing, horse riding, cycle hire, wine tasting, aromatherapy massage, golf and clay pigeon shoots. Private dinner parties available by arrangement. For more information please contact Barry and Josephine Harvey.

Bed & Breakfast per night: single occupancy £39.00; double room £54.00

Bedrooms: 3 double, 2 triple
Bathrooms: 5 en-suite
Parking: 20 spaces
Cards accepted: Mastercard, Visa, Switch/Delta, Eurocard

365 The Hunters Rest

◆◆◆◆◆ Silver Award

King Lane, Clutton Hill, Bristol BS39 5QL **Tel:** (01761) 452303 **Fax:** (01761) 453308
Web: www.huntersrest.co.uk **E-mail:** paul@huntersrest.co.uk

The Hunters Rest Inn was originally built in 1755 as a hunting lodge for the Earl of Warwick. Conveniently located for Bath, Bristol and Wells, this privately-owned free house is renowned for its home-made food, well-stocked cellar and warm welcome. Furnished to the highest standards, our luxury bedrooms include: a four-poster suite, antique furniture, stunning bathrooms, direct dial telephones with modem links, colour televisions, videos and all have wonderful views.

Bed & Breakfast per night: single room from £49.50–£65.00; double room from £75.00–£105.00
Dinner, Bed & Breakfast per person, per night: £65.00–£85.00
Lunch available: 1200–1400

Evening meal: 1830 (last orders 2130)
Bedrooms: 3 single/double, 1 twin/family
Bathrooms: 4 en-suite
Parking: 50 spaces
Cards accepted: Mastercard, Visa, Switch/Delta

366 The Old Court

 ◆◆◆◆◆ Silver Award

Main Road, Temple Cloud, Bristol BS39 5DA **Tel:** (01761) 451101 **Fax:** (01761) 451224
Web: www.theoldcourt.com **E-mail:** oldcourt@gifford.co.uk

Situated nine miles from Bath, Wells and Bristol, overlooking the beautiful Chew Valley, this Grade II listed former court house and police station has recently opened following extensive renovation. Now a family-run bed and breakfast, it retains original features with en-suite bedrooms, power showers and satellite television. Sit by the fire in the magnificent courtroom with vaulted ceilings and cathedral windows. Lovely walled gardens. Have a sauna or jacuzzi prior to your evening meal. Groups by arrangement (we specialise in family reunions, birthday parties and weddings).

Bed & Breakfast per night: single room from £40.00–£65.00; double room from £50.00–£120.00

Bedrooms: 4 single, 6 double, 3 twin, 3 family
Bathrooms: 8 en-suite, 1 private
Parking: 8 spaces
Cards accepted: Mastercard, Visa

367 The Full Moon at Rudge

 ◆◆◆◆

Bath BA11 2QF **Tel:** (01373) 830936 **Fax:** (01373) 831366
Web: www.thefullmoon.co.uk **E-mail:** fullmoon@lineone.net

A wonderful 17th-century inn, in a small hamlet just ten miles from Bath, with traditional settles and flagged floors, the smell of polish and fresh flowers and a warm welcome from friendly staff. A superb à la carte menu, a daily changing fresh fish board, home-made breads, jams and chutneys, delicious puddings and cheeses and comfortable en-suite bedrooms overlooking the gardens – all are memorable features of this lovely inn. Take a drive into the beautiful city of Bath, a walk in the woods at Longleat, a visit to Wells or David Sheppard's studio at Cranmore – all are within easy reach.

Bed & Breakfast per night: single occupancy from £45.00–£55.00; double room from £60.00–£75.00
Dinner, Bed & Breakfast per person, per night: £49.50–£65.00
Evening meal: 1800 (last orders 2130)

Bedrooms: 4 double, 2 family
Bathrooms: 6 en-suite
Parking: 50 spaces
Cards accepted: Mastercard, Visa, Switch/Delta, Amex

368 The Old Stores

 ◆◆◆◆

Westbury-sub-Mendip, Wells, Somerset BA5 1HA **Tel:** (01749) 870817 or 07721 514306 **Fax:** (01749) 870980
E-mail: moglin980@aol.com

This charming cottage, once the village stores, is set in the heart of the village, mid-way between the scenic attractions of Wells and Cheddar Gorge. It is ideally situated for exploring this area of outstanding scenic beauty. All guest rooms are equipped with television, facilities for making hot drinks and have en-suite private facilities. There is also a guest sitting room with television and books and maps of the local area.

Bed & Breakfast per night: single occupancy from £21.00–£22.00; double room from £42.00–£44.00

Bedrooms: 2 double, 1 twin
Bathrooms: 2 en-suite, 1 private
Parking: 5 spaces

369 Beryl

◆◆◆◆◆ Silver Award

Wells, Somerset BA5 3JP **Tel:** (01749) 678738 **Fax:** (01749) 670508
Web: www.beryl-wells.co.uk **E-mail:** stay@beryl.co.uk

'Beryl' – a precious gem in a perfect setting. Small 19th-century Gothic mansion, set in peaceful gardens, one mile from the centre of Wells. Well placed for touring the area. Offers comfortable, well-equipped bedrooms and relaxed use of the beautifully furnished reception rooms. Dinner is served with elegant style using fresh produce from the vegetable garden and local supplies. Children and pets are welcome. Outdoor heated pool, June–September. Chair lift to first floor bedrooms.

Bed & Breakfast per night: single occupancy from £50.00–£65.00; double room from £65.00–£95.00
Dinner, Bed & Breakfast per person, per night: £52.50–£67.50 (min 2 sharing)
Evening meal: 1930

Bedrooms: 5 double, 3 twin
Bathrooms: 8 en-suite
Parking: 16 spaces
Open: all year except Christmas
Cards accepted: Mastercard, Visa, Switch/Delta

Arthurian Legends of the South West

No one knows if Arthur actually existed. What is certain is that when the Romans left Britain in the early 5th century AD, recorded history went with them, at least for several hundred years. So the shadowy figures from these 'Dark Ages' are inevitably reconstructions by later clerics or deductions by latter-day archaeologists.

In fact, historians think Arthur did exist, probably a 5th- or 6th-century British chieftain who fought the invading Anglo-Saxons. His base – Camelot? – may have been at South Cadbury, near Sherborne, since excavations have revealed that this Iron Age hillfort on the troubled frontline between Saxon and Briton, was reoccupied and refortified in the late 5th or early 6th century.

The complex web of Arthurian myth, however, claims earlier beginnings. One story has Joseph of Arimathea sailing to Cornwall, perhaps to trade in tin. With him on one trip to the West Country is the young Christ who walks on the Mendips at Priddy. Another version has Joseph hiding the Holy Grail, the cup Christ used at the Last Supper, on Glastonbury Tor, his staff, stuck firmly into the ground miraculously

growing shoots and known as the Glastonbury Thorn. The quest for the Holy Grail – a metaphor for the search for spiritual perfection – preoccupies many of Arthur's knights in several myths.

The British king is said to have visited Glastonbury at least twice, once to rescue his wife Guinevere from the clutches of Melwas, and again when he went to Avalon (often equated with Glastonbury) to die. Glastonbury Tor indeed resembles the description of the Isle of Avalon, looming dramatically above the Somerset wetlands, which in Arthur's day were regularly inundated by the sea. In 1191 the monks of Glastonbury Abbey (shown here) found a tomb, apparently inscribed with the words 'Here lies the famous King Arthur in the Isle of Avalon'. Only the cynical would see this as a clever (and successful) ploy to attract pilgrims to an abbey recently devastated by fire.

Other West Country Arthurian sites can be found at Amesbury (where Guinevere became abbess after Arthur's death), Dozmary Pool on Bodmin Moor (where Excalibur was caught by a mysterious hand), Tintagel (Arthur's birthplace) and Badbury Rings in Dorset (one of a number of possible locations for the site of the Battle of Mount Badon, at which Arthur was mortally wounded).

370 Bowlish House

Coombe Lane, Shepton Mallet, Somerset BA4 5JD **Tel:** (01749) 342022 **Fax:** (01749) 342022

An elegant Georgian restaurant with rooms, wonderfully counterbalanced by the relaxed atmosphere. The award-winning restaurant and wine list are famous for their range and eclectic mix of modern classics. Shepton Mallet is a market town on the south-west slopes of the Mendip Hills, just ten minutes from the cathedral city of Wells. It is an ideal centre for exploring nearby Bath, Stourhead, Longleat, Glastonbury and Cheddar. Member of the Master Chefs of Great Britain.

Bed & Breakfast per night: single occupancy from £55.00–£60.00; double room from £65.00–£75.00
Dinner, Bed & Breakfast per person, per night: £54.45–£66.95
Evening meal: 1900 (last orders 2130)

Bedrooms: 2 double, 1 twin
Bathrooms: 3 en-suite
Parking: 10 spaces
Cards accepted: Mastercard, Visa, Switch/Delta

371 Bugley Barton

 Silver Award

Victoria Road, Warminster, Wiltshire BA12 8HD **Tel:** (01985) 213389 **Fax:** (01985) 300450
E-mail: bugleybarton@aol.com

Bugley is a Georgian farmhouse set in a beautiful formal garden. The house is traditionally furnished and the spacious and well equipped en-suite (shower) rooms have views overlooking the fountain. Well situated for trips to Bath, Salisbury, Stonehenge, Stourhead, Wells, Longleat and Center Parcs. Ample parking. Easy access to train station. Good selection of local pubs. One room on ground floor with separate access. Delicious breakfast cooked on the Aga, home-made cake and an idyllic stay awaits.

Bed & Breakfast per night: single occupancy from £40.00–£42.50; double room from £60.00–£65.00

Bedrooms: 2 double, 1 twin
Bathrooms: 2 en-suite, 1 private
Parking: unlimited

372 Porlock Vale House

★★ Silver Award

Porlock Weir, Somerset TA24 8NY **Tel:** (01643) 862338 **Fax:** (01643) 863338
Web: www.porlockvale.co.uk **E-mail:** info@porlockvale.co.uk

Formerly a hunting lodge, now a magnificent Edwardian country house hotel in a wonderful situation. Set in twenty five acres of grounds which sweep down to the sea, Porlock Vale House nestles at the foot of the ancient wooded fringe where Exmoor meets the coast. A friendly, unpretentious hotel where you can enjoy good food and fine wines served in a relaxed, informal atmosphere, with beautiful, uninterrupted views across Porlock Bay. Whether you enjoy the great outdoors or sitting by a log fire, Porlock Vale is the perfect place for a short break at any time of the year.

Bed & Breakfast per night: single room/occupancy from £45.00–£56.00; double room from £90.00–£120.00
Dinner, Bed & Breakfast per person, per night: £65.00–£85.00
Lunch available: 1200–1330

Bedrooms: 1 single, 9 double, 5 twin
Bathrooms: 15 en-suite
Parking: 20 spaces
Cards accepted: Mastercard, Visa, Switch/Delta, Amex, Eurocard, JCB

373 Channel House Hotel   ★★ Gold Award

Church Path, Off Northfield Road, Minehead, Somerset TA24 5QG **Tel:** (01643) 703229 **Fax:** (01643) 708925
Web: www.channelhouse.co.uk **E-mail:** channel.house@virgin.net

An elegant Edwardian country house perfectly located for exploring the beauty of Exmoor and situated on the lower slopes of Exmoor's picturesque North Hill where it nestles in two acres of award-winning gardens. The high standards of cuisine and accommodation will best suit those seeking superior quality and comfort. If you would like to experience smiling service in the tranquil elegance of this lovely hotel, we will be delighted to send you our brochure and sample menu. A non smoking hotel.

Bed & Breakfast per night: single occupancy from £56.00–£69.00; double room from £97.00–£108.00
Dinner, Bed & Breakfast per person, per night: £56.00–£69.00 (min 2 sharing)
Evening meal: 1900 (last orders 2030)

Bedrooms: 2 double, 5 twin, 1 triple
Bathrooms: 8 en-suite **Parking:** 10 spaces
Open: March–November and Christmas
Cards accepted: Mastercard, Visa, Switch/Delta, Amex, Diners, Eurocard, JCB, Maestro, Visa Electron

374 Ilex House   ◆◆◆◆

102 Main Road, West Huntspill, Highbridge, Somerset TA9 3QZ **Tel:** (01278) 783801 or (07989) 601705 **Fax:** (01278) 794254
E-mail: rogwyn@onetel.net.uk

Ilex House is a Grade II listed Georgian house with large garden, built around 1800 and furnished appropriate to the period. Accommodation comprises one double and one twin room, both en-suite, and a double room with private bathroom. Central heating throughout. Each room has colour television, radio, hairdryer and hospitality tray. Tea or coffee with home-made cakes served on arrival. Full English breakfast or fruit platter together with home-made bread, jam and marmalade.

Bed & Breakfast per night: single occupancy from £25.00–£35.00; double room from £50.00–£60.00

Bedrooms: 2 double, 1 twin
Bathrooms: 2 en-suite, 1 private
Parking: 4 spaces
Cards accepted: Mastercard, Visa, Switch/Delta, JCB, Maestro, Visa Electron

375 Meare Manor   ◆◆◆◆

60 St Marys Road, Meare, Glastonbury, Somerset BA6 9SR **Tel:** (01458) 860449 **Fax:** (01458) 860449
Web: www.mearemanor.co.uk **E-mail:** info@mearemanor.co.uk

Meare Manor, a rediscovered 300-year-old manor house in the centre of King Arthur country, offers a warm welcome, quiet surroundings, a good breakfast and beautiful en-suite rooms. We welcome the disabled community, small dogs (apartments only) and children. Lift, ample parking and cycle lock-up. Near Glastonbury, Cheddar, Wells Cathedral, Clarks Shopping Village at Street, the M5, Weston-super-Mare, Taunton, Yeovil, Bath, Bristol and the sea.

Bed & Breakfast per night: single room from £30.00–£45.00; double room from £60.00–£75.00

Bedrooms: 1 single, 3 double, 2 twin, 2 family
Bathrooms: 8 en-suite
Parking: 20 spaces
Cards accepted: Mastercard, Visa, Switch/Delta, JCB, Maestro, Visa Electron

Entries are cross referenced by number to the maps on pages 150–151

376 Gurney Manor Mill

Gurney Street, Cannington, Bridgwater, Somerset TA5 2HW **Tel:** (01278) 653582 **Fax:** (01278) 653993
Web: www.gurneymill.freeserve.co.uk **E-mail:** gurneymill@yahoo.co.uk

"There's an old mill by a stream, where you can stay and dream." A converted old watermill and barn, alongside a stream with waterfall and widlife, in the picturesque village of Cannington at the foot of the Quantock Hills. Cannington has five pubs (four with restaurants), a café, shops, a visitor centre for golf, cycle hire, horse riding and heritage gardens. An ideal location for touring the south west. Dogs welcome. Private fishing.

Bed & Breakfast per night: single occupancy from £25.00–£30.00; double room from £40.00–£50.00

Bedrooms: 1 double, 1 twin, 2 family
Bathrooms: 4 en-suite
Parking: 20 spaces
Cards accepted: Mastercard, Visa, Switch/Delta

377 Model Farm

Perry Green, Wembdon, Bridgwater, Somerset TA5 2BA **Tel:** (01278) 433999
Web: www.modelfarm.com **E-mail:** info@modelfarm.com

Richard and Carol Wright invite you to share the peaceful setting of their licensed Victorian country house. Set in two acres of garden and surrounded by fields, Model Farm is an ideal location in which to unwind. Relax in spacious en-suite bedrooms – all with tea/coffee making facilities, or enjoy a pre-dinner drink in the lounge by an open fire. Dine by candlelight, with your hosts, around an oak refectory table beside a roaring log fire.

Bed & Breakfast per night: single occupancy from £35.00–£40.00; double room from £50.00–£60.00
Dinner, Bed & Breakfast per person, per night: £37.00–£53.00
Evening meal: by arrangement

Bedrooms: 1 double, 2 twin
Bathrooms: 3 en-suite
Parking: 6 spaces
Cards accepted: Mastercard, Visa, Switch/Delta

378 Combe House Hotel

★★ Silver Award

Holford, Bridgwater, Somerset TA5 1RZ **Tel:** (01278) 741382 **Fax:** (01278) 741322
E-mail: enquiries@combehouse.co.uk

In the heart of the Quantock Hills (renowned as an area of outstanding natural beauty) lies this 17th-century house of great character. Once a tannery, this cottage-style hotel offers absolute peace and quiet in beautiful surroundings. Inside the beamed building, with its charming collection of pictures, pottery and period furniture, the visitor will find the relaxed atmosphere and friendly service ideal to enjoy Combe House, its restaurant, the Quantocks and the many attractions in the area.

Bed & Breakfast per night: single room from £33.00–£41.00; double room from £66.00–£93.00
Dinner, Bed & Breakfast per person, per night: £51.00–£60.50 (min 2 nights)
Lunch available: 1100–1400
Evening meal: 1930 (last orders 2030)

Bedrooms: 4 single, 5 double, 7 twin
Bathrooms: 16 en-suite
Parking: 20 spaces
Open: All year except January
Cards accepted: Mastercard, Visa, Switch/Delta, Amex, Maestro, Visa Electron, Solo

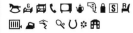

379 Conygar House

◆◆◆◆ Silver Award

2A The Ball, Dunster, Minehead, Somerset TA24 6SD **Tel:** (01643) 821872 **Fax:** (01643) 821872
Web: http://homepage.virgin.net/bale.dunster **E-mail:** bale.dunster@virgin.net

Conygar House is situated in a quiet road just off the main street of the medieval village of Dunster. Restaurants, bars and shops are all within one minute walking distance. A delightful sunny garden and patio with views overlooking the village. Ideal for exploring Exmoor and the coast. All rooms are decorated and furnished to a high standard. Colour television and tea/coffee making facilities in all rooms.

Bed & Breakfast per night: double room from £46.00–£48.00

Bedrooms: 2 double, 1 twin
Bathrooms: 3 en-suite
Open: February–October

Exmoor

Exmoor's coastline is stupendous, a series of high, 'hogsback' cliffs, dropping precipitously from 1,300ft to a rocky shoreline. Where rivers have carved a path to the sea, the great cliffs are intersected by valleys: peaceful Heddon's Mouth, accessible only on foot, the narrow defile of the Lyn where the river tumbles noisily over its stony bed, and the great wide sweep of Porlock Bay. The dramatic Valley of the Rocks, near Lynmouth, was another such riverbed until the Lyn took another course and left the extraordinary geological formations high and dry 500 ft above sea level. From Foreland Point to Porlock, the steep coastal slopes are softened by a mantle of oak woodlands – and on a spring day there are few more delightful sights than the blue sea glinting through a mist of unfurling young leaves.

ERJ Davey

The South-West Coastal Path, of course, offers the perfect means of exploring Exmoor's northern fringe. Inland, two other long-distance paths, the Tarka Trail and the Two Moors Way, lead through some of the region's wild and exquisite scenery. In all, there is a network of some 600 miles (1,000km) of rights-of-way criss-crossing the landscape to create rewarding walks of all lengths and terrains. And of these, some 288 miles (464km) are bridleways offering endless scope for horse-rider and mountain-biker.

Exmoor's interior is a vast, high tableland, sloping imperceptibly from its high cliffs to the gentle farmland of mid-Devon. The higher ground is covered in heather or bracken, grazed by sheep or rugged Exmoor ponies. South of Lynmouth, the Chains – a boggy hump of moorland – is as remote a spot as any in the South. Exmoor's highest point is Dunkery Beacon (1,704ft, 519m), a rounded shoulder of land commanding a superb panorama, encompassing, on a clear day, the distant Black Mountains to the north, and the jagged tors of Dartmoor to the south. Less apparent from the wide, bald heights are the deep wooded combes which form unexpected clefts in the flat 'table' above. Entering them is to reach a different world, for the contrast between the windswept heaths and the luxuriant woodland, all cushioned with moss, loud with birdsong and dappled with light and shade, could hardly be greater. Follow the streams into the wider valleys and the landscape changes again as cosier farmland encroaches into the wilderness, replacing brown moor and dark forest with a higgledy-piggledy patchwork of bright green.

380 Cutthorne

♦♦♦♦ Gold Award

Luckwell Bridge, Wheddon Cross, Minehead, Somerset TA24 7EW **Tel:** (01643) 831255 **Fax:** (01643) 831255
Web: www.cutthorne.co.uk **E-mail:** durbin@cutthorne.co.uk

Tucked away in the heart of Exmoor, hidden in its own private valley, Cutthorne is a country house which is truly 'off the beaten track'. Share our peaceful home and enjoy the tranquillity of the countryside. Lynton and Lynmouth, Torr Steps and Dunster are close by. Spacious and comfortable accommodation. Log fires. En-suite bathrooms. Four-poster bedroom. Candlelit dinners. Licensed. No smoking. Excellent choice of breakfasts. Traditional and vegetarian cooking. Fly fishing. Dogs welcome.

Bed & Breakfast per night: single occupancy from £25.00–£34.00
Dinner, Bed & Breakfast per person, per night: £39.00–£48.00
Evening meal: 1930 (last bookings 1800)

Bedrooms: 3 double/twin
Bathrooms: 3 en-suite
Parking: 6 spaces

All this has been subtly shaped and embellished by human hand. Bronze Age burial mounds and standing stones are often found on the high ground: Five Barrows near Sherracombe, for example, or the famous Caractacus Stone near Winsford. Of the many Iron-Age hill forts, Cow Castle, below Simonsbath, commands an impressive position above the river Barle. But the clapperbridge at Tarr Steps, long thought to be a prehistoric monument, is probably medieval.

From Norman times, Exmoor was a royal hunting ground, ensuring habitats – and their wildlife – have long been preserved. Indeed, red deer are still common, and Exmoor is the only place in England where stags are hunted on horseback, much as they were 900 years ago with hounds. Conceding Exmoor's uselessness as a tree-growing area, the Crown in 1818 sold the land to John Knight, who, followed by his son Frederic, settled at Simonsbath House (now a hotel) and began an ambitious programme of land improvement. In the family's most enduring legacy, Frederic Knight promoted a sturdy windbreak for cattle by planting beech hedges on wide earth banks. Today rows of vast, wind-sculpted trees still cling to the hillsides, their knotted roots binding the banks below.

Ironically, the Knights were engaged in taming the landscape just when tourists began to arrive in ever greater numbers, driven by an appreciation of the area's romantic wildness. Many visitors came to explore 'Doone Country', a fictional area based on Richard Blackmore's novel *Lorna Doone* (1869) and centred on the remote Badgworthy Valley where the band of outlaws, the Doones, supposedly had their hideout. Many local landmarks quickly acquired spurious

Doonish titles, such as Lorna's Cott and Lorna Doone Farm, which endure today. As the tourists arrived, the twin villages of Lynton, perched on its huge cliff, and Lynmouth, down by the sea, became genteel seaside resorts, linked, in 1890, by a hair-raising cliff railway.

Today, the towns and villages of Exmoor have much to offer the visitor, their whitewashed cottages and mellow churches focal points in the intricate patchwork of this lovely landscape. Dunster's great castle dominates the town, but also here are a beautiful wool market, 15th-century nunnery and splendid priory church, complete with 13th-century dovecote. Dulverton, in the south, is a charming, busy market town, set in glorious countryside, while nearby Bury attracts photographers with its rustic packhorse bridge, pretty ford, and Norman castle. Many picture-postcard settlements cluster in Porlock Vale: Allerford, Bossington, Horner, Luccombe and the model village of Selworthy on the Holnicote Estate. Intriguing churches include remote Stoke Pero, clinging to the hillside miles from anywhere; the parish church at Oare, famous as the scene of Lorna Doone's shooting; and the tiny church at Culbone, at 12ft x 35ft, said to be the smallest complete parish church in the country.

Exmoor became a National Park in 1954 and is administered by the National Park Authority which works closely with local people, landowners, farmers and other organisations, offering wide-ranging advice and support. As custodians of Exmoor, the Authority is committed to maintaining the delicate balance between conservation and recreation. There are National Park Visitor Centres at Combe Martin, Lynmouth, County Gate, Dunster and Dulverton.

381 Northam Mill

◆◆◆◆ Silver Award

Water Lane, Stogumber, Taunton, Somerset TA4 3TT **Tel:** (01984) 656916 or (01984) 656146 **Fax:** (01984) 656144
Web: www.northam-mill.co.uk **E-mail:** bmsspicer@aol.com

Hidden for 300 years! This converted corn mill and trout stream (bordering five acres and beautiful gardens) is set in an area of outstanding natural beauty, one mile from Exmoor National Park at the foot of the Brendons and at the neck of the Quantock Hills, providing some of the best walking in the country. The sounds of the waterfall and abundance of wildlife are interrupted only by the whistle of the occasional steam train. All food, including bread, is home made and served in a beamed dining room/library. Licensed with a fine cellar. A five course dinner menu changes daily. All rooms are individually furnished en-suite plus separate garden suite. RAC 'Little Gem' award winner.

Bed & Breakfast per night: single occupancy from £25.50–£47.50; double room from £51.00–£75.00
Dinner, Bed & Breakfast per person, per night: £48.00–£70.00
Evening meal: 1930 (last orders 2000)

Bedrooms: 2 double, 1 twin
Bathrooms: 3 en-suite
Parking: 12 spaces
Open: All year except Christmas
Cards accepted: Mastercard, Visa, Amex, Diners

382 Castle of Comfort Country House

◆◆◆◆ Silver Award

Dodington, Nether Stowey, Bridgwater, Somerset TA5 1LE **Tel:** (01278) 741264 or (07050) 642002 **Fax:** (01278) 741144
Web: www.castle-of-comfort.co.uk **E-mail:** reception@castle-of-comfort.co.uk

The Castle of Comfort is believed to date from the 16th century. Once described as 'a stone inn at the foot of the Quantock Hills where it is rumoured that pirates off the English coast used to dispose of their loot', it is now a small country house hotel set in four acres of grounds. Luxuriously refurbished, offering accommodation of the highest standard for families, business people and honeymoon couples. À la carte dinner and sunday lunches.

Bed & Breakfast per night: single room from £33.00–£69.00; double room from £79.00–£106.00
Dinner, Bed & Breakfast per person, per night: £61.50–£78.50
Evening meal: 1900 (last bookings 1200)

Bedrooms: 2 single, 3 double, 1 family
Bathrooms: 6 en-suite
Parking: 10 spaces
Cards accepted: Mastercard, Visa, Switch/Delta, JCB, Maestro

383 Staddlestones Guest House

◆◆◆◆ Silver Award

3 Standards Road, Westonzoyland, Bridgwater, Somerset TA7 0EL **Tel:** (01278) 691179 **Fax:** (01278) 691333
Web: www.staddlestonesguesthouse.co.uk **E-mail:** staddlestones@euphony.net

Located in the historic village of Westonzoyland and close to Junction 23 of the M5 motorway, Staddlestones provides an ideal base for exploring Somerset. Scenically beautiful and rich in history, natural life and country crafts, this lesser known area of England will delight those not already familiar with its many treasures. An elegant, friendly Georgian home with a 17th-century wing and large secluded garden, Staddlestones offers spacious and interesting accommodation, warm hospitality and every comfort.

Bed & Breakfast per night: single occupancy from £30.00–£35.00; double room £52.00
Dinner, Bed & Breakfast per person, per night: £40.00–£45.00

Bedrooms: 2 double, 1 twin
Bathrooms: 2 en-suite, 1 private
Parking: 4 spaces
Cards accepted: Mastercard, Visa, Switch/Delta, Eurocard, JCB, Maestro, Visa Electron, Solo

384 Manor Farm

Burcombe, Salisbury, Wiltshire SP2 OEJ **Tel:** (01722) 742177 **Fax:** (01722) 744600

A warm welcome awaits you at Manor Farm. A comfortable farmhouse set in the middle of the village with the River Nadder and meadows to the north and Downs with wonderful walks including views of Salisbury Cathedral to the south. An ideal location for Salisbury, Wilton and Wilton House, Stonehenge, the New Forest, Bath and Thomas Hardy country. A variety of eating establishments are within a few miles and the Ship Inn a five minute walk.

Bed & Breakfast per night: double room from £44.00–£46.00

Bedrooms: 1 double, 1 twin
Bathrooms: 2 en-suite
Parking: 6 spaces
Open: March–November
Cards accepted: Mastercard, Visa

385 The Old Mill

 Silver Award

Roughmoor, Bishops Hull, Taunton, Somerset TA1 5AB **Tel:** (01823) 289732 **Fax:** (01823) 289732

Relax and enjoy the ambience of our Grade II listed former corn mill in a lovely riverside setting, on the edge of a conservation village, and still retaining much of the original timbers and workings. Both bedrooms are attractively appointed, with river views and thoughtful extras. Start your day with a choice from our extensive breakfast menu, set amidst the wheels and cogs of a bygone era. Non-smoking throughout. Exmoor and coast 35 minutes' drive away.

Bed & Breakfast per night: single occupancy from £35.00–£40.00; double room from £44.00–£48.00

Bedrooms: 2 double
Bathrooms: 1 en-suite, 1 private
Parking: 4 spaces
Open: all year except Christmas and New Year

386 Handley Farm Accommodation

♦♦♦ Silver Award

Waterrow, Taunton, Somerset TA4 2BE **Tel:** (01398) 361516 **Fax:** (01398) 361516
Web: www.handleyfarm.co.uk **E-mail:** leigh-firbank.george@ntlworld.com

Treat yourself to something special in unspoilt and idyllic countryside situated between Exmoor National Park and the Vale of Taunton Deane. So come and unwind in one of our two luxury bed and breakfast suites created from an original stone barn, with lounge area, door to veranda and garden. Join us in our period farmhouse for wholesome Aga-cooked breakfasts. Games room, two well-stocked course fishing lakes for the exclusive use of our residents. See also our self-catering accommodation on page 199.

Bed & Breakfast per night: single occupancy from £25.00–£28.00; double room from £45.00–£50.00

Bedrooms: 1 double, 1 family
Bathrooms: 2 en-suite
Parking: 4 spaces

387 Muchelney Ham Farm

◆◆◆◆◆ Gold Award

Muchelney, Langport, Somerset TA10 0DJ **Tel:** (01458) 250737
Web: www.muchelneyhamfarm.co.uk

Beautiful luxury farmhouse. Tastefully furnished to a high standard with period and antique furniture, beams and inglenook. The bedrooms are individually decorated with many thoughtful extras and are all en-suite and heated throughout. Country house atmosphere. Lovely views over unspoilt countryside on the Somerset Levels. Muchelney Ham is a quiet hamlet near the Abbey. Peaceful relaxing garden. Ideal for touring, business,cycling and visiting National Trust properties. We pride ourselves on our quality accommodation.

Bed & Breakfast per night: single occupancy from £30.00–£35.00; double room from £555.00–£65.00
Dinner, Bed & Breakfast per person, per night: £45.00–£48.00

Bedrooms: 2 double, 1 twin
Bathrooms: 3 en-suite
Parking: 12 spaces

388 Newton Farm House

◆◆◆◆◆ Silver Award

Southampton Road, Whiteparish, Salisbury, Wiltshire SP5 2QL **Tel:** (01794) 884416 **Fax:** (01794) 884416
Web: www.newtonfarmhouse.co.uk **E-mail:** reservations@newtonfarmhouse.co.uk

Historic listed 16th-century farmhouse, originally part of the Trafalgar Estate. Near the New Forest and convenient for Salisbury, Stonehenge, Romsey, Winchester, Portsmouth and Bath. Delightful en-suite bedrooms (five with genuine four-poster beds). Beamed dining room with flagstones, inglenook and bread oven plus Nelson memorabilia. Superb breakfasts include home-made breads and preserves, fresh fruit and free-range eggs. Extensive grounds with swimming pool. Dinner by arrangement using garden produce. AA 3 Egg Cups and Ladle.

Bed & Breakfast per night: single occupancy from £25.00–£30.00; double room from £38.00–£60.00
Dinner, Bed & Breakfast per person, per night: £45.00–£50.00 (min 2 nights at weekends)
Evening meal: 1900 (by arrangement)

Bedrooms: 3 double, 2 twin, 2 triple, 1 family
Bathrooms: 8 en-suite
Parking: 10 spaces

389 Stoneleigh Barn

◆◆◆◆ Silver Award

North Wootton, Sherborne, Dorset DT9 5JW **Tel:** (01935) 815964
E-mail: stoneleigh@ic24.net

A handsome 18th-century converted stone barn, situated two miles from the historic abbey town of Sherborne. Stoneleigh Barn is a non-smoking establishment set in secluded grounds and within easy walking distance of a good eating pub. Accommodation comprises a large double four-poster en-suite room and en-suite suite of two double rooms. The owners are both qualified local guides and are happy to share their extensive knowledge of the area. A special place.

Bed & Breakfast per night: double room from £50.00–£55.00

Bedrooms: 3 double
Bathrooms: 3 en-suite
Parking: 6 spaces

390 Stafford Barton Farm

◆◆◆◆◆

Broadhembury, Honiton, Devon EX14 3LU **Tel:** (01404) 841403

A warm welcome awaits you at Stafford Barton which is a short walk from the picturesque thatched village of Broadhembury. Our lovely modern home is set in beautiful grounds with splendid views towards the Blackdown Hills and the delightful Devon countryside. From here you can enjoy scenic walks, beautiful gardens, attratcive beaches, historic houses, popular tourist attractions and excellent shopping. The accommodation is on the ground floor and a traditional English breakfast is served.

Bed & Breakfast per night: double room from £45.00

Bedrooms: 1 double, 1 twin
Bathrooms: 2 en-suite
Parking: 3 spaces

391 Goodmans House

◆◆◆◆

Furley, Membury, Axminster, Devon EX13 7TU **Tel:** (01404) 881690 **Fax:** (01404) 881690

An elegant Georgian country house, with five individually converted stone cottages. All have access to eight acres of delightful grounds, planted with many unusual specimen trees and shrubs, and all enjoying outstanding views over beautiful, secluded valley. Family owned for 14 years. A warm welcome awaits. Goodmans' 15th-century arched dining room with inglenooks is renowned for consistently outstanding food and imaginative menus using fresh local produce, many of which are organic. Unusually flexible tarrif offers freedom and choice on inclusive breaks, bed and breakfast or self-catering. Easily accessible east Devon/west Dorset coasts etc.

Bed & Breakfast per night: single room from £28.50–£33.50; double room from £57.00–£70.00
Dinner, Bed & Breakfast per person, per night: £45.50–£55.00
Evening meal: 1830 (last orders 1900)

Bedrooms: 1 single, 6 double/twin
Bathrooms: 7 en-suite
Parking: 7 spaces

392 Beam Cottage

◆◆◆◆

16 North Street, Beaminster, Dorset DT8 3DZ **Tel:** (01308) 863639
E-mail: margie@beam-cottage.fsnet.co.uk

Very attractive Grade II listed cottage with large secluded garden in the centre of Beaminster. Also available is a pretty, twin-bedded cottage in garden with all facilities. Near historic houses and lovely walks. Private sitting room and television in all rooms. Children and dogs welcome.

Bed & Breakfast per night: single occupancy from £30.00–£35.00; double room from £50.00–£65.00
Dinner, Bed & Breakfast per person, per night: £37.50–£42.50
Evening meal: 1900 (last orders 2100)

Bedrooms: 1 double, 2 twin, 1 family
Bathrooms: 2 en-suite, 1 shared
Parking: 4 spaces

393 The Poachers Inn ◆◆◆◆

Piddletrenthide, Dorchester, Dorset DT2 7QX **Tel:** (01300) 348358 **Fax:** (01300) 348153
Web: www.thepoachersinn.co.uk **E-mail:** thepoachersinn@piddletrenthide.fsbusiness.co.uk

A country inn, set in the heart of the lovely Piddle Valley, eight miles from Dorchester and within easy reach of all Dorset's attractions. All rooms are en-suite and have a colour television, tea/coffee making facilities and telephone. Outdoor swimming pool from May to September. The Riverside Garden restaurant is where half-board guests choose from the à la carte menu at no extra cost. Short breaks: three nights for the price of two (half board), October to April. Please send for a brochure.

Bed & Breakfast per night: single occupancy £35.00; double room £60.00
Dinner, Bed & Breakfast per person, per night: £42.00 (based on 2 sharing)
Lunch available: all day
Evening meal: 1700 (last orders 2100)

Bedrooms: 14 double, 3 twin, 1 family
Bathrooms: 18 en-suite
Parking: 30 spaces
Cards accepted: Mastercard, Visa, Switch/Delta

394 Kerrington House Hotel ◆◆◆◆◆ Silver Award

Musbury Road, Axminster, Devon EX13 5JR **Tel:** (01297) 35333 and 35345 **Fax:** (01297) 35333 and 35345
Web: www.kerringtonhouse.com **E-mail:** ja.reaney@kerringtonhouse.com

On the Devon/Dorset borders, close to Lyme Regis and the heritage coast, a fine period house, lovingly restored and furnished with comfort and style. Sumptuous bedrooms with lots of little luxuries, stunning drawing room overlooking the delightful landscaped gardens. Elegant dining room in which to enjoy fine wines and good food, freshly cooked with flair using local produce. Conveniently located on the edge of town and ideal for exploring this beautiful region.

Bed & Breakfast per night: single occupancy from £54.00–£59.00; double room from £88.00–£98.00
Dinner, Bed & Breakfast per person, per night: £69.00–£84.00

Bedrooms: 3 double, 2 twin
Bathrooms: 5 en-suite
Parking: 6 spaces
Cards accepted: Mastercard, Visa

395 Britmead House ◆◆◆◆

West Bay Road, Bridport, Dorset DT6 4EG **Tel:** (01308) 422941 **Fax:** (01308) 422516
Web: www.britmeadhouse.co.uk **E-mail:** britmead@talk21.com

An elegant and spacious detached house. Situated between Bridport and West Bay harbour with its beaches, Chesil Beach and the Dorset Coastal Path. An ideal base from which to discover Dorset. The spacious south-west facing dining room and lounge overlook an attractive garden and open countryside beyond. Well-appointed en-suite bedrooms, all with many thoughtful extras. Quite simply everything, where possible, is tailored to suit your needs. Children welcome, non-smoking rooms, private parking.

Bed & Breakfast per night: single occupancy from £28.00–£42.00; double room from £44.00–£64.00

Bedrooms: 3 double, 2 twin, 2 family
Bathrooms: 7 en-suite
Parking: 8 spaces
Cards accepted: Mastercard, Visa, Switch/Delta, Eurocard, Visa Electron

396 Roundham House Hotel

★★ Silver Award

Roundham Gardens, West Bay Road, Bridport, Dorset DT6 4BD **Tel:** (01308) 422753 **Fax:** (01308) 421500
Web: www.roundhamhouse.co.uk **E-mail:** cyprencom@compuserve.com

An Edwardian country house hotel set in an acre of gardens on elevated ground overlooking the rolling West Dorset hills, the majestic coastline and the sea. Many awards for quality and cuisine. Spacious en-suite bedrooms with glorious sea and country views. The hotel is just a short walk from either West Bay and the sea (along a country path by the side of the hotel) or the rustic country markets and the West Country charm of Bridport. RAC dining award.

Bed & Breakfast per night: single room from £35.00–£40.00; double room from £64.00–£80.00
Dinner, Bed & Breakfast per person, per night: £46.00–£58.00
Evening meal: 1930 (last orders 2030)

Bedrooms: 1 single, 3 double, 2 twin, 2 family
Bathrooms: 7 en-suite, 1 private
Parking: 12 spaces
Open: March–December
Cards accepted: Mastercard, Visa, Switch/Delta, Eurocard, JCB, Maestro, Visa Electron, Solo

397 The Old Rectory

◆◆◆◆ Silver Award

Winterbourne Steepleton, Dorchester, Dorset DT2 9LG **Tel:** (01305) 889468 **Fax:** (01305) 889737
Web: www.trees.eurobell.co.uk **E-mail:** trees@eurobell.co.uk

Genuine 1850 Victorian rectory situated in a quiet hamlet, surrounded by breathtaking countryside. Close to historic Dorchester and Weymouth's sandy beaches. We specialise in providing a quiet comfortable night's sleep followed by a copious English, vegetarian or continental breakfast with fresh organic produce, home-made jams, yoghurt and bread. Enjoy our superbly appointed guest drawing room, croquet, putting green and badminton lawns. Local pub within walking distance and excellent restaurants within a short drive.

Bed & Breakfast per night: single occupancy from £45.00–£55.00; double room from £50.00–£110.00

Bedrooms: 3 double, 1 twin
Bathrooms: 4 en-suite
Parking: 8 spaces

398 Church Cottage

◆◆◆◆ Silver Award

West Knighton, Dorchester, Dorset DT2 8PF **Tel:** (01305) 852243
Web: www.church-cottage.com **E-mail:** info@church-cottage.com

A charming listed 300 year old thatched cottage providing comfortable and up-to-date accommodation with full English or continental breakfast with home-made jams, local honey and free range eggs. Situated in the peace and quiet of an attractive conservation village ten minutes from the historic town of Dorchester and five miles from the beautiful Dorset coast. Next to a 12th-century church renovated by Thomas Hardy. Good walking, village pub and plenty of local eating places.

Bed & Breakfast per night: single occupancy from £35.00–£45.00; double room from £50.00–£60.00

Bedrooms: 1 double, 1 twin
Bathrooms: 2 en-suite
Parking: 2 spaces
Open: All year except January

399 Royal York and Faulkner Hotel ★★ Silver Award

Esplanade, Sidmouth, Devon EX10 8AZ **Tel:** 0800 220714 or (01395) 513043 **Fax:** (01395) 577472
Web: www.royalyorkhotel.net **E-mail:** info@royalyorkhotel.net

Charming Regency hotel on the centre of Sidmouth's delightful Esplanade and adjacent to the picturesque town centre. Long-established family-run hotel offering all amenities and excellent facilities, coupled with renowned personal, efficient service. 68 well appointed en-suite bedrooms, many enjoying sea views. Ample tastefully furnished lounge and bar areas. Sea-facing dining room offering excellent cuisine with a varied choice of menu. Attractive leisure complex comprising jacuzzi, sauna, solarium and exercise equipment. Indoor short-mat bowls, rink and full-size snooker table. Free swimming at local indoor pool (200 yards away).

Bed & Breakfast per night: single room from £30.00–£54.00; double room from £60.00–£108.00
Dinner, Bed & Breakfast per person, per night: £38.00–£62.00 (min 2 nights)
Lunch available: 1200–1400
Evening meal: 1915 (last orders 2030)

Bedrooms: 22 single, 9 double, 29 twin, 8 triple
Bathrooms: 68 en-suite
Parking: 20 spaces
Open: All year except January
Cards accepted: Mastercard, Visa, Switch/Delta, Eurocard, Visa Electron, Solo

400 Hotel Riviera ★★★★ Gold Award

The Esplanade, Sidmouth, Devon EX10 8AY **Tel:** (01395) 515201 **Fax:** (01395) 577775
Web: www.hotelriviera.co.uk **E-mail:** enquiries@hotelriviera.co.uk

Splendidly positioned at the centre of Sidmouth's esplanade, overlooking Lyme Bay. With its mild climate and the beach just on the doorstep, the setting echoes the south of France and is the choice for the discerning visitor. Behind the hotel's fine Regency façade lies an alluring blend of old-fashioned service and present-day comforts. Glorious sea views can be enjoyed from the recently redesigned en-suite bedrooms, which are fully appointed and have many thoughtful extras. In the elegant bay-view dining room guests are offered a fine choice of dishes from extensive menus, prepared by French and Swiss-trained chefs, with local seafood being a particular speciality.

Bed & Breakfast per night: single room from £79.00–£109.00; double room from £138.00–£194.00
Dinner, Bed & Breakfast per person, per night: £80.00–£108.00 (includes 7-course dinner)
Lunch available: 1230–1400

Evening meal: 1900 (last orders 2100)
Bedrooms: 7 single, 6 double, 14 twin
Bathrooms: 27 en-suite
Parking: 26 spaces
Cards accepted: Mastercard, Visa, Switch/Delta, Amex, Diners

401 Farmborough House ◆◆◆◆ Silver Award

Old Exeter Road, Chudleigh, Newton Abbot, Devon TQ13 0DR **Tel:** (01626) 853258 **Fax:** (01626) 853258
Web: www.farmborough-house.com **E-mail:** holidays@farmborough-house.com

Comfortable Edwardian house hidden away from the road in a secluded ten acre rural setting of a former organic vineyard, providing a peaceful retreat for nature lovers. Situated between Haldon Forest and Dartmoor, with easy access from the A38, Farmborough is the ideal base for exploring South Devon, with golfing, fishing or walking nearby. Breakfast is not for the faint-hearted! A hearty traditional breakfast comes from the Aga, with vegetarian or continental alternatives. Non-smoking.

Bed & Breakfast per night: double room from £45.00–£52.00

Bedrooms: 2 double, 1 twin
Bathrooms: 3 en-suite
Parking: 6 spaces

402 Elmdene Hotel ◆◆◆◆

Rathmore Road, Chelston, Torquay TQ2 6NZ **Tel:** (01803) 294940
Web: www.s-h-systems.co.uk/hotels/elmdene.html **E-mail:** elmdenehoteltorqy@amserve.net

A privately-run Victorian hotel situated on level ground close to the railway station and all local amenities. Well presented en-suite rooms with tea and coffee tray, colour television and hairdryer. Full licence and own car park. Quality and service are our priority. Well-balanced evening meal menu available – optional or as part of a package. Out-of-season and Christmas breaks.

Bed & Breakfast per night: single room from £22.50–£27.00; double room from £45.00–£54.00
Dinner, Bed & Breakfast per person, per night: £32.00–£42.00
Evening meal: 1815 (last orders 1845)

Bedrooms: 2 single, 5 double, 1 twin, 3 family
Bathrooms: 7 en-suite, 1 shared
Parking: 12 spaces
Open: all year except February
Cards accepted: Mastercard, Visa, Switch/Delta

403 Roundham Lodge ◆◆◆◆◆ Silver Award

16 Roundham Road, Paignton, Devon TQ4 6DN **Tel:** (01803) 558485 **Fax:** (01803) 553090
Web: www.smoothhound.co.uk/hotels/round1.html **E-mail:** alan@vega68.freeserve.co.uk

Situated in the heart of the English Riviera, we are a family-run bed and breakfast with a warm and friendly atmosphere, offering fine English breakfasts. Close to Paignton Harbour, our lodge affords magnificent sea views from most rooms, and some have balconies. Roundham Lodge provides an ideal centre from which to explore the south west, visit the wide expanses of Dartmoor, take a boat trip from the harbour, or just relax on the many beaches. Non-smoking establishment.

Bed & Breakfast per night: double room from £50.00–£75.00

Bedrooms: 3 double, 1 twin, 1 triple
Bathrooms: 5 en-suite
Parking: 9 spaces
Open: All year except Christmas and New Year

404 Royal Castle Hotel ★★★ Silver Award

11 The Quay, Dartmouth, Devon TQ6 9PS **Tel:** (01803) 833033 **Fax:** (01803) 835445
Web: www.royalcastle.co.uk **E-mail:** enquiry@royalcastle.co.uk

A 17th-century coaching inn in the heart of historic Dartmouth – an unrivalled location ideal for short breaks at any time of year. 25 luxuriously appointed en-suite bedrooms, all individually decorated and furnished, some with four-poster or brass beds and jacuzzi. The elegant restaurant on the first floor overlooks the estuary and specialises in select regional produce and locally-caught seafood. Two bars serve delicious food, traditional ales and a good choice of wines. We look forward to welcoming you.

Bed & Breakfast per night: single room from £56.45; double room from £97.90–£129.90
Dinner, Bed & Breakfast per person, per night: £58.95–£74.95
Lunch available: 1200–1430
Evening meal: 1845 (last orders 2200)

Bedrooms: 4 single, 10 double, 8 twin, 3 triple
Bathrooms: 25 en-suite
Parking: 17 spaces
Cards accepted: Mastercard, Visa, Switch/Delta, Amex, Visa Electron, Solo

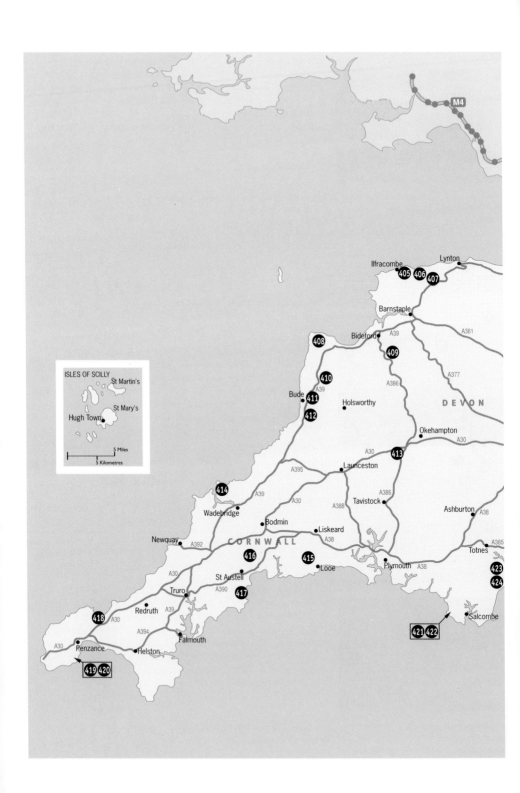

ISLES OF SCILLY
St Martin's
St Mary's
Hugh Town

5 Miles
5 Kilometres

M4

Lynton
Ilfracombe 405 406 407
Barnstaple
A39   A361
Bideford
408   A377
409
410   A386
A39
Bude 411
412 Holsworthy
Okehampton
A30
DEVON
A395   A30   413
Launceston
A386
414   Tavistock
A39   A388   Ashburton
A30   A38
Wadebridge
Bodmin
Newquay   Liskeard   Totnes
A392 CORNWALL A38   A385
416   Plymouth A38   423
St Austell 415 Looe   424
A30   417
Truro A390
Redruth A39   Salcombe
418 A30   421 422
A394
Falmouth
Penzance Helston
A30
419 420

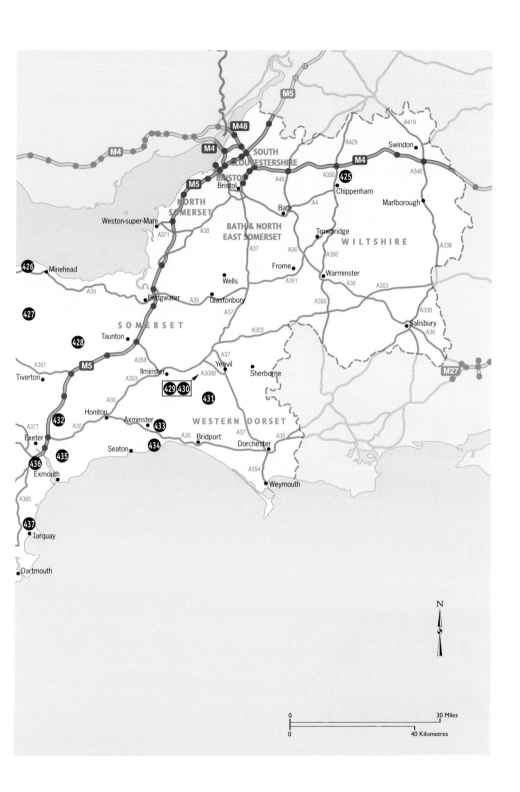

405 The Admirals House   ★ ★ ★ ★

c/o Ilfracombe Carlton Hotel, Runnacleave Road, Ilfracombe, Devon
Contact: The Ilfracombe Carlton Hotel, Runnacleave Road, Ilfracombe, Devon EX34 8AR
Tel: (01271) 862446 **Fax:** (01271) 865379

A harbourside Georgian manor house, now converted to five self catering apartments. Superb view over Ilfracombe's heritage harbour. All comforts including spa baths etc. Open all year.

Low season per week: £180.00–£350.00
High season per week: £300.00–£530.00
Short breaks: from £120.00–£300.00

5 apartments: sleeping 2–6 people
Cards accepted: Mastercard, Visa, Switch/Delta, Amex

406 Pretoria   ★ ★ ★ ★

Seaside, Combe Martin, Ilfracombe, Devon
Contact: Mrs H C Trueman, 6 Crossmead, Lynton, Devon EX35 6DG
Tel: (01598) 753517 **E-mail:** russ@crown-inn.freeserve.co.uk

Pretoria is a three-storey, Victorian, comfortably furnished, fisherman's cottage, situated approximately 70 yards from the sandy and rock pool beach and harbour. Shops, pubs and restaurants are within yards, as is the South-West Coastal Path. The large rear garden, complete with garden furniture, lighting and brick-built barbecue, has access to the beach car park and free parking for two cars is provided. All heating, lighting and linen is included. There are no hidden extras.

Low season per week: £170.00–£285.00
High season per week: £310.00–£495.00
Short breaks: from £90.00 (3 nights, low season only)

1 cottage: sleeping 6 people

407 Voley Farm   ★ ★ ★ ★

Parracombe, Barnstaple, Devon **Web:** www.voleyfarm.com
Contact: Ms J Killen, Voley Farm, Parracombe, Barnstaple, Devon EX31 4PG
Tel: (01598) 763315 **Fax:** (01598) 763660 **E-mail:** voleyfarm@tesco.net

Two spacious cottages, sympathetically converted from a fine Victorian barn, overlooking a pretty cobbled courtyard, on a peaceful Exmoor farm in its own valley. Canopied bedrooms, high beamed ceilings, central heating, wood-burning stoves, panoramic views, superb walks from your door to Exmoor and the sea. A short drive to sandy beaches. There is a wide variety of local attractions for all weathers, games room and laundry room. Help feed our friendly Shetland sheep and rare breed hens.

Low season per week: £200.00–£310.00
High season per week: £310.00–£490.00
Short breaks: from £100.00–£200.00 (low season only)

2 cottages: sleeping 6 people
Open: March–December

DW

408 Rosedown Cottages   ★ ★ ★ ★

Rosedown Farm, Hartland, Bideford, Devon **Web:** www.rosedown.co.uk
Contact: Miss M du Toit, Rosedown Farm, Hartland, Bideford, Devon EX39 6AH
Tel: (01237) 441333 **E-mail:** michelle@rosedown.co.uk

Two comfortably furnished detached cottages nestled in a secluded wooded valley within 90 acres of farmland. They are situated in an Area of Outstanding Natural Beauty, close to the South-West Coastal Path, near Clovelly. Westdown has two pretty bedrooms, whilst Rosebarn has four bedrooms (including an easily accessible downstairs single bedroom with en-suite). Fully equipped kitchen, fireplace/woodburner, beamed ceilings, enclosed garden and shared children's play area. Electricity, linen and central heating included.

Low season per week: £210.00–£610.00
High season per week: £325.00–£732.00
Short breaks: from £120.00–£348.00 (low season only)

2 cottages: sleeping 2–7 people

409 Hill Farm Cottages   ★ ★ ★ ★

Weare Trees Hill, Torrington, Devon **Web:** www.hillfarmcottages.co.uk
Contact: Mrs M Vickery, Hill Farm, Weare Trees Hill, Torrington, Devon EX38 7EZ
Tel: (01805) 622432 **Fax:** (01805) 622432 **E-mail:** info@hillfarmcottages.co.uk

A friendly welcome awaits you. Five cottages with heated indoor pool, play areas and games room. Meet and feed the animals, collect eggs – children will love the farm experience. Ideal for a peaceful and relaxing holiday, near to beaches, RHS Rosemoor, Dartington Crystal and for the more energetic, cycle or walk the Tarka Trail, fishing and golf. Local shops and restaurants nearby. Our well equipped cottages provide the ideal holiday you will want to remember.

Low season per week: £260.00–£480.00
High season per week: £355.00–£625.00
Short breaks: from £150.00–£190.00 (low season only)

5 cottages: sleeping 4–6 people + cot

410 Lympscott Farm Holidays   ★ ★ ★ ★

Bradworthy, Holsworthy, Devon
Contact: Lympscott Farm Holidays, Bradworthy, Holsworthy, Devon EX22 7TR
Tel: (01409) 241607 **Fax:** (01409) 241607 **E-mail:** jon.furse@btclick.com

Large wing of 18th-century farmhouse, on farm bordering the Upper Tamar Lake, which provides fishing and water sports. The magnificent Cornish coast with its excellent surf and sandy beaches are only five miles away. You can also explore Dartmoor and Exmoor, or visit local attractions such as the unique village of Clovelly. The Big Sheep, Milky Way and Killarney Springs are all great family adventure parks. Then return to badminton, volley ball, putting or a barbecue on the lawn. ♿ **Category 2**

Low season per week: £350.00–£550.00
High season per week: £550.00–£850.00
Short breaks: from £250.00–£300.00

1 house: sleeping 11+ people

411 Broomhill Manor Country Estate ★ ★ ★ ★

Broomhill Manor, Bude, Cornwall **Web:** www.broomhillmanor.co.uk
Contact: Mr C B Mower, Broomhill Manor Country Estate, Broomhill Manor, Bude, Cornwall EX23 9HA
Tel: (01288) 352940 **Fax:** (01288) 356526 **E-mail:** chris@broomhillmanor.co.uk

Luxurious and cosy 4-Star cottages nestling at the end of a long leafy drive in one of Cornwall's most attractive Georgian country estates. Set in 40 acres of secluded grounds, our facilities include tropically heated indoor pool, Jacuzzi, sauna, gymnasium, floodlit tennis and own riding stables. Close to the sea, several golf courses and magnificent coastal walks. All cottages are well heated and with Cornwall's mild climate, we are ideal for out of season breaks.

Low season per week: £245.00–£480.00
High season per week: £595.00–£1105.00
Short breaks: from £125.00–£250.00

18 cottages: sleeping 2–6 people
Cards accepted: Mastercard, Visa

412 Kennacott Court ★ ★ ★ ★ ★

Widemouth Bay, Bude, Cornwall **Web:** www.kennacottcourt.co.uk
Contact: Mr & Mrs R H Davis, Kennacott Court, Widemouth Bay, Bude, Cornwall EX23 0ND
Tel: (01288) 361766 or (01288) 361683 **Fax:** (01288) 361434 **E-mail:** maureen@kennacottcourt.co.uk

Set in the midst of 75 acres with magnificent views overlooking the sea at Widemouth Bay, Bude, Kennacott Court is an outstanding collection of holiday cottages with unrivalled leisure and recreational facilities. Every cottage is extremely comfortable, beautifully furnished and comprehensively equipped. We have a leisure centre with large indoor pool, snooker, sauna, mini gym and games room. In the grounds we have two all-weather tennis courts, golf course, nature walk and lots more. Open all year for an unforgetable holiday. ↟ **Category 3**

Low season per week: £220.00–£651.00
High season per week: £460.00–£1860.00
Short breaks: from £125.00–£400.00

18 cottages: sleeping 2–10 people
Cards accepted: Mastercard, Visa, Switch/Delta, JCB, Maestro, Solo, Visa Electron, Fortoak

413 Little Bidlake Barns ★ ★ ★ ★

Bridestowe, Okehampton, Devon **Web:** www.littlebidlakefarm.co.uk
Contact: Mrs J Down, Little Bidlake Barns, Bridestowe, Okehampton, Devon EX20 4NS
Tel: (01837) 861233 **Fax:** (01837) 861233 **E-mail:** bidlakefrm@aol.com

Six luxury, fully equipped, barn conversions on the fringe of Dartmoor. Original beams, arched windows and underfloor heating. Most rooms en-suite with television. Perfect for touring Devon and Cornwall. Meals available. Local shop and pubs. Cycling, golf, fishing, riding, walking or water pursuits easily accessible. Pets and horses welcome. Sleeps 2, 4, 6 +12.

Low season per week: £240.00–£600.00
High season per week: £360.00–£875.00

6 barn conversions: sleeping 2–12 people
Cards accepted: Mastercard, Visa, Switch/Delta

414 Highcliffe

★ ★ ★ ★

Trebetherick, Wadebridge, Cornwall **Web:** www.highcliffeholidays.co.uk
Contact: Highcliffe Agency Ltd, Bosneives, Withiel, Bodmin, Cornwall PL30 5NQ
Tel: (01208) 831167 **Fax:** (01208) 831198 **E-mail:** sales@highcliffeagency.com

The fashionable Highcliffe holiday cottages are situated in the heart of the popular north coast resort. Polzeath and Rock are nearby, with three beautiful beaches within easy walking distance. Sitting amongst charming landscaped grounds are lawns, play areas and two sheltered tennis courts. The cottages are modern wih a Meditteranean feel, spacious and airy and boast all modern conveniences. Brochures available on request.

Low season per week: £300.00–£450.00
High season per week: £600.00–£950.00

24 cottages: sleeping up to 7 people

Clapperbridges

Near Ashway in Exmoor, the River Barle flows wide and shallow over its brown stony bed. On either side, the road ends abruptly in a somewhat intimidating ford, but walkers may remain dry-shod, crossing the Barle via a magnificent walkway of vast stone slabs, known as Tarr Steps.

Tarr Steps is a type of ancient bridge known as a clapperbridge, and at 177ft (54m) in length is the longest and most elaborate of its type in England. The term 'clapperbridge' is used for any bridge constructed from large, flat slabs of stone forming a level pathway over a river or stream; the word probably developed from the Anglo Saxon *cleaca* meaning 'stepping stones'. Indeed a number of clapperbridges may well have begun as simple stepping-stones, which later formed the piers upon which linking slabs of stone were balanced. While some clapperbridges consist simply of a single slab thrown across the stream, multi-span bridges have typically between two and five spans (Tarr Steps with its magnificent 17 spans, is actually something of an anomaly).

No-one knows exactly when Tarr Steps was built, and, although for many years considered a pre-historic monument, it is now thought to be of much more recent construction. Most clapperbridges were built in the 14th century on packhorse routes, but a few appeared as late as the 18th and 19th centuries. They were simple and functional, and when routes changed or more superior structures superseded

them, they were very often allowed to disappear. Today, only about 40 remain in England.

Clapperbridges are found in parts of the country where the local rock yields large slabs of strong stone. There are consequently two main concentrations: one in North and West Yorkshire, the other in Devon and Cornwall. The greatest number are in Dartmoor, which boasts a wide range of variations. Postbridge, a lonely village in the heart of the Moor, has one of the finest of its type (shown above). It consists of three vast slabs of granite, some 17ft (5m) by 7ft (2m) in size, supported by four piers of granite blocks. Also on Dartmoor are Teignhead's bridge, built in 1790, and one over the Cowsic River at Two Bridges, built in 1837. At Wallabrook is a single-span clapperbridge, while the bridge at Yar Tor Down, Hexworthy, has three spans. Runnage bridge, near Postbridge, is a late example fitted with parapets.

415 Well Meadow Cottage ★★★★

Coldrinnick Farm, Duloe, Liskeard, Cornwall **Web:** www.cornishcottage.net
Contact: Mrs K Chapman, Coldrinnick Farm, Duloe, Liskeard, Cornwall PL14 4QF
Tel: (01503) 220251 **E-mail:** kaye@coldrinnick.fsnet.co.uk

Well Meadow Cottage is an attractively converted barn set in a large secluded garden on a working dairy farm. Outstanding views, many woodland walks, close to moors and coast and many attractions including the Eden Project. An excellent locality for walking and relaxing. The cottage sleeps two/four people and comprises of a double en-suite bedroom and a loft bedroom. Well equipped throughout. Heating, electricity and bedlinen etc inclusive. ⚡ **Category 3**

Low season per week: £150.00–£260.00
High season per week: £300.00–£395.00
Short breaks: from £75.00–£264.00 (mid September–mid May only)

1 cottage: sleeping 2/4 people

416 Higher Menadew Farm Cottages ★★★★

Higher Menadew, St Austell, Cornwall **Web:** www.stayingincornwall.com
Contact: Andrew and Anita Higman, Higher Menadew, St Austell, Cornwall PL26 8QW
Tel: (01726) 850310 **Fax:** (01726) 850310 **E-mail:** mail@stayingincornwall.com

Delightful, comfortable, superbly equipped traditional barn conversions in Cornish countryside just north of St Austell Bay, perfect for a relaxing and enjoyable holiday. Ideally situated for Cornwall's attractions. Close to Eden Project, coast, beautiful beaches, picturesque fishing villages and numerous glorious gardens. Stylish cottages have exposed wooden beams, classic pine floors and welcoming woodburners. One cottage even has a group dining table suitable for ten. There is always plenty to do and friendly advice on the locality is only a question away.

Low season per week: from £200.00
High season per week: max £660.00

3 cottages: sleeping 4–6 people + cot

417 Treleaven Farm Cottages ★★★★

Treleaven Farm, Mevagissey, St Austell, Cornwall **Web:** www.treleavenfarm.co.uk
Contact: Mr L Hennah, Treleaven Farm, Mevagissey, St Austell, Cornwall PL26 6RZ
Tel: (01726) 843558 **Fax:** (01726) 843558 **E-mail:** linda.hennah@btinternet.com

Treleaven Farm stands at the head of the valley overlooking Mevagissey. Only a short stroll to the village and harbour. Close to Heligan and the Eden Project, central for visiting all Cornwall and near to safe, sandy beaches. Three luxurious converted barns, retaining all their original charm. Equipped to the highest standard. Games barn, friendly farm animals and putting green.

Low season per week: £216.00–£387.00
High season per week: £400.00–£661.00
Short breaks: from £100.00–£160.00 (low season only)

3 cottages: sleeping 2–6 people

418 Rotorua Apartments ★★★★

Carbis Bay, St Ives, Cornwall **Web:** www.stivesapartments.com
Contact: Rotorua Apartments, Trencrom Lane, Carbis Bay, St Ives, Cornwall TR26 2TD
Tel: (01736) 795419 **Fax:** (01736) 795419 **E-mail:** rotorua@btconnect.com

Luxury apartments situated in a quiet wooded lane, within walking distance of Carbis Bay and other local beaches. Ideally situated for touring Cornwall. Large outdoor heated pool and garden areas. Each apartment has its own parking space. The apartments are very well equipped, including dishwasher, coffee maker, fridge/freezer, electric cooker and microwave. There is a colour television and video in the lounge and all bedrooms have colour televisions and hairdryers. Sorry, no pets.

Low season per week: £150.00–£300.00
High season per week: £400.00–£550.00

8 apartments: sleeping 6 people
Cards accepted: Mastercard, Visa, Switch/Delta

The Leach Pottery

A large artists' colony had been established in St Ives for several decades when in 1920 Bernard Leach returned to England from Japan and set up a pottery here with his lifelong Japanese friend, Shoji Hamada. Leach was born in Hong Kong, of English parents, in 1887 and lived in the Far East as a child. He returned to Japan in 1909 to study pottery, one of the first Westerners to learn the techniques of Oriental pottery. Leach and Hamada chose a site three-quarters of a mile up the hill from the town centre, by the Stennack stream. They wanted to produce 'genuine handicrafts of quality rather than machine craft in quantity', the aim being to combine the traditions of craftsmanship that were still alive in the East with pre-Industrial Revolution English handcrafted pottery. Leach was ideally suited to this, a man able to bridge the spirit of the West and the East, and he was quickly established as the leader of the studio pottery movement. He proved too to be an inspirational teacher, passing on not only practical skills but his philosophy of what it meant to be an artist potter, and always attracted visitors and students from all over the world, the first being Michael Cardew, who later built Wenfordbridge pottery, near Bodmin. In 1923 Hamada went back to Japan, but remained in close touch with Leach. Bernard's son David joined the pottery in 1930, aged 19, and worked as his father's right-hand man for 25 years before starting up on his own in Bovey Tracey, Devon. David's brother, Michael, also worked in St Ives between 1950 and 1955, when he moved to Yelland, North Devon. His son John maintains the family tradition at Mulchelney Pottery in Somerset.

In 1956 Bernard married an American potter, Janet Darnell, and she took over the management of the pottery, showroom and students, while continuing to pot in her own right. Bernard was therefore freed up for more writing and travel, only giving up potting when his sight began to fail in the mid-1970s. After his death in 1979, Janet Leach kept the pottery going, a mecca for collectors and admirers of the art. There is a big collection of Leach and Hamada pots, and work for sale by Trevor Corser and Joanna Wason, who work there (tel: 01736 796398).

419 Harbourside Cottage   ★ ★ ★ ★

The Wharf, Mousehole, Penzance, Cornwall
Contact: Mr and Mrs P Hall, Exmoor House, Porlock, Somerset TA24 8EY
Tel: (01643) 863155 **Fax:** (01643) 863371

This Grade II listed fisherman's cottage is just yards away from Mousehole's picturesque harbour and safe sandy beach. Not only is this beautifully appointed three bedroom cottage perfect in summer for those lazy, sunny days, but it is the cottage for viewing the world-renowned Christmas lights. The cosy, comfortable sitting room has a large inglenook fireplace with woodburner stove and the kitchen is large and very well equipped. Heating, electricity, VAT all included.

Low season per week: £325.00–£395.00
High season per week: £425.00–£750.00

1 cottage: sleeping 6 people

---

420 Tide's Reach   ★ ★ ★ ★

Fisherman's Square, Mousehole, Penzance, Cornwall
Contact: Mr & Mrs P Hall, Exmoor House, Porlock, Somerset TA24 8EY
Tel: (01643) 863155 **Fax:** (01643) 863371 **E-mail:** cornishcottages@its-fts.com

Tide's Reach is an idyllic 250 year-old, Grade II listed fisherman's cottage nestling alongside Mousehole's picturesque harbour and beach. A panoramic 15-foot wide sitting room window and bedroom windows overlook the patio and the nautical vista of bobbing, colourful boats in the harbour. Beyond is a spectacular 180 degree unobstructed sea view towards mystical St Michael's Mount with its fairytale castle rising from the sea. Woodburner stove. Central heating, electricity and VAT included.

Low season per week: £450.00–£550.00
High season per week: £650.00–£950.00

1 cottage: sleeping 4 people

---

421 Hope Barton Barns   ★ ★ ★ ★

Hope Cove, Kingsbridge, Devon **Web:** www.hopebarton.co.uk
Contact: Hope Barton Barns, Bolberry Road, Hope Cove, Kingsbridge, Devon TQ7 3HT
Tel: (01548) 561393 **Fax:** (01548) 560938 **E-mail:** info@hopebarton.co.uk

Nestling in a secluded valley of 35 acres, just a short walk from the sandy cove, are an exclusive group of 17 stone barns in two courtyards, and three apartments in the converted farmhouse. Indoor heated pool, sauna, gym, lounge bar, tennis court, trout lake and play barn. Superbly furnished and fully equipped, each cottage is unique and vary from a studio to four bedrooms, sleeping from 2 to 10. Cottage meals available from extensive menu. Perfect setting for family holidays, coastal walking or just a get-away-from-it-all break. Well behaved dogs welocme. Colour brochure avaiblable.

Low season per week: £200.00–£600.00
High season per week: £400.00–£1200.00
Short breaks: from £100.00–£600.00 (low–mid season only)

20 cottages: sleeping 2–10 people
Cards accepted: Mastercard, Visa, Switch/Delta

---

422 Ocean View ★ ★ ★ ★

Hope Cove, Kingsbridge, Devon
Contact: Mrs PA Chaffe, Atlantic Lodge, Hope Cove, Kingsbridge, Devon TQ7 3HH
Tel: (01548) 561873

This exceptional, well equipped bungalow is in an outstanding position on the south Devon coast, commanding one of the best views of the sea that Britain has to offer. Situated in a small fishing village surrounded by National Trust property, with the beach just three minutes' walk away. All front rooms have full command of the sea. Four double bedrooms, one en-suite, further bathroom and cloak room – all fully tiled. Includes a corner bath, shower, toilet, washbasin. Large lounge, kitchen/diner, patio.

Low season per week: £265.00–£400.00
High season per week: £600.00–£795.00
Short breaks: from £120.00–£150.00 (low season only)

1 bungalow: sleeping 8 people

423 Little Coombe Cottage ★ ★ ★ ★ ★

Dittisham, Dartmouth, Devon
Contact: Mr & Mrs Unitt, Little Coombe Farm, Dittisham, Dartmouth, Devon TQ6 OJB
Tel: (01803) 722599 **Fax:** (01803) 722599

Top quality rating. Idyllic cottage tucked away on small 20-acre estate, overlooking stream-fed pools and woodland. Near Dittisham, yet totally private, with rare breeds of geese, poultry and highland cattle. Lovely walks nearby. Extensive decking area provides picnic seating area and superb views. Two en-suite bedrooms, one four-poster, one twin. Well fitted kichen with separate lounge/dining room. Central heating, double glazing and woodburner make for cosy winter breaks. No steps throughout. Non-smoking. 10% discount for two people, 10% discount for two consecutive weeks.

Low season per week: from £230.00
High season per week: max £525.00

1 cottage: sleeping 4 people

424 Higher Bowden ★ ★ ★ ★

Bowden, Dartmouth, Devon **Web:** www.higherbowden.com
Contact: Mrs & Mr M&P Khosla, Higher Bowden, Bowden, Dartmouth, Devon TQ6 0LH
Tel: (01803) 770745 **Fax:** (01803) 770262 **E-mail:** cottages@higherbowden.com

Thirteen comfortable quality cottages nestling peacefully on a south-facing hillside, one mile from award-winning Blackpool Sands beach and four miles from picturesque Dartmouth. All have a full-range of kitchen appliances including dishwasher, washer/dryer, microwave plus wood-burning stove and direct dial telephone, 13 television channels, video etc. On-site facilities include indoor swimming pool, jacuzzi, sauna, solarium, gym, under 5's playroom, games room, snooker room, two children's playgrounds, tennis court, trampoline and more. Out of season short breaks are available.

Low season per week: £257.00–£495.00
High season per week: £605.00–£1449.00

13 cottages: sleeping 2–8 people + cot

425 Roward Farm   ★ ★ ★ ★

Draycot Cerne, Chippenham, Wiltshire
Contact: Mr D Humphrey, Roward Farm, Roward Farm, Draycot Cerne, Chippenham, Wiltshire SN15 4SG
Tel: (01249) 758147 **Fax:** (01249) 758149 **E-mail:** d.humphrey@roward.demon.co.uk

Three character cottages converted from traditional farm buildings and retaining many original features. Set in a courtyard, they overlook open fields and enjoy privacy and quiet without being isolated. The cottages are all warm, spacious and well equipped, with high quality fittings. Each has a private patio and ample parking space. Excellent centre for the many atttractions of north Wiltshire, the Cotswolds and Bath, or for enjoying the peace of the surrounding countryside.

Low season per week: £190.00–£250.00
High season per week: £275.00–£345.00

3 cottages: sleeping 2–4 people
Cards accepted: Mastercard, Visa, Switch/Delta

426 Hartshanger Holidays   ★ ★ ★ ★

Toll Road, Porlock, Minehead, Somerset **Web:** www.hartshanger.com
Contact: Mrs A Edward, Hartshanger, Toll Road, Porlock, Minehead, Somerset TA24 8JH
Tel: (01643) 862700 **Fax:** (01643) 862700 **E-mail:** hartshanger@lineone.net

Wonderful coastal views greet your arrival here, where Exmoor National Park meets the sea. Beautifully equipped accommodation set peacefully in five acres, yet ony five minutes walk to Porlock with all its pubs, shops and restaurants. Relax and unwind, play tennis, ride or walk the local hills, moors and coastal path; visit the many interesting attractions for the family. Allow us to welcome you to England's best kept secret.

Low season per week: £189.00–£420.00
High season per week: £431.00–£532.00

1 cottage and 1 apartment: sleeping 4/5 people
Cards accepted: Mastercard, Visa, Switch/Delta, Amex, JCB, Solo, Visa Electron

427 Northmoor House & Lodge   ★ ★ ★ ★

Northmoor, Dulverton, Somerset **Web:** www.northmoorhouse.co.uk
Contact: Tim Tarling (Manager), Northmoor, Dulverton, Somerset TA22 9QG
Tel: (01398) 323720 **Fax:** (01398) 324537 **E-mail:** timtarling@northmoor.fsnet.co.uk

Large Victorian country house, set in three acres of secluded gardens surrounded by woodland of the River Barle Valley, within Exmoor National Park. Two miles from Dulverton. Perfect for family gatherings, walking, birdwatching or just relaxing! Sleeps 22 in 12 rooms, plus three cots. One twin room with shower is equipped to Access Category 2. Two sitting rooms. Dining room for 24, small library. Large, well equipped kitchen with Aga and LPG cooker. Snooker room, children's snooker, table tennis, darts, croquet and two barbecues. Northmoor Lodge, sleeping 4 + 1, is also available.
♿ **Category 2**

Low season per week: from £1400.00
High season per week: max £2500.00
Short breaks: from £910.00–£1450.00
(3 nights, low season only)

2 houses: sleeping 22 and 5 people
Cards accepted: Mastercard, Visa, Switch/Delta

428 Handley Farm ★★★★

Venn Cross, Waterrow, Taunton, Somerset **Web:** www.handleyfarm.co.uk
Contact: Mr & Mrs G&L Leigh-Firbank, Handley Farm, Waterrow, Taunton, Somerset TA4 2BE
Tel: (01398) 361516 **Fax:** (01398) 361516 **E-mail:** leigh-firbank.george@ntlworld.com

Tucked away from it all, but easy to find, in an unspoilt and idyllic setting close to Exmoor, the Vale of Taunton Deane and much more. Come and relax in one of our two cottages with woodburners for those chilly evenings, four-poster bed and a private gardens. Central heating. Games room. Children's climbing frames. Course fishing for resident use only. Friendly farm animals. Farm walks. See also our serviced accommodation on page 181.

Low season per week: £165.00–£240.00
High season per week: £240.00–£480.00
Short breaks: from £110.00–£160.00

2 cottages: sleeping 2–6 people

429 The Stable ★★★★

Norton Sub Hamdon, Stoke sub Hamdon, Somerset
Contact: Mr & Mrs J H Fisher, Brook House, Norton Sub Hamdon, Stoke sub Hamdon, Somerset TA14 6SR
Tel: (01935) 881789 **Fax:** (01935) 881789

Our village lies just beneath Ham Hill Country Park in a peaceful countryside dotted with pretty villages built of our local honey-coloured stone and close to many historic houses and classic gardens. The Stable conversion, in the very attractive gardens of 17th-century Brook House, has a large high beamed bedroom with both a double and single bed, kitchen, bathroom and living room with sofa bed.

Low season per week: £125.00–£250.00
High season per week: £260.00–£275.00
Short breaks: from £100.00–£150.00

2 cottages: sleeping 4 people

430 Weavers Cottage ★★★★

West Chinnock, Crewkerne, Somerset
Contact: Gordon and Tricia Piper, 48 Higher Street, West Chinnock, Crewkerne, Somerset TA18 7QA
Tel: (01935) 881370 **E-mail:** thepipers@btinternet.com

A traditionally restored and welcoming flax weaver's cottage, with a wealth of original features. Easy access to National Trust houses, classic gardens, walking, golfing and the Dorset/Devon coastline. Comfortably spacious and ideal for discerning couples. Weavers Cottage has full central heating with unlimited hot water and no hidden extras. Linen and towels are provided. Fresh flowers, wine, chocolates and a warm welcome await you. "The best we have found yet."

Low season per week: £180.00–£220.00
High season per week: £220.00–£260.00
Short breaks: from £150.00 (min 3 nights)

1 cottage: sleeping 2 people

431 Stable Cottage ★ ★ ★ ★

Meerhay Manor, Beaminster, Dorset **Web:** www.meerhay.co.uk
Contact: Mrs D M Clarke, Meerhay Manor, Beaminster, Dorset DT8 3SB
Tel: (01308) 862305 **Fax:** (01308) 863972 **E-mail:** meerhay@aol.com

Situated in the stable yard close to the main house, an old thatched manor, set in a 4 acre plantsman's garden surrounded by 40 acres of farmland, 1 mile from the centre of Beaminster. Ground floor conversion in barn, spacious living room with high ceiling and exposed beams. Fully fitted modern kitchen. Twin bedded bedroom with en-suite bathroom. The accommodation is specially modified for wheelchair users. Sleeps 2/3 people. Sofa bed in living room. Babies' cots can be hired locally. The cottage includes use of owner's garden and tennis court by arrangement. ♿ **Category 2**

Low season per week: £150.00
High season per week: £250.00–£375.00
Short breaks: from £150.00

1 cottage: sleeping 2/3 people

Cerne Abbas Giant

Even without its most famous landmark, Cerne Abbas in Dorset has many attractions. The town grew up around a Benedictine abbey founded in 987, and although only a few ancient remains of the abbey still stand, many of the prettiest houses date from the abbey's 500-year domination of the community. Later, the town flourished as a small market centre, but its decline in the 19th century meant that it never grew large or industrialised, and today it ranks as one of the prettiest villages in Dorset, complete with duckpond, village stocks, a holy well in the churchyard and a superb 14th-century tithe barn.

But what makes Cerne Abbas uniquely memorable is the enormous and extraordinary figure cut into the chalky hillside near by. Brandishing a knobbly club, the Cerne giant strides across the turf, arms outstretched, his naked form leaving little to the imagination. His origins and identity are obscure. Strangely, given that the abbey was a centre of literacy, there is no written record of the figure before 1754, but the current opinion is that the giant is most likely to be a representation of the Roman god Hercules, carved during the first few centuries AD.

Only two other similarly ancient hill-carvings exist in Britain – the White Horse of Uffington, Oxfordshire, and the Long Man of Wilmington, East Sussex. These were probably not the only ones; perhaps a whole panoply of colossal figures and beasts once marched across the English downland, only to be slowly smothered in vegetation and lost forever. The giant

has survived through regular and rigorous 'scourings', usually at seven-year intervals, a practice which was presumably, and rather surprisingly, condoned by the Benedictines despite the giant's obviously pagan nature and indecent nakedness. Today the National Trust is responsible for maintenance.

For obvious reasons the Cerne giant has always been regarded as something of a fertility symbol. It is thought that the village's annual spring revelries were held on a site near by, and to this day it is claimed that merely sitting on the giant's impressive 30ft (9m) member is a certain cure for infertility. This is not to be encouraged, however, because of the risk of eroding the carving's most prominent feature! Perhaps the best view of the Cerne giant is to be had from a viewpoint at the junction where Duck Street meets the A352 Sherborne–Dorchester road.

432 Coach House Farm ★ ★ ★ ★ ★

Moor Lane, Broadclyst, Exeter

Contact: Mr J Bale, Coach House Farm, Moor Lane, Broadclyst, Exeter, EX5 3JH

Tel: (01392) 461254 **Fax:** (01392) 460931 **E-mail:** meadowview@mpprops.fsnet.co.uk

Surrounded by the National Trust Killerton Estate, the converted stables of our Victorian coach house provide comfortable ground floor accommodation with private entrance and garden overlooking sheep meadows. The spectacular east Devon coastline from Lyme Regis to Torquay and the wooded valleys of Exmoor and rugged granite terrain of Dartmoor are quickly reached. Central heating, television/video, washer/dryer, dishwasher, fridge/freezer, microwave. Easy access from the M5 and A30. Ideal for the elderly and wheelchair users. ♿ **Category 2**

Low season per week: £182.00–£355.00
High season per week: £410.00–£480.00
Short breaks: from £140.00–£315.00

1 cottage: sleeping 4 people + cot

433 Champernhayes Cottages ★ ★ ★ ★ ★

Champernhayes, Wootton Fitzpaine, Bridport, Dorset **Web:** www.champernhayes.com

Contact: Mrs E R Thompson, Champernhayes, Wootton Fitzpaine, Bridport, Dorset DT6 6DF

Tel: (01297) 560853 **Fax:** (01297) 561155 **E-mail:** champhayes@aol.com

Perched on the slopes of a west Dorset hillside and surrounded by lush woodland and verdant countryside, only a short drive to the historic coastlines of Lyme Regis and Charmouth. While all guests can share a heated, indoor swim-spa, two cottages have their own heated outdoor pools by the patio, guaranteeing privacy and shelter. Comfortably designed, high quality, well equipped accommodation to provide you with modern comfort whilst retaining the ambience of the original buildings.

Low season per week: £275.00–£519.00
High season per week: £321.00–£1299.00
Short breaks: from £150.00–£450.00
(September–April only)

1 farmhouse and 4 cottages: sleeping 2–8 people

Cards accepted: Mastercard, Visa

434 Sea Tree House ★ ★ ★ ★

Broad Street, Lyme Regis, Dorset **Web:** lymeregis.com/seatreehouse

Contact: Mr D Parker, Sea Tree House, 18 Broad Street, Lyme Regis, Dorset DT7 3QE

Tel: (01297) 442244 **Fax:** (01297) 442244 **E-mail:** seatree.house@ukonline.co.uk

Experience Georgian elegance with a touch of romance in the heart of Lyme Regis. These spacious, completely private, one-bedroom apartments have large bright sitting rooms. Each has south-facing bay windows with magnificent sea views. Ideal for couples wanting to celebrate an anniversary or special occasion in style. Your kitchen is fully equipped with extras such as washer-dryer and dishwasher. We are minutes' walk from the beach, shops, restaurants and heritage coastal walks.

Low season per week: £210.00–£330.00
High season per week: £379.00–£545.00
Short breaks: from £160.00–£250.00

2 apartments: sleeping 2/3 people

435 Squirrel Cottage ★★★★★

Woodbury, Devon **Web:** www.thethatchedcottagecompany.com
Contact: The Thatched Cottage Company, 56 Fore Street, Otterton, Budleigh Salterton, Devon EX9 7HB
Tel: (01395) 567676 **Fax:** (01395) 567440

Squirrel Cottage is a 16th-century thatched cottage in a quiet part of Woodbury, close to the church. There are two double bedrooms and one single bedroom. The cottage has quality furnishings throughout, paintings and antiques. It is an excellent base for touring most of the West Country and is close to restaurants, pubs and the beach. Well behaved dogs welcome.

Low season per week: from £300.00
High season per week: max £1250.00
Short breaks: from £150.00

9 houses and cottages: sleeping 2–8 people
Cards accepted: Mastercard, Visa

436 Fairwinds Holiday Bungalow ★★★★

Rayners, Kennford, Exeter, Devon
Contact: Mrs M Price, Fairwinds Hotel, Kennford, Exeter, Devon EX6 7UD
Tel: (01392) 832911 **E-mail:** fairwindshotbun@aol.com

Exclusively for non-smokers. The perfect holiday home in the heart of a pretty village, just below the Haldon Forest hills, five miles south of Exeter. Delightful secluded garden. Fully equipped kitchen: fridge/freezer, oven/hob, microwave, washing machine. Stylish lounge/diner with colour television, video, stereo, telephone. Central heating throughout. Garage and drive. Sorry no pets. The village store/Post Office and village inn are just a stroll away. Please send for a brochure.

Low season per week: £230.00–£340.00
High season per week: £360.00–£460.00

1 bungalow: sleeping 5 people
Open: all year except December

437 Bay Fort Mansions ★★★★

Warren Road, Torquay **Web:** www.bayfortapartments.co.uk
Contact: Mr P Freeman, Bay Fort Mansions, Warren Road, Torquay TQ2 5TN
Tel: (01803) 213810 **Fax:** (01803) 209057 **E-mail:** freeman@bayfortapartments.co.uk

Elegant, stylish and comfortable south-facing apartments, complemented by probably the finest views of Torquay and the English Riviera. Our 15 non-smoking apartments, 12 of which are sea-facing, many with patios and balconies, have recently been refurbished and equipped to a high standard, designed to provide you with a memorable holiday experience. Each apartment has Sky television and direct dial telephone. Our gardens overlook the bay and marina. Daily service available. Cots and high chairs provided.

Low season per week: £135.00–£440.00
High season per week: £360.00–£725.00
Short breaks: from £65.00–£280.00

15 apartments: sleeping 2–5 people
Cards accepted: Mastercard, Visa, Switch/Delta

South and South East England

When Gerald Tyrwhitt-Wilson, 14th Baron Berners, opened his 140ft (43m) folly to his friends in 1935 he displayed the following notice above the entrance: 'Members of the public committing suicide from this tower do so at their own risk'. Berners was an aristocratic eccentric, an accomplished painter, writer and composer, who entertained lavishly. Those who climb his folly (just outside Faringdon) are rewarded by a panoramic view of several counties stretching to the Berkshire Downs and the White Horse of Uffington. Contact Faringdon Tourist Information Centre (tel: 01367 242191) for more information.

► **Castles of the Weald**

The Weald is the wooded, fertile area of Kent and East Sussex lying between the North and South Downs. The region's historic prosperity and its proximity to London have ensured an array of impressive buildings, many of them castles. These include the fairy-tale Leeds Castle, near Maidstone, perched on two islands in the River Len, and, equally picturesque, ruined Scotney Castle (near Lamberhurst), the centrepiece of a stunning hillside garden. Hever, Knole, Penshurst (all Kent) and Bodiam (East Sussex) are other magnificent examples.

Ancient and modern

History pervades every pore of south eastern England. Despite the prosperity and modernity of these bustling counties, there lies a Roman villa, Saxon church, Tudor cottage, Georgian townhouse or Victorian railway station around almost every corner. Sometimes, the juxtaposition of old and modern is striking; at Folkestone, for example, visitors can choose to marvel at the engineering triumph of the Channel Tunnel or descend the steep cliffs to the Maritime Gardens in a lift built in 1885 and powered by water pressure. On other occasions, you will be hard-pushed to realise that you are now in the 21st century. Stroll through Chiddingstone, near Tonbridge (and not that far from the M25), and you leave the modern world behind. The houses are half-timbered, many dating from the Elizabethan and Jacobean periods, though the feel is of an idyllic, timeless age. Or hire a rowing boat at Odiham and explore the Basingstoke Canal. Trees shade the calm, quiet backwaters, the only sounds the gentle splash of oar and rustle of leaves.

An Englishman's home...

The region specialises in gorgeous villages. Some, such as Chiddingstone, are celebrated, others less so. Into this latter category fall the following. Wherwell (near Andover) is a shrine to the thatcher's art that also enjoys a magnificent setting on the banks of the Test. Across the Solent on the Isle of Wight lies sleepy Shorwell, sheltering in a wooded valley beneath the closely grazed downs. In West Sussex, just three miles from Petworth – itself a delightful small town dominated by the majestic Petworth House – is Fittleworth, a straggling settlement that offers another group of picturesque stone or brick cottages at each twist of the woodland lanes. Flint is the prevailing material at Piddinghoe, just inland from Newhaven, where St John's Church has one of only three Norman round towers in Sussex. East Clandon, about four miles east of Guildford, is a compact community of brick-and-tile houses surrounding two of the staples of village life – the church and

the inn. Milton Abbas is all tranquillity now, but two centuries ago Lord Dorchester provoked outrage from its residents when he razed it to the ground – in order to improve his view – and rebuilt it in a wooded valley a mile away. The replacement, six miles (10km) from Blandford Forum, is made up of regularly spaced, thatched cob cottages, allowing later generations to benefit from the landlord's ruthlessness. Pusey, down a 'no through road' east of Faringdon, is another appealing estate village, this one guarded by venerable beech and horse chestnut trees. Swanbourne, in the Vale of Aylesbury, has been attractively rebuilt since an 18th-century fire. Smithfield Close, however, survived the conflagration, and is a handsome group of whitewashed, 16th-century thatched cottages.

Choose a clear day...

All these villages make excellent centres to walk from, and most offer a pub for well-earned refreshment. If you believe all good walks should include some fine vistas, then try one of these four: Ditchling Beacon, a couple of miles north of Brighton, is arguably the best viewpoint in the South Downs. The stretch of the South Downs Way, leading west to the pair of windmills familiarly known as Jack and Jill, makes a rousing afternoon's hike. At the western end of the Way, and competing for the accolade of best viewpoint, is Butser Hill, highest point in the South Downs. The fort at Ditchling dates from the Iron Age; here Stone Age men and women flourished. The Queen Elizabeth Country Park – of which Butser hill is a part – provides leaflets for waymarked trails. Towards the northern end of the Chilterns – and at the end of the Ridgeway, a track used before the Romans arrived – is Ivinghoe Beacon; views extend to London, out over the Bedfordshire plain and south west to the Chilterns, home to glorious, underrated countryside. The final vantage point is beside the Cerne Abbas giant, that uncompromising symbol of male fertility etched on the Dorset Downs. And Dorset comprises the entire view: untaxing, unspoilt and ineffably beautiful.

Walk this way

Many of the long-distance paths in south eastern England follow the ridges of chalk downland, leading you past countless such viewpoints. With other rights-of-way criss-crossing these paths at regular intervals, it is a simple matter to devise shorter, circular walks. The 100 mile (160km) South Downs Way follows ancient tracks and old droveways in East and West Sussex and Hampshire. The North Downs Way, running 153 miles (246km) from Farnham to Canterbury, explores scenery of such splendour – sometimes wooded, sometimes grassland – it is hard to believe that for much of its length London lies less than 30 miles (48km) away. The Ridgeway keeps to the tops of the Chilterns for its eastern stretch, descending to cross the Thames at Goring Gap, where it meets the Thames Path. A recent creation, this trail follows England's most famous river from its source in Gloucestershire to the Thames Barrier at Woolwich, availing itself of 126 footbridges en route. The region has other longer paths that seek out the remoter corners of the countryside. Hampshire has the Hangers Way (17 miles (27km) through beechwoods between Alton and Petersfield) and the Solent Way (60 miles (96km) from Milford-on-Sea to Emsworth), and others besides. The Isle of Wight Coast Path circles the island in 69 glorious miles (110km).

How the other half lived

Those who enjoy that most compelling of pastimes – having a good look round somebody else's house – can indulge themselves to their heart's content and without conscience. The choice is so wide that it can be a matter

▶ **Pallant House**

Built in 1712, Chichester's Pallant House (tel: 01243 774557) is an interesting setting for a modern-art collection. Each room, lovingly restored, reflects a period in the house's history and contains furniture, porcelain, textiles, even pictures from the period. But amongst all this grace and refinement, the raw colour and abstract form of the modern paintings on its walls strike an exciting note of contrast. Picasso, Sutherland, Nash, Piper, Moore and others are represented, most donated by Walter Hussey, Dean of Chichester Cathedral from 1955 to 1977.

▶ **Brownsea Island**

A trip from busy Poole Quay across Poole Harbour to Brownsea Island is a voyage to a different world. Though once the site of a (failed) china clay industry, for most of its history Brownsea has remained isolated, even neglected. For some crucial years, between 1925 and 1961, the island was cut off from all outside influences by a reclusive owner. Now owned by the National Trust, it has remained unspoilt and undeveloped, a haven for red squirrels and the secretive sika deer (tel: 01202 707744).

► The Bloomsbury Group in Sussex

Inside the 12th-century church at Berwick, near Eastbourne, a surprise awaits. Its walls are covered with astonishing modern murals, created in the 1940s by Duncan Grant, Vanessa Bell and her son, Quentin Bell. The three, who lived at nearby Charleston Farmhouse, were members of an eccentric affiliation of writers and artists, the Bloomsbury Group. Charleston became a gathering place for the group and was vividly decorated in accordance with their artistic ideals. Virginia Woolf lived not far away, at Monk's House (NT), Rodmell (tel: 01892 890651).

► Mad Jack Fuller

Nineteenth-century patron of the arts, bon viveur and local squire, 'Mad' Jack Fuller lives on thanks to his abiding passion for follies. His grave in the churchyard at Brightling, East Sussex, is a 25ft (7.5m)-high stone pyramid. Despite his wish to be interred at table, dressed for dinner and resplendent in top hat, he rests – in conventional repose – in the ground below. Nearby edifices include the Tower, a gothic-looking building with a battlemented top, and the Sugar Loaf, reputedly built in a night to enable Fuller to 'win' a bet that the spire of Dallington church was visible from his windows.

of choosing your scale, which starts at the very, very grand, such as Windsor Castle, Blenheim Palace, Osborne House, Waddesdon Manor and Goodwood House, and includes some comparatively modest houses. Closer to this end of the spectrum is the 14th-century Alfriston Clergy House, the very first property purchased by the National Trust, for just £10, in 1896. Lamb House, in the near-perfect town of Rye, was the home of the novelist Henry James; the 18th-century building is surrounded by an attractive garden. Other less celebrated historic homes include: Rousham House, a 17th-century Oxfordshire mansion now full of portraits but once used as a Royalist garrison in the Civil War; Haseley Manor, a rambling house of several periods happily rescued from dereliction in the 1970s; Dorney Court, Windsor, a 15th-century brick-and-timber house in the same ownership for almost 500 years; Chettle House, near Blandford Forum, an appealingly idiosyncratic, small Baroque country-house that feels – and is – very much a family home.

The coast is clear

England's southern coast has long been a playground for London, ensuring that most resorts offer a bewildering array of amenities. Margate, Eastbourne, Brighton, Bournemouth and Shanklin, amongst others, have long welcomed large numbers of visitors. Escaping the hurly-burly can be more of a challenge on this stretch of coastline, but try Minnis Bay, on Kent's north-facing shore, west of Margate; Pevensey Bay, between Bexhill and Eastbourne; the sand dunes west of Littlehampton; Bracklesham Bay, near Selsey Bill; Lepe, a small stretch of sand and shingle facing the Isle of Wight; Luccombe Bay, ten minutes' walk from Shanklin; and Shipstal Point, giving on to a quiet stretch of Poole Harbour.

The artistic year

The cultural capital for livelier, broad-minded souls is Brighton, with its avant-garde galleries, arthouse cinemas and never-ending supply of clubs. The Brighton Festival – held each May, and one of England's largest celebrations of the arts – includes events such as conducted walks through Victorian cemeteries, dance, theatre, jazz and classical music. Not far away, Arundel puts out the bunting in August and invites you to open-air theatre in the castle grounds, jazz, fireworks and classical concerts. The centrepiece of the Canterbury Festival is the cathedral – used for operatic performances – while other venues host drama, dance and much more, each October. Similarly, Chichester Festival's focal point is its Norman cathedral, though the refurbished ballroom of Goodwood House has also been called into service in the past; the July festivities add exhibitions of contemporary sculpture and lectures to the round of concerts and plays. Guildford holds two festivals each year: music in March and books in October. Henley makes the most of its superb Thames-side setting when theatre takes to the streets and bridges of the town each July. At the end of September and in early October, it is the turn of Windsor to stage musical and literary events, some held in the Castle itself. And for four weeks in February and March, the dance world turns its attention to north western Surrey, the home of the Woking Dance Umbrella.

A break with history

Most of the festival towns and cities are ideal for short breaks. There are a hundred other attractive bases suitable for a weekend away, of which these form an eclectic sample. Winchester, the nation's capital until the reign of Canute, claims the longest cathedral in Europe, and an impressive collection of Georgian townhouses too. Midhurst, a busy market town beneath the South Downs, seems only to have glorious 16th-, 17th- and 18th-century buildings, some of the best in the appealingly named Knockhundred Row. Tunbridge Wells' prosperity arrived with the discovery of chalybeate springs in 1606, and it has barely looked back since. Modern-day visitors can approach the springs along The Pantiles, a shopping area of sublime beauty. Arrive in early June and a cricket festival at one of the country's most picturesque grounds is in full swing. Hungerford, on the banks of the Kennet and close to more superb walking country, is a paradise for antique hunters. Thame, on the river of the same name, is equally popular with those happy to spend an evening in a fine old coaching inn; the town boasts four that date from the 15th century.

Some useful contact numbers

Basingstoke Canal (tel: 01252 370073)
The South Downs Way (tel: 02392 597618)
The North Downs Way (tel: 01622 221526)
The Ridgeway National Trail (tel: 01865 810224)
The Thames Path National Trail (tel: 01865 810224)
Hangers Way (tel: 01962 870500)
Solent Way (tel: 01962 870500)
Isle of Wight Coast Path (tel: 01983 813800)
Windsor Castle (tel: 01753 831118)
Blenheim Palace, Woodstock (tel: 01993 811325)
Osborne House, Isle of Wight (tel: 01983 200022)
Waddesdon Manor, Aylesbury (tel: 01296 653211)
Goodwood House, Chichester (tel: 01243 755000)
Alfriston Clergy House (tel: 01323 870001)
Lamb House, Rye (tel: 01892 890651)
Rousham House, Bicester (tel: 01869 347110)
Dorney Court, Windsor (tel: 01628 604638)
Brighton Festival (tel: 01273 700747)
Arundel Festival (tel: 01903 883690)
Canterbury Festival (tel: 01227 452853)
Chichester Festivities (tel: 01243 785718)
Guildford International Music Festival (tel: 01483 879167)
Guildford Book Festival (tel: 01483 444334)
Henley Festival (tel: 01491 843400)
Woking Dance Umbrella (tel: 01483 545900)

► **Sandham Memorial Chapel**

This chapel, at Burghclere in Berkshire, was built to house an extraordinary series of wall-paintings by the artist Stanley Spencer. He served in the army medical corps during World War I, and the murals record the soldiers' everyday humdrum duties: floor-cleaning, bed-making, laundry-sorting and a whole variety of other chores, but painted with exaggerated proportions and stylised perspective so that the scenes take on an aura of significance and horror. The chapel is dominated by a great Resurrection on the wall behind the altar (tel: 01635 278394).

Sir Stanley Spencer CBE RA

► **The Gardens of Stowe**

Perhaps the finest statement of the art of the 18th-century garden lives on at Stowe, near Buckingham. John Vanbrugh, William Kent, James Gibbs and 'Capability' Brown – the most talented gardeners and architects of their day – went to great lengths to create a landscape remodelled and replanted to look as natural as possible, in order to match the aesthetic blueprint of ancient Rome. To this end, grottoes were built, lakes dug, columns erected and monuments – thirty, all told – sited with consummate care. These majestic gardens are now in the care of the National Trust (tel: 01280 822850).

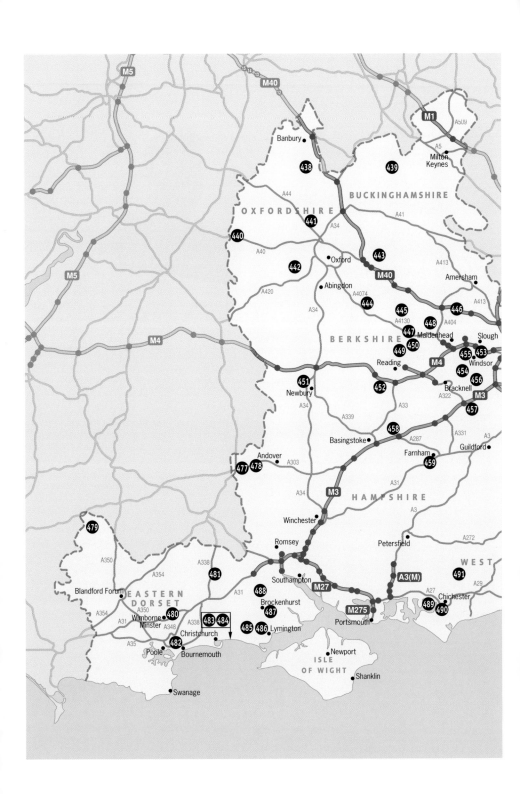

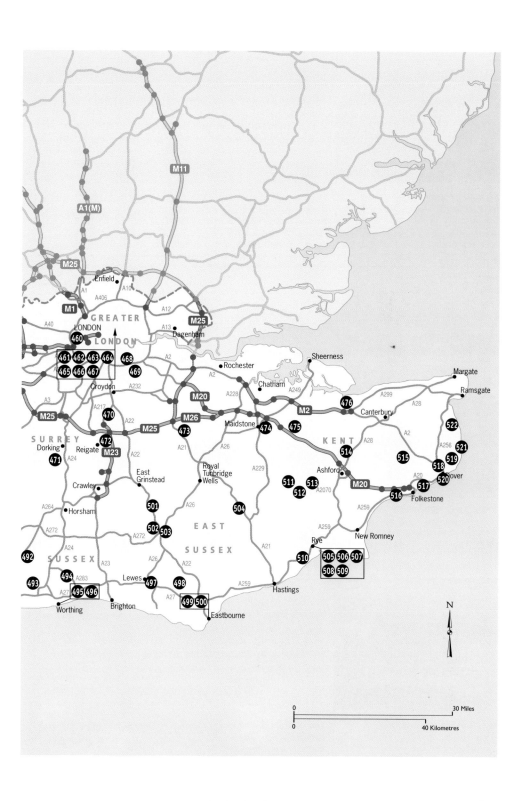

438 Holcombe Hotel & Restaurant

★★★ Silver Award

High Street, Deddington, Banbury, Oxfordshire OX15 0SL **Tel:** (01869) 338274 **Fax:** (01869) 337167
Web: www.holcombehotel.com **E-mail:** reception@holcombehotel.freeserve.co.uk

Delightful 17th-century, family-run hotel offering personal attention and traditional hospitality in a relaxed atmosphere. 17 en-suite bedrooms, each with its own character and every amenity including direct phone, PC socket and satellite television. The restaurant, known locally for its fine cuisine, offers modern and traditional English menus that can best be described as 'honest' food and holds an AA Rosette for the seventh consecutive year. Golfing can be arranged locally at a superb 18-hole course. Meeting room for up to 20 delegates. Free car park for 30 cars. Convenient to the M40 (junctions 10 or 11) on the A4260.

Bed & Breakfast per night: single room from £68.00–£85.00; double room from £89.00–£112.00
Dinner, Bed & Breakfast per person, per night: £65.00–£75.00 (min 2 nights, 2 sharing)
Lunch available: 1200–1400

Evening meal: 1900 (last orders 2200)
Bedrooms: 2 single, 8 double, 6 twin, 1 triple
Bathrooms: 17 en-suite
Parking: 30 spaces
Cards accepted: Mastercard, Visa, Switch/Delta, Amex, Eurocard, JCB, Visa Electron

439 Villiers Hotel

★★★ Silver Award

3 Castle Street, Buckingham, Buckinghamshire MK18 1BS **Tel:** (01280) 822444 **Fax:** (01280) 822113
E-mail: villiers@villiers-hotels.demon.co.uk

When we created Villiers Hotel from the old Swan and Castle Inn, we set out to build a very special and individual hotel. Drawing upon the character of the 400-year-old hostelry we included the highest quality facilities and services, with comfort a priority for you, our guest – a home away from home. Henry's, our elegant air-conditioned restaurant, has been awarded AA 2 Rosettes for exceptional cuisine.

Bed & Breakfast per night: single room from £90.00–£110.00; double room from £115.00–£180.00
Lunch available: 1200–1400
Evening meal: 1900 (last orders 2230)

Bedrooms: 3 single, 27 double, 16 twin
Bathrooms: 46 en-suite
Parking: 46 spaces
Cards accepted: Mastercard, Visa, Switch/Delta, Amex, Diners, Eurocard

440 Burford House Hotel

◆◆◆◆◆ Gold Award

99 High Street, Burford, Oxford, Oxfordshire OX18 4QA **Tel:** (01993) 823151 **Fax:** (01993) 823240
Web: www.burford-house.co.uk **E-mail:** stay@burfordhouse.co.uk

Situated in one of the Cotswold's most historic towns, Burford House is perfectly placed for exploring this lovely area. Run with care by owners Jane and Simon Henty, importance is placed on comfort, a relaxed atmosphere and attention to detail, and the house is cosy and intimate with a wealth of personal touches. Wonderful breakfasts are served and guests can return to traditional afternoon tea in the sitting rooms or delightful courtyard garden. A warm welcome awaits.

Bed & Breakfast per night: single occupancy from £75.00–£95.00; double room from £95.00–£130.00
Lunch available: 1200–1415

Bedrooms: 3 four-poster, 3 double, 2 twin
Bathrooms: 8 en-suite
Cards accepted: Mastercard, Visa, Switch/Delta, Amex

441 Shipton Glebe

Woodstock, Oxford, Oxfordshire OX20 1QQ **Tel:** (01993) 812688 **Fax:** (01993) 813142
Web: www.shipton-glebe.com **E-mail:** stay@shipton-glebe.com

This lovely country house, set in nine acres of garden/parkland, is situated on the edge of historic Woodstock, close to Blenheim Palace. All the rooms are luxuriously furnished, and incorporate sitting room facilities. Breakfasts are served in the conservatory overlooking the gardens. You will find that Shipton Glebe is the perfect setting for that special and relaxing few days away. Winner of the Best Bed & Breakfast in the Southern region.

Bed & Breakfast per night: single occupancy from £65.00–£70.00; double room from £75.00–£90.00

Bedrooms: 2 double, 1 twin
Bathrooms: 3 en-suite
Open: March-October
Cards accepted: Mastercard, Visa, Switch/Delta

The Eastern Cotswolds

Mirroring the geography of the whole country, the Cotswolds slope gently down from west to east. Oxfordshire and the Eastern Cotswolds may not have great blustery tops and panoramic vistas, but the towns and villages – the true beauty of the area – continue to be of the highest level. The rivers – the Evenlode and Windrush (shown here) – are older and wiser here, flowing serenely through broader valleys and under stone bridges. Both are headed for the Thames and for Oxford, outside the Cotswolds proper, but an ideal basecamp for tackling the eastern fringes.

Southernmost of these Cotswold valleys is the Thames (known here as the Isis). The river is navigable as far as Lechlade on the Gloucestershire border, and is a popular attraction in its own right. Those who prefer dry land can follow almost the same route on the Thames Path. Buscot, west of the attractive market town of Faringdon, is perhaps the highlight of the upper Thames. An unspoilt estate village, it has a riverside church and two 18th-century properties belonging to the National Trust: the Old Parsonage (open by appointment only) and the larger Buscot Park, containing an important collection of paintings and set within fine parkland. Five miles downstream are Pusey House Gardens.

The evocatively named river Windrush flows over grey stone which has been used for St Paul's Cathedral,

many Oxford colleges and – on a more modest scale – the houses of Burford, a real Cotswold gem. Just south is the Cotswold Wildlife Park. Between Burford and Witney, an appealing town whose prosperity derived from blanket-making, is Minster Lovell, a charming, tucked-away village that conceals a gruesome legend. Desperate to escape capture after involvement in a failed insurrection, a 15th-century Lord Lovell had himself walled up by a servant, who suddenly died. The lord's remains were supposedly discovered in 1718. The ruined hall is open to the public.

The Evenlode makes its meandering way through remnants of the ancient Wychwood Forest towards Charlbury, where the quaint museum presents the history of this peaceful, former weaving town. The valley is good walking country – the Oxfordshire Way long-distance path follows the riverbank for some miles, as does the Oxford–Worcester railway line, which makes a good, leisurely vantage point. The Glyme, a tributary of the Evenlode, feeds the lakes of the sumptuous Blenheim Palace, given to the Duke of Marlborough by a grateful nation in the early 18th century after he had proved victorious in the War of the Spanish Succession. Nearby Woodstock is another magnificent village to dawdle in.

The greater part of the Cotswolds lie to the west – see feature on pages 116 & 117.

442 Pinkhill Cottage

45 Rack End, Standlake, Witney, Oxfordshire OX29 7SA **Tel:** (01865) 300544
E-mail: pinkhill@madasafish.com

A charming 17th-century thatched cottage in half-acre gardens fronting the River Windrush in a quiet Oxfordshire village, offering exclusive, private bed & breakfast accommodation for two. The old stable has been transformed into a sitting room from which leads a staircase to the hayloft – now an airy double bedroom with en-suite shower room. Many of the original beams are a feature of our cottage. Standlake is ideal for touring Oxford and the Cotswolds.

Bed & Breakfast per night: single occupancy from £32.00–£35.00; double room from £48.00–£50.00

Bedrooms: 1 double
Bathrooms: 1 en-suite shower
Parking: 1 space

The Landmarks of White Horse Hill

The Lambourn Downs of South Oxfordshire, rising up bare and smooth from the Vale of the White Horse, are steeped in ancient history. Around 5,000 years ago our ancestors settled here, built their forts, buried their dead and walked their pathways; today the Downs are liberally sprinkled with the relics of their existence. Some sites have been excavated, but alongside the scant archaeological evidence, a vein of myth and legend has come down over the centuries to provide explanations for the mysterious landmarks.

Dominating the valley which is named after it, the strange elongated shape of a galloping horse is cut into the chalk near Uffington. The Iron Age tribes who lived in the nearby hillfort are believed to have carved it in about 50BC as a representation of the horse goddess, Epona. Possibly the oldest chalk carving in the country, it is, intriguingly, the only one which faces right. In more recent centuries the white horse became the focus of a seven-yearly tradition: people would climb the hill to 'scour' the accumulated weeds and debris from the horse to the accompaniment of fairground revels.

Just below the horse is a mound known as Dragon's Hill. Whether natural or man-made is unknown, but local legend asserts that this is where St George killed the dragon. The patches of bare chalk on its top and sides, the story goes, were formed by hot streams of dragon's blood, over which the grass can never grow.

Running along the ridge of the Downs, just south of the White Horse, is the Ridgeway. This track – used by people of the New Stone Age, the builders of Stonehenge – is one of the oldest roads in Britain. It leads south west past Wayland's Smithy, a neolithic burial chamber dating from around 2800BC. This remote spot is one of many places throughout Europe (usually either caves or burial mounds) imagined as the home of Wayland, the fearsome Saxon blacksmith-god.

The figure of the smith is also associated, somewhat menacingly, with another curiosity: a strangely-shaped stone beside the road leading south from Kingston Lisle, just east of the White Horse. The 'Blowing Stone', as it is called, was supposedly brought here by a blacksmith living in the nearby cottage who could blow into its many holes to create a gruesome, moaning roar. Another legend grew up that King Alfred summoned his troops to battle by blowing through the stone.

443 The Dairy

♦♦♦♦♦ Gold Award

Moreton, Thame, Oxfordshire OX9 2HX **Tel:** (01844) 214075 **Fax:** (01844) 214075
Web: www.thedairy.freeuk.com **E-mail:** thedairy@freeuk.com

This former milking parlour, set in over four acres, provides a beautiful, peaceful and comfortable stay. All bedrooms are bright and airy and include hairdryers, writing tables, fresh flowers, biscuits and comfortable sofas and chairs. There is a large open plan lounge with views of the Chilterns. The property is very convenient for London, either by train (50 minutes from local station), coach or car. Oxford is 20 minutes by car.

Bed & Breakfast per night: single occupancy from £62.00; double room from £86.00

Bedrooms: 3 single/double
Bathrooms: 3 en-suite
Parking: 6 spaces
Cards accepted: Mastercard, Visa, Amex

444 Fyfield Manor

♦♦♦♦ Silver Award

Benson, Wallingford, Oxfordshire OX10 6HA **Tel:** (01491) 835184 **Fax:** (01491) 825635
E-mail: chris@fifield-software.demon.co.uk

Fyfield Manor is a most interesting house with 12th-century origins, medieval dining hall and many 18th-century features. Each bedroom, with en-suite facilities, is tastefully restored to reflect its individual period and provides spacious comfortable accommodation. Set in seven acres of natural and informal gardens, it is essentially a family home offering a warm welcome. It is ideally situated between Henley and Oxford, with easy access to the M40 and M4. Local pubs offer excellent food.

Bed & Breakfast per night: single occupancy from £35.00–£40.00; double room from £55.00–£60.00

Bedrooms: 1 double, 1 twin
Bathrooms: 2 en-suite
Parking: 6 spaces
Open: all year except Christmas

445 The Stonor Arms Hotel

★★★ Silver Award

Stonor, Henley-on-Thames, Oxfordshire RG9 6HE **Tel:** (01491) 638866 **Fax:** (01491) 638863
Web: www.stonor-arms.co.uk **E-mail:** stonorarms.hotel@virgin.net

A privately-owned country hotel and restaurant, the 18th-century Stonor Arms is the perfect retreat, with its award-winning restaurant, elegant accommodation and intimate walled garden. We offer all the charms of a country home away from home in a peaceful, yet accessible, setting. Scenic Henley-on-Thames, the Royal Regatta and the university town of Oxford are a comfortable drive away. The village of Stonor itself offers stunning countryside and excellent walks.

Bed & Breakfast per night: single occupancy from £120.00–£155.00; double room from £145.00–£175.00
Lunch available: 1200–1400

Bedrooms: 4 double, 6 double/twin
Bathrooms: 10 en-suite
Parking: 26 spaces
Cards accepted: Mastercard, Visa, Switch/Delta, Amex

446 Rosemary Cottage Bed & Breakfast ◆◆◆◆

99 Heath End Road, Flackwell Heath, High Wycombe, Buckinghamshire HP10 9ES **Tel:** (01628) 520635 **Fax:** (01628) 520635
Web: www.reservation.co.uk **E-mail:** mike.1@virgin.net

Charming character cottage situated on the edge of the Chiltern Hills, 350 feet above sea level with uninterrupted views over the Thames Valley. An ideal base to explore Buckinghamshire and Berkshire, yet less than 30 miles from London. Our rooms are light and spacious with breathtaking views. Indulge yourself in our hearty full English or continental breakfast and at the end of the day relax by our pool and watch the sun go down.

Bed & Breakfast per night: double room from £50.00–£60.00

Bedrooms: 2 double, 1 twin
Bathrooms: 1 en-suite, 1 shared
Parking: 5 spaces
Open: all year except Christmas

447 Coldharbour House ◆◆◆◆

3 Coldharbour Close, Henley-on-Thames, Oxfordshire RG9 1QF **Tel:** (01491) 575229 **Fax:** (01491) 575229
E-mail: coldharbourhouse@cs.com

Coldharbour House stands in a quiet close on the outskirts of the renowned riverside town of Henley-on-Thames. It is built in a pretty farmhouse style with character features but up-to-the-minute amenities, and a walled garden surrounds the house. There are three bedrooms, one double with en-suite shower, one twin and one single with shared bathroom. Full English and continental breakfast is served in the dining room overlooking the garden. There is off street parking.

Bed & Breakfast per night: double room from £55.00–£65.00

Bedrooms: 1 single, 1 double, 1 twin
Bathrooms: 1 en-suite, 1 shared
Parking: 2 spaces

448 Danesfield House Hotel and Spa ★★★★ Silver Award

Medmenham, Marlow-on-Thames, Buckinghamshire SL7 2EY **Tel:** (01628) 891010 **Fax:** (01628) 890408
Web: www.danesfieldhouse.co.uk **E-mail:** sales@danesfieldhouse.co.uk

Danesfield House offers one of England's finest award-winning country house hotels, ideally set within the Chiltern Hills in an area of outstanding natural beauty, and yet within only one hour of London. Panoramic views of the River Thames from luxurious bedrooms, a beautiful terrace brasserie and the AA 2 Rosette Oak Room restaurant have helped establish Danesfield as a very popular destination. Luxurious spa with 20 metre pool, sauna, steam room, gymnasium and treatment rooms available. Visit our website for more information.

Bed & Breakfast per night: single room from £185.00; double room from £225.00
Lunch available: 1200–1400
Evening meal: 1830 (last orders 2200)

Bedrooms: 9 single, 59 double, 16 twin, 3 family
Bathrooms: 87 en-suite **Parking:** 130 spaces
Cards accepted: Mastercard, Visa, Switch/Delta, Amex, Diners, JCB

449 Holmwood

◆◆◆◆

Shiplake Row, Binfield Heath, Henley-on-Thames, Oxfordshire RG9 4DP **Tel:** (0118) 947 8747 **Fax:** (0118) 947 8637

Holmwood is an elegant Georgian country house with a galleried hall, mahogany doors and marble fireplaces. The house is set in three acres of beautiful gardens with extensive views over the Thames Valley. The large bedrooms are furnished with antique and period furniture – all have bathrooms en-suite, colour television and tea/coffee making facilities. Holmwood is convenient for Windsor, Oxford, London and Heathrow. Nearby are several pubs offering excellent evening meals.

🚶 **Category 3**

Bed & Breakfast per night: single room £45.00; double room £65.00

Bedrooms: 1 single, 2 double, 2 twin
Bathrooms: 5 en-suite
Parking: 8 spaces
Cards accepted: Mastercard, Visa, Switch/Delta

450 The Knoll

◆◆◆◆

Crowsley Road, Shiplake, Henley-on-Thames, Oxfordshire RG9 3JT **Tel:** (01189) 402705 or 07885 755437 **Fax:** (01189) 402705
Web: www.theknollhenley.com **E-mail:** theknollhenley@aol.com

The Knoll provides the perfect accommodation for an idyllic holiday or short stay. Relax after a day's sightseeing or riverside walk in this private home with extensive landscaped gardens. The Knoll is just two miles from Henley-on-Thames. Only 28 miles from London, you are also within easy driving distance of Windsor and Oxford. Free internet access. Top finalist of the 'Landlady of the Year' awards, nominated for 'Best British Breakfast' and winner of the South of England 'Bed & Breakfast of the Year' excellence award.

Bed & Breakfast per night: single occupancy £45.00; double room from £56.00–£60.00 (min 2 nights)

Bedrooms: 1 double, 1 twin/family suite
Bathrooms: 2 en-suite
Parking: 4 spaces

451 Rookwood Farmhouse

◆◆◆◆

Stockcross, Newbury, Berkshire RG20 8JX **Tel:** (01488) 608676 **Fax:** (01488) 608676

This charming and comfortable former farmhouse combines ease of access with rural views and a large garden. The guest bedrooms are in a newly converted coach house which is traditionally furnished and yet affords all modern facilities. In the winter there is a welcoming log fire in the guest sitting room and in the summer breakfast is served in the conservatory overlooking the swimming pool. An ideal place to relax.

Bed & Breakfast per night: single occupancy from £40.00–£45.00; double room from £55.00–£60.00
Evening meal: 1830 (last orders 2030)

Bedrooms: 2 double, 2 twin
Bathrooms: 3 en-suite, 1 private
Parking: 3 spaces
Cards accepted: Mastercard, Visa, Switch

452 The Old Manor
◆◆◆◆◆ Silver Award

Whitehouse Green, Sulhamstead, Reading, Berkshire RG7 4EA **Tel:** (01189) 832423 **Fax:** (01189) 836262
E-mail: raga-r@theoldmanor.fsbusiness.co.uk

A 17th-century manor house with later additions. Large and elegant bedrooms include one with a four-poster bed and jacuzzi bath and one with a dressing room and bathroom with shower. The drawing room is light and relaxing and the dining room is gracious. Breakfast is taken in a cosy morning room. Gardens and grounds of ten acres surround the property.

Bed & Breakfast per night: single room from £35.00; double room £70.00

Bedrooms: 2 double
Bathrooms: 2 en-suite
Parking: 6 spaces
Open: all year except Christmas

453 Sir Christopher Wren's House, Hotel & Business Centre
★★★ Silver Award

Thames Street, Windsor, Berkshire SL4 1PX **Tel:** (01753) 861354 **Fax:** (01753) 860172
Web: www.wrensgroup.com **E-mail:** reservations@wrensgroup.com

Steeped in history and uniquely situated on the historic Eton Bridge, the hotel is overlooked by the towers of Windsor Castle. On the banks of the RIver Thames, the hotel is the original home of the celebrated 17th-century architect, Sir Christopher Wren. A short walk into Windsor reveals a lively, stylish shopping centre, bustling with pavement cafés, bars and restaurants. A leisurely stroll over the bridge into Eton leads to Dickensian cobbled streets, antique shops and pubs.

Bed & Breakfast per night: single room from £109.00–£170.00; double room from £150.00–£325.00
Dinner, Bed & Breakfast per person, per night: £102.75–£190.25
Lunch available: 1230–1430

Evening meal: 1900 (last orders 2200)
Bedrooms: 12 single, 47 double, 9 twin, 18 family **Bathrooms:** 86 en-suite
Parking: 25 spaces
Cards accepted: Mastercard, Visa, Switch/Delta, Amex, Diners

454 Stirrups Country House Hotel
★★★ Silver Award

Maidens Green, Bracknell, Berkshire RG42 6LD **Tel:** (01344) 882284 **Fax:** (01344) 882300
Web: www.stirrupshotel.co.uk **E-mail:** reception@stirrupshotel.co.uk

Set in ten acres of beautifully landscaped grounds, Stirrups, with its Tudor origins, provides the perfect combination of a traditional inn with 29 luxurious, individually designed bedrooms and three modern conference and banqueting rooms. The relaxed bar and award-winning candlelit restaurant, with discrete and personal service, complete the picture. Ideally situated between Windsor, Ascot and Bracknell, Stirrups boasts a location within eay reach of a host of leisure opportunities including Legoland and the surrounding Berkshire countryside.

Bed & Breakfast per night: single occupancy from £105.00–£120.00; double room from £110.00–£170.00
Dinner, Bed & Breakfast per person, per night: £57.50–£80.00
Evening meal: 1900 (last orders 2200)

Bedrooms: 20 double, 5 twin, 4 family
Bathrooms: 29 en-suite
Parking: 100 spaces
Cards accepted: Mastercard, Visa, Switch/Delta, Amex, Diners

455 Beaumont Lodge

◆◆◆◆

1 Beaumont Road, Windsor, Berkshire SL4 1HY **Tel:** (01753) 863436 or (07774) 841273 **Fax:** (01753) 863436
Web: www.beaumontlodgeguesthouse.co.uk **E-mail:** bhamshere@beaumontlodge.demon.co.uk

Built at the beginning of the 19th century, Beaumont Lodge is situated in a quiet, residential area and is beautifully adapted with full central heating. An ideal base from which to explore Windsor itself and the surrounding area. The town centre and Windsor Castle are both within walking distance – as is the River Thames. All the rooms are equipped with an en-suite bathroom, the main double room also has a spa bath (wonderfully relaxing!), colour television with video recorder (with a library of tapes), tea and coffee making facilities, trouser press, hair dryer, radio alarm clock and telephone point. There is a comfortable breakfast room and a residents' lounge to relax in.

Bed & Breakfast per night: single occupancy from £60.00–£65.00; double room from £65.00–£75.00

Bedrooms: 1 double, 2 twin, 1 family
Bathrooms: 3 en-suite, 1 private
Cards accepted: Mastercard, Visa

456 Ascot Corner

◆◆◆◆ Silver Award

Wells Lane, Ascot, Berkshire SL5 7DY **Tel:** (01344) 627722 **Fax:** (01344) 873965
E-mail: susan.powell@easynet.co.uk

We offer informal luxury in an elegant, non-smoking family home close to Heathrow/Gatwick, M3, M4, and M25. Mainline station to London Waterloo/Eurostar. Room rate includes minibar, savoury/sweet snacks, fruit/cheese plates, towelling robes, sound/visual systems, iron and hairdryer. Ten minutes drive to Windsor/Eton. Excellent pubs/restaurants within walking distance, as well as horse riding, polo and golf. Splendid walks and bicycle trails through Windsor Great Park. Heated, outdoor, inground swimming pool.

Bed & Breakfast per night: double room from £70.00–£90.00

Bedrooms: 3 double, 2 twin
Bathrooms: 5 en-suite
Parking: 8 spaces
Open: all year except Christmas and New Year
Cards accepted: Mastercard, Visa, Switch/Delta

457 Carlton Guest House

◆◆◆◆

63-65 Macdonald Road, Lightwater, Surrey GU18 5XY **Tel:** (01276) 473580 **Fax:** (01276) 453595
Web: www.carltonguesthouse.co.uk **E-mail:** carltongh@aol.com

Convenient, peaceful location just off junction 3 of the M3. Ideal for Hampton Court, Windsor, Ascot Races and well known golf courses. Comfortable, quality accommodation in a warm and welcoming environment. With 13 en-suite rooms, all fully equipped, we endeavour to ensure our guests enjoy their stay with us. Guests may wish to relax in our spacious lounge and conservatory. As a licensed establishment, drinks are available. For dining out, there are plenty of restaurants within easy reach.

Bed & Breakfast per night: single room from £40.00–£55.00; double room from £50.00–£65.00

Bedrooms: 6 single, 7 double/twin
Bathrooms: 13 en-suite
Parking: 16 spaces
Cards accepted: Mastercard, Visa, Switch/Delta, Amex

458 Tylney Hall Hotel

★★★★ Gold Award

Rotherwick, Hook, Hampshire RG27 9AZ **Tel:** (01256) 764881 **Fax:** (01256) 768141
E-mail: sales@tylneyhall.com

Amidst sixty six acres of Hampshire countryside lies Tylney Hall, an independently-owned, Grade II listed country house hotel. The one hundred and ten bedrooms are beautifully decorated and fitted with all modern amenities. The award-winning Oak Room Restaurant offers innovative menus for those dining for business or pleasure, complemented by an extensive wine cellar and attentive, yet discreet, service. Twelve individually designed function suites cater for up to one hundred people, whilst extensive and exclusive leisure facilities allow guests to relax in the luxurious surroundings.

Bed & Breakfast per night: single occupancy from £130.00–£400.00; double room from £165.00–£430.00
Dinner, Bed & Breakfast per person, per night: £112.50–£210.00 (min 2 nights, 2 sharing)
Lunch available: 1230–1400

Evening meal: 1930 (last orders 2130)
Bedrooms: 95 double, 15 twin
Bathrooms: 110 en-suite
Parking: 120 spaces
Cards accepted: Mastercard, Visa, Switch/Delta, Amex, Diners

459 The Bishop's Table Hotel & Restaurant

★★★ Silver Award

27 West Street, Farnham, Surrey GU9 7DR **Tel:** (01252) 710222 **Fax:** (01252) 733494
E-mail: bishops.table@btinternet.com

An elegant, award-winning hotel where hospitality is at its best. All bedrooms are individually decorated. The walled garden is a walk into another world. The restaurant is well known and offers an excellent cuisine, including a full vegetarian menu.

Bed & Breakfast per night: single room from £65.00–£95.00; double room from £90.00–£165.00
Lunch available: 1230–1345
Evening meal: 1900 (last orders 2145)

Bedrooms: 6 single, 9 double, 2 twin
Bathrooms: 17 en-suite
Cards accepted: Mastercard, Visa, Amex, Diners

460 Cavendish Guest House

◆◆◆◆

24 Cavendish Road, London NW6 7XP **Tel:** (020) 8451 3249 **Fax:** (020) 8451 3249

Small, friendly Victorian family house in a quiet residential conservation area. Five minutes' walk from Kilburn underground station (Jubilee line), with 15 minutes' travelling time to the West End. Easy access to Wembley Stadium, Heathrow, Gatwick and Luton. Ten minutes from the M1. Shops, restaurants, theatres and pubs nearby. Free parking. Special emphasis is given to cleanliness and hospitality. Multi-lingual.

Bed & Breakfast per night: single room from £33.00–£45.00; double room from £52.00–£59.00

Bedrooms: 2 single, 1 double, 1 twin, 2 triple
Bathrooms: 3 en-suite, 2 shared
Parking: 4 spaces

461 Avonmore Hotel   ◆◆◆◆

66 Avonmore Road, Kensington, London W14 8RS **Tel:** (020) 7603 3121 or (020) 7603 4296 **Fax:** (020) 7603 4035
Web: www.avonmorehotel.co.uk **E-mail:** reservations@avonmorehotel.co.uk

Avonmore Hotel is the winner of a national award for the best private hotel in London. Refurbished to the highest standards with all in-room facilities – hairdryer, minibar with drinks, tea and coffee making facilities, colour television, telephone and a large bathroom with bath and shower! We are situated in Kensington in a quiet street, yet just a short walk from West Kensington station and buses. Avonmore Hotel is small enough to provide that personal touch where we look after our clients with care and courtesy. Visit our website for more information.

Bed & Breakfast per night: single room from £70.00–£95.00; double room from £95.00–£105.00

Bedrooms: 1 single, 2 double, 3 twin, 3 triple
Bathrooms: 7 en-suite, 1 shared
Cards accepted: Mastercard, Visa, Switch/Delta, Amex, Diners, Eurocard, JCB

462 The Milestone Hotel and Apartments   ★★★★★ Gold Award

1 Kensington Court, Kensington, London W8 5DL **Tel:** (020) 7917 1000 **Fax:** (020) 7917 1010
Web: www.redcarnationhotels.com **E-mail:** guestservicesms@rchmail.com

Quoted as 'one of the best hotels in the world' in Architectural Digest, The Milestone combines the finest of traditional services with the most creative innovations. In London's heart, with magnificent views across Kensington Gardens and Palace, this unique mansion blends luxury and comfort with exceptional attention from all staff. The hotel's extraordinary touches far exceed guest expectations – from the welcome drink, personal soap selection, guest floor butlers and fresh fruit, to the departing gift.

Bed & Breakfast per night: single occupancy from £312.00–£358.00; double room from £328.00–£376.00
Dinner, Bed & Breakfast per person, per night: £350.00–£395.00
Lunch available: 1230–1430

Evening meal: 1730–2300 (Sunday 1900–2200)
Bedrooms: 55 double, 8 twin
Bathrooms: 63 en-suite
Cards accepted: Mastercard, Visa, Switch/Delta, Amex, Diners, JCB

463 The Goring   ★★★★ Gold Award

15 Beeston Place, London SW1W 0JW **Tel:** (020) 7396 9000 **Fax:** (020) 7834 4393
Web: www.goringhotel.co.uk **E-mail:** reception@goringhotel.co.uk

For three generations the Goring family have harmonised traditional standards of hotel keeping with progressive management. In a small side street next door to Buckingham Palace, The Goring – now fully air conditioned – has one of London's best and quietest locations. The Garden Bar and a number of delightfully decorated rooms overlook its beautiful grounds. The combination of dedicated staff, excellent service and superb facilities create a unique atmosphere which makes The Goring special.

Bed & Breakfast per night: single room from £230.00–£237.00; double room from £290.00–£315.00
Evening meal: 1800 (last orders 2200)

Bedrooms: 20 single, 43 double, 4 twin, 7 suites
Bathrooms: 74 en-suite
Parking: 8 spaces
Cards accepted: Mastercard, Visa, Switch/Delta, Amex, Diners

464 Five Sumner Place Hotel ◆◆◆◆

South Kensington, London SW7 3EE **Tel:** (020) 7584 7586 **Fax:** (020) 7823 9962
Web: www.sumnerplace.com **E-mail:** reservations@sumnerplace.com

This delightful award-winning hotel (awarded best small hotel) is situated in South Kensington, one of the most fashionable areas of London. The hotel itself has been sympathetically restored to recreate the ambience and style of a bygone era. Family-owned and run, it offers excellent service and personal attention. All rooms are luxuriously appointed and come with private en-suite facilities, telephone, colour television, trouser press and full buffet breakfast.

Bed & Breakfast per night: single room from £99.00; double room from £152.00

Bedrooms: 3 single, 5 double, 5 twin
Bathrooms: 13 en-suite
Cards accepted: Mastercard, Visa, Switch/Delta, Amex, Eurocard, JCB

465 Aster House ◆◆◆◆◆ Silver Award

3 Sumner Place, London SW7 3EE **Tel:** (020) 7581 5888 **Fax:** (020) 7584 4925
Web: www.AsterHouse.com **E-mail:** AsterHouse@btinternet.com

Aster House, 'Best Bed and Breakfast in London 2001' is an entirely 'no smoking' establishment. All our fully air-conditioned guestrooms are en-suite and are individually decorated in English country style. Buffet style breakfast is served in the L'Orangerie, our elegant yet homely conservatory. We are located in the heart of South Kensington with easy transport access to all major sights of London. South Ken famous museums and restaurants, Knightsbridge and Chelsea shops are all within walking distance.

Bed & Breakfast per night: single room from £75.00–£99.00; double room from £135.00–£180.00

Bedrooms: 3 single, 4 double, 7 twin
Bathrooms: 14 en-suite
Cards accepted: Mastercard, Visa, Switch/Delta

466 Dolphin Square Hotel ★★★★ Silver Award

Dolphin Square, Chichester Street, London SW1V 3LX **Tel:** (020) 7834 3800 **Fax:** (020) 7798 8735
Web: www.dolphinsquarehotel.co.uk **E-mail:** reservations@dolphinsquarehotel.co.uk

Dolphin Square Hotel is set in three and a half acres of glorious private gardens, bordered by the River Thames and surrounded by Westminster. One of the few 4 Star all-suite hotels in London. The hotel is home to Zest! health and fitness spa and acclaimed chef Gary Rhodes' award-winning restaurant 'Rhodes in the Square'. Warm and welcoming, discreet and never stuffy, Dolphin Square Hotel offers service with style and always with a smile.

Bed & Breakfast per night: single occupancy from £120.00–£155.00; double room from £150.00–£400.00
Dinner, Bed & Breakfast per person, per night: £150.00–£450.00
Evening meal: 1800 (last orders 2230)

Bedrooms: 148 suites
Bathrooms: 148 en-suite
Parking: 18 spaces
Cards accepted: Mastercard, Visa, Switch/Delta, Amex, Diners, JCB

467 Windermere Hotel

◆◆◆◆ Silver Award

142–144 Warwick Way, Victoria, London SW1V 4JE **Tel:** (020) 7834 5163 or (020) 7834 5480 **Fax:** (020) 7630 8831
Web: www.windermere-hotel.co.uk **E-mail:** windermere@compuserve.com

Award-winning, recently refurbished hotel situated a short walk from Victoria Station, Buckingham Palace, The Tate Gallery, Westminster Abbey and the Houses of Parliament. Individually designed comfortable rooms, all with direct dial telephone, remote control satellite television, in-room safe, hairdryer and tea/coffee making facilities. A scrumptious English breakfast and gourmet dinner is served in the relaxed atmosphere of the 'Pimlico Room', our elegant restaurant and bar. Windermere Hotel won the BTA trophy and the RAC dining award and was one of the Bed and Breakfast of the Year 2000 finalists in the London Tourism awards (ETC).

Bed & Breakfast per night: single room from £69.00–£96.00; double room from £89.00–£139.00
Evening meal: 1730 (last orders 2230)

Bedrooms: 4 single, 10 double, 5 twin, 1 triple, 2 family
Bathrooms: 20 en-suite, 2 shared
Cards accepted: Mastercard, Visa, Switch/Delta, Amex, Eurocard, JCB

468 Shepherd's

◆◆◆◆

39 Marmora Road, London SE22 0RX **Tel:** (020) 8693 4355 or 07946 319027 **Fax:** (020) 8693 7954
Web: www.shepherdslondon.com **E-mail:** dulwichdragon@hotmail.com

Brian and Penny Shepherd give a wonderful welcome at their beautiful Victorian home. Spacious bedrooms are bright and luxuriously furnished with fruit, flowers, books, welcome drinks tray, television, bathrobe and slippers. Meals are served in the Aga-warmed kitchen. The sitting room has a log fire, library and piano. The French windows open out onto a mature garden which leads to several acres of parkland. Pick-up service is available. Christmas packages available. 'London's Finest B&Bs' Homes & Gardens.

Bed & Breakfast per night: single room from £40.00–£55.00; double room from £50.00–£70.00
Dinner, Bed & Breakfast per person, per night: £40.00–£55.00
Evening meal: by arrangement

Bedrooms: 2 double, 1 twin
Bathrooms: 1 en-suite, 2 private
Parking: 2 spaces

469 Melrose House

◆◆◆◆

89 Lennard Road, London SE20 7LY **Tel:** (020) 8776 8884 **Fax:** (020) 8325 7636
Web: www.uk-bedandbreakfast.com **E-mail:** melrose.hotel@virgin.net

We are a family-run guest house in a beautifully refurbished, traditionally built Victorian town house with parking,, situated in a quiet and pretty suberb only 15 minutes from the centre of London by public transport. The house has been carefully preserved with its 120 year old cornices and fireplaces still in place. The rooms are all charmingly furnished with private bathrooms. One room has a private marble bathroom with antique fittings and another has a king size, four-poster bed. We also have accommodation for disabled people.

Bed & Breakfast per night: single occupancy from £35.00–£45.00; double room from £50.00–£65.00

Bedrooms: 1 single, 3 double, 2 twin, 1 family
Bathrooms: 5 en-suite, 1 private
Parking: 4 spaces
Cards accepted: Mastercard, Visa, Switch/Delta

470 Coulsdon Manor Hotel

★★★★ Silver Award

Coulsdon Court Road, Coulsdon, Croydon, Surrey CR5 2LL **Tel:** (020) 8668 0414 **Fax:** (020) 8668 3118
Web: www.marstonhotels.com **E-mail:** coulsdonmanor@marstonhotels.com

Set in 140 acres of parkland, a large part of which is laid down as a challenging 18-hole golf course. Fifteen miles from central London and Gatwick, and easily accessible from all parts of the South East via the M25, M23, A23 or A22. A restored manor house with thirty five delightful bedrooms – many with enchanting views over the golf course – an award-winning restaurant and Reflections Leisure Club offering squash, sunbed, gymnasium, racketball, aerobics, sauna and steam.

Bed & Breakfast per night: single occupancy from £104.00–£115.00; double room from £127.00–£149.00
Dinner, Bed & Breakfast per person, per night: £66.00–£82.50 (min 2 nights)
Evening meal: 1900 (last orders 2130)

Bedrooms: 16 double, 19 twin
Bathrooms: 35 en-suite
Parking: 200 spaces
Cards accepted: Mastercard, Visa, Switch/Delta, Amex, Diners, Eurocard

471 Leylands Farm

◆◆◆◆

Leylands Lane, Abinger Common, Dorking, Surrey RH5 6JU **Tel:** (01306) 730115 **Fax:** (01306) 731675

Beautifully furnished, self-contained annexe within period farmhouse. Large, comfortable lounge with television and log fire; stairs leading to double bedroom with en-suite bathroom. Access all day. Tea/coffee making facilities, fridge provided for self-service continental breakfast. The farmhouse is set in lovely seven acre gardens, surrounded by National Trust land. Ideal base for sightseeing and walking; total seclusion yet easy access to Heathrow, Gatwick, M25 and London.

Bed & Breakfast per night: single occupancy from £40.00; double room from £110.00

Bedrooms: 1 suite
Bathrooms: 1 en-suite
Parking: 4 spaces

472 Nutfield Priory

★★★★ Gold Award

Nutfield, Redhill, Surrey RH1 4EL **Tel:** (01737) 824400 **Fax:** (01737) 823321
Web: www.nutfield-priory.com **E-mail:** nutfield@arcadianhotels.co.uk

Set high on Nutfield Ridge in 40 acres of grounds, the hotel has far-reaching views of the Sussex and Surrey countryside. Nutfield Priory boasts elegant Victorian lounges, a grand library and individual bedrooms and suites furnished in a comfortable country house style. Set in the grounds, the exclusive Priory Health and Leisure Club offers facilities which include an indoor pool, gym, squash, spa, steam room and beauty treatments. Located 5 miles from the M25 and 15 minutes from Gatwick.

Bed & Breakfast per night: single room from £120.00–£170.00; double room from £160.00–£280.00
Dinner, Bed & Breakfast per person, per night: £90.00–£140.00 (min 2 nights, 2 sharing)
Evening meal: 1900 (last orders 2200)

Bedrooms: 8 single, 40 double, 12 twin
Bathrooms: 60 en-suite
Parking: 170 spaces
Cards accepted: Mastercard, Visa, Switch/Delta, Amex, Diners

473 Hornshaw House

♦♦♦♦

47 Mount Harry Road, Sevenoaks, Kent TN13 3JN **Tel:** (01732) 465262
Web: www.hornshaw-house.co.uk **E-mail:** embates@hornshaw47.freeserve.co.uk

A wonderful base for exploring Kent's castles, gardens and countryside, also for central London which is only 30 minutes away by train. Hornshaw House is a quiet family home, surrounded by trees and pleasant gardens and is only five minutes walk from the railway station. The well-heated bedrooms have large, comfortable beds, radio, television and en-suite bathrooms. The house is furnished with family paintings and antique furniture.

Bed & Breakfast per night: single occupancy from £35.00; double room from £45.00–£55.00
Dinner, Bed & Breakfast per person, per night: £31.00–£55.00 (depending upon number of people/nights)

Bedrooms: 2 double/twin
Bathrooms: 2 en-suite
Parking: 3 spaces
Open: all year except Christmas

Dickens' Kent

For eight days in late June, Broadstairs, on Kent's eastern coast, is thronged with characters in Victorian dress, parading the streets and participating in period cricket matches, bathing parties and other amusements. They are here for the Dickens festival, a literary event first staged in 1937 to mark the centenary of Dickens' first visit, and held annually ever since.

When Dickens came to Broadstairs he was 25 years old and on the point of achieving nationwide fame with the publication of *The Pickwick Papers*. He had spent part of his childhood in the Kent town of Chatham and had become well-acquainted with the county from accompanying his father on long country walks. For 14 years he frequently spent summer and autumn months in Broadstairs, eventually leasing Fort House, a fine residence overlooking Viking Bay. Now called Bleak House and open to the public as a museum (tel: 01843 862224), it is thought to have inspired its namesake in Dickens' famous novel, for it stands, tall and solitary, on the cliffs far above Broadstairs. Visitors may see rooms inhabited by the author, including the study where he completed *David Copperfield* and planned *Bleak House*. Also in Broadstairs is the Dickens House Museum (tel: 01843 862853) once the home of Miss Mary Strong, an eccentric woman who was probably the inspiration for one of Dickens's most colourful creations, Miss Betsey Trotwood, David Copperfield's aunt.

In 1856, Dickens purchased Gad's Hill Place, near Rochester, which he had admired as a boy, and

always dreamed of owning. This substantial house, now a private school, is occasionally open to the public (details from Rochester's Tourist Information Centre, tel: 01634 843666). The town also provided inspiration for many places in Dickens' works. Eastgate House was both Nun's House School in *The Mystery of Edwin Drood* and Westgate House in *The Pickwick Papers*. Now the Rochester Dickens Centre (tel: 01634 844176), it recreates scenes and characters from the author's best-known works. In its gardens an elaborately carved Swiss chalet was a gift to Dickens from an actor friend who sent it to Higham station in 58 packing cases. It once stood in the shrubbery at Gad's Hill and in it Dickens wrote his last words before his death in 1870. Further Dickensian associations may be followed up using The Dickens Trail, available from local tourist information centres.

474 Grove House   ◆◆◆◆

Grove Green Road, Weavering Street, Maidstone, Kent ME14 5JT **Tel:** (01622) 738441 **Fax:** (01622) 735927

Attractive, detached comfortable home in quiet surroundings, with parking for six. Comfortable, double en-suite room and double and twin rooms with attractive guest bathroom. All rooms have their own colour television and tea/coffee making facilities. Easy access to motorways for London or the Channel Tunnel. Leeds Castle, Kent County Show Ground, restaurants and golf courses all nearby. Non-smoking.

Bed & Breakfast per night: single occupancy from £35.00–£40.00; double room from £45.00–£50.00

Bedrooms: 2 double, 1 twin
Bathrooms: 1 en-suite, 1 shared
Parking: 6 spaces
Open: all year except Christmas and New Year

475 The Ringlestone Inn & Farmhouse Hotel   ◆◆◆◆◆ Gold Award

Ringlestone Hamlet, Harrietsham, Maidstone, Kent ME17 1NX **Tel:** (01622) 859900 or 07973 612261 **Fax:** (01622) 859966
Web: www.ringlestone.com **E-mail:** bookings@ringlestone.com

Situated on the North Downs in the heart of Kent, just ten minutes from Leeds Castle, this character Kentish farmhouse is surrounded by eight acres of tranquil gardens and farmland. Luxuriously furnished in rustic oak throughout, with a canopied four-poster bed in the Elderflower Room. Opposite, the famous 16th-century Ringlestone Inn is recommended in major guides for help-yourself buffet lunch and interesting evening Kentish fare incorporating English fruit wines in the traditional recipes.

Bed & Breakfast per night: single occupancy from £97.00–£107.00; double room £119.00
Lunch available: 1200–1400
Evening meal: 1900 (last orders 2130)

Bedrooms: 2 double, 1 family
Bathrooms: 3 en-suite
Parking: 74 spaces
Cards accepted: Mastercard, Visa, Switch/Delta, Amex, Diners, Eurocard

476 Preston Lea   ◆◆◆◆ Silver Award

Canterbury Road, Faversham, Kent ME13 8XA **Tel:** (01795) 535266 **Fax:** (01795) 533388
Web: http://homepages.which.net/~alan.turner10 **E-mail:** preston.lea@which.net

This beautiful spacious house, built a century ago, was designed by a French architect and has many unique and interesting features, including two turrets, an oak-panelled hall, staircase, dining room and guest drawing room. Situated in lovely secluded gardens but by the A2, it is convenient for Canterbury, all the Channel ports, the M2 to London and beautiful countryside. Each bedroom is individually designed and all are large and sunny. A warm welcome is assured by caring hosts.

Bed & Breakfast per night: single occupancy from £35.00–£40.00; double room from £55.00–£60.00

Bedrooms: 2 double, 1 twin
Bathrooms: 2 en-suite, 1 private
Parking: 11 spaces
Cards accepted: Mastercard, Visa, Switch/Delta, Eurocard, JCB, Maestro, Visa Electron, Solo

477 Lains Cottage ◆◆◆◆

Quarley, Andover, Hampshire SP11 8PX **Tel:** (01264) 889697 **Fax:** (01264) 889227
Web: www.lainscottage.co.uk **E-mail:** enquiries@lainscottage.co.uk

Lains Cottage is a charming thatched house combining modern comforts with traditional cottage style. An ideal base from which to explore Stonehenge, Salisbury, the New Forest, Winchester and the South coast. The house is set in a quiet situation, yet only half a mile from the A303, giving access to London and the West Country.

Bed & Breakfast per night: single occupancy from £45.00; double room from £55.00

Bedrooms: 1 double, 2 twin
Bathrooms: 3 en-suite
Parking: 6 spaces

478 May Cottage ◆◆◆◆ Silver Award

Thruxton, Andover, Hampshire SP11 8LZ **Tel:** (01264) 771241 or 07768 242166 **Fax:** (01264) 771770

May Cottage dates back to 1740 and is situated in the heart of this picturesque tranquil village with old inns. A most comfortable home, set in a pretty garden with a stream, with en-suite rooms, all having colour television, radio and tea tray. Guests' own sitting/dining room. Just off the A303, an ideal base for visiting ancient cities, stately homes and gardens, yet within easy reach of ports and airports. A non-smoking establishment.

Bed & Breakfast per night: double room from £55.00–£70.00

Bedrooms: 1 double, 2 twin
Bathrooms: 2 en-suite, 1 private
Parking: 4 spaces

479 Kington Manor Farm ◆◆◆◆

Church Hill, Kington Magna, Gillingham, Dorset SP8 5EG **Tel:** (01747) 838371 **Fax:** (01747) 838371
Web: www.smoothhound.co.uk/hotels/kingtonmanor.html

We are a family-run working farm of approximately 100 acres, converting to 'organic' with our suckler cow herd. An attractive farmhouse in a quiet, pretty village with splendid views over the Blackmore Vale, one mile from the A30. An ideal area for walking, cycling, fishing in the River Stour and visiting Stourhead and Longleat. A warm welcome, comfort and healthy, hearty breakfasts are our priorities. Guests may use the outdoor pool, heated from May to September.

Bed & Breakfast per night: single occupancy from £24.00; double room from £44.00

Bedrooms: 1 double, 1 twin, 1 family
Bathrooms: 1 en-suite, 2 private
Parking: 4 spaces
Open: January–November

480 Beechleas Hotel and Restaurant   ★★ Silver Award

17 Poole Road, Wimborne Minster, Dorset BH21 1QA **Tel:** (01202) 841684 **Fax:** (01202) 849344

A delightful Georgian Grade II listed hotel. Beautifully restored, tastefully furnished en-suite bedrooms of quality and an RAC Blue Ribbon and Double Dining Award, AA Rosette award-winning restaurant, Good Hotel and Which? Hotel Guides. Log fires in autumn and winter, elegant conservatory overlooking the walled garden. National Trust properties nearby include Kingston Lacey, Corfe Castle Badbury Rings and Brownsea Island. Walking, fishing, golf, sandy beaches, the New Forest, Purbeck Hills, Thomas Hardy country, Poole and Bournemouth are all nearby. Sailing on the hotel's yacht out of Poole Harbour. Recommended by all leading guides.

Bed & Breakfast per night: single occupancy from £69.00–£99.00; double room from £79.00–£119.00.
Dinner, Bed & Breakfast per person, per night: £59.00–£76.00 (min 2 nights)
Evening meal: 1900 (last orders 2100)

Bedrooms: 7 double, 2 twin
Bathrooms: 9 en-suite
Parking: 12 spaces
Cards accepted: Mastercard, Visa, Switch/Delta, Amex, Eurocard, JCB, Diners

481 The Three Lions   ◆◆◆◆◆ Gold Award

Stuckton, Fordingbridge, Hampshire SP6 2HF **Tel:** (01425) 652489 **Fax:** (01425) 656144
E-mail: the3lions@btinternet.com

Built in 1863, The Three Lions nestles on the edge of the New Forest and is personally owned and run by Mike and Jayne Womersley. The rooms are all en-suite, airy and very peaceful, overlooking well-manicured gardens and the forest behind. There is also an open-air whirlpool therapy spa for residents' use. The restaurant is highly rated in all major UK food guides (Highly Commended Restaurant of the Year, 2001 *Good Food Guide*) with 3 AA Rosettes and a 150-bin wine list.

Bed & Breakfast per night: single occupancy from £59.00–£75.00; double room from £65.00–£85.00.
Dinner, Bed & Breakfast per person, per night: £50.00–£62.50 (min 2 nights)
Lunch available: 1200–1400

Evening meal: 1900 (last orders 2100)
Bedrooms: 2 double, 1 twin
Bathrooms: 3 en-suite
Parking: 40 spaces
Cards accepted: Mastercard, Visa, Switch/Delta, Amex, JCB, Maestro

482 The Connaught Hotel   ★★★ Silver Award

West Hill Road, West Cliff, Bournemouth, Dorset BH2 5PH **Tel:** (01202) 298020 **Fax:** (01202) 298028
Web: www.theconnaught.co.uk **E-mail:** sales@theconnaught.co.uk

This impressive hotel is central to the town centre, BIC, the pier and sandy beaches. Magnificent indoor leisure centre with large swimming pool, spa, saunas, steam rooms, gym and games room. Superb en-suite bedrooms, some with balconies. Honeymoon Suite with traditional four-poster bed and jacuzzi air bath. VIP Suite with separate lounge and balcony. Enjoy fine food and wine in The Cameo Restaurant. A unique blend of traditional good service and modern facilities.

Bed & Breakfast per night: single room from £40.00–£70.00; double room from £80.00–£140.00.
Dinner, Bed & Breakfast per person, per night: £46.00–£85.00
Evening meal: 1830 (last orders 2100)

Bedrooms: 9 single, 24 double, 14 twin, 9 family
Bathrooms: 56 en-suite
Parking: 44 spaces
Cards accepted: Mastercard, Visa, Switch/Delta, Amex, Diners

483 The White House ◆◆◆◆

428 Lymington Road, Highcliffe, Christchurch, Dorset BH23 5HF **Tel:** (01425) 271279 **Fax:** (01425) 276900
Web: www.thewhite-house.co.uk **E-mail:** thewhitehouse@themail.co.uk

The proprietors, Eileen and Fred, welcome you to their beautiful Victorian house which is decorated and furnished to a very high standard. Just a short walk from Highcliffe beach with its wonderful views of The Needles. Scenic cliff-top walks. Restaurants, shops and pubs are also within walking distance. Being close to the New Forest and golf courses makes this an ideal location. Colour television and tea/coffee facilities in all rooms. Generous breakfasts served in the delightfully decorated dining room. Private car park front and rear (free).

Bed & Breakfast per night: single occupancy from £27.00–£32.00; double room from £44.00–£54.00

Bedrooms: 4 double, 2 twin
Bathrooms: 5 en-suite, 1 shared
Parking: 6 spaces

484 Chewton Glen Hotel, Health & Country Club ★★★★★ Gold Award

Christchurch Road, New Milton, Hampshire BH25 6QS **Tel:** (01425) 275341 **Fax:** (01425) 272310
Web: www.chewtonglen.com **E-mail:** reservations@chewtonglen.com

A very warm welcome awaits you here. Great emphasis is placed on service, with the restaurant being renowned for the quality of its food and wines. All bedrooms are individually designed, and most have a balcony or terrace with a beautiful view. The health club offers a full range of health and fitness facilities, including an indoor pool and gymnasium. Beauty therapy appointments also available. Nine-hole, par 3 golf course within grounds.

Room only per night: single or double occupancy from £250.00–£720.00
Dinner, Bed & Breakfast per person, per night: £197.50–£435.00 (2 sharing)
Lunch available: 1230–1345
Evening meal: 1930 (last orders 2130)

Bedrooms: 60 double
Bathrooms: 60 en-suite
Parking: 125 spaces
Cards accepted: Mastercard, Visa, Switch/Delta, Amex, Diners

485 Miranda ◆◆◆◆

Vaggs Lane, Hordle, Lymington, Hampshire SO41 0FP **Tel:** (01425) 621561

Shirley Davis at Miranda Bed & Breakfast provides her visitors with a unique, unforgetable stay in the New Forest. Miranda is set in three acres, with pretty gardens to relax in, and all home comforts. En-suite bedrooms with colour television and tea/coffee making facilities. There is a guest sitting room and a warm welcome awaits you along with delicious food! Evening meals by arrangement. There is a no smoking policy at Miranda. Parking spaces available.

Bed & Breakfast per night: single occupancy from £26.00–£28.00; double room from £48.00–£50.00
Dinner, Bed & Breakfast per person, per night: £35.00–£42.00

Bedrooms: 1 double, 1 twin
Bathrooms: 2 en-suite
Parking: 6 spaces

486 Rosefield House

♦♦♦♦♦ Gold Award

Sway Road, Lymington, Hampshire SO41 8LR **Tel:** (01590) 671526 **Fax:** (01590) 689007

Rosefield House offers a most enjoyable way to explore the Forest and nearby coastal resorts or 'just a night or two away from home'. Luxury accommodation in a beautiful country house. Large indoor heated swimming pool. Luxurious en-suite bedrooms all with super king-size beds, television, video, telephone and many other pampering ingredients. Superb lounge with wood-burning fire. Delicious breakfasts with our own free range eggs. Mid-week three night breaks available, £105.00 per person.

Bed & Breakfast per night: double room
£80.00

Bedrooms: 2 double, 1 twin
Bathrooms: 3 en-suite
Parking: 6 spaces
Open: February-October
Cards accepted: Mastercard, Visa, Switch/Delta

The New Forest

The New Forest is the largest tract of uncultivated land in lowland Britain, escaping, by various accidents of history, the agricultural changes that have transformed most of southern England into fertile farmland. It was first granted special status in 1079 when William the Conqueror made it a Royal hunting preserve, imposing fierce and unpopular laws to protect his royal playground. His son, William Rufus, met his death here, killed by an arrow in the heart, but whether by accident or design remains a mystery. The Rufus Stone (actually made of cast iron – shown below) was erected in 1865 by Earl de la Warr at a lonely place in the Forest near Upper Canterton to commemorate the event, though there is scant evidence that this was actually the spot where Rufus died.

There is no record of any sovereign hunting here after James II, but by this time the status of the Forest had changed, from royal hunting ground to valuable timber resource. The Forest's trees, many planted by William I as coverts for his deer, were felled to supply timber for houses and for ships, and today large areas are devoted to the commercial cultivation of fast-growing conifers. But ancient broad-leaved woodland still clothes many parts of the New Forest, some of the finest undisturbed deciduous forest in Western Europe. At Mark Ash Wood, near Boldrewood, and Denny Wood, near Lyndhurst, for example, the mighty oaks and beeches have stood for hundreds of years, their leaves creating a vast canopy of dappled light and shade, their decayed trunks a rich habitat for fungi, insects and woodland-dwelling birds. These magnificent woodlands, however, are just one part of the New Forest's natural picture. Drive along the B3078 near Godshill, and a vista opens up of endless undulating heather-covered wilderness.

Explore on foot, and the diversity of flora and fauna becomes apparent. Rain collects in the ill-drained hollows of the heath to create acidic peat bogs, where the eagle-eyed may spot sundews, march gentian and bog orchid, rare types of dragonfly and damselfly, or all three of Britain's species of newt. The air is specked with butterflies, and loud with the call of the heathland and marshland birds – evening may even bring the churr of the shy and very rare nightjar. To learn more about aspects of the Forest's wildlife, visit the Holiday Hills Reptiliary, near Lyndhurst, or the New Forest Nature Quest, near Longdown.

487 Whitley Ridge Country House Hotel

★★★ Silver Award

Beaulieu Road, Brockenhurst, Hampshire SO42 7QL **Tel:** (01590) 622354 **Fax:** (01590) 622856
Web: www.whitleyridge.co.uk **E-mail:** whitleyridge@brockenhurst.co.uk

A charming Georgian country house hotel, formerly a royal hunting lodge, in five acres of New Forest parkland, Whitley Ridge has a very good reputation for its cuisine and friendly service. All en-suite bedrooms have recently been refurbished to a high standard and overlook extensive grounds which include a tennis court. In winter, log fires burn on cooler evenings, and the candlelit dining room (AA 2 Rosettes) creates a special atmosphere. Special midweek inclusive rates available.

Bed & Breakfast per night: single room from £65.00–£70.00; double room from £105.00–£140.00
Dinner, Bed & Breakfast per person, per night: £70.00–£85.00
Lunch available: 1200–1400 (Sunday only)

Evening meal: 1900 (last orders 2030)
Bedrooms: 2 single, 9 double, 3 twin
Bathrooms: 14 en-suite
Parking: 28 spaces
Cards accepted: Mastercard, Visa, Switch/Delta, Amex, Diners, Eurocard

The whole New Forest is criss-crossed by footpaths and bridleways, and well provided with car parks and signposts, making this a paradise for walkers of all staminas, as well as horse-riders and mountain-bikers. At Rhinefield and Boldrewood ornamental trees and shrubs have been planted along the roadside, creating a spectacular splash of autumn colour; for more natural surroundings follow on foot the well-marked paths along the lovely Ober Water, near Brockenhurst, one of the Forest's finest beauty spots.

The New Forest also has a unique cultural heritage rooted in old custom and law. When William the Conquerer made the forest his own, he granted the commoners special rights, such as cutting turf, collecting fallen wood, and, in particular, grazing animals. Today, cows, sheep and ponies are permanent residents, their voracious nibbling continually re-shaping the landscape. The wild ponies are a breed found nowhere else – it is said they are descended from animals who swam ashore from the Spanish Armada. In autumn you may chance upon a pony 'drift', a frenetic round-up at which ponies' tails are cut in a special pattern to record payment for grazing rights, and new foals are branded with their owner's number. For 60 days in autumn pigs, too, are allowed to forage in the woodlands for green acorns, poisonous to deer and cattle, an ancient privilege known as 'pannage'.

From Norman times, the laws were administered by a Forest Court presided over by ten elected verderers, whose job it was to administer justice in Forest disputes. Today the Court has changed little, and still sits regularly at the Queen's House in Lyndhurst. The sessions are not heard in public, but visitors can learn all about the Forest laws and customs at the excellent New Forest Museum and Visitor Centre near by.

Right in the heart of the Forest, Lyndhurst is considered its capital, a busy, important little town, with many picturesque old buildings, and a fine church noted for its pre-Raphaelite stained-glass. Not far away, Brockenhurst's medieval church is one of the oldest in the area. Its churchyard is dominated by the famous Brockenhurst yew, said to be over 1000 years old, but don't miss the fascinating Victorian monument to a disreputable local character, the snakecatcher Henry 'Brusher' Mills.

To the east is Beaulieu; its famous stately home, Beaulieu Abbey, was built upon the remains of a Cistercian monastery, and is still the ancestral home of the Montagu family, who created its fascinating motor museum. 5 miles (8km) downstream Buckler's Hard, once an important shipbuilding settlement, lies tranquilly beside the water. Amongst its mellow brick houses are a Maritime Museum and a house furnished with late 18th century interiors, interesting reminders of this once-great Forest industry.

488 Clayhill House

♦♦♦♦ Silver Award

Clayhill, Lyndhurst, Hampshire SO43 7DE **Tel:** (02380) 282304 **Fax:** (02380) 282093
Web: www.clayhillhouse.demon.co.uk **E-mail:** bookings@clayhillhouse.demon.co.uk

A warm welcome awaits you at Clayhill House. Built in 1830, this Georgian house has been tastefully decorated with all rooms en-suite, plus lots of extras to make your stay more comfortable. Ideally situated for walking and cycling, within walking distance of the village of Lyndhurst, where there is a wide range of eating places. Alternatively, you could try our local pub which is only two minutes away and where they serve a very good meal.

Bed & Breakfast per night: single occupancy from £25.00–£45.00; double room from £46.00–£50.00

Bedrooms: 3 double/twin
Bathrooms: 3 en-suite
Parking: 6 spaces
Cards accepted: Mastercard, Visa, Switch/Delta

489 Millstream Hotel and Restaurant

★★★ Gold Award

Bosham Lane, Bosham, Chichester, West Sussex PO18 8HL **Tel:** (01243) 573234 **Fax:** (01243) 573459
Web: www.millstream-hotel.co.uk **E-mail:** info@millstream-hotel.co.uk

A beautifully appointed country house dating from 1701, set in a picturesque quayside village, only four miles west of Chichester. The friendly staff will make you feel very welcome. Bedrooms are all individually furnished, with every modern facility. The Millstream Restaurant is renowned for its superb food and extensive wine list and has been awarded an AA Rosette for culinary excellence. Enjoy walking on the beautiful shoreline or the rolling South Downs. Fishbourne Roman Villa, Goodwood House and Chichester Festival Theatre are all within easy reach.

Bed & Breakfast per night: single room from £75.00–£80.00; double room from £120.00–£125.00
Dinner, Bed & Breakfast per person, per night: £60.00–£85.00 (min 2 nights)
Lunch available: 1230–1400
Evening meal: 1900 (last orders 2130)

Bedrooms: 5 single, 14 double, 10 twin, 2 family, 3 suites
Bathrooms: 35 en-suite
Parking: 44 spaces
Cards accepted: Mastercard, Visa, Switch/Delta, Amex, Diners, Eurocard

490 Friary Close

♦♦♦♦ Silver Award

Friary Lane, Chichester, West Sussex PO19 1UF **Tel:** (01243) 527294 **Fax:** (01243) 533876
E-mail: friaryclose@btinternet.com

Friary Close is a Grade II listed Georgian house built astride the ancient city wall in central Chichester. The house stands in its own grounds and has a large walled garden. It is convenient for all city centre amenities, cathedral, theatre and Roman palace. Within a short drive it is possible to visit Chichester harbour (sailing and walking), Pagham harbour nature reserve and Goodwood (horse racing, golf and walking). Bus and mainline train station nearby.

Bed & Breakfast per night: double room from £50.00

Bedrooms: 3 twin
Bathrooms: 3 en-suite
Parking: 3 spaces
Cards accepted: Mastercard, Visa

491 The Coach House

Pilleygreen Lodge, Goodwood, Chichester, West Sussex PO18 0QE **Tel:** (01243) 811467 **Fax:** (01243) 811408
Web: www.sussexlive@enta.net **E-mail:** coachhouse@pilleygreen.demon.co.uk

High on the South Downs with distant views of the sea, this fascinating Grade II listed building gives a unique opportunity to get away from it all. Sample the glorious, historic countryside or come to the major local events. This totally sef-contained accommodation comprises of a lovely sitting room, opening onto a private terrace, a spiral staircase leading to a galleried bedroom with either a king-size or twin beds, a luxury bathroom, kitchen area and secluded parking. Breakfast provided in fridge stocked with a good selection of food.

Bed & Breakfast per night: single occupancy from £35.00–£42.00; double room from £70.00–£84.00

Bedrooms: 1 double/twin
Bathrooms: 1 private
Parking: 2 spaces

492 Moseleys Barn

 Silver Award

Hardham, Pulborough, West Sussex RH20 1LB **Tel:** (01798) 872912 **Fax:** (01798) 872912
Web: www.smoothhound.co.uk/hotels/moseleys

Converted 17th-century barn with galleried beamed hall and panoramic views of the South Downs. Situated in the hamlet of Hardham, near the church with its 12th-century wall paintings. Conveniently placed for RSPB Reserve, South Downs Way, Arundel, Petworth, Chichester, Goodwood and the coast. Accommodation at the barn consists of two ground floor en-suite double bedrooms and a twin room with private bathroom. All rooms have television, tea/coffee making facilities and are non-smoking.

Bed & Breakfast per night: single occupancy from £37.00–£45.00; double room from £55.00–£70.00

Bedrooms: 3 double/twin
Bathrooms: 2 en-suite, 1 private
Parking: 6 spaces

493 Burpham Country House Hotel

 ★★★ Silver Award

Burpham, Arundel, West Sussex BN18 9RJ **Tel:** (01903) 882160 **Fax:** (01903) 884627

Nestling in a fold of the famous Sussex South Downs, the hotel offers the most perfect location for a 'Stress Remedy Break'! The hamlet of Burpham is totally peaceful and unspoilt and the walks are truly spectacular. The dining room offers a regularly changing menu using only the best ingredients. The resident owners are justly proud of their AA Rosette award-winning cuisine offered in the restaurant and brand new conservatory. The comfort offered here is truly memorable. Please mention this guide when booking. Special breaks available.

Bed & Breakfast per night: single room from £58.50; double room from £86.50–£120.00
Dinner, Bed & Breakfast per person, per night: £64.00–£78.00 (min 2 nights)
Evening meal: 1915 (last orders 2045)

Bedrooms: 1 single, 6 double, 3 twin
Bathrooms: 10 en-suite
Parking: 12 spaces
Cards accepted: Mastercard, Visa, Amex, Eurocard

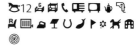

494 The Old Tollgate Restaurant & Hotel

★★★ Silver Award

The Street, Bramber, Steyning, West Sussex BN44 3WE **Tel:** (01903) 879494 **Fax:** (01903) 813399
Web: www.oldtollgatehotel.com **E-mail:** otr@fastnet.co.uk

In a lovely old Sussex village nestling at the foot of the South Downs, standing on the original Tollhouse site, a perfect blending of the old with the new. Award-winning, carvery-style restaurant – a well-known and popular eating spot – offers a magnificent hors d'oeuvres display followed by a vast selection of roasts, pies and casseroles, with delicious sweets and cheeses to add the final touch. Luxuriously-appointed bedrooms, including two four-posters with jacuzzi baths, and two suites.

Bed & Breakfast per night: single occupancy from £82.65–£127.65; double room from £90.30–£135.30
Lunch available: 1200–1345
Evening meal: 1900 (last orders 2130)

Bedrooms: 21 double, 10 twin
Bathrooms: 31 en-suite **Parking:** 60 spaces
Cards accepted: Mastercard, Visa, Switch/Delta, Amex, Diners, Eurocard, JCB, Maestro, Visa Elect

495 Angel Lodge

◆◆◆◆

19 Malvern Close, Worthing, West Sussex BN11 2HE **Tel:** (01903) 233002 or (07779) 217734 **Fax:** (01903) 233002
Web: www.angellodge.co.uk **E-mail:** angellodge19@aol.com

An ideal base for touring beautiful Sussex! Very friendly atmosphere. 15 years of bed and breakfast experience. Attractive detached house, one minute from seafront in a very quiet road. Own keys allowing access at all times. Beautiful bedroom with television, tea/coffee/chocolate, biscuits and fresh milk. Private bathroom with jacuzzi. Excellent full English breakfast with all the trimmings, or continental. Open all year except Christmas. Beautiful landscaped gardens to relax in. Hope to see you sometime soon!

Bed & Breakfast per night: single occupancy from £37.00–£40.00; double room from £46.00–£54.00

Bedrooms: 1 double
Bathrooms: 1 private
Open: all year except Christmas

496 Rosedale House

◆◆◆◆

12 Bath Road, Worthing, West Sussex BN11 3NU **Tel:** (01903) 233181
E-mail: rosedale@amserve.net

Delightful Victorian house run by the friendly Nightingale family. Quality comfortable en-suite accommodation, ideally situated for enjoying coast and countryside. Nestling by a delightful seaside town. Full grilled English breakfast. Ground floor room available. Centrally heated throughout. Hairdryer, tea/coffee making facilities. Guests' pay phone. A non-smoking house.

Bed & Breakfast per night: single room from £24.00–£26.00; double room from £48.00–£54.00

Bedrooms: 2 single, 2 double/twin
Bathrooms: 3 en-suite

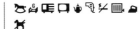

497 Shelleys Hotel

★★★ Silver Award

High Street, Lewes, East Sussex BN7 1XS **Tel:** (01273) 472361 **Fax:** (01273) 483152
E-mail: info@shelleys-hotel-lewes.com

The town of Lewes, which is well known to opera lovers who attend the celebrated annual Glyndebourne Opera Festival, is nestled among the picturesque South Downs. Shelleys offers the highest standard of comfort. A short break can offer you the chance to explore some beautiful scenery, shop for antiques and visit the attractions of Brighton – about twenty minutes away – before returning to a peaceful country house hotel, renowned for its service and cuisine.

Bed & Breakfast per night: single room from £90.00–£158.50; double room from £116.00–£277.00
Dinner, Bed & Breakfast per person, per night: £86.50–£98.50 (min 2 nights)
Lunch available: 1215–1415

Evening meal: 1900 (last orders 2115)
Bedrooms: 1 single, 9 double, 9 twin
Bathrooms: 19 en-suite **Parking:** 25 spaces
Cards accepted: Mastercard, Visa, Switch/Delta, Amex, Diners, Eurocard, JCB, Maestro, Visa Elect

498 Eckington House

◆◆◆◆ Silver Award

Ripe Lane, Ripe, Lewes, East Sussex BN8 6AR **Tel:** (01323) 811274 or 07720 601347 **Fax:** (01323) 811140
Web: www.eckingtonhouse.co.uk **E-mail:** sue@eckingtonhouse.co.uk

Beautiful 16th-century house with peaceful, mature garden in a rural village close to the South Downs and South coast. Facilities include oak-panelled guest sitting room with inglenook fireplace, croquet lawn and four-poster suite. Breakfast is served on the terrace during warm weather, with vegetarians catered for. Historic Lewes, famous Glyndebourne Opera House, and the coastal towns of Brighton and Eastbourne are nearby. London is one hour by rail from Lewes. Excellent for cycling, walking and sightseeing. Pub/restaurant within walking distance.

Bed & Breakfast per night: single occupancy from £35.00–£40.00; double room from £50.00–£60.00

Bedrooms: 3 double
Bathrooms: 3 en-suite
Open: March–October

499 Lansdowne Hotel

★★★ Silver Award

King Edward's Parade, Eastbourne, East Sussex BN21 4EE **Tel:** (01323) 725174 **Fax:** (01323) 739721
Web: www.the.lansdowne.btinternet.co.uk **E-mail:** the.lansdowne@btinternet.com

Traditional, privately-owned seafront hotel close to theatres and shops. The dining room offers the best of English cooking supported by a comprehensive wine list from around the world. Two lifts, two snooker rooms and games room. Sky Sports television in public room. Elegant lounges and foyer facing the sea. 22 lock-up garages and unrestricted street parking nearby. At lunchtime, enjoy our bar/lounge menu or traditional lunch on Sunday. Social/duplicate bridge weekends. Golfing breaks. Attractive Regency bar.

Bed & Breakfast per night: single room from £45.00–£69.00; double room from £78.00–£132.00
Dinner, Bed & Breakfast per person, per night: £41.75–£82.00 (min 2 nights)
Lunch available: 1200–1400
Evening meal: 1830 (last orders 2030)

Bedrooms: 36 single, 23 double, 44 twin, 9 triple
Bathrooms: 112 en-suite
Parking: 22 spaces
Cards accepted: Mastercard, Visa, Switch/Delta, Amex, Diners, JCB, Maestro, Visa Electron, Solo

At-a-glance symbols are explained on the flap inside the back cover

500 Pinnacle Point

◆◆◆◆◆ Gold Award

Upper Duke's Drive, Foyle Way, Eastbourne, East Sussex BN20 7XL **Tel:** (01323) 726666 or 0796 7209958 **Fax:** (01323) 643946
Web: www.pinnaclepoint.co.uk

'One feels like an honoured guest rather than a paying visitor'. Peter and Elspeth Pyemont invite their guests to enjoy the Pinnacle Point experience. Pinnacle Point is a luxury house with unrivalled views overlooking the English Channel. It has a unique position on the cliffs near the foot of the South Downs. Used by stars of theatre and television and international sports stars – it is special.

Bed & Breakfast per night: single occupancy from £60.00; double room from £100.00

Bedrooms: 2 double, 1 twin
Bathrooms: 3 en-suite
Parking: 4 spaces

501 Ashdown Park Hotel

★★★★ Gold Award

Wych Cross, Forest Row, East Sussex RH18 5JR **Tel:** (01342) 824988 **Fax:** (01342) 826206
Web: www.ashdownpark.co.uk **E-mail:** sales@ashdownpark.co.uk

Ashdown Park Hotel is an impressive Victorian mansion set in the heart of Ashdown Forest - home to 'Pooh Bear' yet within easy reach of London, Gatwick Airport and the South coast. Each of the bedrooms and suites is beautifully decorated, many with breathtaking views of the surrounding gardens and parklands. The award-winning Anderida Restaurant offers an unforgettable dining experience which can be enjoyed following an energetic or relaxing visit to our extensive country club.

Bed & Breakfast per night: single room from £130.00–£330.00; double room from £165.00–£360.00
Dinner, Bed & Breakfast per person, per night: £112.50–£210.00 (min 2 nights, 2 sharing)
Lunch available: 1230–1400

Evening meal: 1930 (last orders 2130)
Bedrooms: 6 single, 34 double, 31 twin, 36 suites **Bathrooms:** 107 en-suite
Parking: 140 spaces
Cards accepted: Mastercard, Visa, Switch/Delta, Amex, Diners, Eurocard

502 South Paddock

◆◆◆◆◆ Silver Award

Maresfield Park, Uckfield, East Sussex TN22 2HA **Tel:** (01825) 762335

South East England Tourist Board 'Best Bed & Breakfast' runner up award. A comfortable country house, beautifully furnished with an atmosphere of warmth and elegance. All rooms face south, overlooking three and a half acres of mature gardens, landscaped for attractive colouring throughout the year. A peaceful setting for relaxing on the terrace, beside the fishpond and fountain or in spacious drawing rooms with log fires. Centrally located, 41 miles from London and within easy reach of Gatwick, the Channel ports, Glyndebourne, Nymans, Sissinghurst and Chartwell. Good restaurants locally.

Bed & Breakfast per night: single occupancy £40.00; double room £61.00

Bedrooms: 1 double, 1 twin
Bathrooms: 2 private
Parking: 6 spaces

503 Huckleberry   ◆◆◆◆

Perrymans Lane, High Hurstwood, Uckfield, East Sussex TN22 4AG **Tel:** (01825) 733170

A pretty house set in a prize-winning garden in a quiet country lane. Very near the Ashdown Forest with its many walks. Tunbridge Wells is a 20 minute drive away. Chartwell, Hever Castle, the Bluebell Railway and various National Trust houses are all only a short distance away. Comfortable rooms and a friendly atmosphere. All rooms have tea/coffee making facilities. Two television lounges. Parking for six cars. Children and dogs welcome.

Bed & Breakfast per night: single room from £25.00–£35.00; double room from £50.00–£60.00

Bedrooms: 1 single, 2 double, 1 twin, 1 family
Bathrooms: 3 en-suite, 1 shared
Parking: 6 spaces

504 Dale Hill Hotel & Golf Club   ★★★★ Silver Award

Ticehurst, Wadhurst, East Sussex TN5 7DQ **Tel:** (01580) 200112 **Fax:** (01580) 201249
Web: www.dalehill.co.uk **E-mail:** info@dalehill.co.uk

The 4 Star Dale Hill Hotel is situated in an area of outstanding natural beauty, high on the Kentish Weald. All of our 36 en-suite bedrooms offer comfort and luxury, many have magnificent views overlooking our 18-hole golf courses, one of which was designed to USGA specification by former US Masters Champion Ian Woosnam. Our award-winning Fairway restaurant and leisure facilities, which include an indoor swimming pool, sauna and gymnasium, complements the hotel.

Bed & Breakfast per night: single room from £70.00–£100.00; double room from £80.00–£140.00
Evening meal: 1900 (last orders 2145)

Bedrooms: 6 single, 20 double/twin
Bathrooms: 26 en-suite
Parking: 220 spaces
Cards accepted: Mastercard, Visa, Switch/Delta, Amex

505 Playden Cottage Guesthouse   ◆◆◆◆◆ Silver Award

Military Road, Rye, East Sussex TN31 7NY **Tel:** (01797) 222234
Web: www.smoothhound.co.uk/hotels/playden.html

On the old Saxon shore, less than a mile from Rye town and on what was once a busy fishing harbour, there is now only a pretty cottage with lovely gardens, a pond and an ancient right of way. The sea has long receded and, sheltered by its own informal gardens, Playden Cottage looks over the River Rother and across the sheep-studded Romney Marsh. It offers comfort, peace, a care for detail – and a very warm welcome.

Bed & Breakfast per night: single occupancy from £45.00–£51.00; double room from £60.00–£68.00
Dinner, Bed & Breakfast per person, per night: £45.00–£53.00

Bedrooms: 3 double/twin
Bathrooms: 3 en-suite
Parking: 7 spaces
Cards accepted: Mastercard, Visa, JCB

506 Rye Lodge Hotel

★ ★ ★ Silver Award

Hilders Cliff, Rye, East Sussex TN31 7LD **Tel:** (01797) 223838 or (01797) 226688 **Fax:** (01797) 223585
Web: www.ryelodge.co.uk **E-mail:** info@ryelodge.co.uk

Premier position on East Cliff, close to the historic 14th-century Landgate, High Street teashops, antique and art galleries, in this charming medieval Cinque port with its cobbled streets and picturesque period buildings. Rye Lodge offers elegance and charm in a relaxed atmosphere. The luxurious de luxe bedrooms are all en-suite. Room service – breakfast in bed as late as you like! Candlelit dinners in the elegant marble-floored Terrace Room, delicious food and fine wines, attentive caring service, and an indoor swimming pool!

Bed & Breakfast per night: single room from £55.00–£95.00; double room from £90.00–£150.00
Dinner, Bed & Breakfast per person, per night: £60.00–£90.00 (min 2 nights)
Evening meal: 1900 (last orders 2100)

Bedrooms: 2 single, 11 double, 7 twin
Bathrooms: 20 en-suite
Parking: 20 spaces
Cards accepted: Mastercard, Visa, Switch/Delta, Amex, Diners, Eurocard, JCB, Maestro, Visa Elect

507 Jeake's House

◆ ◆ ◆ ◆ ◆ Silver Award

Mermaid Street, Rye, East Sussex TN31 7ET **Tel:** (01797) 222828 **Fax:** (01797) 222623
Web: www.jeakeshouse.com **E-mail:** jeakeshouse@btinternet.com

Jeake's House stands on the most famous cobbled street in medieval Rye. Bedrooms have been individually restored to create a very special atmosphere, combining traditional elegance and luxury with modern amenities. Oak-beamed and panelled bedrooms with brass, mahogany or four-poster beds overlook the marsh and rooftops to the sea. Vegetarian or traditional breakfast is served in the galleried former chapel where soft chamber music and a roaring fire will make your stay a truly memorable experience. Private car park nearby.

Bed & Breakfast per night: single room from £32.50–£68.00; double room from £63.00–£105.00

Bedrooms: 1 single, 7 double, 1 twin, 2 triple, 1 family
Bathrooms: 9 en-suite, 1 private, 2 shared
Cards accepted: Mastercard, Visa, Switch/Delta, Eurocard

508 Mountsfield

◆ ◆ ◆ ◆ ◆ Silver Award

Rye Hill, Rye, East Sussex TN31 7NH **Tel:** (01797) 227105 **Fax:** (01797) 227106

Set in formal grounds on the edge of the ancient Cinque Port town of Rye, East Sussex, Mountsfield is a rare example of a country villa - circa 1776. A few minutes' walk from Rye, this Grade II listed mansion, of great historical and architectural interest, is mentioned in Pevsner and is perfectly situated for visiting the variety of castles, gardens, historical sites and nearby golf courses to be found in the beautiful countryside of East Sussex.

Bed & Breakfast per night: double room from £76.00–£110.00

Bedrooms: 3 double
Bathrooms: 3 en-suite
Open: All year except Christmas

509 Little Orchard House

◆◆◆◆◆ Silver Award

West Street, Rye, East Sussex TN31 7ES **Tel:** (01797) 223831 **Fax:** (01797) 223831
Web: www.littleorchardhouse.com

Elegant Georgian townhouse in a quiet cobbled street at the heart of ancient Rye. Perfectly situated for many excellent restaurants, shops, art/antique galleries as well as country/seaside walks, birdwatching or touring nearby National Trust properties like Sissinghurst. Antique furniture throughout, open fires, fine art, books and bears create a relaxed house-party atmosphere. Large, secluded walled garden for guests' use. Generous country breakfasts feature local organic and free range products. Parking available.

Bed & Breakfast per night: single occupancy from £45.00–£65.00; double room from £64.00–£90.00

Bedrooms: 2 double
Bathrooms: 2 en-suite
Cards accepted: Mastercard, Visa, Switch/Delta, Eurocard, JCB, Maestro, Visa Electron, Solo

510 Manor Farm Oast

◆◆◆◆◆ Gold Award

Windmill Orchard, Workhouse Lane, Icklesham, Winchelsea, East Sussex TN36 4AJ **Tel:** (01424) 813787 **Fax:** (01424) 813787
E-mail: manor.farm.oast@lineone.net

A three roundel oasthouse built in the 19th century and nestling in acres of apple and cherry orchards. A truly peaceful haven of luxury, ideally situated for country walks or coastal visits. Set in 1066 Country, within easy reach of Rye, Winchelsea, Battle and Hastings. Birthdays and anniversarys a speciality. Credit cards accepted. Licensed. Five-course dinner by arrangement.

Bed & Breakfast per night: single occupancy from £35.00–£40.00; double room from £55.00–£64.00
Dinner, Bed & Breakfast per person, per night: £44.50–£49.00
Evening meal: 1900 (last orders 2000)

Bedrooms: 2 double, 1 twin
Bathrooms: 2 en-suite, 1 private
Parking: 10 spaces
Cards accepted: Mastercard, Visa, Switch/Delta, Eurocard, JCB, Visa Electron, Solo

511 Heron Cottage

◆◆◆◆

Biddenden, Ashford, Kent TN27 8HH **Tel:** (01580) 291358

Peacefully set in unspoilt countryside, surrounded by trees, a walled garden, a pond for fishing and animals to visit. Heron Cottage is situated between the historic village of Biddenden and Sissinghurst Castle and reached by an unmade road through farmland. Easy access to local footpaths. Warmth and comfort are assured with central heating and log fires in season. Home cooking is traditional with emphasis on fresh and local produce. Many historic properties to visit.

Bed & Breakfast per night: single occupancy from £25.00–£35.00; double room from £35.00–£50.00
Dinner, Bed & Breakfast per person, per night: £30.00–£47.50

Bedrooms: 2 double, 1 twin
Bathrooms: 3 en-suite
Open: March–October

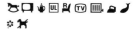

512 Little Silver Country Hotel
★★★ Silver Award

Ashford Road, St Michaels, Tenterden, Kent TN30 6SP **Tel:** (01233) 850321 **Fax:** (01233) 850647
Web: www.little-silver.co.uk **E-mail:** enquiries@little-silver.co.uk

Little Silver Country Hotel is set in its own landscaped gardens. The restaurant provides an intimate, tranquil atmosphere where local produce is enjoyed, pre-dinner drinks and after dinner coffee are offered in the beamed sitting room with its log fire. Breakfast is served in a Victorian conservatory overlooking the waterfall rockery. Luxury bedrooms, tastefully and individually designed, some with four-posters and jacuzzi baths, others with brass beds. Facilities for disabled. Personal attention, care for detail, warmth and friendliness create a truly memorable experience. RAC Restaurant Award. ⋔ **Category 3**

Bed & Breakfast per night: single occupancy from £60.00–£75.00; double room from £90.00–£115.00
Dinner, Bed & Breakfast per person, per night: £60.00–£70.00 (min 2 nights)
Lunch available: 1200–1400 (pre-booked only)

Evening meal: 1830 (last orders 2200)
Bedrooms: 5 double, 3 twin, 1 triple, 1 family
Bathrooms: 10 en-suite
Parking: 50 spaces
Cards accepted: Mastercard, Visa, Switch/Delta, Amex, Visa Electron, Solo

513 Shirkoak Farm
◆◆◆◆ Silver Award

Bethersden Road, Woodchurch, Ashford, Kent TN26 3PZ **Tel:** (01233) 860056 **Fax:** (01233) 861402
Web: www.shirkoakfarm.com **E-mail:** shirkoakfarm@aol.com

18th-century Gerogian farmhouse in quiet rural setting with landscaped gardens, small lake and tennis court. Comfortably furnished en-suite bedrooms with television, tea tray etc. Luxurious, spacious drawing room, elegant dining room furnished with antiques. Adjacent barn with billiard room and smoking lounge. A peaceful retreat; perfect for the more discerning guest, offering a warm, genuine welcome, a comfortable night's sleep and a superb breakfast selection. Perfectly situated for touring Kent and within easy reach of Sissinghurst and Leeds Castle. Convenient for all cross-channel transportation.

Bed & Breakfast per night: single occupancy from £35.00–£45.00; double room from £50.00–£60.00

Bedrooms: 3 double/twin
Bathrooms: 3 en-suite
Parking: 6 spaces
Cards accepted: Mastercard, Visa, Switch/Delta

514 Eastwell Manor Hotel
★★★★ Gold Award

Eastwell Park, Boughton Lees, Ashford, Kent TN25 4HR **Tel:** (01233) 213000 **Fax:** (01233) 635530
Web: www.eastwellmanor.co.uk **E-mail:** eastwell@btinternet.com

Breathtaking Eastwell Manor enjoys seclusion and tranquillity in the heart of the Garden of England. The 62 bedroom hotel is set within 62 acres of its own landscaped gardens and woodland, but within a 3000 acre working estate. The Manor Restaurant holds 3 AA Rosettes for food. Eastwell Mews, a conversion of 18th-century stable blocks, provides 19 courtyard apartments, all fully en-suite. The Pavilion is close by and offers a 20m heated pool, hydrotherapy pool, sauna, steam room, state of the art gymnasium, bar and brasserie, and 'Dreams', our beauty salon, with 12 treatment rooms and hairdressers to complete your luxurious stay. Situated close to junction 9 of the M20 at Ashford.

Bed & Breakfast per night: single occupancy from £170.00–£325.00; double room from £200.00–£355.00
Dinner, Bed & Breakfast per person, per night: £202.00–£357.00 (min 2 nights)
Lunch available: 1200–1430
Evening meal: 1930 (last orders 2130)

Bedrooms: 14 double, 13 twin, 35 family
Bathrooms: 62 en-suite
Parking: 112 spaces
Cards accepted: Mastercard, Visa, Switch/Delta, Amex, Diners, Maestro, Visa Electron, Solo

515 Molehills

◆◆◆◆

Bladbean, Canterbury, Kent CT4 6LU **Tel:** (01303) 840051
E-mail: molehills84@hotmail.com

The house, with one acre of gardens, is situated in a peaceful hamlet, off the beaten track, within the beautiful Elham Valley. We are within easy reach of the historic city of Canterbury and the Channel terminals. We produce good home-grown food and excellent home cooking. Our comfortable accommodation includes ground floor bedrooms, a sitting room with wood-burning stove, a conservatory and verandah for the use of our guests.

Bed & Breakfast per night: single occupancy £25.00; double room from £45.00–£50,00
Dinner, Bed & Breakfast per person, per night: £28.50–£35.00

Bedrooms: 1 double, 1 twin
Bathrooms: 2 en-suite
Parking: 3 spaces

516 The Hythe Imperial

★★★★ Silver Award

Prince's Parade, Hythe, Kent CT21 6AE **Tel:** (01303) 267441 **Fax:** (01303) 264610
Web: www.marstonhotels.com **E-mail:** hytheimperial@marstonhotels.com

An impressive sea-front resort hotel set within fifty acres in the historic Cinque port of Hythe. All the rooms enjoy sea or garden views with executive, four-poster, half-tester or jacuzzi rooms and suites available. Conference facilities available for up to two hundred and fifty, as well as superb leisure facilities, including 9-hole golf course, indoor swimming pool, luxurious spa bath, steam room, sauna, gym, sunbed, tennis, croquet, beauty salon and hairdressing. AA Rosette.

Bed & Breakfast per night: single room from £91.00–£127.00; double room from £127.00–£199.00
Dinner, Bed & Breakfast per person, per night: £82.50–£107.50 (min 2 nights)
Lunch available: 1230–1400

Evening meal: 1900 (last orders 2100)
Bedrooms: 17 single, 45 double, 38 twin
Bathrooms: 100 en-suite
Parking: 202 spaces
Cards accepted: Mastercard, Visa, Switch/Delta, Amex, Diners

517 Harbourside Hotel

◆◆◆◆◆ Gold Award

12/14 Wear Bay Road, Folkestone, Kent CT19 6AT **Tel:** (01303) 256528 or 07768 123884 **Fax:** (01303) 241299
Web: www.harboursidehotel.com **E-mail:** joy@harboursidehotel.com

Three beautifully restored Victorian houses on the East Cliff, overlooking sea and harbour, provide luxury en-suite accommodation. The quality, hospitality, and value for money are truly special. We can be your perfect base from which to tour South East England, the best stop-over when crossing the Channel, or the centre point for a relaxing holiday. Phone, fax or e-mail to reserve your room or ask for more details, or see all the detail on www.harboursidehotel.com.

Bed & Breakfast per night: single occupancy from £40.00–£60.00; double room from £60.00–£100.00

Bedrooms: 4 double, 2 twin
Bathrooms: 5 en-suite, 1 private
Cards accepted: Mastercard, Visa, Switch/Delta, Amex, Diners, Eurocard, Maestro, Visa Electron

518 The Park Inn   ◆◆◆◆

1–2 Park Place, Ladywell, Dover, Kent CT16 1DQ **Tel:** (01304) 203300 **Fax:** (01304) 203324
Web: www.theparkinnatdover.co.uk **E-mail:** theparkinn@cs.com

An extremely high standard of Victorian style decoration, furnishings and facilities prevails in our five en-suite rooms which complement our successful inn and restaurant. All rooms are cosy and comfortable and include satellite television and direct dial telephone with fax/modem points. Doubles, twins and superb four-poster rooms are available. All rooms are strictly non-smoking. The Park Inn offers an extensive à la carte and snack menu with a wide choice of ales and wines.

Bed & Breakfast per night: single room from £35.00–£45.00; double room from £54.00–£74.00
Dinner, Bed & Breakfast per person, per night: £39.55–£49.55
Evening meal: 1130–2200

Bedrooms: 1 single, 1 double, 2 twin, 1 family
Bathrooms: 5 en-suite
Parking: secure parking by arrangement
Cards accepted: Mastercard, Visa, Switch/Delta, Amex, Diners, Eurocard, JCB, Visa Electron, Solo

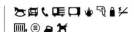

519 Wallett's Court Country House Hotel & Restaurant   ★★★ Silver Award

Westcliffe, St-Margarets-at-Cliffe, Dover, Kent CT15 6EW **Tel:** (01304) 852424 **Fax:** (01304) 853430
Web: www.wallettscourt.com **E-mail:** wc@wallettscourt.com

Wallett's Court Country House is a 17th-century manor with 16 luxurious rooms, some with four-posters, others with sea views. Noted in major guides, the restaurant serves the finest local and organic produce, including some of the finest fish and seafood on the South Coast. In the grounds is a health spa with indoor pools, saunas and sun terrace set in seven acres of beautiful gardens in a tranquil, rural area of outstanding natural beauty on the White Cliffs of Dover.

Bed & Breakfast per night: single occupancy from £75.00–£115.00; double room from £90.00–£150.00
Dinner, Bed & Breakfast per person, per night: £80.00–£110.00
Lunch available: 1200–1400

Evening meal: 1900 (last orders 2100)
Bedrooms: 11 double, 2 twin, 3 triple
Bathrooms: 16 en-suite
Parking: 20 spaces
Cards accepted: Mastercard, Visa, Switch/Delta, Amex, Diners, Eurocard, JCB, Maestro, Visa Elect

520 Loddington House Hotel   ◆◆◆◆

14 East Cliff, (Seafront - Marine Parade), Dover, Kent CT16 1LX **Tel:** (01304) 201947 **Fax:** (01304) 201947

Loddington House is a Regency Grade II listed building on the seafront, with panoramic views over the harbour and English Channel. The famous Dover Castle and White Cliffs form a spectacular backdrop to the property. Canterbury, Sandwich and Deal are all a short distance away, making it an excellent holiday choice for exploring Kent, or for a trip to France. Freshly prepared quality food, table d'hôte or à la carte, with a good selection of wines, by arrangement.

Bed & Breakfast per night: single room from £45.00–£50.00; double room from £54.00–£60.00
Evening meal: 1830 (last orders 2000)

Bedrooms: 1 single, 3 double, 2 twin
Bathrooms: 4 en-suite, 2 private
Parking: 3 spaces
Cards accepted: Mastercard, Visa, Amex

521 Hardicot Guest House

◆◆◆◆

Kingsdown Road, Walmer, Deal, Kent CT14 8AW **Tel:** (01304) 373867 **Fax:** (01304) 389234
E-mail: guestboss@talk21.com

This spacious, detached Victorian house stands 100 yards from the Channel in three quarters of an acre of sheltered gardens with a garage and parking. Sea views, comfortable bedrooms with private facilities, substantial breakfasts with home-made preserves and a very warm welcome in elegant surroundings, guarantee a memorable visit. The area is steeped in history with Dover, Deal and Walmer Castles nearby and Canterbury a short drive away. Ideally situated for cliff walks, golf and cross-channel trips.

Bed & Breakfast per night: single occupancy £25.00; double room from £44.00–£50.00

Bedrooms: 1 double, 2 twin
Bathrooms: 1 en-suite, 2 private
Parking: 4 spaces

---

522 Ilex Cottage

◆◆◆◆

Temple Way, Worth, Deal, Kent CT14 0DA **Tel:** (01304) 617026 **Fax:** (01304) 620890
Web: www.ilexcottage.com **E-mail:** info@ilexcottage.com

This carefully modernised home dating from 1736 retains many character features. Our well-appointed, spacious en-suite guest rooms have co-ordinated furnishings and rural views. The Georgian conservatory provides a delightful reception area for relaxing and enjoying refreshments. Non-smoking throughout. Children and pets welcomed. Secluded, peaceful location, yet conveniently near picturesque conservation village centre. Sandwich and Deal are five minutes away, and Canterbury, Dover and Ramsgate are 20 minutes away. Numerous local tourist attractions and leisure facilities. An idyllic holiday base.

Bed & Breakfast per night: single occupancy from £30.00–£35.00; double room from £50.00–£55.00

Bedrooms: 1 double, 2 twin
Bathrooms: 3 en-suite
Parking: 6 spaces
Cards accepted: Mastercard, Visa, Switch/Delta, Visa Electron, Solo

---

Key to Symbols

For ease of use, the key to symbols for hotels and guest accommodation appears on the back of the cover flap and can be folded out while consulting individual entries. The symbols are designed to enable you to see at a glance what's on offer. Most of the symbols are clear, simple icons and few require any further explanation, but the following points may be useful:

Alcoholic drinks: Alcoholic drinks are available at all types of serviced accommodation listed in the guide unless the symbol [UL] (unlicensed) appears. However, even in licensed premises there may be some restrictions on the serving of drinks, such as being available to diners only.

Smoking: Some establishments prefer not to accommodate smokers, and if this is the case it will be indicated by the symbol ⤬. Other establishments may offer facilities for non-smokers such as no smoking bedrooms and parts of communal rooms set aside for non-smokers. Please check at the time of booking if the non-smoking symbol does not appear.

Pets: The symbol 🐕 is used to show that dogs are not accepted in any circumstances. Some establishments will accept pets, but we advise you to check this at the time of booking and to enquire as to whether any additional charge will be made to accommodate them.

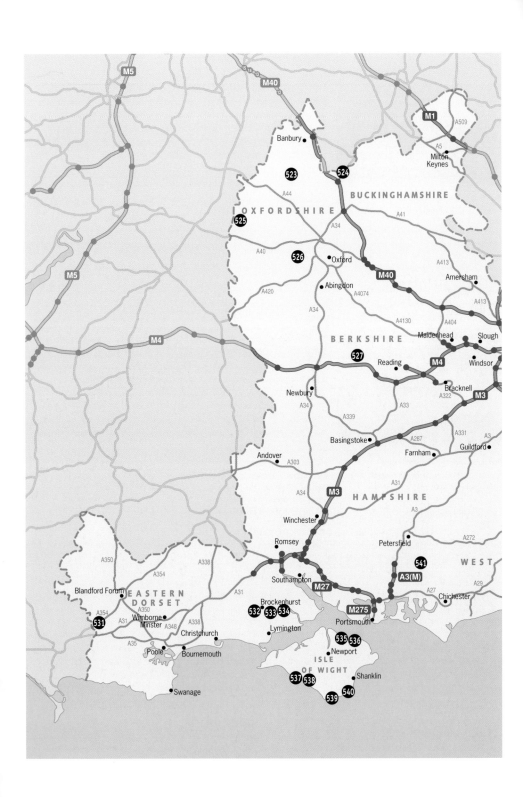

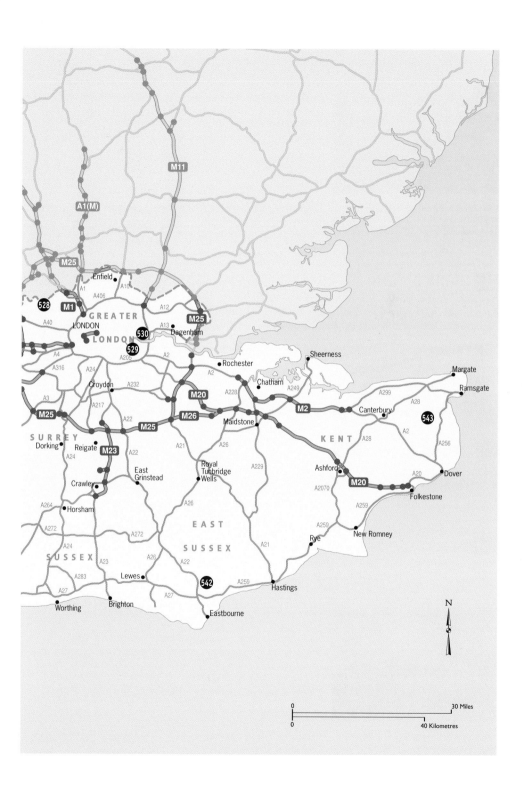

523 Heath Farm Holiday Cottages ★ ★ ★ ★

Heath Farm, Swerford, Chipping Norton, Oxfordshire **Web:** www.heathfarm.com
Contact: Mr & Mrs D Barbour, Heath Farm, Swerford, Chipping Norton, Oxfordshire OX7 4BN
Tel: (01608) 683270 or (01608) 683240 **Fax:** (01608) 683222 **E-mail:** barbours@heathfarm.com

Award-winning stone cottages set in 70 acres of woodland and flower meadows. Glorious views over unspoilt Cotswold countryside. Extensive use of local hardwoods in hand-crafted furniture and fittings. Stunning paved courtyard with water garden. Oxford, Stratford and all Cotwold attractions within easy reach. Exclusive, unusual, luxurious. Spoil yourself.

Low season per week: £238.00–£375.00	**5 cottages:** sleeping 2–4 people
High season per week: £327.00–£505.00	**Cards accepted:** Mastercard, Visa,
Short breaks: from £155.00–£328.00	Switch/Delta

524 Pimlico Farm Country Cottages ★ ★ ★ ★

Pimlico Farm, Tusmore, Bicester, Oxfordshire **Web:** www.pimlicofarm.co.uk
Contact: Mr & Mrs J Harper, Pimlico Farm, Tusmore, Bicester, Oxfordshire OX27 7SL
Tel: (01869) 810306 **Fax:** (01869) 810309 **E-mail:** enquiries@pimlicofarm.co.uk

Seven top quality cottages situated on two working farms within easy day trips to London, Oxford, Warwick, Cambridge and world class attractions such as Blenheim Palace, The Cotswolds, Shakespeare's birthplace at Stratford-upon-Avon and numerous National Trust properties. The fully furnished cottages reflect taste, warmth and charm with fully equipped modern kitchens and bathrooms. Every booking is considered individually to ensure personal requirements. The resident owners ensure a warm welcome.
Category 2

Low season per week: £232.00–£365.00	**7 cottages:** sleeping 6 people
High season per week: £315.00–£512.00	**Cards accepted:** Mastercard, Visa,
Short breaks: from £180.00–£320.00 (low season only)	Switch/Delta

525 Bruern Stable Cottages ★ ★ ★ ★ ★

Bruern, Chipping Norton, Oxfordshire **Web:** www.bruern.co.uk
Contact: Ms F Curtin, Red Brick House, Bruern, Chipping Norton, Oxfordshire OX7 6PY
Tel: (01993) 830415 **Fax:** (01993) 831750 **E-mail:** enquiries@bruern.co.uk

Sole winners of the English Tourism Council's 'England for Excellence' Award 1998. Bruern Stable Cottages contain every modern convenience that you would have in a contemporary city apartment, coupled with the open log fires, antiques and four-poster beds that you would find in a grand country house. There is a swimming pool, tennis court, games room and a children's play area. The gardens and interiors have been featured in The Sunday Times, Country Living, Condé Nast Traveller and The Lady.

Low season per week: £365.00–£786.00	**10 cottages:** sleeping 2–8 people
High season per week: £744.00–£2012.00	**Cards accepted:** Mastercard, Visa,
Short breaks: from £255.00–£655.00	Switch/Delta

526 Akers

Sutton, Stanton Harcourt, Oxfordshire **Web:** www.oxfordshirecottages.com
Contact: Ms B J Harding, Lower Farm, Duck End Lane, Sutton, Stanton Harcourt, Oxfordshire OX29 5RH
Tel: (01865) 881553 **E-mail:** barbaraharding@yahoo.co.uk

Stunning Grade II listed thatched house, privately situated at the end of a no-through-lane, on the edge of an historic village. Only 15 minutes to Oxford/ Burford. Sympathetically and stylishly restored. No chintz. Heavily beamed, two inglenooks, two sitting rooms, large lavishly equipped kitchen diner, separate utility room. Five bedrooms, three bathrooms, free standing ball and claw baths. Colonial furniture, Egyptian cotton bed linen, silk and velvet throws. Three acres of landscaped gardens. Garden pond complete with duck island.

Low season per week: £750.00–£1000.00
High season per week: £1100.00–£1650.00
Short breaks: from £650.00–£850.00

1 house: sleeping 9/10 people

527 Pennycroft

★ ★ ★ ★

Upper Basildon, Reading, Berkshire **Web:** www.pennycroft.com
Contact: Mrs G V Collingwood, 34 Ambleside Avenue, London SW16 1QP
Tel: (020) 8769 2742 **Fax:** (020) 8677 3023 **E-mail:** info@pennycroft.com

Pennycroft is an Edwardian cottage set in the woodland and fields of the Berkshire Downs above the Thames, between Pangbourne and Goring, made famous by Kenneth Grahame in 'The Wind in The Willows'. It has log fires, is centrally heated and is fully modernised with dishwasher, washing machine and dryer, and microwave, hi-fi, television and video. London is about 50 miles, Oxford and Heathrow about 25 miles, pubs and restaurant about one mile away. Pennycroft has lawns and gardens for picnics/ barbeques and backs onto the woods and parkland of the historic Basildon Park. See www.pennycroft.com for the many amenities and attractions close by.

Low season per week: £350.00–£420.00
High season per week: £420.00–£630.00

1 house: sleeping 6–8 people
Cards accepted: Mastercard, Visa, Switch/Delta

528 Moss Cottage

★ ★ ★ ★

Moss Lane, Pinner, Middlesex **Web:** www.moss-lane-cottages.com
Contact: Mr and Mrs C Le Quesne, 31 Paines Lane, Pinner, Middlesex HA5 3BU
Tel: (020) 8868 5507 **Fax:** (020) 8868 5507 **E-mail:** bemail2@aol.com

Moss Cottage is a 17th-century listed building in Pinner, an historic and picturesque village, 12 miles from central London. The property overlooks a large garden with lawns and mature trees. It is conveniently located for local underground, rail and bus services, London's Heathrow airport and the M25. The self-contained accommodation offers three bedrooms and two separate toilets. Nearby there are supermarkets, restaurants, pubs, theatres, cinemas and sports facilities.

Low season per week: £600.00–£700.00
High season per week: £700.00–£800.00
Short breaks: from £300.00–£450.00

1 cottage: sleeping 4–5 people
Cards accepted: Mastercard, Visa

529 Bridge House - London Docklands ★ ★ ★ ★

Falcon Way, Clippers Quay, London **Web:** www.johnkgraham.com
Contact: Mr J K Graham, 31 Falcon Way, London E14 9UP
Tel: (020) 7538 8980 **Fax:** (020) 7538 8980 **E-mail:** john@johnkgraham.com

Two bedrooms to sleep four in a peaceful waterscaped environment. Sunny patio-garden leading to water. Master bedroom balcony overlooks water. Private parking. 100 metres to underground. 20 minutes to West End. Short walk to Canary Wharf. Conveniently close to 30 restaurants, cafés, supermarket, London Arena, Multiplex cinema and Excel. Internally, every modern facility available. No smoking in the house. No pets. Nightly rates. Bookings taken for any number of nights all year.

Low season per week: £595.00
High season per week: £651.00
Short breaks: from £300.00 (3 nights)

1 house: sleeping 4 people
Cards accepted: Mastercard, Visa

Epsom Derby

The Derby, the most famous horserace in the world, was first run in 1780, and has attracted huge audiences of ordinary people ever since. 'On Derby Day,' wrote Charles Dickens, 'a population rills and surges and scrambles through the place, that may be counted in millions.' Dickens was surely exaggerating, but so great was the race's popularity in the second half of the 19th century that Parliament was suspended for the day. Currently crowds of some 100,000 or so attend the race, held on the first Saturday in June.

The Derby is named after the 12th Earl of Derby, Edward Smith Stanley, who, together with his colourful uncle, General John Burgoyne, organised the first contest for three-year old fillies in 1779. The race over Epsom Downs was named 'The Oaks' after Burgoyne's rambling house, once a pub, near Epsom, and was won by Derby's filly, Bridget. At the celebration dinnner which followed, Derby planned a second race for three-year-old colts and fillies, to be named after himself. On 4 May 1780 the first Derby took place – and a great English tradition was born. Both races continue to run, with The Oaks taking place the day before the Derby.

During its long history the race has had more than its fair share of dramatic occurrences. In 1913 the suffragette, Emily Davison, was killed when she threw herself in front of the King's horse, a deliberate act of martyrdom designed to generate maximum publicity. More recently, in 1981, the crowds thrilled

to the most dramatic Derby win ever, when the legendary colt Shergar, ridden by Walter Swinburn, won effortlessly by a clear 10 lengths. Two years later Shergar was kidnapped from the Aga Khan's stud in Ireland, and to this day his fate remains a mystery.

From a racing point of view, the course over the Epsom Downs is supremely challenging. Run early in the season when the going can be heavy, the undulating and twisting 1½mile (2.4km) course requires great stamina. Rising 150ft (46m) in the first four furlongs, it then falls 100ft (30.5m) in varying gradients to the famous Tattenham Corner, before rising again towards the finishing post. The difficulties of winning such an event make the Derby a true test of equine greatness.

Tickets for the Derby and Oaks may be obtained by ringing 01372 470047. 'Derby Experience' tours of the racecourse (tel: 01372 726311) are available throughout the year.

530 River Thames Apartment ★ ★ ★ ★

London Docklands
Contact: Gretta Paull
Tel: (020) 8530 2336 **Fax:** (020) 8530 2336

First floor, with all rooms overlooking the river. Undercover parking. Double bedroom en-suite, twin bedroom, bathroom and lounge/dining room. Kitchen with microwave, fridge/freezer and washer/dryer. Canary Wharf with shops and restaurants is just a walk away. Supermarket close by. Trains to city, West End and Greenwich. Free bus from Canary Wharf to London City airport with daily flights to Europe and Ireland.

Low season per week: £400.00–£550.00
High season per week: £550.00–£700.00

1 apartment: sleeping 6 people

531 Little Hewish Barn ★ ★ ★ ★ ★

Milton Abbas, Blandford Forum, Dorset
Contact: Terry Dunn, 2 Little Hewish Cottages, Milton Abbas, Blandford Forum, Dorset DT11 0DP
Tel: (01258) 881235 **Fax:** (01258) 881393 **E-mail:** terry@littlehewish.co.uk

Recently converted 150 year-old brick and flint barn, in lovely rural setting. Spacious open-plan living/dining area featuring original beams, wood-burning stove and fully equipped kitchen. There are two double bedrooms, both with full en-suite facilities and full central heating. Refreshments and first-day breakfast are included. Children welcome. Well behaved dogs by arrangement. Small, private, patio garden (fully enclosed) and ample off-road parking. Pre-arrival shopping/baby sitting available at cost. Flexible family-run business. Fully inclusive prices – no hidden extras!

Low season per week: from £330.00
High season per week: max £550.00

1 barn conversion: sleeping 4/6 people

532 Heywood House ★ ★ ★ ★

Sway Road, Brockenhurst, Hampshire **Web:** www.newforestcottages.co.uk
Contact: Adam Ogilvie, 4 Quay Hill, Lymington, Hampshire SO41 3AR
Tel: (01590) 697655

The owners have created a newly equipped and spacious self-contained annexe to their large family home for the use of holiday visitors and guests. Located on the outskirts of Brockenhurst on the road to Sway, the property offers ready access to both open forest and the centre of Brockenhurst. Large sitting/dining room with colour television and video. Kitchen area with gas hob, electric oven, microwave, fridge, dishwasher and washing machine. Two double bedrooms sleep five + one. Heating and electricity included. Linen/towels for hire. Non-smoking, regret no pets, no children under five.

Low season per week: £235.00–£275.00
High season per week: £310.00–£395.00

1 house: sleeping 5 people
Cards accepted: Mastercard, Visa, Switch/Delta

533 Gorse Cottage ★★★★★

Balmer Lawn Road, Brockenhurst, Hampshire **Web:** www.gorsecottage.co.uk
Contact: Mr & Mrs J Bareford, Whins, Hook Heath Avenue, Woking, Surrey GU22 0HN
Tel: (01483) 760803 **Fax:** (01483) 764227 **E-mail:** jon@bareford.com

Beautifully appointed cottage/bungalow, set in secluded garden opposite open forest, close to the village of Brockenhurst in the New Forest. Spacious yet cosy accommodation, lounge, dining hall with wood-burning stove and attractive conservatory. Small luxurious bathroom with whirlpool bath. Two well designed bedrooms, well equipped kitchen with microwave, Miele washer/dryer, dishwasher etc. Baxi clean air system. Ideal location for lovers of the countryside. Many fine amenities and attractions close by.

Low season per week: from £360.00
High season per week: max £650.00

1 bungalow: sleeping 4 people

534 Mares Tails Cottage ★★★★

Beaulieu, Brockenhurst, Hampshire
Contact: Mrs A Barber, Mares Tails, Furzey Lane, Beaulieu, Brockenhurst, Hampshire SO42 7WB
Tel: (01590) 612160 **E-mail:** marestails612160@cs.com

Well appointed modern cottage with own secluded garden in the grounds of architect's house. One mile from the lovely village of Beaulieu with direct access to the open forest and backing onto farmland. The cottage is fully carpeted and comprises of lounge, bedroom with en-suite bathroom and unusual sit-in bath with hand-held shower, galley kitchen, 30ft conservatory. Gas central heating or curl up beside a lovely log fire. Ideal for walking, birdwatching. Two miles from the Solent shore. Peace and quiet.

Low season per week: £280.00–£320.00
High season per week: £330.00–£345.00

1 cottage: sleeping 2 people
Open: May–October

535 Oak Lawn Holiday Cottages ★★★★

Woodside, Wootton, Ryde, Isle of Wight
Contact: Mrs L M Haywood, Corner House, Oak Lawn, Woodside, Wootton Bridge, Ryde, Isle of Wight PO33 4JR
Tel: (01983) 884080 **Fax:** (01983) 880072 **E-mail:** oaklawn@talk21.com

Comfortable, well equipped two and three bedroom Victorian cottages set in an Area of Outstanding Natural Beauty, with views of the Solent through the trees. Private gardens with barbecues and patio furniture. The cottages are equipped to a high standard with dishwasher, microwave, washer/dryer, colour television and video. Use of outdoor swimming pool (May–September). Ample parking adjacent. Linen provided. Electricity and heating included. Sorry no pets or smoking.

Low season per week: £250.00–£400.00
High season per week: £500.00–£650.00

2 cottages: sleeping 6 + 1 people

536 Kemphill Barn ★ ★ ★ ★ ★

Stroudwood Road, Upton, Ryde, Isle of Wight **Web:** www.kemphill.com
Contact: Kemphill Farm, Stroudwood Road, Upton, Ryde, Isle of Wight PO33 4BZ
Tel: (01983) 563880 **Fax:** (01983) 563880 **E-mail:** ron.holland@farming.co.uk

Built in 1769 as a 2 storey building with hay stored above shire horses, Kemphill Barn has been lovingly converted into a beautiful holiday home. It still overlooks the original duck pond and commands wonderful views across the 300 acre working farm. The four en-suite bedrooms comfortably sleep up to ten guests. The lounge, with all its original beams is on the first floor. The large, farmhouse style kitchen opens onto its own private patio and garden.

Low season per week: £600.00–£800.00
High season per week: £900.00–£1500.00
Short breaks: from £300.00

1 barn conversion: sleeping 10 people

---

537 Casses ★ ★ ★ ★

Main Road, Brighstone, Isle of Wight
Contact: Mr & Mrs J K Nesbitt, Kerrich House, Peartree Court, Old Orchards, Lymington, Hampshire SO41 3TF
Tel: (01590) 679601 **E-mail:** jkn@casses.fsbusiness.co.uk

Delightful 17th-century listed smugglers cottage enjoying a spacious garden with apple trees. Described by guests as 'excellent location, lovely cottage, very picturesque village'. The fully equipped kitchen/dining area includes an Aga/Rayburn range and halogen cooker with comfortable seating for eight adults. Woodstove with logs provided. The generous south-facing garden is approximately 250 yards from the village pub and shops, less than a mile from sandy beaches and many beautiful forest walks.

Low season per week: £325.00–£695.00
High season per week: £495.00–£865.00
Short breaks: from £125.00–£190.00 (low season only)

1 cottage: sleeping 11 people

---

538 Rose Cottage ★ ★ ★ ★ ★

Brighstone, Newport, Isle of Wight
Contact: Mr J B Russell, Thorncross Farm, Brighstone, Newport, Isle of Wight PO30 4PN
Tel: (01983) 740291 **Fax:** (01983) 741408

17th-century, semi-detached, thatched cottage. Beautifully renovated to a high standard. One large family bedroom sleeps four comfortably. Near Brighstone in the heart of the south west side of the island, in wonderful walking countryside. Large garden and parking. Sorry, no smoking or pets.

Low season per week: £300.00–£400.00
High season per week: £400.00–£495.00

1 cottage: sleeping 4 people (1 bedroom)

539 Puckaster House ★ ★ ★ ★ ★

Niton Undercliff, Ventnor, Isle of Wight **Web:** www.islandcottageholidays.com
Contact: Island Cottage Holidays, The Old Vicarage, Kingston, Wareham, Dorset BH20 5LH
Tel: (01929) 480080 **Fax:** (01929) 481070 **E-mail:** enq@islandcottageholidays.com

This beautiful 'Cottage Ornee' style house, is surrounded by six acres of peaceful garden with lovely lawns going down towards the sea. It provides superb and spacious accommodation. The variety of antiques, books, ornaments and pictures produce a delightful country house atmosphere. Relax in front of an open wood fire in the panelled library or drawing room.

Island Cottage Holidays have additional quality properties situated throughout the Isle of Wight.

Low season per week: £995.00–£1189.00
High season per week: £1240.00–£1499.00
Short breaks: from £750.00 (low season only)

1 cottage: sleeping 8 people
Cards accepted: Mastercard, Visa, Switch/Delta

540 Uppermount ★ ★ ★ ★

Bonchurch, Isle of Wight **Web:** www.islandcottageholidays.com
Contact: Island Cottage Holidays, The Old Vicarage, Kingston, Wareham, Dorset BH20 5LH
Tel: (01929) 480080 **Fax:** (01929) 481070 **E-mail:** enq@islandcottageholidays.com

Uppermount is delightfully situated in the picturesque village of Bonchurch and is only five minutes' walk from the sea. It is furnished in a traditional style, with many antiques and items of furniture from across the world. Four-poster bed. Spacious sitting room with wood-burning stove. Lovely well established garden.

Island Cottage Holidays have additional quality properties situated throughout the Isle of Wight.

Low season per week: £329.00–£499.00
High season per week: £599.00–£835.00
Short breaks: from £229.00–£295.00 (low season only)

1 cottage: sleeping 7 + 1 people
Cards accepted: Mastercard, Visa, Switch/Delta

541 3 The Old School House ★ ★ ★ ★

Compton, Chichester, West Sussex **Web:** www.comptoncottage.co.uk
Contact: Mr & Mrs B&V Parkinson, 47-48 Castle Garden, Swan Street, Petersfield, Hampshire GU32 3AG
Tel: (01730) 233747 **E-mail:** val@comptoncottage.co.uk

In a tranquil and unspoilt South Downs valley, our Grade II listed, flint and brick cottage was once part of the village school. Walk to open downland or stroll to the village shop, pub and restaurant, just two minutes away. Comfortably furnished, light, spacious, yet cosy accommodation, with open stone hearth for log fires. Pine spiral staircase to large bedroom under eaves. Very well equipped kitchen with oven, microwave, dishwasher and washing machine etc. Sun-trap courtyard with barbecue, plus garden.

Low season per week: £285.00–£325.00
High season per week: £325.00–£450.00
Short breaks: from £190.00–£300.00

1 cottage: sleeping 2 people

542 Little Marshfoot Farmhouse   ★ ★ ★ ★

Mill Road, Hailsham, East Sussex

Contact: Ms K Webster, Little Marshfoot Farmhouse, Mill Road, Hailsham, East Sussex BN27 2SJ
Tel: (01323) 844690 **E-mail:** kew@waitrose.com

Located in the grounds of a former farmhouse, this purpose-built wooden eco-building offers the highest standards of comfort and convenience. Enjoy breakfasts on the covered loggia, play croquet, boules and other garden games, hear birds and watch other wildlife in a quiet rural location adjacent to the Pevensey Levels. Ideal for 1066 Country, Eastbourne, the sea, the South Downs and Sussex Weald. Suitable for families, walkers, gardeners, birdwatchers and cyclists, we offer full weeks and short breaks.

Low season per week: £225.00–£275.00
High season per week: £300.00–£375.00
Short breaks: from £50.00 per night

1 chalet: sleeping 4 people + cot

Rudyard Kipling and Bateman's

As soon as Rudyard Kipling set eyes upon Bateman's he knew he wanted it as his home: 'That's her! The only she!' he exclaimed, 'Make an honest woman of her – quick!' He then explored every room, finding 'no shadow of ancient regrets, stifled miseries, nor any menace'.

The beautiful manor house near Burwash in Sussex (tel: 01435 882302) indeed has an atmosphere of venerable serenity. Built from warm local sandstone, its rooms all dark panelling and polished old wood, it is a perfect example of the English Jacobean manor house, almost unaltered since its completion in 1634. Of its early history little is known save that it may have been built by a prosperous Wealden ironmaster (17th-century Burwash was at the heart of a thriving iron industry). A large, rambling place with an oddly asymmetrical frontage, it is surrounded by large trees and the beautiful gardens the Kiplings created there.

Kipling was a successful author when he came to Bateman's. Literary acclaim had come early and by his late twenties he was already well known in London's intellectual circles. In 1892 he married Caroline Balestier and spent the next four years at her family's estates in America, where he wrote his famous *Jungle Book*. Kipling then returned to England and settled at Rottingdean, a village not far from Burwash, where a beautiful public garden has been created in his memory, adjacent to his former home, The Elms. The years there, however, were clouded by the death of his six-year-old daughter from pneumonia, and after only a year or so

the hunt began for a new house. After years of searching, Bateman's became his next, and final, home.

The Bateman's years were productive: here he wrote, amongst other works, *Traffics and Discoveries, Puck of Pooks Hill, Rewards and Fairies,* and the poems *If* and *The Glory of the Garden.* After his death in 1936, Caroline Kipling lived on at Bateman's for a further three years, finally bequeathing the house to the National Trust as a memorial to her husband. Many of the furnishings now on display belonged to the Kiplings, and particularly evocative is the author's study, barely touched since the day of his death. The table where he wrote, in front of the window, still bears his writing implements and paraphernalia, and the view is of a little grassy knoll, immortalised in his writings as Pooks Hill.

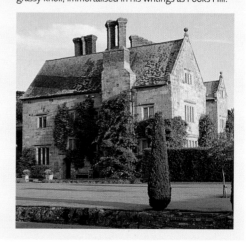

543 Piglet Place

★ ★ ★ ★

Barnsole, Staple, Canterbury, Kent
Contact: Mr & Mrs R Barber, Greengage Cottage, Lower Road, Barnsole, Staple, Canterbury, Kent CT3 1LG
Tel: (01304) 813321 **Fax:** (01304) 812312

A delightful converted barn, in a rural location in the hamlet of Barnsole, four miles from Sandwich Cinque Port. Set adjacent to the owner's home, in nine acres of young woodlands. A quiet, private location with a covered patio and secluded garden. The cottage has two double bedrooms: one with en-suite shower and toilet, the second with single beds and an adjacent bathroom. Fully fitted large kitchen and cosy lounge. Ideally situated for France, Kent coast and Canterbury.

Low season per week: £250.00–£300.00
High season per week: £350.00–£450.00
Short breaks: from £75.00–£100.00 per night

1 cottage: sleeping 4 people

Flemings and Huguenots

The distinctive Flemish flavour of the streets of Sandwich, one of Southern England's most pleasant small towns, is difficult to miss. The clearest sign is the prevalence of Dutch gables – there are some on the corner of the church of St Peter (now the Tourist Information Centre during summer months) and others on Manwood Court, built in 1564 as a grammar school. Another indication is part of the local vocabulary; 'polder' – taken straight from the Dutch – is the word used by the townsfolk to describe the low-lying marshes between Sandwich and Canterbury.

In fact, the Flemings (as the immigrants from the Low Countries were known) were first invited by Edward III in the 14th century, since they were especially skilled in the art of weaving. The economy of this part of Kent had for some time been dependent upon trade through the port of Sandwich and upon cloth-making. The silting up of the harbour over many years (Sandwich is now some two miles from the sea) and the inefficiency of the old cloth-manufacturing techniques meant that the new arrivals were particularly welcome. Business boomed, and Sandwich's density of substantial timbered houses (Strand Street boasts some of the finest) bears witness to the fact that the town prospered greatly. The immigrants also brought other trades to this fertile corner of the land, such as hop-growing for the production of beer, and commercial market gardening; trades which have since become synonymous with Kent.

By the 16th century, many were fleeing the Low Countries to escape persecution for their Calvinist beliefs. Some French Protestants, too, had left their native land, but the Edict of Nantes in 1598 afforded them a measure of religious freedom. When in 1685 this was revoked, nearly half a million Protestants abandoned their homeland, many to cross the Channel to the South Coast. These new exiles, known as Huguenots, tended to stay on the eastern side of England, a significant number never leaving Kent. Echoing the achievements of their earlier Flemish counterparts, the Huguenots established in England the silk-weaving industry. At the peak of the trade, as many as 2,000 people were employed in the silk business in Canterbury alone. Indeed the contribution of the Huguenot community to the city was such that they were granted their own chapel within the cathedral.

Useful Information

Booking checklist

When enquiring about accommodation make sure you check prices and other important details. You will also need to state your requirements clearly and precisely – for example:

- Your intended arrival and departure dates, with acceptable alternatives if appropriate.
- The type of accommodation you require.
- The number of people in your party and the ages of any children.
- Any particular requirements, such as a special diet or a ground-floor room.
- If you think you are likely to arrive late in the evening, mention this when you book. Similarly, if you are delayed on your journey a telephone call to inform the management may well help avoid any problems on your arrival.
- If you are asked for a deposit or the number of your credit card, find out what the proprietor's policy is if, for whatever reason, you can't turn up as planned – see 'cancellations' overleaf.
- Exactly how the establishment's charges are levied – see opposite.

Misunderstandings can easily occur over the telephone, so it is advisable to confirm in writing all bookings, together with special requirements. Please mention that you learnt of the establishment through *Somewhere Special*. Remember to include your name and address, and please enclose a stamped, addressed envelope – or an international reply coupon if writing from outside Britain. Please note that the English Tourism Council does not make reservations; you should address your enquiry directly to the establishment.

Prices

The prices given throughout this publication will serve as a general guide, but you should always check them at the time of booking.

- Prices were supplied during the autumn of 2001 and changes may have occurred since publication.
- Prices include VAT where applicable.
- Prices are often much cheaper for off-peak holidays; check to see whether special off-season packages are available.

For hotels and guest accommodation the following information may also prove useful when determining how much a trip may cost:

- You should check whether or not a service charge is included in the published price.
- Prices for double rooms assume occupancy by two people; you will need to check whether there is a single person supplement if a single occupancy rate is not shown.
- A full English breakfast may not always be included in the quoted price; you may be given a continental breakfast unless you are prepared to pay more.
- Establishments with at least four bedrooms or eight beds are obliged to display in the reception area or at the entrance overnight accommodation charges.
- Reduced prices may apply for children; check exactly how these reductions are calculated, including the maximum age for the child.

Deposits and advance payments

When booking a hotel or guest accommodation, reservations made weeks or months ahead will usually require a deposit which will be deducted from the total bill at the end of your stay.

Some establishments, particularly the larger hotels in big towns, will require payment for the room upon arrival if a prior reservation has not been made. This is especially likely to happen if you arrive late and have little or no luggage. If you are asked to pay in advance, it is sensible to see your room before payment is made to ensure that it meets your requirements.

When booking self-catering accommodation, the proprietor will normally ask you to pay a deposit immediately and then to pay the full balance before your holiday date. This is to safeguard the proprietor in case you decide to cancel at a late stage, or simply do not turn up. He or she may have turned down other bookings on the strength of yours and may find it hard to re-let.

If you book by telephone and are asked for your credit card number, you should note that the proprietor may charge your credit card account even if you subsequently cancel the booking. Ask the owner what his or her usual practice is.

Credit/charge cards

Any credit/charge cards that are accepted by the establishment are indicated at the end of the written description. If you intend to pay by either credit or charge card you are advised to confirm this at the time of booking.

Please note that when paying by credit card, you may sometimes be charged a higher rate for your accommodation in order to cover the percentage paid by the proprietor to the credit card company. Again find this out in advance.

When making a booking, you may be asked for your credit card number as 'confirmation'. The proprietor may then charge your credit card account if you have to cancel the booking, but if this is the policy, it must be made clear to you at the time of booking – see overleaf.

Cancellations

When you accept offered accommodation, including over the telephone, you are entering into a legally binding contract with the proprietor. This means that if you cancel a reservation or fail to take up all or part of the accommodation booked, the proprietor may be entitled to compensation if the accommodation cannot be re-let for all or a good part of the booked period. If you have paid a deposit, you will probably forfeit this, and further payment may well be asked for.

However, no such claim can be made by the proprietor until after the booked period, during which time every effort should be made to re-let the accommodation. It is therefore in your interests to advise the management immediately in writing if you have to cancel or curtail a booking. Travel or holiday insurance, available quite cheaply from travel agents and some hotels, will safeguard you if you have to cancel or curtail your stay.

And remember, if you book by telephone and are asked for your credit card number, you should check whether the proprietor intends charging your account should you later cancel your reservation. A proprietor should not be able to charge for a cancellation unless he or she has made this clear at the time of your booking and you have agreed. However, to avoid later disputes, we suggest you check whether he or she intends to make such a charge.

Hotels and guest accommodation

Service charges and tipping

Some establishments levy a service charge automatically, and, if so, must state this clearly in the offer of accommodation at the time of booking. If the offer is accepted by you, the service charge becomes part of the contract. If service is included in your bill, there is no need for you to give tips to the staff unless some particular or exceptional service has been rendered. In the case of meals, the usual tip is 10% of the total bill.

Telephone call charges

There is no restriction on the charges that can be made by hotels for telephone calls made from their premises. Unit charges are frequently considerably higher than telephone companies' standard charges in order to defray the costs of providing the service. It is a condition of the National Rating Standard that unit charges are displayed by the telephone or with the room information. But in practice it is not always easy to compare these charges with standard telephone rates. Before using a hotel telephone, particularly for long-distance calls, it is advisable to ask how the charges compare.

Security of valuables

It is advisable to deposit any valuables for safe keeping with the management of the establishment in which you are staying. If the management accept custody of your property they become wholly liable for its loss or damage. They can however restrict their liability for items brought on to the premises and not placed in their special custody to the minimum amounts imposed by the Hotel Proprietors Act, 1956. These are the sum of £50 in respect of one article and a total of £100 in the case of one guest. In order to restrict their

liability the management must display a notice in the form required by the Act in a prominent position in the reception area or main entrance of the premises. Without this notice, the proprietor is liable for the full value of the loss or damage to any property (other than a motor car or its contents) of a guest who has booked overnight accommodation.

Code of Conduct

All establishments appearing in this guide have agreed to observe the following Code of Conduct:

1. To ensure high standards of courtesy and cleanliness; catering and service appropriate to the type of establishment.

2. To describe fairly to all visitors and prospective visitors the amenities, facilities and services provided by the establishment, whether by advertisement, brochure, word of mouth or any other means. To allow visitors to see accommodation, if requested, before booking.

3. To make clear to visitors exactly what is included in all prices quoted for accommodation, meals and refreshments, including service charges, taxes and other surcharges. Details of charges, if any, for heating or for additional services or facilities available should also be made clear.

4. To adhere to, and not to exceed, prices current at time of occupation for accommodation or other services.

5. To advise visitors at the time of booking, and subsequently, of any change, if the accommodation offered is in an unconnected annexe, or similar, or by boarding out, and to indicate the location of such accommodation and any difference in comfort and amenities from accommodation in the main establishment.

6. To give each visitor, on request, details of payments due and a receipt if required.

7. To deal promptly and courteously with all enquiries, requests, reservations, correspondence and complaints from visitors.

8. To allow an English Tourism Council representative reasonable access to the establishment, on request, to confirm that the Code of Conduct is being observed.

Feedback

Let us know about your break or holiday. We welcome suggestions about how the guide itself may be enhanced or improved and you will find our addresses on page 4 of the guide.

Details listed were believed correct at time of going to press (December 2001), but we advise telephoning in advance to check that details have not altered and to discuss any specific requirements.

Most establishments welcome feedback. Please let the proprietor know if you particularly enjoyed your stay. We sincerely hope that you have no cause for complaint, but should you be dissatisfied or have any problems, make your complaint to the management at the time of the incident so that immediate action may be taken.

In certain circumstances the English Tourism Council may look into complaints. However, the Council has no statutory control over establishments or their methods of operating. The Council cannot become involved in legal or contractual matters.

If you do have problems that have not been resolved by the proprietor and which you would like to bring to our attention, please write to:
Quality Standards Department
English Tourism Council
Thames Tower
Black's Road
Hammersmith
London W6 9EL

The *Safeway*
Excellence in England
AWARDS 2002

The Safeway Excellence in England Awards are all about blowing English tourism's trumpet and telling the world what a fantastic place England is to visit, whether it's for a two week holiday, a weekend break or a day trip.

Formerly called England for Excellence, the Awards are now in their 13th year and are run by the English Tourism Council in association with England's ten regional tourist boards. There are 13 categories including B&B of the Year, Hotel of the Year and Visitor Attraction of the Year. New for 2002 are Short Break Destination of the Year and Most Improved Seaside Resort.

Winner of the 2002 awards will receive their trophies at a fun and festive event to be held on St George's Day (23 April) at the Royal Opera House in London. The day will not only celebrate excellence in tourism but also Englishness in all its diversity.

For a truly exceptional experience, look out for accommodation and attractions displaying a Safeway Excellence in England Award from April 2002 onwards.

Safeway, one of the UK's leading food retailers, is delighted to be sponsoring these awards as a part of a range of initiatives to help farming communities and the tourism industry.

For more information on Safeway Stores please visit: www.safeway.co.uk
For more information about the Excellence in England Awards visit: www.englishtourism.org.uk